OPERATION: WORLD WAR III

OPERATION: WORLD WAR III

The Secret American Plan 'Dropshot' for War with the Soviet Union, 1957

Edited by Anthony Cave Brown

Arms and Armour Press
London—Melbourne

First published 1979 by
Arms and Armour Press
Lionel Leventhal Limited
2-6 Hampstead High Street
London NW3 1QQ
and at
4-12 Tattersalls Lane
Melbourne Victoria 3000

British Library Cataloguing in Publication Data:
Operation World War III.
1. United States—Military policy 2. United
States—Foreign relations—Russia 3. United
States—Foreign relations—1945-1953 4. Russia
—Foreign relations—United States
I. Brown, Anthony Cave
355.03'35'73   UA23
ISBN 0-85368-123-6

Printed in Great Britain

CONTENTS

List of Maps / vi

Editor's Prologue / 1

Volume 1

The outbreak of the war,
disaster, and defense / 31

Volume 2

Holding the last line of defense, preparing for the counter-offensive / 63

Volume 3

The strategic counter-offensive and the defeat
and occupation of the USSR / 183

Editor's Epilogue / 247

Appendices

A: Summary Strategic Estimate as of the end of Phase 1 / 259
B: Western hemisphere fighter defenses and control and early warning
coverage / 283
C: Antiaircraft defense of the continental United States / 285
D: A typical strategic air offensive program / 289
E: Offensive mining requirements / 298
F: The Soviet Union (a military survey) / 302
G: The NATO Powers / 308
H: Memorandum for the Secretary of Defense from the Planning
Committee for Plan Dropshot / 318
I: Final Report on Plan Dropshot / 321

Glossary / 329

LIST OF MAPS

Allied Strategy 58

Total Estimated Volume of U.S. Supply of
Strategic and Critical Materials by World
Areas in the Event of War with the U.S.S.R.,
1957–1959 86

Estimated Relative Importance to the U.S. of
World Areas as Sources of Strategic and
Critical Materials in the Event of War with the
U.S.S.R., 1957–1959 88

Soviet Capabilities in Europe and the Near and
Middle East 127

Priority Facilities in the U.S. 188

U.S.-Canadian Fighter Intercept Capabilities 196

Deployment of Allied Forces for the Defense of
the Western Hemisphere 198

Centers of Control and Mining Targets 204

Deployment of Forces for Conducting the Allied
Air Offensive 208

Deployment of Forces for Conducting Allied
Offensive Operations to Destroy Enemy Naval
Forces 210

Deployment of Allied Forces for Holding the
Rhine-Alps-Piave Line 216

Deployment of Forces for Holding Southeast
Turkey, Tigris Valley, and the Persian Gulf 222

Deployment of Allied Forces in the Pacific and
Indian Oceans 226

Sea and Air Lines of Communication (LOC's) 232

Deployment of Allied Forces in the Barents-
Norwegian Sea, Atlantic Ocean, Mediter-
ranean-Arabian Sea Areas 234

Employment of Allied Forces for Major Land
Offensive in Europe 260

Soviet Electric Power System, 1957 290

Known Soviet Petroleum Refineries, 1957 294

Soviet Steel Ingot Capacity, 1957 296

EDITOR'S PROLOGUE

Plan Dropshot was the United States' plan for world war with the Soviet Union. It was prepared by a committee of the Joint Chiefs of Staff in 1949 with the authority and knowledge of President Harry S Truman. The chairman of the Joint Chiefs was General of the Army Omar N. Bradley, and Dropshot's basis was that atomic war would break out on 1 January 1957. The date was politically irrelevant; it was selected for planning purposes only. However, Dropshot was the main military planning production of the times, and its existence was the outcome of the menacing events of the first years of the Cold War. As such, Dropshot (the code name was deliberately meaningless and was selected to confuse the Soviet intelligence agencies) is a document of immense importance. It was, after all, the flow sheet for Armageddon.

Dropshot was promulgated in three volumes of green-colored paper late in 1949. It became public property in 1977 through the United States' Freedom of Information Act and may now be purchased at the National Archives for fifteen cents a page. This incongruous fact belittles its importance, for at the time nothing could have been more secret. Indeed, the parts of it pertaining to purely conventional war might, one would have thought, still be considered secret. After all, military geography does not change. And conventional weapons change only in the degree of their destructiveness. Therefore the battlefields of 1949–1957 could well be the battlefields of a future war.

These obvious facts lead to a critical question: Was it not folly to make Dropshot public? I have thought extensively about this point, and I am bound to conclude that it was folly to release this document. It should have been burned, buried, or preserved in some secret vault, for it cannot endear America to Russia. As will be seen, not only was Dropshot the blueprint for the atomization of Russia, but it provided also for the occupation by American armies of that vast continent—and for the eradication by the roots of Bolshevism. Doubtless, at this critical time—the Cold War may have ended, if only temporarily, but the political and ideological war goes on with undiminished intensity—the Russians will argue that Dropshot constitutes an example of America's continuing bellicosity toward Russia and that therefore Russia must maintain and expand her armed forces.

Why, therefore, was Dropshot made public? The Joint Chiefs were not required by law to declassify it. The law expressly states that certain documentation may remain secret if the national interest so dictates. The question, therefore, becomes a tantalizing one in which several conjectures are possible. The first is that there was no point in keeping it secret because the Russians already knew all about it. This is conceivable; Dropshot was hatched at a time of considerable Soviet intelligence activity. But this conjecture may be a little too fanciful—although frequently in 1948 Stalin did refer to American war plans, and his representative at the United Nations, Andrei Vishinsky, did allege that America was planning atomic war against Russia over Berlin.

But we should look elsewhere for the reason that this document was made public. Is it possible that Dropshot was some gigantic blind, that it was created to hide some other more relevant plan? This conjecture borders upon paranoia. Is it possible that it was released by somebody in the Pentagon (1) to torpedo detente or (2) to alarm and inform the American people? Certainly Dropshot is an alarming and informative document—for the document and its associated papers, when read together, shows that (1) the United States might well have lost World War III; (2) Russia would probably have succeeded in occupying all Western Europe in twenty days; (3) the U.S. Air Force thought that Russia would be able to knock Britain—then America's principal ally with bases of the first importance to the successful conduct of the atomic riposte—out of the war within sixty days; (4) Russian atomic attacks combined with Communist guerrilla warfare within the United States would have gravely impaired America's ability and will to make war; (5) America could not defend her own cities; (6) it would have taken America at least two years to bring her industry and armed forces to a pitch that would have enabled her military to return to Europe; and (7) America intended to occupy Russia and thereby risk interminable guerrilla warfare in that country.

But alarm and information may have been only part of the decision to release Dropshot—if indeed there was a motive. My personal view is that there was no motive in the Joint Chiefs' astounding action in declassifying Dropshot. The simple fact is that in all respects Dropshot was considered obsolete; that given the state of weaponry today it is no longer relevant; that we have reached the edge of doomsday; and that therefore Dropshot does not matter.

If this was the case, then we must proceed to the next major questions about Dropshot. Why was it necessary to write Dropshot at all? And what was its history? Obviously generals exist to protect their country, and to protect their country they must have plans. But surely it is one thing to plan for the defense of one's frontiers and another to plan for a world war. I do not think this plan was written for a preventive war (although clearly preventive war crossed the minds of the generals, as we shall see). Nor do I believe the old Kremlin bogey that America intended to start a war before Russia got too powerful. I believe that Dropshot was written because global war seemed likely at the time; indeed it seemed the only kind of war. This thinking was clearly wrong, and it demonstrates how easily global war might arise through miscalculation—for when Korea erupted, the conflict was confined to that peninsula, and while the world was politically involved, it was not militarily involved.

To repeat, Dropshot was little more than a contingency plan for a war that might arise through the Cold War. It is necessary therefore to examine briefly what was meant by that term and how it arose.

The Cold War was that state of no war, no peace in which the globe found itself at the end of World War II. The editor believes that that conflict—which produced much smoke but little fire—was a historical inevitability. As surely as commotion is produced when two of the earth's plates rub together, two mighty forces, capitalism and Communism, found themselves rubbing together dangerously in many parts of the world.

The consequences of this friction were predictable. Truman felt the cold wrath and malevolence (only some of it justified) of his late ally in the war against Hitler, Josef Stalin. This produced a state of labyrinthine, shrill political warfare that gradually deteriorated into a state of near war. In turn, the United States began a form of war planning purely as insurance. But these plans could not compare with the Rainbow and Pot of Gold series produced by the U.S. Army and Navy for the war with Hitler, Mussolini, and Tojo.

General Eisenhower, then still Commander-in-chief of U.S. forces in Europe, produced a plan for war with Russia in Europe called Totality. That was late in 1945. But the plan was an incongruous document: there were few troops, fewer aircraft, no armies to give it teeth. It was, therefore, hardly worth the paper it was written on.

The Pentagon's Joint Intelligence Staff promulgated a study entitled *Strategic Vulnerability of Russia to a Limited Air Attack,* and only fifty-one days after the Russo-American alliance dissolved with the surrender of Japan, the Staff presented its report. In brief it visualized a limited air attack with atomic bombs on twenty Russian cities in the event that war developed between Russia and America in Europe. This seems to have been the first serious joint study for an air war against Russia, and its objective was to destroy Russia's capacity to make and sustain land warfare by wrecking her industrial and research-and-development centers.

There were other plans, or variations of existing plans. But none of them amounted to much. Then, late in 1946, Winston Churchill surveyed the bitter animosities in a speech at Fulton, Missouri, and proclaimed the Cold War. Stalin retaliated by making it clear that he believed that coexistence between the capitalist and Communist systems was not possible. The result of these speeches was that America moved further to the right while the rest of the world moved further to the left.

As happened after World War I, the victors seemed unable to agree on a peace—and were therefore in danger of losing it. The position was complicated by the fact that Europe had lost the political leadership of the world, and the British, French, and Dutch empires were collapsing irremediably. The United Nations began to seem as fruitless a forum as had been the League of Nations; the atomic tests at Bikini increased people's apprehensions about the future of mankind; the Gouzenko spy case in Canada demonstrated that sinister Russian quality called stealth—and showed that she meant business over the atomic bomb; the Russians hamstrung the Security Council nine times in its first year of trying to preserve the peace; and there were dangerous frictions between the Western democracies and Communism everywhere they met—in Germany, Austria, Indochina, China, Malaya, Indonesia, Burma, Turkey, Greece, Persia,

Korea. Weapons technology leaped ahead against a prospect of political disintegration. In particular, biological warfare showed that diseases of humans, animals, and plants could be spread on a wholesale scale. Secretary of State James F. Byrnes announced a "firm" policy toward Russia, America was wracked by strikes that seemed to many to have been organized by the Communists, the Soviet-sponsored party swamped Berlin's first postwar elections, and Britain was bankrupt.

All around, everywhere, there was disorder and chaos. But these elements in 1946 were inconsequential as against those of 1947.

In that year the great schism opened between East and West, and it was clear that an epic struggle for world hegemony was beginning between America and Russia. Two worlds had emerged: one led by the White House, the other by the Kremlin.

The United Nations was shaken to its foundations, and the attempt to write a peace treaty for Germany was postponed, seemingly indefinitely. Britain granted independence to India, which promptly dissolved into a large-scale religious war in which millions were killed. Palestine produced further similar tensions as the British partitioned the country into one Arab and one Jewish community. Europe hovered on the edge of bankruptcy, famine, the plague, and anarchy. A serious recession set in in America; the Communists were hyperactive throughout the world and especially in Latin America—which seemed to present a direct threat to the United States. Greece and Turkey appealed to the United States for assistance against Communist menaces. And Truman enunciated his Doctrine—the most important step in the Cold War after Churchill's speech at Fulton.

The Albanian Communist militia mined some British warships in the Corfu Channel. Yugoslavia, Bulgaria, and Albania were accused in the UN of giving aid and comfort to the outlawed Greek Communist guerrillas. The Communists took over in Hungary in a brief, violent *coup d'état*. Secretary of State George C. Marshall announced his plan to help Europe recover economically in a speech at Harvard, and Stalin reestablished the old Comintern as a riposte. British Foreign Secretary Ernest Bevin announced in London that British appeasement of Russia was at an end; the Dutch attacked in the Indonesian islands; Stalin's representative at the United Nations accused the United States of warmongering, and his Foreign Minister in Moscow hinted that Russia now had the atomic bomb; and on the last day of the year Romanian Communists forced King Michael to abdicate.

At home, Truman urged Congress to agree to universal military training and ordered loyalty checks on all executive-branch employees. The armed forces were unified; the House Un-American Activities Committee began its investigation of Communism in America; Truman asked Congress for $17 billion to help put Europe back on her feet; and the Secretary of State expressed the gravest concern over Communist maneuvers in France and Italy.

To meet all these challenges and menaces, Congress passed the National Security Act of 1947, which, among other things, led to the formation of the National Security Council and the Central Intelligence Agency. This same act also permitted the Joint Chiefs to begin planning for war. This planning—which led to Dropshot—began against this warning by Major General Curtis Le May: the United States possessed the means to "depopulate vast areas of the earth's surface, leaving only vestigial remnants of man's material works."

An additional impetus to war planning came through the events of 1948. In that year a shooting war seemed inevitable. The Communists seized Czechoslovakia, and the capitalists began building their military, political, and economic alliances in Europe—the alliances that led to NATO. The Communists completed their conquest of North China and supported revolutions or continued warfare in Greece, Indonesia, Burma, Korea, Indochina, and Malaya. The capitalists announced their plans for a government in West Germany, and the Communists retaliated by blockading Berlin, which brought on the Anglo-American airlift. In East Berlin, the Communists established their own government and began rearming the German army, and the Allied Council for Germany and the Berlin Kommandatura collapsed.

The United States accused Russia of massive espionage in the United States and of violating thirty-seven different treaties, and the Hiss case began. Vishinsky accused the United States of planning an atomic attack on the USSR—an allegation that was denied at the time but now seems to have been proved true. Stalin accused the West of wanting to make war over Berlin. This was not true, although the Pentagon had made a plan for such a war. It was called Broiler. It was a limited edition of Dropshot. But one question did emerge out of Stalin's and Vishinsky's allegations: Was somebody at the Pentagon, or attached to it, leaking these plans to Russia? I have already examined that postulation, and my conclusions remain the same. However, each of these allegations did have a grain of truth to them; so the possibility becomes somewhat more tenable, although, of course, it was a simple matter to guess—every general in the West was making some sort of war plan, big or small, at that time.

In Italy the Reds lost, and in Hungary they won—and arrested Cardinal Mindszenty. The UN indicted Greece's Communist neighbors for meddling in Greek affairs. In China the U.S. position collapsed entirely toward the end of the year. The Reds lost in Indonesia but won in Burma—they staged an uprising and the British quit. The Koreans quickly crushed a Red revolt in South Korea, and in the north the Communists proclaimed a Red republic. In Malaya, the Communists were defeated by British troops and the British system, but in Indochina the Communists under Ho Chi Minh continued their revolt.

There was violence throughout the Middle East as the Jews established the state of Israel in 1948; Marshal Tito broke with the Kremlin—Stalin's largest defeat so far; in the United States there was a stock-market crash and Truman seized the railways to prevent economic chaos and further labor trouble.

The best the State Department could tell the President in the middle of the year was that world war was not likely in the next thirty days.

Against this background of commotion on a global scale, the Joint Chiefs authorized the writing of the first global emergency war plan, Charioteer. Its premise was that Europe had been overrun by the Red Army and that the overwhelming strength of Russia was such that only an atomic riposte would restore the authority and power of the Western democracies. Charioteer's political appreciation made the attitude of the United States toward Russia very clear. The plan stated:

> Never before have the intentions and strategic objectives of an aggressor nation been so clearly defined. For a hundred years, victory in the class struggle of the proletariat versus the bourgoisie has been identified as the means by which communism would dominate the world.

The Charioteer planners felt that "the USSR may be entering an era wherein the ultimate objective (of communism) might be gained by military force if all other methods fail."

Therefore the United States must have the plans and capabilities to:

> (a) destroy the war-making capacity of the USSR to the extent and in such manner as to permit the accomplishment of the following objectives. (1) To compel the withdrawal of Soviet military and political forces from areas under their control or domination within 1939 boundaries. (2) To create conditions within the Soviet Republic which will insure (a) abandonment of any ideology which advocates world domination or violation of the sovereignty of one or more states by another state (b) the creation of governments which will practice goodwill toward nations to the end that the principle of the United Nations can become effective.

Among the ways that these political objectives would be obtained was to:

> Initiate strategic air operations as soon as possible after the outbreak of hostilities by launching a concerted attack employing atomic bombs against governmental, political and administrative centers, urban industrial areas, and selected petroleum targets within the USSR from bases in the western hemisphere and the United Kingdom.

The Strategic Air Command plan associated with Charioteer planned for the delivery of 133 atomic weapons on seventy Russian cities or industrial conurbations, all within thirty days: eight such weapons would be unloaded on Moscow to destroy approximately forty square miles of that city's center; at the same time, a further seven atomic bombs would be delivered to Leningrad, to atomize some thirty-five square miles of Russia's second city and largest port.

Over the ensuing twenty-four months, Russia would then—assuming that she did not surrender immediately, the objective of the first strike—be "treated" to a combination of atomic and conventional warfare. In this phase, which was to continue until she did surrender, some 200 atomic bombs would be employed with some 250,000 tons of high-explosive bombs. It was expected that the first strike would destroy some 30–40 percent of Soviet industry, destroy the petroleum industry entirely together with some 6.7 million workers, and bring the Soviet advance in Europe to a halt.

Charioteer was followed by numerous plans and estimates—among them, Cogwheel, Gunpowder, Doublestar, ABC 101, Dualism, and Fleetwood. Fleetwood was by far the most interesting for two reasons: it was part of the planners' response to the Soviets' blockade of Berlin, and it was Dropshot's principal antecedent. We should therefore deal with Fleetwood at length.

The first part of the Fleetwood intelligence plan consisted of a discussion of political factors concerning Russia and her satellites. This was a somber document:

> The ultimate object of Soviet policy is the establishment of Communism, directed from Moscow, throughout the world.

Therefore:

> In a war between the Soviet Union and the Anglo-American Powers before the end of 1949, the political objectives of the Soviet leaders will be to check the threat to the Soviet orbit inherent in the growing stabilization of the non-Communist world, and to establish Soviet-dominated governments in areas occupied by Soviet forces. The political instruments used in the attainment of these objectives would be:—
>
> (a) Intensification of the propaganda program which will be designed particularly to undermine the United Front of the Western Allies, to portray the Soviet Union as the defender of all "true democracies" and "peace loving" peoples of the world and to convince the peoples of the world that war has been forced on the Soviet Union by the "imperialistic designs" of the United States and the United Kingdom.
>
> (b) Maximum exploitation of the Communist parties and dissatisfied minority groups of all countries and their dependencies outside of the Soviet orbit for subversion and sabotage.

The Joint Intelligence Committee estimated the "significant political strengths and weaknesses of the Soviet orbit" to be . . .

STRENGTHS

(1) The native courage, stamina, and patriotism of the Russian population.
(2) The elaborate and ruthless machinery by which the Kremlin exercises centralized control in the Soviet orbit, employing police forces, propaganda, and economic and political duress.
(3) The ideological appeal of theoretical Communism.
(4) The apparent ability of the Soviet regime to mobilize native Russian patriotism behind a Soviet war effort.
(5) The ability of the people and the administration to carry on a war under circumstances of extreme disorganization, demonstrated in the early years of World War II.

WEAKNESSES

(1) Disillusionment and embitterment among the masses throughout the Soviet orbit, resulting from ruthless Soviet and Communist oppression and exploitation.

(2) The fear pervading all elements in Soviet and Satellite society, which tends to destroy independent thinking and paralyze initiative.

(3) The traditional admiration of many of the Soviet Union and Satellite peoples for Western democracy in general and the United States in particular.

(4) Influence of religious groups, especially among the Satellites.

(5) The native nationalism of the Satellite populations and of certain ethnic groups in the Soviet Union.

(6) Demoralization which would result from military and occupation duties outside their own country.

(7) The extreme concentration of power in the Politburo of the Communist Party, which heads the bureaucratic machinery, tends to preclude the assumption of initiative and to discourage individuals at lower levels in the system from making decisions.

But as the evaluation went on to concede, while the strengths "constitute an actual and present advantage to the Soviet Union" the weaknesses "in most cases, are potential rather than actual." Therefore, during the early stages of the war, the weaknesses would not have an early and decisive effect on the outcome of a Soviet military venture. Only slowly would the weaknesses come to be a burden upon Russia's machinery for political control; only slowly would they come to impair the Kremlin's economic and administrative capabilities. In fact, the report warned, during the early stages of war, native Soviet morale "might improve somewhat with reports of spectacular victories and the prospects of booty from Western Europe." It was

> unlikely that the psychological weaknesses in the Soviet and Satellite structure would produce serious consequences unless (a) The Soviet orbit were subjected to intensive and effective aerial attack from the West. (b) The prospect for ultimate victory further diminished because of the continued pressure of sea power as exercised through blockade and commerce destruction, although a sea blockade of the Soviet Union would not be as effective as against a more insular power. (c) Or it seemed to them that the Soviet Union was faced with a protracted war doomed to end in Soviet defeat.

Lastly, in the context of potential Russian weakness, the intelligence team thought it "extremely doubtful that the forces of resistance within the Soviet orbit would effectively assert themselves unless and until they received guidance and material support from the West, and saw hope for early liberation by Western forces."

The Fleetwood planners turned to the Communist economic factors. Although in the recent war Russia was estimated to have lost some 20 million dead, most of them able-bodied men, there remained 33 million workers in her national economy—more than enough to maintain a war economy and agricul tural forces and armies that would be larger than the combined forces of the Allies. She was deficient in certain war materials—including industrial diamonds, tungsten, tin, cobalt, molybdenum, and some special types of machine tools and precision equipment—but none of these deficiences was likely to impair Russia's capacity for war, at least in the first stages. In both men and materials Russia would have the resources of her satellites at her disposal, and neither should be discounted.

In general, therefore, the Joint Intelligence Committee conceded to Russia the men and the industry to fight a prolonged major war. However, there was one Achilles' heel in Russian might: her railway system. Russia moved 90 percent of her goods and people by rail, and her rails had been very seriously damaged during the world war. The committee estimated that in 1949 she would be able to move only the same number of trains that she had run in 1940, and because of steel shortages and poor management, rehabilitation and new rails construction would remain well behind their plan. The Trans-Siberian railway could not sustain a major war in Asia for very long, and the difference in gauges between the Russian system and that of Eastern and Central Europe would plague a railway system that was already poorly distributed. At known and easily attacked points, Russia had to tranship goods or change the bogeys from the Russian to the European gauge. And if these points were destroyed by air attack, guerrillas, or sabotage, then the Soviet war plan would be seriously discommoded. As the Joint Intelligence Committee declared, this was a weak factor that "cannot be over-emphasized." Nor could Russia readily overcome this problem—and certainly not with trucks and aircraft.

In terms of the production of major military equipment, the Joint Intelligence Committee thought that in 1948 Russia would produce 12,000 aircraft, 270,000 motor vehicles, and 6,210 tanks and self-propelled guns—a considerable advance over 1945 figures, and larger by far than the combined production of America, England, Canada, and France, the major figures in the alliance. Thus, despite her Achilles' heel, Russia was the world's major land power. And as the Joint Intelligence Committee put it:

> The Soviet Armed Forces, by the close of World War II, had been developed into a powerful military machine. This formidable force was not demobilized in the same sense that the forces of the Western Powers were demobilized. Instead, it was reorganized and put through extensive and intensive training programs and maneuvers with the objective of profiting from the experience gained in the last conflict. Sufficient military industrial support has been kept in being to maintain these forces and to build up reserve stocks.

Therefore, the committee went on:

> It is concluded from consideration of Soviet political, economic, and military strengths and weakness factors, that against probable opposing forces [i.e., the United

States, Great Britain and the nations with which they were allied] the Soviets have the combat power to overrun key areas in Europe and Asia.

Against this somber picture of Soviet strength, therefore, the Joint Intelligence Committee considered what it called the *Strategic Intentions of the Soviet Union*. Its main conclusion was that:

> The Soviet Union will appreciate that her ultimate objects can be attained only through the overthrow of the two main bastions of democratic power—the United States of America and the United Kingdom.

But how were these bastions to be overthrown? As the committee recognized in the intelligence annex of Plan Fleetwood:

> The Soviet leaders will probably appreciate that direct military invasion of the U.S.A. is an almost impossible task. They are likely, therefore, to appreciate that their object can only be achieved in two stages. The first stage would be to defeat the United Kingdom and to complete the domination of [Eurasia]. The second stage would be to consolidate economic and military gains and to put the Soviet Union in an impregnable position, from which the U.S.A. could first be gradually weakened by Communist infiltration or economic exhaustion, and then attacked by armed force.

In short, the U.S. Joint Intelligence Committee conceded to Russia a military position she may never have lost—that Russia, overall, was the world's mightiest power. Her industrial base had been strengthened, not weakened, by the world war, and her ideological position seemed to have global appeal.

By the time this menacing document was in secret circulation, 1948 was turning into Dropshot year: 1949. Nineteen hundred and forty-eight had been such a bad year that the Nobel authorities decided not to award a Peace Prize at all. And if 1948 had been a bad year for the United States, 1949 approached disaster.

The Russians exploded their first atomic bomb, and the great arms race began to produce advanced weapons and the H-bomb. The American position in China finally collapsed, and the largest nation in the world became Communist. Ex-Defense Secretary James V. Forrestal committed suicide, perhaps in despair over the Soviet triumphs. Revolutions broke out in the Latin American republics of Ecuador, Panama, the Dominican Republic, Guatemala, Bolivia, and Paraguay. The smallest state in the world—San Marino (population 12,000)—emerged as Communist. George Bernard Shaw called Stalin "the ablest statesman in Europe" and predicted that the West would go Red. Everywhere it seemed that local Communist parties were triumphant—even in Britain. The pound, that symbol of capitalist supremacy, collapsed. And in America eleven members of the Communist party were convicted of treason—convictions that were, in the context of Dropshot, of considerable significance. For it seemed to the Pentagon planners that they had to consider what was happening not only overseas but also at home.

Alarmed by these cases, the Dropshot planners asked the Joint Chiefs' Joint Intelligence Group to make a study of Communist plans and capabilities in the United States in the event of war with Russia. This they did, presenting the Dropshot planners with a paper entitled *Intelligence Estimate on Espionage, Subversion and Sabotage.*

The group warned that Russia would continue its effort to disrupt the American war potential by infiltrating "Communist agents and/or sympathizers into the armed forces, governments, and the general economic life of the United States and other nations of the western hemisphere":

> Small groups of militant Communists have been able to wield power out of proportion to their numbers. Communist influence in labor organizations is not expected to increase by 1955, but it will be a danger in view of the grave possibilities of paralyzing general economic life.

The Joint Intelligence Group now turned to the involvement of minority and certain other groups in Soviet special actions in America:

> Negroes and elements of recent European origin are receptive targets for Communist subversion as are a number of intelligent people of sound background, who are deceived by misinformation, or have a perennial weakness for "causes" to support. The professions, and various youth and women's organizations, are a fertile field for this subversive effort.

Therefore the group expected that:

> In 1955 [the target date for this study], through open party and cover groups, the Soviets will have a well-organized system of espionage, and adequate channels of communications with the USSR to ensure the collection of essential political, military and economic information.

Moreover:

> They will be capable, through direct and disguised propaganda, of arousing considerable animosity towards, and confusion in, the United States. The Soviets will have well-laid plans for the sabotage of industrial installations and communication facilities—plans which will go into full-scale operation in the event of war or imminent threat of war. By these means the Soviets will seriously interfere with the mobilization and utilization of the United States war potential.

The group thereupon debated another serious threat to the United States:

> It is probable that the Soviets will be able to employ atomic weapons, biological and chemical warfare against the United States in 1955 either covertly or by direct military action. The Soviet capability of applying a wide variety of biological agents harmful to human, animal and/or vegetable life is practically unlimited.

Developing this theme, the Joint Intelligence Group thought that:

> Methods of introduction would probably include infection of food and water supplies, detonation of small bombs at predetermined times, use of natural vectors such as fleas and lice, contamination of the air either directly or via ventilating systems, smearing agents on equipment, counters, and handrails. Animals, crops, and humans could be subjected to biological or chemical agents by covert methods without great difficulty to the saboteur.

To add to the general aura of menace implicit in their report, the group thought it conceivable that:

> unassembled atomic bombs could be clandestinely introduced into the United States prior to a general attack, assembled, and then detonated in accordance with a preconceived plan. There is also a real possibility of Soviet employment of cargo vessels as atomic bomb carriers berthed in ports along both coasts.

The group thought that the primary targets for atomic and biological warfare carried out by both overt and covert means would be U.S. atomic-bomb plants and repositories and the areas around New York City, Washington, Detroit, Pittsburgh, Chicago, Akron, Duluth, San Francisco, Los Angeles, and Puget Sound. And among the other means of disseminating such advanced weapons were one-way suicide bombing missions and submarine-launched guided missiles (the first Russian intercontinental ballistic missile—indeed the world's first such missile—would not be fired until, coincidentally, 1957).

Against this frightening background of menaces explicit and implicit, Dropshot was written. But what was the political basis for even considering war between America and Russia? This was provided by the National Security Council, the watchdogs of the American ideology. Essentially, advised the National Security Council, there were five basic conflicts between capitalism and Communism. As the National Security Council paper NSC/40, *American Objectives vis-à-vis the USSR,* enumerated them, they were:

(1) . . . peaceful coexistence and mutual collaboration of sovereign and independent governments, regarding and respecting eath other, is an illusion and an impossibility.
(2) That regimes which do not acknowledge Moscow's authority and ideological supremacy are wicked and harmful to human progress and that there is a duty on the part of right-thinking people everywhere to work for the overthrow or weakening of such regimes, by any and all methods which prove tactically desirable.
(3) That there can be, in the long run, no advancement of the interests of the communist and the noncommunist world by mutual collaboration, these interests being basically conflicting and contradictory.
(4) That conflict is the basis of international life wherever, as is the case between the Soviet Union and capitalist countries, one country does not recognize the supremacy of the other.

(5) That spontaneous association between individuals in the communist-dominated world and individuals outside that world is evil and cannot contribute to human progress.

Concerning these five conflicts, the National Security Council and the Joint Chiefs of Staff considered the objectives in two forms of war: cold and hot. The objectives for the Cold War with Russia were two:

(1) To reduce the power and influence of Moscow to limits in which they will no longer constitute a threat to the peace and stability of international society; and (2) to bring about a change in the theory and practice of international relations as observed by the government in power in Russia.

These twin pursuits were also the basic objectives for the hot war. But there were also five supplemental war objectives. As the National Security Council determined them, these were:

(a) Eliminate Soviet Russian domination in areas outside the borders of any Russian state allowed to exist after the war.
(b) Destroy the structure of relationships by which the leaders of the All-Union Communist Party have been able to exert moral and disciplinary authority over individual citizens, or groups of citizens, in countries not under communist control.
(c) Assure that any regime or regimes which may exist on traditional Russian territory in the aftermath of a war: (1) Do not have sufficient military power to wage aggressive war. (2) Impose nothing resembling the present iron curtain over contacts with the outside world.
(d) In addition, if any Bolshevik regime is left in any part of the Soviet Union, ensure that it does not control enough of the military–industrial potential of the Soviet Union to enable it to wage war on comparable terms with any other regime or regimes which may exist on traditional Russian territory.
(e) Seek to create postwar conditions which will: (1) Prevent the development of power relationships dangerous to the security of the United States and international peace. (2) Be conducive to the successful development of an effective world organization based upon the purposes and principles of the United Nations. (3) Permit the earliest practicable discontinuance within the United States of war aims.

As this appreciation was being promulgated, the State Department was producing a paper called *Fundamental Common Objectives*. This became part of Dropshot's political content, and it expresses vividly the degree of apprehension within the State Department about Soviet power and intentions. The appreciation warned that:

The existence of free nations, free men and freedom itself is endangered by an aggressively malignant philosophy backed by great material power and organized in monolithic dictatorship. [The free nations] are opposed on a world-wide front, including the home front, by a ruthless, resourceful and determined enemy utilizing every conceivable means, short of direct overt armed combat, to accomplish its aggressive ends.

While the State Department discounted the probability of imminent war, "the possibility that the enemy will resort to open war can never safely be ignored." The Russians respected "only determination backed by force," and while "the threat to freedom has never been more serious," the

> deadly challenge of our times, indeed the survival of freedom, requires essential unity of purpose and action [because] . . . the capacities of Europe, even a United Europe, are inadequate. So are those of the United States. A united effort, spearheaded by the United Kingdom, France and the United States . . . is essential.

But the Western powers were beset by "parliamentary instability, partisan irresponsibility, nationalism, timidity, inertia, wishful thinking, ignorance, distrust, conflicting social and economic philosophies, limited resources and the compelling urge for maximum economy." Therefore the State Department urged that "agreement be sought . . . in the moral, military, political and economic fields . . . to achieve the kind of world in which freedom can endure." The objectives remained the same in the State Department paper as they were in that of the National Security Council, except in the sphere of military objectives. These were detailed as being:

(1) To deter Soviet armed aggression against any of our homelands by making clear in advance . . . our common determination to consider an armed attack on one as an armed attack on all and to reply with all immediately available, and potentially overwhelming, force.

(2) To build and maintain the maximum military strength compatible with sound economic health, and to achieve maximum strength and economy through military integration, since ability to repulse aggression is second in importance only to determination to do so.

(3) To deter aggression against any other area by making clear that such aggression would involve . . . determined action . . . maximum available assistance to the country attacked . . . and the risk of general war.

(4) To defeat existing Communist-dominated armed rebellions, as in Indo-China, Malaya and Burma, and to deter similar Communist adventures in other areas.

These objectives, and the challenges and responses they produced from the Kremlin, produced the Cold War. Gone was the Communist conception of—as Béla Kun, the Hungarian Communist, foresaw the Communist state as becoming—a "garden of flowers in which every man may pick his share." Instead, the world found itself in a noisy, nerve-racking state produced by two hostile ideologies seeking supremacy and survival. As the Dropshot planners acknowledged, in this state of affairs war might arise from accident or miscalculation. Precisely how accident or miscalculation might produce war would not become really clear until 1977, when the Brookings Institution produced a remarkable study entitled *The Use of the Armed Forces as a Political Instrument*.

The authors of this study, Barry M. Blechman and Stephen S. Kaplan, found that between 1945 and 1957 and between 1957 and 1973, war might have begun through accident and/or miscalculation on an alarming number of occasions—far more than is popularly supposed.

Between 1948 and 1957 the United States used its armed forces for political purposes no less than sixty-three times. In that same period Russia used hers on forty-eight occasions. Not all American demonstrations were directed at Russian or Communist activities, although the majority were. On the other hand, in all cases the Russian power demonstrations were wholly directed at America or her allies, mainly Britain, or to menace satellite or client states who showed signs of deviating from the straight-and-narrow of Communist ideology.

These are fearful figures, for in some cases—though not all—there were the seeds of war-through-miscalculation. More fearful still are the number of occasions in which strategic nuclear forces were flourished in one way or another to influence a political end.

In this matter, little or nothing is known about Russia's use of strategic nuclear forces. It is to be assumed that there were such flourishes, although they must have been conveyed privately or secretly to the governments concerned. As is to be expected, much more is known about the American flourishes.

Between 1945 and 1957 there were no less than ten such displays, with nine more occurring between 1957 and 1973. But what are strategic nuclear flourishes? The Brookings Institution study defines this latest form of power demonstration (what the British used to call gunboat diplomacy or showing-the-flag) as: "deliberate nuclear threats, whether implicit or explicit."

According to the study there were five such types of nuclear signals:

(1) An overt and explicit threat directed at the USSR through global actions of U.S. [strategic nuclear forces]. Since the end of World War II there have been two such demonstrations—during the Cuban missile crisis and the October 1973 war in the Middle East.

(2) In ten incidents, USAF strategic bombers were moved either closer to Russia or China, placed on increased alert, or their withdrawal from a region abroad was delayed, in the context of U.S.–Soviet or U.S.–Chinese tension.

(3) In four incidents, Sixth Fleet aircraft carriers were used to help attain political objectives in the Middle East or Europe. In only one of these incidents, however— the 1958–1959 Berlin Crisis—was the nuclear flourish probably deliberate.

(4) In two peculiar incidents, U.S. long-range bombers assigned to Strategic Air Command were flown to Uruguay (1947) and Nicaragua (1954). The purpose was either to reassure allies or in connection with maneuvers to overthrow the Soviet-backed Arbenz government in Guatemala.

(5) In one case, a U.S. strategic submarine visited Turkey to demonstrate that the U.S. retained a strategic presence in the region.

The incidents in which strategic nuclear forces were used were: November 1946, U.S. aircraft shot down by Yugoslavia; February 1947, inauguration of president in Uruguay; January 1948, April 1948, and June 1948, security of

Berlin; July 1950, security of Europe; August 1953, security of Japan and South Korea; May 1954, Guatemala accepts Soviet bloc support; August 1954, China–Taiwan conflict, security of the Tachen Islands; October 1956, Suez crisis. It is to be noted that there were no strategic nuclear flourishes in 1957, the Dropshot year, although there were three in 1958—over the political crisis in Lebanon, the political crisis in Jordan, and the Quemoy and Matsu crisis.

At this time, this form of showing-the-flag seemed to many to bespeak arrogance in America. Indeed some of these demonstrations were both arrogant and unwise—the editor well remembers being with the U.S. Sixth Fleet in 1957 on a power demonstration off Gallipoli in the eastern Mediterranean. The fleet was concentrated and at anchor in the Gulf of Saros when two high-flying Badger bombers approached the fleet from the direction of Bulgaria. Across the editor's desk came this signal to the commander of the carrier division: "Two your way. Intercept and use Sidewinders [air-to-air missiles] as necessary if fleet disposition approached too closely." The signal was signed by the Commander-in-chief of the Sixth Fleet, Admiral Charles H. "Cat" Brown. The interceptors were scrambled but they failed to make the intercept, and so Sidewinders were not used. Nevertheless there was the danger of wider conflict in this action. The Badgers apart, this mighty force was landing very large numbers of Marines on Turkish soil less than a hundred miles from the Bulgarian frontier—as an entire Turkish army was maneuvering near that frontier. What were the Russians and Bulgars expected to think, especially if two of their strategic aircraft were shot down with missiles?

However, in general, fairness demands the acknowledgment that the American flourishes were characterized by both caution and success—they succeeded in obtaining the political point without casualties, commotion, and the ominous atmosphere that so often precedes major war. (A case in point is the landing of fourteen thousand American troops in Lebanon in 1958: in a highly charged and complicated situation President Eisenhower obtained a restoration of the Western position in Arabia, avoided a civil war in Lebanon, prevented the murder of Hussein and an Arab Nationalist–Communist revolution in Jordan, protected the frontiers of Israel, assured the West of its oil, and exposed the Kremlin's impotence to intervene militarily in a region far from its own frontiers—all for the loss of a single American soldier.)

But of course there were two playing the game. And Russia's flourishes were not only cruder and more blatant displays of armed might but were also attended frequently by the four horsemen of the modern apocalypse: sudden, dangerous intensifications of Russo-American antipathy; commotion; and/or bloodshed; and failure of policy.

In 1977, Faith Campbell Johnson attempted to document the instances of Soviet flourishes between 1945 and 1973, as part of the Brookings study. Her findings constitute a valuable survey of Russian power demonstrations. They also show how many times war might have developed if the ripples caused by the flourishes had turned into tidal waves.

Between 1945 and 1947 there were more than forty cases in which American or Allied (usually British) aircraft were shot down within Soviet territory or along its borders. There were seizures of Japanese fishermen in disputed waters north of Hokkaido. There were also extensive Soviet reconnaissance flights, warship patroling, and surveillance of Western military maneuvers—to say nothing of incessant, global, and sometimes highly provocative espionage and general clandestinity. But Ms. Campbell does not include these incidents in her study because all might be considered acts of legitimate national self-protection. Ms. Campbell considers only those Russian military actions that were undertaken to make or obtain a political point or advantage. The catalog makes long, sombrous reading.

Before Dropshot was promulgated, there were nineteen Soviet flourishes: January 1946, China was the target nation, and the action consisted of the occupation of Manchuria; January 1946, Korea, occupation of the north; March 1946, Iran, delay of troop withdrawals contrary to agreements; March 1946, Turkey, the massing of troops on the frontier; 1947, Austria, intimidation of non-Communist political organizations; January 1947, Germany, intimidation of non-Communist political organizations; February 1947, three incidents— Romania, Bulgaria, Hungary—all with the same purpose, to intimidate the non-Communist political elements by delaying the withdrawal of troops; August 1947, Iran, the massing of troops on the border; January 1948, Germany, interdiction of transportation into Berlin; February 1948, Germany, provocative and menacing aerial activities; February 1948, Czechoslovakia, maneuvers on the frontier; April 1948, Germany, interdiction of transportation into Berlin; June 1948, Germany, blockade of Berlin; November 1948, Iran, massing of troops on the frontier; April 1949, Philippines, shipment of arms to insurgents; August 1949, Yugoslavia, massing of troops on the border; October 1949, Hungary, menacing use of Red Army units as escorts for a sports team.

Between the promulgation late in 1949 of Dropshot and the projected 1957 D-Day, Russia rattled her sabers a further twenty-nine times:

1950–1953, Germany, sporadic harassment of traffic into Berlin; June 1950, Korea, naval presence; January 1951, Korea and China, deployment of divisions to northeast China; January 1951, Germany, occupation of two enclaves in Berlin; March 1951, Albania, provision of air-defense assistance against Yugoslavia; June 1951, Iran, massing of troops on the frontiers; August 1951, Czechoslovakia, provision of air-defense assistance against non-Communist forces; August 1951, Germany, provocative troop maneuvers; September 1951, Yugoslavia, massing of troops on the frontier; June 1952, Austria, harassment of American aircraft; 1953, Bulgaria, Romania, and Albania, port visits; April 1953, Great Britain, port visits; June 1953, Germany, crushing political uprisings; July 1954, Sweden, port visit; September 1954, Germany, harassment of air traffic; October 1954, China, withdrawal from naval base; May 1955, Austria, withdrawal of troops; October 1955, Finland, withdrawal from naval base; October 1955, China, port visit; May 1956, Yugoslavia, port visit; May 1956,

Germany, withdrawal of some troops; July 1956, Holland and Denmark, port visit; October 1956, Poland, maneuvers; October 1956, Hungary, intervention in civil war; November 1956, Hungary, crushing unacceptable Communist regime; November 1956, Germany, harassment of traffic; November 1956, Egypt, maneuvers and troop movements in response to Allied military operations; August 1957, Germany, harassment of traffic into Berlin; September 1957, Syria, port visit.

But if all these events were quickly forgotten in the public mind, the generals and admirals did not forget them. They constituted a pattern of arrogance and mayhem that might dissolve into general war at any time. Therefore that war had to be planned for, and among the forms of war the planners had to contemplate was war by action and by miscalculation—*and* preventive war. The last, it is clear, is a bad, thorny problem, for it implies sneak attacks while the enemy sleeps—a tactic foreign, it is said, to the Anglo-Saxon spirit of fair play. However, there is some evidence that preventive war was indeed studied by the Pentagon (as no doubt it was studied by the Kremlin). This Pentagon study seems to have been undertaken just after Russia exploded her first atomic bomb in August 1949.

After that explosion it became clear at the Pentagon that America's superiority in strategic nuclear forces might be very temporary. Given that a war seemed both imminent and inevitable, would it not be foolhardy to wait for Russia to strike first? Would it not be better to get it over with while America was still the stronger of the two powers? After all, America possessed at least 300 atomic bombs at the end of 1949 and had 840 strategic bombers in service with another 1,350 in mothballs—and all Russia had at best was 200 strategic bombers of the B-29 type. The planners looked at the predictions. Russia might have 10 atomic bombs by the end of 1949. That number could not be decisive in any way except, perhaps, against Great Britain. By mid-1950 she might have 25. Still this stockpile could not be decisive. But now the situation began to get menacing. She could have 50 by mid-1951, 75 by mid-1952, 110 by mid-1953. *Those* figures really could be dangerous.

As Major General Truman H. Landon of USAF Operations declared in a study of the effectiveness in 1950 of the Strategic Air Command (a study that was closely associated with Dropshot):

> Successful delivery of ten to fifty atomic weapons on selected targets in the United States could seriously impede our mobilization for war for a considerable period in that the attacks would cause the destruction of the headquarters of the Federal Government, the partial destruction of large cities, and more than one million casualties. It could delay or reduce materially the scale of our planned strategic atomic air offensive and could cause great delay in projecting United States forces and war materials by neutralizing key centers.

With these somber words in mind, it can be seen readily that the Pentagon, given the world political climate, could very easily have decided that a preventive war might not only be necessary but also desirable. Thus in a paper associated with Dropshot these words appear:

> This Government has been forced, for the purposes of the political war now in progress, to consider more definite and militant objectives towards Russia even now, in time of peace, than it was ever called upon to formulate with respect to either Germany or Japan in advance of the actual hostilities with those countries.
>
> The gravest threat to the security of the United States [stems] from the hostile designs and formidable power of the USSR, and from the nature of the Soviet system. The political, economic, and psychological warfare which the USSR is now waging has dangerous potentialities for weakening the relative world position of the United States and disrupting its traditional institutions by means short of war, unless sufficient resistance is encountered in the policies of this and other non-communist countries. The risk of war with the USSR is sufficient to warrant, in common prudence, timely adequate preparation by the United States. Soviet domination of the potential power of Eurasia, whether achieved by armed aggression or by political and subversive means, would be strategically and politically unacceptable to the United States.

Moreover:

> The USSR has already engaged the United States in a struggle for power. While it cannot be predicted with certainty whether, or when, the present political warfare will involve armed conflict, nevertheless there exists a continuing danger of war at any time.

This statement, which was promulgated by the Joint Chiefs on 18 August 1948, shows clearly that the Pentagon had something more in mind than contingency planning. There is some evidence that Louis Johnson, secretary of defense, 1949–1950, backed preventive war—what Hanson Baldwin of *The New York Times* called "instituting a war to compel cooperation for peace." And there was one other statement that shows that the grave political situation in 1948—the Berlin crisis was at its height, Berlin was blockaded, the Kremlin had seized control of Czechoslovakia, Stalin was trying to wreck the Marshall Plan and plunge Europe back into the Dark Ages, and Mao was knocking at the gates of Peking and elsewhere—had caused the American generals to examine their options. This statement was tucked away toward the end of the long paper by the Joint Chiefs, and it said:

> In addition to the risk of war, a danger equally to be guarded against is the possibility that Soviet political warfare might seriously weaken the relative position of the United States, enhance Soviet strength and either lead to our ultimate defeat short of war, or force us into a war under dangerously unfavorable conditions.

This state of affairs, the paper went on, would be

> facilitated by vacillation, appeasement, or isolationist concepts in our foreign policy, leading to a loss of our allies and influence; by internal disunity or subversion; by eco-

nomic instability in the form of depression or inflation; or by excessive or inadequate armament and foreign aid expenditures.

Clearly, therefore, the Joint Chiefs would have thought there was reason and excuse for preventive war in 1948–1949. However, preventive war was not launched. Apart from all else, the United States could not have won such a war in 1949–1950. Strategic Air Command was *not* capable of dealing Russia a single irreparable blow at this time. It was no more than a deterrent force. Uneasy at the lack of real power and good intelligence, the Joint Chiefs began a plan for a war launched by Russia—Dropshot.

The general assumptions for Dropshot were:

a. For the present, it is improbable that the USSR will wage war with military weapons against the United States;

b. United States support to the nations of western Europe cannot be expected to continue indefinitely. Unless their response to our assistance is so accelerated that they soon are capable of assuming a major portion of the responsibility for checking communism in Europe, the international situation may become favorable for major Soviet aggression;

c. Unless a major economic depression develops in the west, or unless differences in the political and economic aims of the western powers permit exploitation by Soviet diplomacy, the Soviets will cautiously attempt to strengthen their position in western Europe and the Middle East for future exploitation; meanwhile they will concentrate on consolidation of the Communist position in eastern Europe and in the USSR itself. In the Far East consolidation of gains and expansion will be pressed;

d. On the basis that the western nations will not voluntarily accept communism, a major war appears to be ultimately inevitable unless one or more of the following occurs:

(1) The Soviet ideology of Communist domination of the world and the aggressive policy of the USSR designed to achieve this domination are radically changed;

(2) The military potential of the United States and other non-Communist nations and their psychological resistance are sufficiently strong to convince the Soviets that a Soviet gamble for achieving world domination by armed forces is unlikely of success; and

(3) Nationalistic deviation, like that of Yugoslavia, becomes a serious weakness of the Soviet bloc. Such a weakness is susceptible to exploitation by the United States. If the United States military position is strong enough to deter the USSR from attack, as an opening wedge the United States might, by undermining Soviet prestige, be able to develop a group of anti-Moscow Communist nations.

e. If the political leaders of the USSR should decide to resort to war to accomplish their aggressive intentions, war will break out either without warning or following a few months' period of political negotiations and increasing tension;

f. As long as the USSR pursues a policy of world aggression and is opposed by the United States, the United Nations alone will not be an effective instrument for the maintenance of world peace and security;

g. Whether or not the USSR remains in the UN cannot be accepted as a clear-cut indication that a decision has been reached by the Central Committee of the Communist Party (Politburo) relative to the use of military forces for major aggression.

h. Allied occupation forces (including Soviet forces) will be maintained in Germany and United States occupation forces may remain in Japan although their military strength and effectiveness may be reduced for political or budgetary reasons. Allied occupation forces in Austria and Anglo-American occupation forces in Trieste may be removed for political reasons. American and Soviet military missions will, in all probability, remain in a divided Korea; and

i. As long as the present regime in the USSR remains in power, the political, economic, and psychological warfare now being waged against the United States will continue and will vary in intensity, although not in intention, from time to time.

The overall strategic concept of Dropshot was:

In collaboration with our allies, to impose the war objectives of the United States upon the USSR by destroying the Soviet will and capacity to resist, by conducting a strategic offensive in Western Eurasia and a strategic defensive in the Far East.

Initially: To defend the Western Hemisphere *and the home territory of our European Allies;* to launch a powerful air offensive; to initiate a discriminate containment of the Soviet Powers within the general area; North Pole–Greenland Sea–Western Scandinavia–Rhine River–Alps–Piave River–Adriatic Sea–Crete–Iskenderun Pocket–Turkish-Syrian border–Iran–Himalayas–South China–East China Sea–Japan Sea–Tsugaru Strait–Bering Sea–Bering Strait–North Pole; to secure and control essential strategic areas, bases and lines of communication; and to wage political, economic, psychological and underground warfare, while exerting unremitting pressure against the Soviet citadel, utilizing all means to force the maximum attrition of Soviet war resources.

Subsequently: To launch coordinated offensive operations of all arms against the USSR as required.

The basic undertakings of Dropshot were:

In collaboration with our Allies:

a. To maintain the security and war-making capacity of the Western Hemisphere.

b. *To defend the U.K. with particular attention to its continued availability as a base for offensive operations.*

c. *To defend western Scandinavia, selected areas in Denmark, and western continental Europe as far east as possible of the line Rhine River–Alps–Piave River.*

d. To conduct, at the earliest practicable date, a strategic air offensive against the vital war-making capacity of the USSR, and other air offensive operations against suitable targets of the Soviet Powers.

e. To expand the over-all power of the armed forces for later offensive operations against the Soviet Powers.

f. To secure and control land and sea areas and bases essential to the accomplishment of the over-all strategic concept.

g. To secure sea and air lines of communication essential to the accomplishment of the over-all strategic concept, and

h. To provide essential aid to our Allies in support of efforts contributing directly to the over-all strategic concept.

The Dropshot air planners then provided the committee with this précis of the air plan:

1. Under the over-all strategic concept it is essential that (a) the air offensive be initiated immediately, (b) it be initiated and sustained in sufficient force to be effective, (c) targets or target systems destroyed be those which contribute most to the reduction of war-making capacity, and (d) the results of the effort be reflected immediately in the reduction of the offensive capabilities of the Soviet military forces, particularly with respect to their capability to employ weapons of mass destruction.

EMPLOYMENT OF THE ATOMIC BOMB

2. The use of atomic weapons in a strategic air campaign against the U.S.S.R. . . . is considered essential to the provision of adequate initial destructive capabilities to that air effort. The extent to which its quantitative use will influence the composition, size, deployment, and the employment of strategic air forces depends on Soviet counter measure development, both offensive and defensive, on the effectiveness of available bombs, and on the ability of either side to deliver atomic bombs against selected targets within definite time periods. For planning purposes herein it is assumed that the development of atomic munitions in the U.S.S.R. will give the U.S. a quantitative advantage, on D-Day, in the order of 10 to 1 and that the Soviets lag slightly behind the U.S. in technical development of both offensive and defensive weapons.

3. Target systems selected for atomic attack, and the timing and magnitude of the initial attack are based on the requirement for early and effective preventative attack if such action becomes feasible and on the requirement for destruction of their offensive capabilities against our own war potential. They are extended to include the early destruction of selected elements of the Soviet war-making capacity. The following general considerations are deemed pertinent to atomic target selection at present and in 1955.

a. Destruction of stockpiles of atomic bombs or other weapons of mass destruction stocks and processing plants of fissionable materiels, and any known operational supplies of such weapons must be destroyed as soon as possible after the outbreak of hostilities.

b. The initial atomic campaign must provide for its employment against the political, governmental, administrative, and technical and scientific elements of the Soviet nation. They include urban areas as an essential element in basic industries. Inseparable from the destruction of urban areas, major destruction would be accomplished on industry itself. No over-all change in the location of Soviet centers of industry and population can be expected to occur during the next 8 years, with the exception of additional development of limited extent, hence, weapon requirements will be modified primarily by the effectiveness of available bombs, and means of delivery, rather than through revision of the over-all target complexes.

c. The use of atomic weapons in reasonable quantity will permit the achievement of great physical destruction with relatively small effort within a short time. In addition to this physical destruction, it seems reasonable to anticipate that the use of the weapon would create a condition of chaos and extreme confusion. The magnitude of this increased effect cannot be accurately evaluated since at least up to this time it will be in the abstract. It seems logical, however, to anticipate that the psychological effect, properly exploited, could become an important factor in the timing of and the effort necessary to cause the cessation of hostilities and indicates the necessity and profitability of concurrently conducting a well-planned and carefully-executed psychological warfare campaign which would take full advantage of the conditions thus created.

d. The importance of the psychological factor in effectuating defeat may be increased between now and 1955 through more detailed analysis of the global after-effects to be anticipated from large scale employment of weapons of great physical destructive power. Should the Western Hemisphere and European economies become sufficiently inter-dependent that material destruction of a large portion of the latter would result in near collapse of the former, it may become advisable to abandon the concept of destruction of the enemy's physical *means* to wage war in favor of a concept involving destruction of his will through selective attack of limited complexes or mass attack of people with, in each instance, a minimum of damage to physical property. This concept has not been analyzed in this study and conclusions as to force requirements are not modified by these considerations. However, continuing development of biological warfare techniques is definitely indicated.

e. It does not appear possible at this time to analyze the psychological vulnerability of the U.S.S.R. in order to arrive at a proper balance between physical and moral effects to be applied in order to assure the attainment of national war objectives in the minimum time at minimum cost. In this campaign emphasis has again been placed on physical destruction of the enemy's ability to resist. It is therefore necessary that weapons of mass destruction be applied as early as possible and to the extent estimated to be necessary for the destruction of the Soviet ability to resist without undue emphasis on their intangible effects. The limited forces which we can anticipate will be available, and the consequences of failure to destroy her offensive capability *early*, require that this course of action be currently contemplated.

TARGET SYSTEMS FOR STRATEGIC (LONG-RANGE) AIR ATTACK

4. Study of the best available basic industrial data and intelligence information indicates that most important segments of the Soviet economy and most important elements of her war-making capacity which are vulnerable to air attack are: a. Stockpiles of weapons of mass destruction, and facilities for their production; b. Key government and control facilities; c. Urban industrial areas; d. Petroleum industry; e. Aerial mining against submarines; f. Submarine bases, construction and repair facilities; g. Transportation system; h. Aircraft industry; i. Coke, iron and steel industry; j. The electric power system.

While the Dropshot planners did contemplate and plan a long war, they hoped and prayed for a short one in which Russia would be demolished by the Strategic Air Command (SAC) in the opening weeks of the campaign. Therefore the principal factors governing Dropshot planning were that the war would be started by Russia and that it would begin with a series of surprise attacks against SAC bases. Since the British bases were then (in 1949) the most vital—

only from there, given the range of the B-29 and the B-50, could Moscow and Leningrad and the other targets in western Russia be atomized—the Dropshot planners had to calculate whether the British bases were secure. The estimates were discouraging for a number of complicated and interrelated reasons. For these reasons the planners decided that the United States would not be able to depend upon the British bases after D+60. The bases (and large areas of England) would certainly be atomized if the Russians had sufficient numbers of atomic bombs by D-Day.

However, SAC hoped that it would have knocked Russia out before D+60. Therefore the Pentagon decided to go ahead and use the British bases. If these could be secured for sixty days, so the rationale went, then America could win.

Now the planners turned to the question of the effectiveness of SAC itself. The strategic air-war plan in Dropshot required that SAC be capable of mounting and succeeding in six thousand sorties against Russia and Russian-occupied territory in the first three months of war. They required that the bombers deliver about 300 atomic bombs and 20,000 tons of high explosive conventional bombs on about 200 targets located in about 100 urban areas. The Dropshot planners required that the atomic phase be completed in thirty days in order to achieve the psychological effect necessary to compel the Russians to surrender. The primary targets would be Soviet atomic, air, petroleum, steel, and munitions industries and primary administrative centers, such as Moscow and Leningrad.

But could SAC do the job? There was no way of telling except through war games, and of course the new weapons—the H-bombs, advanced A-bombs, B-52s, B-47s, ICBM—were an unknown factor. Therefore the Joint Chiefs were compelled to proceed from the basis of what might happen if war came in the period 1948–1951. This they did.

The Joint Chiefs directed Lieutenant General J. E. Hull, an officer highly experienced in the problems of strategic warfare, to form a group and then study and report upon the effectiveness of SAC. For planning purposes the target date for the war they visualized was 1 January 1950, not 1 January 1957. After a year of study Hull produced a report which was called *Evaluation of Effectiveness of Strategic Air Operations*.

This reports shows that, as in so many other fields, the United States' intelligence about Russia was lamentable, for clearly Hull had to make a study of the effectiveness of an attack force on the basis of an almost total ignorance of the defense.

The Hull evaluators were, therefore, compelled to *assume*—a very dangerous thing to do in war or when planning for it—two different levels of Russian defense capability. One was a high level of competence, in which Russia had modernized its World War II apparatus, incorporating the Luftwaffe's experience, equipment, and techniques. The lower estimate assumed that the Russians had not extensively developed their air defenses much beyond the state of the science as it existed in World War II.

Against this background of ignorance and assumption (two of the great offenses in military lore), General Hull and his team examined the evidence to see whether SAC could or could not get through to targets in nine strategic areas: Moscow–Leningrad; the Urals; the Black Sea; the Caucasus; the Archangel area; Tashkent–Alma-Ata; Novosibirsk; Lake Baikal; and Vladivostok.

The Hull team ran very extensive and expensive aerial tests, war games, and computations of many kinds, visualizing every conceivable situation. The sum total of this theoretical experience was then studied and two aerial war games were played.

The first was a daylight raid by 223 B-29s and B-50s, carrying thirty-two atomic bombs against the Black Sea target area. Very large numbers of electronic countermeasure (ECM) aircraft were employed to divert the Soviet defenses from the atom-bomb carriers and to "red-herring" the ground defenses. It was assumed that the area was defended by 270 jet fighters and 550 piston-engined aircraft.

The attackers crossed the frontier at a cruising altitude of thirty-five thousand feet and bombed from thirty-five thousand feet—important factors where piston-engined aircraft were concerned because of their inability to operate with any high degree of effectiveness beyond thirty thousand feet. The higher and lower levels of defense competences were assumed and applied. In terms of SAC casualties, the findings were close to disastrous.

In the case of the more competent level of defense, SAC was judged to have lost thirty-five aircraft to fighters (twenty after they had released their bombs—a point, it should be said, in SAC's favor), two to antiaircraft artillery fire, and five to what were called (without definition) "operational causes." In addition, fourteen aircraft were judged to have aborted before reaching the target. As a result, twenty-four of the thirty-two bombs dispatched were judged to have been dropped on their targets. Three bombs were lost in crashing aircraft, two were returned in the aborted aircraft, and three were dropped outside the intended target area.

The second war game was a night raid, again into the Black Sea area. The more competent defense was assumed. Ninety-six aircraft went in with thirty-two atomic bombs (again the majority of the planes were ECMs, there to baffle the defenses). Fifty night fighters were assumed to be defending the target area. In the raid seven aircraft were lost to night fighters, two to antiaircraft artillery fire, and two to "operational causes." Twenty-three bombs reached their intended aiming points; three were lost; four returned in aborting aircraft—eight aborted; and two fell outside the target areas. In neither war game did the Hull report state how many aircraft were damaged or damaged beyond repair by enemy action, but other evidence indicates that this type of casualty would have been heavy.

In any event, in both cases, about 70 percent of the bombers succeeded in dropping their bombs in the intended target areas, but with this important difference: the night raid was executed with half the bombers used in the daylight raid and with about a quarter of the casualties. The capacity of SAC to get through was distinctly encouraging. But the losses were serious because, if they persisted, SAC would not be able to sustain the campaign without drawing upon the mothballed reserve. Accordingly, the Hull evaluators turned to this reserve and discovered an alarming factor: very few of these aircraft would be airworthy for eighteen months. Here then was another strike to add against the campaign's feasibility—another strike to add to the base question to limit SAC's ability to carry out its mission.

With all the data at hand, the Hull evaluators undertook four atomic offensives to establish just how serious the casualty and replacement situation might become. Their findings were embodied in a chapter entitled "Estimate of Overall Losses and Results for Several Different Hypothetical Atomic Offensives."

In Offensive A, the striking force available consisted of 260 B-29s and B-50s, 30 B-36s, and 72 very-long-range reconnaissance planes.

Against the lower level of defense, 871 sorties on three night attacks resulted in the loss of thirty-three aircraft, with twenty-three damaged beyond repair—fifty-six aircraft, or just over a sixth of the force. These were very heavy casualties and could not be sustained, as we shall see. On the other hand, 186 atomic bombs were delivered to the targets, representing 85 percent of those intended.

With the higher Russian defense capability, 1,039 sorties were launched in four night attacks to deliver 176 bombs on target (80-percent satisfactory delivery). But the losses were grievous: 123 aircraft were lost over enemy territory, with 25 damaged beyond repair. This represented a 32-percent loss factor. Such a rate of loss meant that after the first strikes SAC would become progressively weakened to the point where very rapidly it would not be able to sustain the atomic campaign.

These were grave data. But when the Hull group came to evaluate what would have happened on daylight offensives, the news became even graver.

In four days of massed daylight operations against the higher-level Soviet defense, 1,221 sorties delivered 153 bombs (70-percent completion) with the loss of 222 aircraft over enemy territory and 27 damaged beyond repair. *This was an overall loss of 55 percent of the force available*—catastrophically high and far higher than the worst losses suffered in any strategic attack during World War II. (During that war the worst loss was that suffered by the Royal Air Force Bomber Command when Four Group lost 20.6 percent of its aircraft—twenty out of ninety-seven Halifaxes—in the great attack on Nuremberg on the night of 30–31 March 1944.)

For the lower level of Russian defense competence, the dispersed type of day raids could—Hull judged—be employed. Otherwise daylight raids were out of the question now and in the future. Even so, the dispersed daylight raids would suffer heavier casualties than were encountered at any time during World War II. This war game provided for 993 sorties in four days of operations. The analysis showed that in order to deliver 185 bombs on target (85-percent completion), SAC would lose 168 aircraft over Russia, and 22 would be lost through other causes or damaged beyond repair. This meant 41-percent casualties. This rate was very high indeed—probably unacceptably high—and if such casualties persisted, it meant that SAC would probably be unable to complete the entire Dropshot program.

The Hull group now made a final casualty summary. They decided that the atomic phase of the air campaign could be carried out at night with total losses of the order of 30 percent of the bomber force for 80-percent completion of the program. Dispersed raids in daylight would be possible only against the less effective defense. For the better of the two defense systems, only concentrated raids could be laid on in daylight, and the strike force would lose 55 percent of the bomber force to complete 70 percent of the offensive.

In conclusion, the Hull group turned to the question of logistic factors in the campaign. The analysis showed that a strategic bombing effort of the magnitude of the campaign could *not* be supported by the supplies of aircraft, parts, fuel, ordnance, personnel, and transportation that would exist on 1 May 1950—even assuming that the bases would be available. However, the evaluators agreed, a more limited effort, which included the whole of the atomic phase of the air attack, could be executed beginning 1 May 1950. This involved the delivery of some 300 atomic bombs, including a second-strike allocation of some 70 such weapons. They found that one of the key factors preventing the execution of the entire aerial attack program was the current strategic reserves of fuel. These were *not* adequate; indeed sufficient fuel only for two thousand sorties would be available—enough to complete only the atomic phase of the campaign.

Secondly, Hull reported that in the opinion of his group the bomber force allocated to SAC for the air campaign was too small to complete the plan satisfactorily, given the expected casualty rates of the campaign. Moreover, additional bombers could be made available only at the expense of those committed to training, testing, command support, and administration. Hull warned that if these were used, the Phase 2 of the campaign would be seriously delayed.

To add to SAC's difficulties, the airlift needed to deploy SAC units overseas in Phase 1 was in excess of Military Air Transport Service capacity. The only way the emergency deployment could be undertaken was by the use of bombers to help move the men and the equipment needed to launch the air attack—and this in turn would affect the bombers' ability to launch the immediate retaliation which war with Russia would demand. In all, Hull reported, the attack would require "considerable modification to make it logistically feasible."

As for the British bases, Hull went on, an inspection revealed that they were "exceedingly vulnerable" to air attack, that no organized defense would exist at the time SAC began to execute its war plan, and that the British would require thirty days' warning to organize such a defense. Hull noted that "Since the Soviets realize the significance of these bases and appreciate the difficulties of a tight air defense, it is not unlikely that their first hostile move would be to attack these bases" and deny them to SAC. Such an attack, of course, would wreck not only the aerial campaign but also the other counterblows in Dropshot.

On this somber note the study ended. Two months later, on 11 April 1950, Major General S. E. Anderson, Director of USAF plans and operations, commenting upon the Hull report, wrote a memorandum to W. Stuart Symington, the Secretary of the Air Force. Given the acute political tensions that existed, it must have been an extremely disturbing document for the President, the Cabinet, and the Joint Chiefs.

General Anderson agreed that the SAC campaign was not entirely a feasible operation of war. He agreed that only the atomic phase could be carried out with the men and materiel available on D-Day, but even so SAC would not be able to guarantee a primary requirement built into the air plan: that the atomic attack be compressed into the shortest possible time "in order to create the greatest possible shock effect on the USSR." Such was the state of SAC in those days that Plan Trojan, for example, did not propose to atomize either Moscow or Leningrad until the ninth day of the war. But why would SAC's counteroffensive as planned be so slow in getting airborne? Because, as Anderson reported, of "insufficient bases overseas [and] insufficient prestocked fuel supplies overseas."

But there were also other factors: too few Military Air Transport Command planes to ferry the ground crews, weapons, and ground handling equipment; sabotage and bombardment at both ends of the flight; political negotiations with the governments concerned; and the general effects and shock of the surprise attack the Russians were expected to launch.

These matters were, of course, corrected later, and SAC did soon afterward reach a degree of efficiency that was almost superhuman. However, at that time Anderson was compelled to declare that: "In the event of war in 1950, the Air Force can (a) complete the atomic phase of the planned strategic air offensive (b) provide inadequate air defense for the United States and Alaska (c) initiate mobilization and training." The Air Force could not "(a) complete the entire air offensive called for in Trojan or (b) provide the air defense for the United States and Alaska with the maximum risk we can afford to take."

To sum up, if the Hull and Anderson reports are accepted as being in the realm of accurate forecasting and analysis, then the aerial campaign as planned could not have succeeded. It was true that appalling damage could have been inflicted on Russia, but only at appalling loss to the U.S. Air Force. Presumably Truman, the Cabinet, and the Joint Chiefs would have accepted this loss, but would SAC have done so? If the evidence of World War II and the Vietnam war has validity, air crews are prepared to accept serious losses up to a point. But as was demonstrated after the terrible losses suffered by the Royal Air Force Bomber Command at Nuremberg during the raid of 30–31 March 1944, a form of mutiny spreads through even elite forces when casualties become catastrophic—and as the above figures show, Dropshot losses would have been catastrophic.

Even assuming that SAC would have stuck to its task, there remains the considerable body of evidence that through lack of bases, crews, aircraft, stockpiles, and transportation, the campaign probably would not have succeeded. In that case it is not unreasonable to postulate that Dropshot would have failed. And what would this have meant if war had broken out in 1957—or at any other time during the period that Dropshot was being conceived and written?

It would have meant that America would have been in for a very long war that would have been fought, in all likelihood, much as George Orwell thought it would be fought in his novel *1984:* two exhausted giants hurling missiles at each other from time to time in an interminable and inconclusive war that ruined the world. Moreover, it is reasonable to suppose that had America failed—had Dropshot failed—then the Red Army would have emerged the master of Europe.

Dropshot did not, of course, change the world by itself. But the circumstances surrounding it most certainly did. The major consequence was that it made America realize that it was not as powerful as it thought it was, and this realization catapulted the world into the twenty-first century with a rapidity and dynamism that is to be compared with the Industrial Revolution—and the October Revolution. It created a Titan—even though the Kremlin thought and thinks that that Titan may be made of paper.

Anthony Cave Brown,

VOLUME 1

THE OUTBREAK OF THE WAR, DISASTER, AND DEFENSE.

CONTENTS

1. MISSION / 35

2. BASIC ASSUMPTION / 35

3. NATIONAL WAR OBJECTIVES OF THE UNITED STATES
Report by the National Security Council on U.S. Objectives with Respect to
the U.S.S.R. to Counter Soviet Threats to U.S. Security / 36
The Problem / 37
Analysis of the Nature of the Threats / 37
Conclusions / 42

4. SPECIAL ASSUMPTIONS / 45

5. OVERALL STRATEGIC CONCEPT / 47

6. BASIC UNDERTAKINGS / 47

7. PHASED CONCEPT OF OPERATIONS
Phase I. In collaboration with our allies
Secure the Western Hemisphere / 49
Conduct an air offensive against the Soviet powers / 49
Conduct offensive operations to destroy enemy naval forces, shipping,
naval bases, and supporting facilities / 50
Hold the United Kingdom / 50
Hold the Rhine–Alps–Piave line / 50
Hold the area southeastern Turkey–Tigris Valley–Persian Gulf / 50
Hold maximum areas of the Middle East and Southeast Asia consistent with
indigenous capabilities supported by other Allied courses of action / 51
Hold Japan, less Hokkaido / 51
Secure sea and air lines of communications essential to the accomplish-
ment of the overall strategic concept / 51
Secure overseas bases essential to the accomplishment of the overall
strategic concept as follows / 51
Expand the overall power of the armed forces for later operations against
the Soviet powers / 55
Provide essential aid to our allies in support of efforts contributing directly
to the overall strategic concept / 55
Initiate or intensify psychological, economic, and underground
warfare / 55
Establish control and enforce surrender terms in the USSR and satellite
countries / 55

Phase II. In collaboration with our allies

Continue the air offensive to include the intensification of the air battle with the objective of obtaining air supremacy / 56

Maintain our holding operations along the general line of discriminate containment, exploiting local opportunities for improving our position thereon and exerting unremitting pressure against the Soviet citadel / 56

Maintain control of other essential land and sea areas and increase our measure of control of essential lines of communications / 56

Reenforce our forces in the Far East as necessary to contain the Communist forces to the mainland of Asia and to defend the southern Malay Peninsula / 56

Continue the provision of essential aid to Allies in support of efforts contributing directly to the overall strategic concept / 56

Intensify psychological, economic, and underground warfare / 56

Establish control and enforce surrender terms in the USSR and satellite countries (in the event of capitulation during Phase II) / 56

Generate at the earliest possible date sufficient balanced forces, together with their shipping and logistic requirements, to achieve a decision in Europe / 56

Phase III. In collaboration with our allies

Initiate a major land offensive in Europe to cut off and destroy all or the major part of the Soviet forces in Europe / 56

Continue offensive operations of all arms, as necessary to force capitulation / 56

Phase IV. In collaboration with our allies

Establish control and enforce surrender terms in the USSR and satellite countries / 56

EDITOR'S ASSESSMENT / 56

Assumptions for Peacetime Preparations for War or Emergency / 60
War Planning Assumptions / 61

1:MISSION

1. To impose the national war objectives of the United States on the USSR and her allies.

2:BASIC ASSUMPTION

2. On or about 1 January 1957, war against the USSR has been forced upon the United States by an act of aggression of the USSR and/or her satellites.

3:NATIONAL WAR OBJECTIVES OF THE UNITED STATES

3. The conclusions of NSC 20/4,* approved by the President, state the aims and objectives of the United States with respect to the USSR. . . .

---

* See Appendices.

November 23, 1948

REPORT BY THE NATIONAL SECURITY COUNCIL*

on

U.S. OBJECTIVES WITH RESPECT TO THE USSR TO COUNTER SOVIET THREATS TO U.S. SECURITY

*Editor's Note: This report was one of the earliest to be made by the National Security Council, a body that met for the first time on 26 September 1947. The Council (along with the Central Intelligence Agency and the National Security Resources Board) was established by the National Security Act of 1947. The establishment of the NSC was a direct outcome of the darkening international horizons caused by Soviet bloc threats to Greece and Turkey, the failure of Russia to keep pace with the Western powers in demobilization, the collapse of the Council of Foreign Ministers' meeting in Moscow (called to draft the peace treaties with Germany and Austria), and the Soviet walkout from the Allied Control Council. It was a period of intense Soviet intransigence at the United Nations and a time in which Russia generally tightened its hold on Eastern Europe while Stalin's agents sought to undermine Western Europe and Great Britain with intensive class and political agitation. Faced with the loss of all Europe, Truman promulgated his Doctrine and Marshall launched his Plan.

The members of the first NSC—the men who wrote this report—consisted of Alben Barkley, the Vice-President; George C. Marshall, the Secretary of State; James Forrestal, the Secretary of Defense; Kenneth Royall, the Secretary of the Army; J. L. Sullivan, the Secretary of the Navy; W. Stuart Symington, the Secretary of the Air Force; Rear Admiral Roscoe Hillenkoetter, the first Director of the Central Intelligence Agency (which was formed at the same time as the NSC); and John Steelman, the Secretary of the National Security Resources Board. The Executive Secretary was Admiral Sidney W. Souers.

The NSC was formed out of the old Committee of Three, which consisted of the Secretaries of State, War, and the Navy—a body noted for the elegance and brevity of its meetings. The new Council's function was—and remains—to plan, coordinate, and evaluate the defense policies of the United States and also to exercise general direction over the CIA.

THE PROBLEM

1. To assess and appraise existing and foreseeable threats to our national security currently posed by the USSR; and to formulate our objectives and aims as a guide in determining measures required to counter such threats.

ANALYSIS OF THE NATURE OF THE THREATS

2. The will and ability of the leaders of the USSR to pursue policies which threaten the security of the United States constitute the greatest single danger to the United States within the foreseeable future.

3. Communist ideology and Soviet behavior clearly demonstrate that the ultimate objective of the leaders of the USSR is the domination of the world. Soviet leaders hold that the Soviet Communist party is the militant vanguard of the world proletariat in its rise to political power and that the USSR, base of the world Communist movement, will not be safe until the non-Communist nations have been so reduced in strength and numbers that Communist influence is dominant throughout the world. The immediate goal of top priority since the recent war has been the political conquest of Western Europe. The resistance of the United States is recognized by the USSR as a major obstacle to the attainment of these goals.

4. The Soviet leaders appear to be pursuing these aims by:

a. Endeavoring to insert Soviet-controlled groups into positions of power and influence everywhere, seizing every opportunity presented by weakness and instability in other states, and exploiting to the utmost the techniques of infiltration and propaganda, as well as the coercive power of preponderant Soviet military strength.

b. Waging political, economic, and psychological warfare against all elements resistant to Communist purposes and in particular attempting to prevent or retard the recovery of and cooperation among Western European countries.

c. Building up as rapidly as possible the war potential of the Soviet orbit in anticipation of war, which in Communist thinking is inevitable.

Both the immediate purposes and the ultimate objective of the Soviet leaders are inimical to the security of the United States and will continue to be so indefinitely.

5. The present Soviet ability to threaten U.S. security by measures short of war rests on:

a. The complete and effective centralization of power throughout the USSR and the international Communist movement.

b. The persuasive appeal of a pseudoscientific ideology promising panaceas and brought to other peoples by the intensive efforts of a modern totalitarian propaganda machine.

c. The highly effective techniques of subversion, infiltration, and capture of political power, worked out through a half century of study and experiment.

d. The power to use the military might of Russia, and of other countries already captured, for purposes of intimidation or, where necessary, military action.

e. The relatively high degree of political and social instability prevailing at this time in other countries, particularly in the European countries affected by the recent war and in the colonial or backward areas on which these European areas are dependent for markets and raw materials.

f. The ability to exploit the margin of tolerance accorded the Communists and their dupes in democratic countries by virtue of the reluctance of such countries to restrict democratic freedoms merely in order to inhibit the activities of a single faction and by the failure of those countries to expose the fallacies and evils of Communism.

6. It is impossible to calculate with any degree of precision the dimensions of the threat to U.S. security presented by these Soviet measures short of war. The success of these measures depends on a wide variety of currently unpredictable factors, including the degree of resistance encountered elsewhere, the effectiveness of U.S. policy, the development of relationships within the Soviet structure of power, etc. Had the United States not taken vigorous measures during the past two years to stiffen the resistance of Western European and Mediterranean countries to Communist pressures, most of Western Europe would today have been politically captured by the Communist movement. Today, barring some radical alteration of the underlying situation which would give new possibilities to the Communists, the Communists appear to have little chance of effecting at this juncture the political conquest of any countries west of the Lübeck–Trieste line. The unsuccessful outcome of this political offensive has in turn created serious problems for them behind the Iron Curtain, and their policies are today probably motivated in large measure by defensive considerations. However, it cannot be assumed that Soviet capabilities for subversion and political aggression will decrease in the next decade, and they may become even more dangerous than at present.

7. In present circumstances the capabilities of the USSR to threaten U.S. security by the use of armed forces* are dangerous and immediate:

---

* Soviet military capabilities as set forth in this paper, while constituting potential threats to U.S. security which must be recognized, do not represent an evaluated estimate of Soviet intentions to utilize these capabilities, do not take into account the effect of counteraction, *and are based upon the assumption of no important change in the territory under Soviet control or in the type of that control.* (Italics added by editor.)

a. The USSR, while not capable of sustained and decisive direct military attack against U.S. territory or the Western Hemisphere, is capable of serious submarine warfare and of a limited number of one-way bomber sorties.

b. Present intelligence estimates attribute to Soviet armed forces the capability of overrunning in about six months all of Continental Europe and the Near East as far as Cairo, while simultaneously occupying important continental points in the Far East. Meanwhile, Great Britain could be subjected to severe air and missile bombardment.

c. Russian seizure of these areas would ultimately enhance the Soviet war potential, if sufficient time were allowed and Soviet leaders were able to consolidate Russian control and to integrate Europe into the Soviet system. This would permit an eventual concentration of hostile power which would pose an unacceptable threat to the security of the United States.

Editor's Note: Between 1940 and 1948 the Soviets annexed or came to control 115.9 million people in 575,947 square miles of new territory. They annexed or placed under Soviet administration 24 million people and 182,000 square miles in parts of Finland, Estonia, Latvia, Lithuania, part of German East Prussia, part of Poland, part of Czechoslovakia, and part of Romania. Also, by 1948 Russia had come to control 91.9 million people in 393,547 square miles of territory in Bulgaria, Romania, Poland (including German territories under Polish administration), Hungary, the Soviet zone of Germany, Czechoslovakia, and Albania. At this time Russia was also exerting heavy pressure in northern Iran, Turkey, and Greece, and she had also extended considerably her influence in Asia by occupying the greater part of Manchuria and North Korea. In addition, Communist agitation was being intensified throughout the whole of Southeast Asia, especially in Indochina, Malaya, Burma, and the Philippines. China itself was about to be taken over completely by the Chinese Communist party.

8. However, rapid military expansion over Eurasia would tax Soviet logistic facilities and impose a serious strain on [the] Russian economy. If at the same time the USSR were engaged in war with the United States, Soviet capabilities might well, in face of the strategic offensives of the United States, prove unequal to the task of holding the territories seized by the Soviet forces. If the United States were to exploit the potentialities of psychological warfare and subversive activity within the Soviet orbit, the USSR would be faced with increased disaffection, discontent, and underground opposition within the area under Soviet control.

9. Present estimates indicate that the current Soviet capabilities . . . will progressively increase and that by no later than 1955 the USSR will probably be capable of serious air attacks against the United States with atomic, biological, and chemical weapons, of more extensive submarine operations (including the launching of short-range guided missiles), and of airborne operations to seize advance bases. However, the USSR could not, even then, successfully

undertake an invasion of the United States as long as effective U.S. military forces remained in being. Soviet capabilities for overrunning Western Europe and the Near East and for occupying parts of the Far East will probably still exist by 1958.

10. The Soviet capabilities and the increases thereto set forth in this paper would result in a relative increase in Soviet capabilities vis-à-vis the United States and the Western democracies unless offset by factors such as the following:

a. The success of ERP*
b. The development of Western Union† and its support by the United States.
c. The increased effectiveness of the military establishments of the United States, Great Britain, and other friendly nations.
d. The development of internal dissension within the USSR and disagreements among the USSR and orbit nations.

*Editor's Note: The European Recovery Program (ERP; also called the Marshall Plan) was the idea of General George C. Marshall, the Secretary of State, and "the architect of victory in World War II." He promulgated his idea in a speech at Harvard University on 5 June 1947, and it was the outcome of the situation in Europe: despite extensive aid to the Western European countries from the United States, the mechanism of the European economy remained badly jammed, and it seemed that all Western Europe was on the brink of economic collapse. The plan lasted until 1951 and goods, services, and financial assistance totaling some $12 billion were dispensed. The participating countries were Austria, Belgium, Denmark, France, West Germany, Great Britain, Greece, Iceland, Luxembourg, the Netherlands, Norway, Sweden, Switzerland, Turkey, and the United States. Together they formed the Organization of European Economic Cooperation. While one object was undoubtedly the containment of the Communist parties in Czechoslovakia, France, and Italy, Marshall said in his speech that the policy was "not directed against any country or doctrine but against hunger, poverty, desperation and chaos." The Marshall Plan was open to Russia and the countries behind the Iron Curtain. But Stalin refused all American aid for the USSR and, despite initial interest on the part of Poland and Czechoslovakia, compelled the satellite governments to do likewise. Instead Stalin set up the Cominform (an organization not unlike the prewar Comintern in its aspirations) to fight the Marshall Plan as "an instrument of American imperialism." The world thus found itself split into two blocs. The results were NATO and the Warsaw Pact—and this first postwar U.S. war plan.

†Editor's Note: Western Union: On 4 March 1948, representatives of Belgium, France, Luxembourg, Holland, and Great Britain met in Brussels to consider the terms of a treaty of mutual assistance in answer to the menaces implicit in the establishment of the Cominform by Russia in September 1947. The Western discussions soon met with success, and the

Brussels Treaty was signed on 17 March 1948. This was the seed from which NATO sprang. The signatories pledged themselves to build up a common defense system and to strengthen their cultural and economic ties. The basis of the pact was that an attack upon one signatory would be deemed an attack upon all and that all would respond. The Brussels Treaty was scarcely signed when the Russians started the blockade of West Berlin in June 1948. This move hastened the establishment of the Western Union Defense Organization, which was set up in September 1948. The U.S. and Canadian governments had observers at Brussels Treaty meetings from July 1948 onward. Field Marshal Bernard L. Montgomery was appointed chairman of the commanders-in-chief committee of the WUDO and established his headquarters at Fontainebleau, France. The commanders-in-chief were General de Lattre de Tassigny (France) for the land forces; Air Chief Marshal Sir James Robb (Great Britain) for the air forces; and Vice Admiral Jaujard (France) for the naval forces. This committee did much valuable work despite serious personality differences between Montgomery and de Lattre de Tassigny. The Atlantic Alliance, with the United States as a full member, was effectively established on 4 April 1949.

11. The USSR has already engaged the United States in a struggle for power. While it cannot be predicted with certainty whether, or when, the present political warfare will involve armed conflict, nevertheless there exists a continuing danger of war at any time.

a. While the possibility of planned Soviet armed actions which would involve this country cannot be ruled out, a careful weighing of the various factors points to the probability that the Soviet government is not now planning any deliberate armed action calculated to involve the United States and is still seeking to achieve its aims primarily by political means, accompanied by military intimidation.

b. War might grow out of incidents between forces in direct contact.

c. War might arise through miscalculation, through failure of either side to estimate accurately how far the other can be pushed. There is the possibility that the USSR will be tempted to take armed action under a miscalculation of the determination and willingness of the United States to resort to force in order to prevent the development of a threat intolerable to U.S. security.

12. In addition to the risk of war, a danger equally to be guarded against is the possibility that Soviet political warfare might seriously weaken the relative position of the United States, enhance Soviet strength, and either lead to our ultimate defeat short of war or force us into war under dangerously unfavorable conditions. Such a result would be facilitated by vacillation, appeasement, or isolationist concepts in our foreign policy, leading to loss of our allies and influence; by internal disunity or subversion; by economic instability in the form of depression or inflation; or by either excessive or inadequate armament and foreign-aid expenditures.

13. To counter threats to our national security and to create conditions conducive to a positive and in the long term mutually beneficial relationship between the Russian people and our own, it is essential that this government formulate general objectives which are capable of sustained pursuit both in time of peace and in the event of war. From the general objectives flow certain specific aims which we seek to accomplish by methods short of war, as well as certain other aims which we seek to accomplish in the event of war.

CONCLUSIONS

Threats to the Security of the United States

14. The gravest threat to the security of the United States within the foreseeable future stems from the hostile designs and formidable power of the USSR and from the nature of the Soviet system.

15. The political, economic, and psychological warfare which the USSR is now waging has dangerous potentialities for weakening the relative world position of the United States and disrupting its traditional institutions by means short of war, unless sufficient resistance is encountered in the policies of this and other non-Communist countries.

16. The risk of war with the USSR is sufficient to warrant, in common prudence, timely and adequate preparation by the United States.

a. Even though present estimates indicate that the Soviet leaders probably do not intend deliberate armed action involving the United States at this time, the possibility of such deliberate resort to war cannot be ruled out.

b. Now and for the foreseeable future there is a continuing danger that war will arise either through Soviet miscalculation of the determination of the United States to use all the means at its command to safeguard its security, through Soviet misinterpretation of our intentions, or through U.S. miscalculation of Soviet reactions to measures which we might take.

17. Soviet domination of the potential power of Eurasia, whether achieved by armed aggression or by political and subversive means, would be strategically and politically unacceptable to the United States.

18. The capability of the United States either in peace or in the event of war to cope with threats to its security or to gain its objectives would be severely weakened by internal developments, important among which are:

a. Serious espionage, subversion, and sabotage, particularly by concerted and well-directed Communist activity.

b. Prolonged or exaggerated economic instability.
c. Internal political and social disunity.
d. Inadequate or excessive armament or foreign-aid expenditures.
e. An excessive or wasteful usage of our resources in time of peace.
f. Lessening of U.S. prestige and influence through vacillation or appeasement or lack of skill and imagination in the conduct of its foreign policy or by shirking world responsibilities.
g. Development of a false sense of security through a deceptive change in Soviet tactics.

U.S. Objectives and Aims Vis-à-Vis the USSR

19. To counter the threats to our national security and well-being posed by the USSR, our general objectives with respect to Russia, in time of peace as well as in time of war, should be:

a. To reduce the power and influence of the USSR to limits which no longer constitute a threat to the peace, national independence, and stability of the world family of nations.
b. To bring about a basic change in the conduct of international relations by the government in power in Russia, to conform with the purposes and principles set forth in the UN charter.

In pursuing these objectives due care must be taken to avoid permanently impairing our economy and the fundamental values and institutions inherent in our way of life.

20. We should endeavor to achieve our general objectives by methods short of war through the pursuit of the following aims:

a. To encourage and promote the gradual retraction of undue Russian power and influence from the present perimeter areas around traditional Russian boundaries and the emergence of the satellite countries as entities independent of the USSR.
b. To encourage the development among the Russian peoples of attitudes which may help to modify current Soviet behavior and permit a revival of the national life of groups evidencing the ability and determination to achieve and maintain national independence.
c. To eradicate the myth by which people remote from Soviet military influence are held in a position of subservience to Moscow and to cause the world at large to see and understand the true nature of the USSR and the Soviet-directed world Communist party and to adopt a logical and realistic attitude toward them.
d. To create situations which will compel the Soviet government to recognize

the practical undesirability of acting on the basis of its present concepts and the necessity of behaving in accordance with precepts of international conduct, as set forth in the purposes and principles of the UN charter.

21. Attainment of these aims requires that the United States:

a. Develop a level of military readiness which can be maintained as long as necessary as a deterrent to Soviet aggression, as indispensable support to our political attitude toward the USSR, as a source of encouragement to nations resisting Soviet political aggression, and as an adequate basis for immediate military commitments and for rapid mobilization should war prove unavoidable.
b. Assure the internal security of the United States against dangers of sabotage, subversion, and espionage.
c. Maximize our economic potential, including the strengthening of our peacetime economy and the establishment of essential reserves readily available in the event of war.
d. Strengthen the orientation toward the United States of the non-Soviet nations and help such of those nations as are able and willing to make an important contribution to U.S. security to increase their economic and political stability and their military capability.
e. Place the maximum strain on the Soviet structure of power and particularly on the relationships between Moscow and the satellite countries.
f. Keep the U.S. public fully informed and cognizant of the threats to our national security so that it will be prepared to support the measures which we must accordingly adopt.

22. In the event of war with the USSR, we should endeavor by successful military and other operations to create conditions which would permit satisfactory accomplishment of U.S. objectives without a predetermined requirement for unconditional surrender. War aims supplemental to our peacetime aims should include:

a. Eliminating Soviet Russian domination in areas outside the borders of any Russian state allowed to exist after the war.
b. Destroying the structure of relationships by which the leaders of the All-Union Communist party have been able to exert moral and disciplinary authority over individual citizens, or groups of citizens, in countries not under Communist control.
c. Assuring that any regime or regimes which may exist on traditional Russian territory in the aftermath of a war:
   (1) Do not have sufficient military power to wage aggressive war.
   (2) Impose nothing resembling the present Iron Curtain over contacts with the outside world.

d. In addition, if any Bolshevik regime is left in any part of the Soviet Union, ensuring that it does not control enough of the military–industrial potential of the Soviet Union to enable it to wage war on comparable terms with any other regime or regimes which may exist on traditional Russian territory.

e. Seeking to create postwar conditions which will:
   (1) Prevent the development of power relationships dangerous to the security of the United States and international peace.
   (2) Be conducive to the successful development of an effective world organization based upon the purposes and principles of the United Nations.
   (3) Permit the earliest practicable discontinuance within the United States of wartime controls.

23. In pursuing the above war aims, we should avoid making irrevocable or premature decisions or commitments respecting border rearrangements, administration of government within enemy territory, independence for national minorities, or postwar responsibility for the readjustment of the inevitable political, economic, and social dislocations resulting from the war. . . .

4:SPECIAL ASSUMPTIONS

4. The North Atlantic Pact nations (the United States, Canada, the United Kingdom, France, Belgium, Netherlands, Luxembourg, Italy, Norway, Denmark, Iceland, and Portugal), non-Communist China, the other nations of the British Commonwealth (except India and Pakistan), and the Philippines will be allied. . . .

5. Ireland, Spain, Switzerland, Sweden, Greece, Turkey, the Arab League (Egypt, Transjordan, Syria, Lebanon, Iraq, Saudi Arabia, Yemen), Israel, Iran, India, and Pakistan will attempt to remain neutral but will join the Allies if attacked or seriously threatened.

6. Allied with the USSR, either willingly or otherwise, will be Poland, Finland, Latvia, Estonia, Lithuania, Czechoslovakia, Hungary, Yugoslavia,* Albania, Romania, Bulgaria, Mongolian People's Republic (Outer Mongolia), Manchuria, Korea, and Communist China (hereinafter denoted the Soviet powers).

7. Except for Soviet satellites, other countries of the Eastern Hemisphere

---

* If the present defection of Yugoslavia from the Soviet satellite orbit should continue to 1957, it is not likely that Yugoslavia would ally with the Soviet Union but would attempt to remain neutral and would be committed to resist Soviet and/or satellite attack.

will attempt to remain neutral, but will submit to adequate armed occupation by either side rather than fight.

8. The Latin American countries will remain neutral or join the Allies. Those that remain noncombatant probably will make their economic resources and possibly their territories available to the Allies.

9. United States programs for European [economic and fiscal] recovery have been completed by 1953 and have been effective to the extent that, by 1957, countries participating therein have achieved political stability and are mutually self-supporting economically.

10. The armed forces of the Western European Allies have been regenerated to the extent that by 1957 they are capable of substantial coordinated defensive military action in Western Europe.*

*Editor's Note: This was not as vain a hope as it might have seemed at the time. When the NATO treaty was signed in Washington on 4 April 1949, the military position of the Western powers was very weak. Most of the ground forces available were badly equipped and were deployed not for defense but for the occupation of Germany. There were less than one thousand aircraft and about twenty airfields. Within ten years—that is, by the 1957 D-Day— NATO's powers had changed very considerably. The ground forces in Europe consisted of twenty of the thirty divisions planned, and they were equipped with nuclear missiles. NATO had about five thousand aircraft, excluding strategic bombers, and some 220 bases. POL (petrol, oil, and lubricants) and logistical organizations had been established, joint production of modern weapons had begun, there was talk of a NATO tank, and— despite personality problems with the land-forces commander, Montgomery, who was in occasional serious argument with the Canadians and the French—there was a most un-European degree of harmony. (For further data see the Institute for Strategic Studies [ISS] study of NATO in 1959 in the appendices.)

11. Allied forces, of substantially the same military strength and effectiveness as at present, will be available for D-Day deployment in, or will be actually stationed in, Germany, Austria, Trieste, and Japan in 1957, either in the role of occupation forces or by other arrangement.

12. Soviet aggression will be planned in advance and Soviet mobilization TO THE EXTENT REQUIRED BY INITIAL PLANS will be practically completed prior to D-Day. Intelligence of heightened war preparation on the part of the USSR has been received, and Allied mobilization and minimum preparatory force dispositions have been initiated, but time has not permitted significant progress prior to D-Day.

13. The [petrol, oil, lubricants] requirements of the Allies will be such that at least part of the finished products of the Near and Middle East oil-bearing areas will be required by the Allies from the start of a war in 1957.

14. Atomic weapons will be used by both sides. Other weapons of mass de-

struction (radiological, biological, and chemical warfare) may be used by either side subject to considerations of retaliation and effectiveness.

15. Between now and 1957 the United States will not suffer from either a major depression or a catastrophic inflation.

16. The political and psychological tension as it existed in 1948 between the USSR and the Western or Allied powers will continue relatively unabated until 1957.

17. Russian military and economic potentials have not been appreciably augmented prior to 1957 by acquisition or exploitation of territory not under their control in 1948. . . .

5: OVERALL STRATEGIC CONCEPT

19. In collaboration with our allies, to impose the Allied war objectives upon the USSR by destroying the Soviet will and capacity to resist, by conducting a strategic offensive in Western Eurasia and a strategic defensive in the Far East.

Initially: To defend the Western Hemisphere; to launch an air offensive; to initiate a discriminate containment of the Soviet powers within the general area: North Pole–Greenland Sea–Norwegian Sea–North Sea–Rhine River–Alps–Piave River–Adriatic Sea–Crete–southeastern Turkey–Tigris Valley–Persian Gulf–Himalayas–Southeast Asia–South China Sea–East China Sea–Japan Sea–Tsugaru Strait–Bering Sea–Bering Strait–North Pole; to secure and control essential strategic areas, bases, and lines of communication; and to wage psychological, economic, and underground warfare, while exerting unremitting pressure against the Soviet citadel, utilizing all means to force the maximum attrition of Soviet war resources.

Subsequently: To launch coordinated offensive operations of all arms against the USSR as required.

6: BASIC UNDERTAKINGS

20. In collaboration with our allies:

a. To secure the Western Hemisphere.
b. To conduct an air offensive against the Soviet powers.

c. To hold the United Kingdom.
d. To hold maximum areas in Western Europe.
e. To conduct offensive operations to destroy enemy naval forces, naval bases, shipping, and supporting facilities.
f. To secure sea and air lines of communication essential to the accomplishment of the overall strategic concept.
g. To secure overseas bases essential to the accomplishment of the overall strategic concept.
h. To expand the overall power of the armed forces for later offensive operations against the Soviet powers, and
i. To provide essential aid to our allies in support of efforts contributing directly to the overall strategic concept.

7: PHASED CONCEPT OF OPERATIONS*

21. In the implementation of the overall strategic concept the conduct of the required operations may be considered to fall into four general phases. These phases will not be distinct and will probably overlap as between areas in both time and operation. They are defined as follows:

PHASE I.   D-Day to stabilization of initial Soviet offensives, to include the initiation of the Allied [atomic] air offensive.
PHASE II.   Stabilization of initial Soviet offensives to Allied initiation of major offensive operations of all arms.
PHASE III.   Allied initiation of major offensive operations until Soviet capitulation is obtained.
PHASE IV.   Establishment of control and enforcement of surrender terms.

*Editor's Note: As has been noted in the Prologue (and will be seen in the appropriate appendix), the United States was not capable in 1949 or in 1957 of guaranteeing the defense of all her territory against air attack. This capability would come only in the very late 1950s and early 1960s. Even then, no guarantee could be given against ICBM strikes. In both cases—air and ICBM—the extraordinary cost and complexity of establishing an early warning and fighter-control apparatus to guard a continent embracing some 3,615,191 square miles of territory, was prohibitive.

In the event the air offensive, together with other operations, results in Soviet capitulation during Phases I or II, the war would pass immediately into Phase IV. . . .

22. Phase I. In collaboration with our allies:

a. *Secure the Western Hemisphere.*

(1) Maintain surveillance of the approaches to the North American continent.

(2) Provide an area air defense of the most important areas of the United States.

(3) Provide the antiaircraft defense of the most vital installations of the United States.

(4) Provide for the protection of Western Hemisphere coastal and intercoastal shipping and of important ports and harbors in the continental United States.

(5) Ensure the security of the refineries on the islands of Curaçao, Aruba, and Trinidad and of associated sources of oil.

(6) Provide the optimum defense against sabotage, subversion, and espionage.

(7) Establish or secure and defend the following peripheral areas and bases necessary to the defense of the continental United States: Alaska, Canada, Greenland, Labrador, Newfoundland, Bermuda, the Caribbean, northeastern Brazil, and Hawaii.

(8) Defend the sea approaches to the North American continent and to its peripheral bases.

(9) Provide the optimum ground-force defense of the most important areas of the continental United States, including a mobile striking force.

b. *Conduct an air offensive against the Soviet powers.*

(1) Initiate, as soon as possible after D-Day, strategic air attacks with atomic and conventional bombs against Soviet facilities for the assembly and delivery of weapons of mass destruction; against LOCs [lines of communications], supply bases, and troop concentrations in the USSR, in satellite countries, and in overrun areas, which would blunt Soviet offensives; and against petroleum, electric power, and steel target systems in the USSR, from bases in the United States, Alaska, Okinawa, the United Kingdom, [and] the Cairo–Suez–Aden area and from aircraft carriers when available from primary tasks.

(2) Initiate, as soon as possible after D-Day, air operations against naval targets of the Soviet powers to blunt Soviet sea offensives, with emphasis on the reduction of Soviet submarine capabilities and the offensive mining of enemy waters.

(3) Extend operations as necessary to additional targets both within and outside the USSR essential to the war-making capacity of the Soviet powers.

(4) Maintain policing of target systems reduced in the initial campaigns.

c. *Conduct offensive operations to destroy enemy naval forces, shipping, naval bases, and supporting facilities.*

(1) Destroy Soviet naval forces, shipping, naval bases, supporting facilities, and their air defenses.

(2) Mine important enemy ports, and focal sea approaches thereto, in the Baltic–Barents–White Sea area, northeast Asia, the Black Sea, the Adriatic, and the Turkish straits.

(3) Establish a sea blockade of the Soviet powers.

d. *Hold the United Kingdom.*

(1) Maintain surveillance of the approaches to the United Kingdom.

(2) Provide the air defense of the most critical areas of the United Kingdom.

(3) Provide the antiaircraft [AA] defense of the most critical areas of the United Kingdom.

(4) Provide for the protection of the United Kingdom coastal shipping and of important ports and harbors in the United Kingdom.

(5) Provide the optimum defense against sabotage, subversion, and espionage.

(6) Provide the optimum ground-force defense of the most critical areas of the United Kingdom.

e. *Hold the Rhine–Alps–Piave line.*

(1) Provide the ground-force defense of the Rhine River line from Switzerland to the Zuider Zee.

(2) Provide the ground-force defense of Italy along the Alps–Piave River line.

(3) Provide tactical air support of Allied ground forces along the Rhine–Alps–Piave line.

(4) Accomplish planned demolitions and interdict Soviet LOCs east of the Rhine–Alps–Piave line.

(5) Provide air defense of areas west of the Rhine–Alps–Piave line.

(6) Provide AA defenses for areas west of the Rhine–Alps–Piave line.

(7) Gain and maintain air superiority over the Rhine–Alps–Piave line.

(8) Provide for the protection of Allied coastal shipping and of important ports and harbors in Western Europe.

f. *Hold the area southeastern Turkey–Tigris Valley–Persian Gulf.*

(1) Provide the ground, air, and AA defenses of the refineries and associated installations at Bahrein and Ras Tanura and the airfield at Dhahran.

(2) Provide the ground, air, and AA defenses of the Abadan refinery, its associated installations and oil fields, and the key communications and port facilities in that area.

(3) Accomplish planned demolitions and air interdiction of the Soviet LOCs leading through Iran and Turkey.

(4) Gain and maintain air superiority over the Iranian mountain passes and over the southeastern Turkey battle areas.

(5) Provide the ground-force defense of the mountain passes leading into Iraq and the Iranian oil areas.

(6) Provide the ground-force defense of southeastern Turkey.

(7) Provide tactical air support of Allied ground forces.

(8) Provide AA protection for Baghdad, Mosul, the Iskenderun–Aleppo area and the LOCs southward from the latter.

(9) Provide naval local-defense forces in the Bahrein–Dhahran area.

(10) Provide a floating reserve of ground forces.

g. *Hold maximum areas of the Middle East and Southeast Asia consistent with indigenous capabilities supported by other Allied courses of action.*

(1) Conduct air attacks against Soviet forces which threaten Bandar Abbas* and interdict the LOC leading thereto.

*Editor's Note: The port of Bandar Abbas is in Iran at the mouth of the Persian Gulf. It is a port of commercial and strategic significance and is the focal point of the trade routes in southern Persia.

(2) Provide ground and air defenses against indigenous Communist forces in Malaya.

(3) Interdict Soviet land and sea LOCs leading into China and neutralize enemy bases in China.

h. *Hold Japan, less Hokkaido.†*

†Editor's Note: Dropshot does not make it clear why the United States was prepared to abandon Hokkaido, the second largest, northernmost, and most sparsely populated of the major islands of Japan. It is rich in coal, iron, and manganese, and the Ishikari coalfield produces most of Japan's coal supply. However, perhaps the planners considered it indefensible. It is separated from Russia by the relatively narrow Soya Strait, and its road and rail net was certainly poor (especially in the north of the island). On the other hand, its climate and terrain would favor an active defense, especially in terms of guerrillas.

(1) Provide ground and air defenses of Honshu and Kyushu.

(2) Organize, train, and equip Japanese forces prior to D-Day.

(3) Defend the sea approaches to Japan.

(4) Provide naval local-defense forces.

(5) Provide AA defenses for the most important areas.

i. *Secure sea and air lines of communication essential to the accomplishment of the overall strategic concept.*

(1) Establish a convoy system and control and routing of shipping.

(2) Provide convoy air and surface escorts.

(3) Provide air defense of convoys within effective range of enemy air.

j. *Secure overseas bases essential to the accomplishment of the overall strategic concept as follows:*

(1) Immediately after D-Day, provide forces by air and sea transport to

occupy or recapture Iceland* and the Azores† and establish necessary air and naval bases thereon.

*Editor's Note: In 1946 Iceland granted the United States the right-to-use in the U.S.-built World War II base at Keflavík. In 1949 she became a member of NATO, and in 1951 she permitted the United States to station troops there. While she has no armed forces, she does have an internal-security police force of about 500 men and a coast guard of five ships and 120 men. A glance at the map will show her importance as an air and sea staging post between the United States, Europe, and Scandinavia, and if Britain were knocked out of World War III early, Iceland would become one of SAC's main attack bases. For this reason the U.S. maintains 3,300 USAF and USN personnel in various air and radar base sites. Moreover, Iceland's civil air fleet—seven jets, four turboprops, and four piston transports—would prove useful to the Military Air Transport Service. However, from 1958, when Iceland extended her territorial waters from four to twelve miles and thereby denied Britain valuable cod fisheries, there has been sporadic minor naval action between her coast guard and the Royal Navy. This has led to some uneasiness concerning U.S. and NATO security of tenure over the bases. Indeed, in 1974 Iceland proposed their removal by 1976, perhaps as the result of strong internal maneuvering by the influential Communist party in the island. In 1953 and 1956 there was considerable discussion in Iceland about whether the U.S. forces should be asked to withdraw. However, had war come in 1957, no doubt Iceland would have remained loyal to its treaty obligations.

†Editor's Note: As is true of Iceland, the Azores constitute an important if not vital link in the chain of bases maintained by the Pentagon between America and Europe. Lying as they do some nine hundred miles off mainland Portugal, SAC would base squadrons there if Britain were knocked out in the opening stages of World War III. They would become extremely important in Stage II of World War III—that part of the war plan in which the United States would begin to build up its strength ready for the strategic counteroffensive visualized in Stage III. Their importance in the restoration of the Western military position in the Near East and Arabia cannot be underestimated. No doubt for that reason the United States has been especially careful and especially generous in its relations with Portugal.

    (a) Immediately after D-Day, or before, if practicable, provide ground, air, and antiaircraft forces to secure and defend Iceland, utilizing airlift as necessary.

    (b) As soon as possible after D-Day, provide ground and air units to secure and defend the Azores.

    (c) Defend the sea approaches to Iceland and the Azores.

    (d) Provide naval local-defense forces for Iceland and the Azores.

    (2) Establish or expand and defend Allied bases as required in northwest Africa and North Africa.‡

‡**Editor's Note:** Under Dropshot it was the Pentagon's intention to hold the line along the African and Arabian shore between Dakar and Tel-Aviv. As it did in World War II, this operation would have involved many hundreds of thousands of Allied troops, perhaps millions. But unlike in World War II the Pentagon would have encountered extremely hostile native armies, especially in Algeria, Libya, and Egypt. Moreover, after 1957 some of these armies were very well equipped, mainly by the Russians or the French, with advanced weapons and armor. And some of the governments and tribes became especially fond of the Russians. Some very hard fighting could be expected, therefore, before the great counteroffensive.

      (a) Provide air defenses and naval local-defense forces for bases at Port Lyautey and Casablanca.

      (b) Provide ground defenses, air defenses, antiaircraft defenses, and naval local-defense forces for Gibraltar, Malta, and Bizerte–Gabes Gulf.*

*Editor's Note: Gibraltar would remain loyal to England in any war, although its principal usefulness—as a naval base—would be limited following any atomic attack, even though all command and communications installations are deeply buried in the Rock. Politically, Malta was much less reliable and equally vulnerable to atomic attack and its consequences. A crown colony, its constitution (which gave it considerable powers of self-government) was revoked by London in 1947 following civil disorders. However, it was given self-rule in 1961. As in World War II, it would be an important though not vital base. Its use would lie mainly in its underground installations. Built mainly in World War II, these were vast. But because of the peculiar geography of Grand Harbor and Sliema, the main naval bases, atomic attack would completely wreck both. Bizerte, the great French naval base in Tunisia, would have proved the most unreliable of all three. Tunisia was swept by strong anti-French nationalism from the end of World War II onward, and as the French were to find out in 1963, Bizerte was not tenable if the Tunisian people did not want it to be. It is probable that the United States would have had to fight for the base, for the French gave Tunisia full independence in 1956. While in general Tunisia maintained pro-Western attitudes, the Russians did succeed in obtaining more influence at Tunis than the NATO powers thought desirable.

      (c) Provide air defenses, antiaircraft defenses, and naval local-defense forces for Oran and Algiers.

      (d) Provide ground defenses, antiaircraft defenses, and naval local-defense forces for Tripoli.

      (3) Ensure the availability of suitable bases required in the Cairo–Suez–Aden area, prior to D-Day.

      (a) Provide ground, air, and antiaircraft defenses of the Cairo–Suez area.

      (b) Defend the sea approaches to the Cairo–Suez–Aden area.

      (c) Provide naval local-defense forces for Alexandria, Port Said, Aden, Massawa, and Port Sudan.

(d) Provide ground, air, antiaircraft, and naval local-defense forces for Crete.*

*Editor's Note: There was considerable Communist guerrila activity in Crete during World War II, and no doubt the Communists would have surfaced again to prevent or disrupt Allied activity on the island. As the Germans and the British found during and after World War II, the Greek guerrilla is a formidable animal.

(e) Provide ground, air, antiaircraft, and naval local-defense forces for Cyprus.†

†Editor's Note: Cyprus, the important island and network of military bases off the Levantine coast, was annexed by Britain in 1914. In 1957, had war come, it would have found the island in a state akin to civil war as the Greek Cypriots fought for independence against very strong British forces—and succeeded. However, the British would probably have succeeded in getting important military enclaves, as they did when they left the island to govern itself. SAC would have found Cyprus very useful in its campaign against southern Russia. However, it would also have found a formidable little Communist party. Guerrillas might have made operations difficult and, at times, impossible.

(4) Have forces in being on D-Day in Okinawa for the security of that island.‡

‡Editor's Note: Okinawa and Guam were SAC's most important bases in the Far East. Okinawa was placed under a U.S. military governor after its capture in 1945 and would presumably have remained dependable. Similarly with Guam, which became little more than a huge floating U.S. military base after 1945—as was demonstrated in the Vietnam war. In general, it is an interesting strategical fact of Dropshot that the United States' bases in the Pacific were a good deal more secure than those in the Atlantic and the Mediterranean.

(a) Provide ground, air, and AA defenses of Okinawa.
(b) Defend the sea approaches to Okinawa.
(c) Provide naval local-defense forces.
(5) Provide necessary minimum protection for other overseas bases essential to the maintenance of sea and air lines of communication.
(a) Provide ground, air, antiaircraft, and naval local-defense forces for Guam.
(b) Provide antiaircraft and naval local-defense forces for Singapore.§

§Editor's Note: The United States would have encountered serious Communist terrorism in Singapore in 1957, although unlike in Greece and Crete this activity could be controlled provided there were strong counterinsurgency forces in the island. The British were still commercially strong here, but already the Indonesians were beginning to eye the island, and in 1963–1964 they attempted to invade on several occasions. Indonesia was a strong Communist bastion in Southeast Asia at that time.

(c) Provide naval local-defense forces for bases in Kwajalein, the Philippines, Ceylon, Australia, New Zealand, and Captetown.*

*Editor's Note: In general the U.S. forces would have found themselves secure in all white, English-speaking countries such as New Zealand, South Africa, and Australia. Ceylon was a different story. Granted full independence within the Commonwealth by Britain in February 1948, at first this major former British naval base in the Indian Ocean seemed pro-Western. But then a Marxist Peoples' Liberation Front—an organization so violent and unstable that even the Russians cooperated when the British and the Indians went in to eradicate it—emerged to make security over the base at Trincomalee a doubtful proposition, at least in 1957. Kwajalein, the largest of the atolls in the Ralik Chain of the Marshall Islands and a headquarters of the U.S. Trust Territory of the Pacific Islands, would have remained secure. The Philippines offered yet another story. She was given full independence from the United States in 1946, but the Communist Huk guerrillas emerged and there was violent and prolonged guerrilla activity until 1954, when the Huk leader, Luis Taruk, surrendered. However, strong cadres of Huks remained, and no doubt Moscow would have brought them into play.

(d) Provide a theater reserve of ground forces for the western Pacific.
   k. *Expand the overall power of the armed forces for later operations against the Soviet powers.*
   1. *Provide essential aid to our allies in support of efforts contributing directly to the overall strategic concept.*
   m. *Initiate or intensify psychological, economic, and underground warfare.*
      (1) Collaborate in the integration of psychological, economic, and underground warfare with plans for military operations.
      (2) Provide assistance as necessary for the execution of psychological, economic, and underground warfare.
   n. *Establish control and enforce surrender terms in the USSR and satellite countries* (in the event of a possible early capitulation of the USSR during Phase I).
      (1) Move control forces to selected centers in the USSR and in satellite countries.
      (2) Establish some form of Allied control in the USSR and in satellite countries.
      (3) Enforce surrender terms imposed upon the USSR and its satellites.
      (4) Reestablish civil government in the USSR and satellite countries.

23. Phase II. In collaboration with our allies:

a. Continue the air offensive to include the intensification of the air battle with the objective of obtaining air supremacy.
b. Maintain our holding operations along the general line of discriminate containment, exploiting local opportunities for improving our position thereon and exerting unremitting pressure against the Soviet citadel.
c. Maintain control of other essential land and sea areas and increase our measure of control of essential lines of communications.
d. Reenforce our forces in the Far East as necessary to contain the Communist forces to the mainland of Asia and to defend the southern Malay Peninsula.
e. Continue the provision of essential aid to Allies in support of efforts contributing directly to the overall strategic concept.
f. Intensify psychological, economic, and underground warfare.
g. Establish control and enforce surrender terms in the USSR and satellite countries (in the event of capitulation during Phase II).
h. Generate at the earliest possible date sufficient balanced forces, together with their shipping and logistic requirements, to achieve a decision in Europe.

24. Phase III. In collaboration with our allies:

a. While continuing courses of action *a* through *f* of Phase II, initiate a major land offensive in Europe to cut off and destroy all or the major part of the Soviet forces in Europe.
b. From the improved position resulting from *a* above, continue offensive operations of all arms, as necessary to force capitualtion.

25. Phase IV. In collaboration with our allies:

Establish control and enforce surrender terms in the USSR and satellite countries.

EDITOR'S ASSESSMENT

The force requirements for these vast military undertakings cannot be estimated. Certainly they would have required a mobilization of the United States, Great Britain, the British Commonwealth, and the entire Western world such as has not been seen before. It is not unreasonable to postulate that as many as 30 million Americans of both sexes aged between sixteen and sixty would be required if all programs were to be met, and it is doubtful that such a requirement could be fulfilled without disrupting industry and/or demolishing the economy. It is in the area of logistical feasibility that Phase I might collapse, and if it had collapsed before SAC had destroyed the Russian industrial and communications complex, then the United States could not have won the war. Several logistical feasibility surveys associated with Dropshot show that if the Soviet attack did develop as visualized, most and possibly all American arms would remain seriously deficient. For example, neither SAC nor the U.S. Navy would be fully mobilized in the first sixty days, by which time, Dropshot estimated, the first phase of the Russian campaign would have ended. Neither the American nor the British forces in being at the onset of the war could have resisted effectively either on the European frontiers between East and West or on the Rhine. The situation was similar in the second critical area of operations: the Middle East. In the critical area of combat and transport aircraft, less than half those needed to execute the air plan would be available on D-Day, and therefore, while this represented a formidable force, the tasks set by the Pentagon were thought to be logistically infeasible. In another important aspect of Trojan, the SAC segment of Dropshot, the Allied forces available were far below those needed for the successful accomplishment of the plan.

The airfields in the Cairo–Suez–Aden area, vital to the successful execution of the southern arm of the SAC plan, would be, the Pentagon estimated, in an unsatisfactory state—for example, the runways and hardstandings would not be capable of supporting extensive landings and takeoffs of very heavy aircraft. Therefore, before these airfields could be used, extensive engineering and construction would be necessary. Yet, as a survey showed, during the first eight months the shortages of construction units would average from 60 to 70 percent of the requirement, with even greater shortages in the first month or so of hostilities. Later and more detailed studies of this problem indicated that the situation was even more acute. Here then was another limiting factor against the success of Trojan, upon which all else hinged.

Similarly serious shortfalls were noted in other manpower areas critical to the success of Trojan—especially in the availability of specialized personnel such as electronics maintenance and repair men and specialized mechanical technicians. This same shortage applied not only to SAC but to all other arms of the services and would have affected all other aspects of Dropshot and Offtackle (another war plan intended to make strategy conform to capabilities) in all areas and all phases. Indeed, studies by the Joint Chiefs of Staff associated with Dropshot show that through manpower and budgetary difficulties no part of the first phase could possibly have succeeded. The outcome, presumably, would have been that while she might be almost mortally wounded, Russia would survive to fight Phase II.

The Joint Chiefs themselves were not confident about the outcome, at least

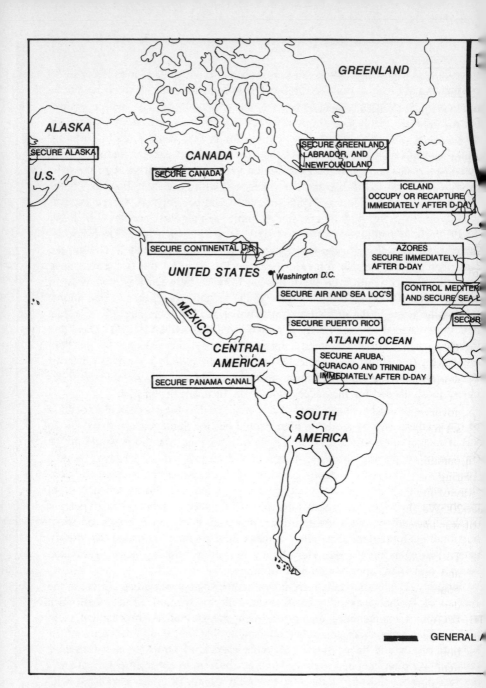

GREENLAND

ALASKA

SECURE ALASKA

U.S.

CANADA

SECURE CANADA

SECURE GREENLAND, LABRADOR, AND NEWFOUNDLAND

ICELAND
OCCUPY OR RECAPTURE IMMEDIATELY AFTER D-DAY

SECURE CONTINENTAL U.S.

UNITED STATES • Washington D.C.

AZORES
SECURE IMMEDIATELY AFTER D-DAY

SECURE AIR AND SEA LOC'S

CONTROL MEDITERR
AND SECURE SEA L

MEXICO

SECURE PUERTO RICO

SECUR

CENTRAL
AMERICA

ATLANTIC OCEAN

SECURE ARUBA, CURACAO AND TRINIDAD IMMEDIATELY AFTER D-DAY

SECURE PANAMA CANAL

SOUTH
AMERICA

GENERAL A

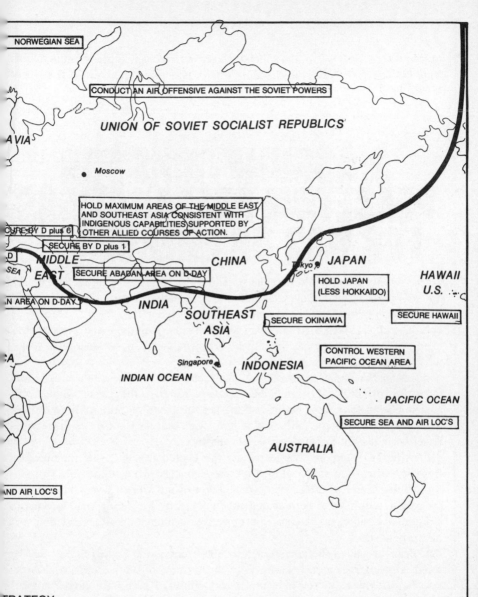

NORWEGIAN SEA

CONDUCT AN AIR OFFENSIVE AGAINST THE SOVIET POWERS

UNION OF SOVIET SOCIALIST REPUBLICS

AVIA

• Moscow

HOLD MAXIMUM AREAS OF THE MIDDLE EAST
AND SOUTHEAST ASIA CONSISTENT WITH
INDIGENOUS CAPABILITIES SUPPORTED BY
OTHER ALLIED COURSES OF ACTION.

CURE BY D plus 6

SECURE BY D plus 1

D MIDDLE

SEA EAST

CHINA

Tokyo JAPAN

HAWAII
U.S.

SECURE ABADAN AREA ON D-DAY

HOLD JAPAN
(LESS HOKKAIDO)

N AREA ON D-DAY

INDIA

SOUTHEAST
ASIA

SECURE OKINAWA

SECURE HAWAII

CA

Singapore

INDONESIA

CONTROL WESTERN
PACIFIC OCEAN AREA

INDIAN OCEAN

PACIFIC OCEAN

SECURE SEA AND AIR LOC'S

AUSTRALIA

AND AIR LOC'S

TRATEGY

AINMENT OF SOVIET POWERS

of Phase I, as is shown in the following excerpt from a JCS paper entitled *Strategic Guidance to Facilitate Planning Within the Joint Agencies* (JCS 1630/14 6 Dec 49).

2. ASSUMPTIONS FOR PEACETIME PREPARATIONS FOR WAR OR EMERGENCY

a. It is highly improbable that the possibility of actual hostilities will be accepted by the United States in time for adequate industrial and manpower mobilization before belligerent action actually begins.

b. Essential United States military requirements, including stockpiles of strategic and critical materiel, will not be adequately met in advance of a major war.

c. In the absence of approved national mobilization plans, both military and industrial, which can be implemented very rapidly, the United States will require considerable time before making her full potential military power effective. The United States will face a long war and early attack with possible losses of industrial facilities, materiel, and lives.

d. Allies will not be able to protect the United States during mobilization from one-way air attack or guided missiles launched from submarines.

e. Before unity of effort of the population of the United States is obtained, the people will have to be prepared psychologically for a long war, for attacks (particularly sabotage) on strategic objectives within the continental limits of the United States.

f. Prior to and in the course of full mobilization, the United States may be faced with internal unrest, particularly in the form of work stoppage, subversion, and sabotage in key industries and facilities, which will hamper conversion to war production and interrupt the flow of materiel to the armed services.

g. It will be more difficult to apply psychological warfare to the people of the USSR than to the people of the United States. However, if properly applied, the effect on the Soviets might be far greater than on the people of the United States.

h. The United States will maintain an advantage over the USSR in military technology and in industrial production but this advantage may, in time, be materially reduced, particularly in the field of military technology.

i. The United States will maintain an advantage in atomic-bomb stockpiling and in the capacity for production of such atomic weapons.

j. Results of research and development in peacetime, both at home and abroad, will necessitate flexibility in war techniques and revision of plans for a war or an emergency.

k. In the absence of a comprehensive statement of long-range national objectives, applicable in general as far as practicable both in peace and in war for use in planning by the various agencies in the Department of Defense and other departments of the government, military plans of the United States will not, in all probability, be fully coordinated and integrated with political, social, and economic plans.

3.WAR PLANNING ASSUMPTIONS

a. Although the North Atlantic Treaty countries of Continental Europe will improve their positions politically, socially, economically, and militarily by means of United States economic and military aid and by mutual military planning and assistance, such improvement will not, for a number of years, ensure their ability to resist effectively being overrun by Soviet forces.

b. The United States will furnish military assistance to friendly nations. This will be done without substantially adversely affecting our capability of initiating current war plans.

c. United States military assistance to Allies in wartime may materially affect adversely later operations envisaged in our current planning because of sharing our industrial output with our allies. However, the capability of these friendly nations to resist aggression by the USSR should, if the military assistance provided is properly utilized, more than offset this curtailment.

d. United States independence in overall strategic planning will at least to some degree be influenced by our participation in the North Atlantic Treaty Organization.

e. The USSR will have a distinct initial advantage over the United States in information, in preparedness, and in freedom to initiate attack without a formal declaration of war.

f. The USSR will seek to destroy the war-making potential of the United States by sabotage, air attack, [and] submarine and guided missile attack or at least to delay the United States in reaching its full industrial output for total war.

g. In the initial stages of the war, the USSR will attempt to use political and psychological means, together with subversion and sabotage, in an endeavor to weaken the support of the United States war effort.

h. The United States and its Allies will possess an initial superiority in sea power, an initial shortage of effective ground-combat units and tactical air power, and for at least the next few years a superiority in long-range strategic air power.

i. Atomic bombs will be used by the United States and by the USSR.

j. The United States will have the capability of launching prompt retaliatory air attack with atomic bombs against critical enemy areas.

k. Other weapons of mass destruction might conceivably be used by either the United States or the USSR, subject to consideration of retaliation.

l. The United States may be denied access to some sources of important strategic and critical materials in the Far East and Southeast Asia if all China falls to the Communists.

m. The need for Middle East oil to meet Allied major war requirements will become progressively more essential.

n. Our advanced bases, lines of communication thereto, and surface expeditionary requirements and requirements for imported strategic materials will make us vulnerable to submarine warfare.

o. The USSR will concentrate on developing and equipping her armed forces with those offensive elements which are presently deficient in her military establishment, notably atomic weapons and guided missiles.

p. A major undertaking of the United States will be the conduct of an extensive psychological-warfare campaign whose basic objective will be to destroy the support accorded by the people of the USSR and her satellites to their present systems of government and to fasten a realization among the peoples of the USSR that the overthrow of the Politburo is an attainable reality.

q. Plans developed prior to outbreak of war or during the course of the war between the United States and the USSR will assume a successful conclusion of our belligerent action and will include the peace terms to be imposed and the controls to be utilized in enforcing the peace terms. . . .

VOLUME 2

HOLDING THE LAST LINE OF DEFENSE, PREPARING FOR THE COUNTER-OFFENSIVE.

CONTENTS

Strategic estimate

Summary of opposing situations

POLITICAL FACTORS 69

USSR and Satellites political aims and objectives / 73

Attitude and moral of Soviet Union / 74

Political strengths and weaknesses of the Soviet orbit / 75

Allied (except *US*)

Political aims and objectives of United Kingdom / 76

Canada / 77

Australia / 77

New Zealand / 78

South Africa / 78

France and Benelux / 78

Germany, Austria, Japan / 78

Italy / 79

Iceland / 79

Portugal / 79

Denmark / 79

Norway / 80

ECONOMIC FACTORS 80

Soviet and satellite

Basic resources / 80

Industrial development / 81

Industrial manpower / 81

Dependence on foreign sources for key commodities / 81

Transport capabilities / 81

Vulnerability of Soviet industry / 82

Summary / 83

Allied nations

General / 83

United States / 83

Oil / 83

United Kingdom / 85

Estimated relative volume of domestic production, stockpile withdrawals, and imports of strategic and critical materials during three years of war, 1957–1959 (Table 1) / 90

Estimate of US average yearly volume of strategic and critical materials from various world areas during three years of war, 1957–1959 (Table 2) / 90

65

Estimated relative importance to the US of world areas as sources of
strategic and critical materials during three years of war, 1957–1959
(Table 3) / 91
Canada / 92
Australia and New Zealand / 92
South Africa / 92
France / 92
Belgium / 93
Netherlands / 93
Luxembourg / 94
The Rhur / 94
Italy / 95
Iceland / 95
Portugal / 95
Denmark / 95
Norway / 96
Relative Combat Power
Soviet and satellite armed forces
Strengths and dispositions / 96
Mobilization capabilities / 102
Combat efficiency / 103
Defenses / 104
Weapons, new and improved
Atomic / 105
Aircraft / 105
Antiaircraft / 106
Biological warfare / 106
Chemical warfare / 106
Guided missiles / 106
Allied armed forces
United States / 108
Heavy and medium bombers / 108
Guided missiles / 110
Anti-Submarine warfare / 112
Chemical and biological warfare / 114
Allied ground forces / 115
Allied naval forces / 117
Allied air forces / 118
Logistics
Soviet and satellite
Soviet Union / 121
Europe / 121
Near and Middle East / 122
Sea transport / 122
Air facilities / 123
Ports / 123
Stockpiles / 123

Probable Soviet strategic objective / 124

Soviet capabilities
Eurasia / 125
Western Europe / 126
Iberian Peninsula / 128
Turkey, Near and Middle East / 129
Far East / 130
British Isles / 131
Canada and the United States / 131
North Atlantic Islands / 132
Alaska, the Aleutians, and the North Pacific / 132
Caribbean / 133
Allied sea communications / 133

Probable Soviet courses of action
Summary of strategic considerations / 135
Initial courses of action / 136
Subsequent courses of action / 137

Allied courses of action
General considerations / 137
Western hemisphere / 139
North Atlantic approaches / 139
Western Europe
United Kingdom / 140
West Germany / 141
France and Italy / 144
Iberia / 146
Italy / 147
Mediterranean islands / 148
North Europe / 149
Norway, Sweden / 150
Denmark / 151
Near and Middle East / 152
Turkey / 152
Cairo–Suez / 154
Retake the oil-bearing areas immediately / 155
Retake the oil-bearing areas subsequently / 156
Hold maximum areas of the Middle East / 157
Far East
General / 157
Japan / 158
Southeast Asia / 159
General courses of action
Conduct an air offensive against the Soviet powers / 159
Secure sea and air lines of communication
General / 161
Mediterranean / 162
Air lines of communication / 162
Conduct offensive operations to destroy enemy naval forces, shipping,
naval bases, and supporting facilities / 163

Expand the overall power of the armed forces for later offensive operations against the Soviet powers / 164
Initiate major offensive land operations against the USSR as required / 165
Establish control and enforce surrender terms in the USSR and satellite countries / 168
Initiate or intensify psychological, economic, and underground warfare / 169
Provide aid to allies / 170

Selection of allied courses of action
Basic undertakings / 171
Western Europe / 172
Suitability of courses of action / 172
Feasibility of courses of action / 173
Acceptability of courses of action / 175
Selected courses of action / 177
Near and Middle East / 178
Northern Europe / 180
North Atlantic approaches / 180
Far East / 181
Consolidation of certain selected courses of action / 181
Summary of selected courses of action / 181

STRATEGIC ESTIMATE
I. SUMMARY OF OPPOSING SITUATIONS

1. Political Factors

a. The gravest threat to the security of the Allies within the foreseeable future stems from the hostile designs and formidable power of the USSR and from the nature of the Soviet system. The political, economic, and psychological warfare which the USSR is now waging has dangerous potentialities for weakening the relative world position of the Allies and disrupting their traditional institutions by means short of war, unless sufficient resistance is encountered in the policies of the Allies and other non-Communist countries. The risk of war with the USSR is sufficient to warrant, in common prudence, timely and adequate preparation by the Allies. Soviet domination of the potential power of Eurasia, whether achieved by armed aggression or by political and subversive means, would be strategically and politically unacceptable to the United States.

b. The USSR has already engaged the Allies in a struggle for power. While it cannot be predicted with certainty whether, or when, the present political warfare will involve armed conflict, nevertheless there exists a continuing danger of war at any time.

(1) While the possibility of planned Soviet armed actions which would involve the United States cannot be ruled out, a careful weighing of the various factors points to the probability that the Soviet government is not now planning any deliberate armed action calculated to involve the Allies and is still seeking to achieve its aims primarily by political means, accompanied by military intimidation.

(2) War might grow out of incidents between forces in direct contact.

(3) War might arise through miscalculation, through failure of either side to estimate accurately how far the other can be pushed. There is the possibility that the USSR will be tempted to take armed action under a miscalculation of the determination and willingness of the Allies to resort to force in order to prevent the development of a threat intolerable to their security.

c. In addition to the risk of war, a danger equally to be guarded against is the possibility that Soviet political warfare might seriously weaken the relative position of the Allies, enhance Soviet strength, and either lead to our ultimate defeat short of war or force us into war under dangerously unfavorable conditions. Such a result would be facilitated by vacillation, appeasement, or isolationist concepts, leading to dissension among the Allies and loss of their influence; by internal disunity or subversion; by economic instability in the form of depression or inflation; or by either excessive or inadequate armament and military-aid expenditures.

d. To counter these threats to Allied national security and to create political, economic, and military conditions leading to containment of Soviet expansion and to the eventual retraction of Soviet domination, the United States has initiated or is supporting the following measures:

(1) The European Recovery Porgram.
(2) The development of Western Union.
(3) The increased effectiveness of the military establishments of probable allies.
(4) The North Atlantic Treaty.

e. Alignment of selected states and areas. In order to establish reasonable limits for an estimate of the 1957 alignment of selected states and areas, it has been necessary to reduce the variables involved. Accordingly, the estimate for 1957 is based on the following premises:

(1) Europe and the Near East * will continue as the primary U.S. security interest, and U.S. policy, including the maintenance of West Germany, will remain approximately as now formulated.
(2) The periphery of Asia will continue as an ever-present but secondary U.S. security interest.
(3) Latin America will remain at its present lower priority as a U.S. security interest.

f. The estimate of probable alignment in 1957 of states and areas of the world is as follows:

State or Area	Probable Alignment in 1957†
United States	
United Kingdom	
Denmark	
Norway	
Iceland	
Greenland	
France	
Benelux Group	Will be allied
Belgium	
Netherlands	
Luxembourg	

* "Near East" includes Greece, Turkey, Cyprus, Lebanon, Syria, Palestine, Egypt, Yemen, Saudi Arabia, British-Arabian protectorates, Transjordan, and Iraq; "Middle East" includes Iran, Afghanistan, Pakistan, India, and Ceylon.

State or Area	Probable Alignment in 1957†
Italy Portugal Philippines Canada Union of South Africa U.K. Colonial Africa Belgian Congo Australia and New Zealand	Will be allied
Republic of Ireland Sweden Switzerland Greece Spain Turkey Syria–Lebanon* Transjordan* Egypt* Arabian peninsula* Israel* Iran India Iraq* Pakistan	Will attempt to remain neutral but will join the Allies if attacked or seriously threatened.‡
Finland Latvia Estonia Lithuania Poland Czechoslovakia Hungary Romania Yugoslavia** Bulgaria Albania Communist China Manchuria Outer Mongolia Korea	Will be allied with the USSR, either willingly or otherwise.
Afghanistan Non-Communist China Siam	Will attempt to remain neutral but will submit to adequate armed occupation rather than fight.

* All estimates for the Arab states and Israel, with the possible exception of the states on the Arabian peninsula, are fundamentally conditioned by the policies of the United States, the United Kingdom, and Soviet powers regarding Palestine.

** If the present defection of Yugoslavia from the Soviet satellite orbit should continue to 1957, it is not likely that Yugoslavia would ally with the Soviet Union but would attempt to remain neutral and would be committed to resist Soviet and/or satellite attack.

State or Area	Probable Alignment in 1957†
Burma Malaya Indochina Indonesia Portugese, Spanish, Italian, and French Colonial Africa Ethiopia	Will attempt to remain neutral but will submit to adequate armed occupation rather than fight.
Caribbean area South America	Will remain neutral or will ally with the United States.
West Germany Austria Trieste Japan	Initially occupied as at present or will join the Allies.

†**Editor's Note:** This estimate would prove fairly accurate. West Germany in fact had become "respectable" again by 1957—largely through Russian and East German military pressures—and she became a member of NATO on 5 May 1955. This more than compensated for the defection of France from NATO in 1966. However, France was to adhere to the Treaty and to the NATO council even though she would withdraw her staff and forces from NATO commands.

‡**Editor's Note:** This estimate was to prove gravely inaccurate. Through massive Soviet agitprop, British and American influence in Arabia suffered grave blows that virtually ended British hegemony, imperiled Western control of or access to Arabian oil, and lost for Britain that precious cord to the East: the Suez Canal. In the entire area, only Israel retained its Western orientation. In 1954, the Ba'ath party emerged as the most powerful in Syria and introduced a program that combined Arab nationalism with socialism. To protect themselves against what the Syrians believed were the military menaces of the Baghdad Pact—the Central Treaty Organization (CENTO) consisting of Great Britain, Pakistan, Iran, Turkey, and Iraq—both Syria and Egypt signed economic and military accords with Russia. As a result, the Syrian Communists gained increasing control of Syria, and the Soviets established bases and supplied the Syrians with large quantities of military equipment and stores. The situation was similar in Egypt, whose air bases were critical in importance to the Strategic Air Command's war plan. In 1952, Egyptian nationalists forced King Farouk to abdicate, and by 1956 all British troops had left the Canal Zone and all bases had been occupied by Egyptian forces. In 1956 the Egyptians suddenly nationalized the Suez Canal and ejected all British diplomatic and oil officials. In turn the British, French, and Israeli armies invaded the Canal Zone in an effort to restore Anglo-French control over the vital waterway. World diplomatic and political opinion forced the invaders to withdraw under ignominious circum-

stances—a withdrawal that marked the end of Britain as a first-rank world power. Thereafter Egypt swung increasingly under direct Soviet control.

The pro-Western regime in Transjordan was gravely destabilized by the seemingly unholy combination of Soviet influence, Arab nationalism, and the Muslims' special brand of socialism. Hussein was compelled to break his treaty relationship with Britain, and such was the turmoil that British paratroopers were sent in with American help to keep him on his throne. There were, in two years, no less than fourteen separate attempts on Hussein's life.

Lebanon was also badly destabilized, generally by the same conflicting forces that threatened Jordan. American troops were landed in strength in 1958 to maintain the *status quo*. These same forces served to bring turmoil to the entire Arabian peninsula, although America's main source of Arabian oil—Saudi Arabia—did remain relatively tranquil. However, even in Saudi Arabia anti-Western feeling over Western policies in Israel ran so high that in 1961 the United States was forced to abandon its great base at Dhahran, a key installation in the Dropshot war plan and in SAC's operations. In the Trucial States and Aden, key points in Anglo-American naval and military strategy, severe riots developed which made various military and political agreements uncertain. Iraq went Red when King Feisal and Premier Nuri-es-Said were murdered in 1958. And as a result the Baghdad Pact collapsed almost entirely. India emerged as a leader of the world's nonaligned states and could not therefore be depended upon to support the West in any war, but Pakistan, despite instability, did remain fairly loyal to the West, and SAC would have had a reasonable welcome had they sought to use the air bases at Lahore, which had been earmarked for use by SAC in its campaign against southern Russia.

In reality, the only encouragement the West could draw from its entire Near Eastern position was the stubborn loyalty of the Turks and the fact that under the Shah of Iran the Persians began to develop closer ties with the West, especially with the United States.

As for Ireland, Sweden, Switzerland, and Greece, only Greece would have made a stand. In general, in all four countries it would have been a war on the telephone.

g. *USSR and Satellites*

(1) *Political Aims and Objectives*

(a) *Soviet Union*

i. Never before have the intentions and strategic objectives of an aggressor nation been so clearly defined. For a hundred years, victory in the class struggle of the proletariat versus the bourgeoisie has been identified as the means by which Communism would dominate the world. The only significant new facts to emerge have been strict control of world Communism by Soviet Russia and the possibility that the USSR may now be entering an era wherein the ultimate objective might be gained by military force if all other methods fail.

ii. The ultimate object of the USSR is domination of a Communist world. In its progress toward this goal, the USSR has employed, and may be expected to employ, the principle of economy of force. World War III is probably regarded by the Kremlin as the most expensive and least desirable method of achieving the basic aim, but the USSR has been, and will continue to be, willing to accept this alternative as a last resort. As time passes, the intense Soviet concentration on increasing its military potential will render the war alternative less hazardous from their point of view.

(b) *Satellite States*. In general, the governments of the satellite states which are completely under Soviet domination and control will have no political aims and objectives distinguishable from those of the USSR.

(2) *Attitude and Morale*

(a) *Soviet Union*

i. The morale of the Soviet people would not become a decisive consideration to the Kremlin until such time as a drastic deterioration of the Soviet military position took place. While certain elements of the Soviet population—particularly ethnic groups in the Baltic states, [the] Ukraine, the Caucasus, and Central Asia—are dissatisfied with Soviet rule and hostile to domination by the Great Russians, the Soviet government through its efficient security-police network would be able to keep these groups under effective control in the early stages of the war. The more protracted the war, the more chance there would be for these subversive influences, already present in the Soviet Union, to manifest themselves and take a more active part in interfering with the Soviet war effort. Effective resistance or uprisings could be expected to occur only when the Western Allies are able to give material support and leadership and assure the dissident elements early liberation from the Soviet yoke.

ii. Soviet patriotism, while less ardent in support of a foreign war than in defense of home territory, would not be greatly shaken as long as military victories and war booty were forthcoming. As hostilities progress, however, and if Soviet military reverses become known within the USSR, the increased hardships and suffering would magnify any existing popular dissatisfaction with the regime. Russian respect for American technical and industrial ingenuity also might prove to be an important factor in affecting the Soviet people's morale and their willingness to make seemingly useless sacrifices for a sustained war effort.

iii. The people of the USSR are very susceptible to psychological warfare. The Soviet Union's most significant weakness in this regard is its policy of keeping its people in complete ignorance of the true conditions both inside and outside the USSR.

iv. Psychological warfare, therefore, can be an extremely important weapon in promoting dissension and defection among the Soviet people, undermining their morale, and creating confusion and disorganization within the country. It could be particularly effective in subversive operations directed toward those ethnic nationalities which would welcome liberation, as well as toward the Soviet Army, especially those elements of it which would be stationed outside the borders of the USSR.

     v. The most effective theme of a psychological-warfare effort directed against the Soviet Union would be that the Western powers are not fighting against the peoples of the USSR but only against the Soviet regime and its policies of enslavement and exploitation.

(b) *Satellite States.* A majority of the native populations in the satellite countries are intensely nationalistic and religious and resent both Moscow domination and Communist regimes with which they are burdened as well as the religious restrictions imposed upon them. This attitude, however, while a source of great potential weakness to the Soviet bloc if shrewdly exploited by the West, would not give rise to effective resistance movements immediately upon the outbreak of hostilities. Initially the dominant attitude among the non-Communist population of the satellite states would be one of increased noncooperation and passive resistance toward their Communist masters. This would result in some reduction of the agricultural, industrial, and military contribution of the satellites to the Soviet war effort. More effective resistance, however, in the form of organized sabotage and guerrilla activity would be unlikely to develop significantly until they were assured of guidance and support from the West. In view of the probable continuance of these conditions, the peoples of the satellite area in 1957 would still prove readily susceptible to psychological appeals and would be particularly influenced by assurances that aid from the West in support of their aspirations for national independence and religious freedom would be forthcoming.

(3) *Political Strengths and Weaknesses.* The significant political strengths and weaknesses of the Soviet orbit are estimated to be as follows:

    (a) *Strengths*

       i. The native courage, stamina, and patriotism of the Soviet people.

       ii. The elaborate and ruthless machinery by which the Kremlin exercises centralized political control throughout the Soviet orbit, employing police forces, propaganda, and economic and political duress.

       iii. The ideological appeal of theoretical Communism.

       iv. The apparent ability of the Soviet regime to mobilize native Russian patriotism behind a Soviet war effort.

       v. The ability of the people and the administration to carry on a war under circumstances of extreme disorganization, demonstrated in the early years of World War II.

    (b) *Weaknesses*

i. Popular disillusionment and embitterment among certain groups throughout the Soviet orbit, resulting from ruthless Soviet and Communist oppression and exploitation.

ii. The fear of the police state pervading all elements of Soviet and satellite society.

iii. The traditional admiration of many of the Soviet and satellite peoples for the living standards of Western democracies in general and of the United States in particular.

iv. Influence of religious groups, especially among the satellites.

v. The native nationalism of the satellite populations and of certain ethnic groups in the USSR.

vi. Probable demoralization which would result from Soviet military and occupation duties in foreign countries.

vii. The extreme concentration of power in the Politburo of the Communist party, which leads the bureaucratic machinery, tends to preclude the assumption of initiative and to discourage individuals at lower levels in the system from making decisions.

(c) It is estimated that the strengths noted above constitute an actual and present advantage to the USSR, while the weaknesses, in most cases, are potential rather than actual. During the early stages of conflict these weaknesses would constitute a substantial burden upon the Soviet Union's machinery for political control and would also impair the Kremlin's economic and administrative capabilities. These weaknesses, however, would not have an early or decisive effect upon the outcome of a Soviet military venture. During the early stages of war native Soviet morale might improve somewhat with reports of spectacular victories and the prospects of booty from Western Europe. It is unlikely that the psychological weaknesses in the Soviet and satellite structure would produce serious consequences unless the prospect for ultimate victory was seriously diminished by effective Allied air attack, resistance to their advances, disruption of coastal commerce, and the threat of increasing Allied strength.

(d) Furthermore it is extremely doubtful that the forces of resistance within the Soviet orbit would effectively assert themselves unless they received guidance and material support from the Allies with tangible hope for early liberation by Allied forces.

h. *Allied Nations (Except U.S.)*

(1) *Political Aims and Objectives*

(a) *United Kingdom*

i. The United Kingdom desires a maximum of international stability in order to achieve economic recovery as rapidly as possible. However, this aim is qualified by a determination to ensure the security of the United Kingdom, her dependent areas and imperial communications, and the Near and Middle East from Soviet encroachment. The United Kingdom firmly intends, in concert with the United States, to check Soviet expansionism.*

Editor's Note: The United States had a gloomy—but probably realistic—
view of Britain's capacity to fight a third world war. Other war plans promulgated in connection with Dropshot estimated that 40 atomic bombs
would knock England to her knees and 120 would destroy her, and SAC
believed that they could depend upon British bases for only sixty days. For a
fascinating Joint Intelligence Committee view of what would happen in any
major war between those two old enemies—England and Russia—see Appendix A. Appendix B is the State Department's assessment for the Joint Intelligence Staff.

     ii. The United Kingdom intends to maintain its imperial position
so far as possible. In the dependent empire it aims to encourage a reasonable rate of progress toward self-government, replacing political
controls with economic, cultural, and security ties. With regard to the
Dominions, it aims to preserve and promote Commonwealth solidar-
ity.

     iii. The United Kingdom intends to encourage Western Union and
increasing unity in Western Europe but at a pace which will not risk
the estrangement of the Dominions.

     iv. The United Kingdom will continue to support the United Na-
tions. Until the United Nations has the power to guarantee collective
security, the United Kingdom will continue to build power-political
relationships based on an intimate association with the United States
and on the Brussels Pact, Commonwealth cooperation, and the North
Atlantic Treaty.

     (b) *Canada.* Canada desires international peace and a high level of in-
ternational trade as conditions prerequisite to the development of its territory and resources.† Canada intends to maintain close relations with the
United States as the best guarantee of its security. Canada also intends to
continue its membership in the British Commonwealth of Nations, seeing
in the Commonwealth a major support of world order and its own participation as a vital link in a North Atlantic security system embracing the
United States and the United Kingdom. Canada desires political stability
and economic recovery in Western Europe because of the area's importance to Canadian security and because of long-standing cultural and commercial ties.

†**Editor's Note:** From time to time in the 1940s and 1950s Canada displayed
a desire—like India—to be nonaligned in the deadly hiatus, as Churchill
called the Cold War. But wisely she remained riveted to the Anglo-American
alliance. For that the Russians have themselves to blame: Igor Gouzenko,
the Soviet cipher clerk at the Ottawa embassy, provided the Canadian government with ample evidence that Russia regarded Canada with an attitude
that was basically hostile.

     (c) *Australia.* Australia desires international peace and a high level of
world trade. It wishes to preserve the Australian continent as an area of

white settlement and secure it against Asiatic imperialism. It desires friendly relations with the United States and close contacts with the United Kingdom and other Commonwealth countries.

(d) *New Zealand*. New Zealand desires peace and a high level of world trade. It desires to preserve the security of the southwest Pacific area and would resist any Asiatic encroachment.

(e) *South Africa*.* South Africa desires to maintain its country free of external influence and internally secure for its dominant white minority. It is interested in seeing as much of the African continent as possible become a "white man's country" in which the Union would be the leading nation.

***Editor's Note:** South Africa's racial problems were yet to make themselves forcibly apparent to the Pentagon planners. But through British criticism of apartheid, South Africa would leave the British Commonwealth in 1961. Long before that date, however, there was considerable uncertainty that South Africa would do in the third world war what she had done in the first and the second: spring to arms in support of the British crown.

(f) *France † and Benelux*. The primary concern of the governments of France, Belgium, the Netherlands, and Luxembourg is security in order to effect the political and economic recovery and stability of their respective peoples. These governments also seek to restore the prestige of their nations to a pre-World War II level and to retain their colonial possessions. All wish to participate in the formation of an economically stable but decentralized West Germany.

†**Editor's Note:** The instability and demoralization of France following World War II, her *folie de grandeur,* the omnipresence of the Communists throughout French society—all made France a very undependable ally. Privately many Pentagon planners believed that France would fight only a telephone war with Russia. The extent of her unreliability, even after accepting massive U.S. aid, was made very clear later on when she left the NATO alliance. American anxieties increased substantially when it was discovered just after World War II that Professor Frédéric Joliot-Curie—the leading French nuclear scientist, who had close connections with the American program through a disciple, Hans von Halban—was a Communist. Not without reason, the Americans suspected him of transmitting von Halban's information to the Russians. For the political appreciation of the French scene (discovered in the Plans and Operations Division files of the Joint Chiefs) see Appendix C. The situation in Italy was equally serious.

(g) *Allied Occupied Areas*. It is assumed that Allied forces either will be available for D-Day deployment in or will be actually stationed in Austria, West Germany, and Japan in 1957. These countries will, in all likelihood, seek to increase their economic and political strength and will desire to be reestablished as self-governing states free of occupation forces.

(h) *Italy*. Italy has two primary objectives: maintenance of political stability through alleviation of economic distress and the resumption of her position as a world power. Two primary considerations keep her aligned with the West, and particularly with the United States, in her attempts to attain these objectives. First is her realization that political stability can be maintained and economic recovery achieved only through very extensive outside assistance and that the West is able to give such assistance. Second is her realization both that her former position as a world power can be achieved only through political alliances and that no alliance with the USSR is possible on any basis of equality or even of independence. While Italy has a history of opportunistic action to fit the needs of the moment, her inborn psychological need for national aggrandizement together with the influence of the church can be counted on to maintain a strong resistance to communization. So long as the Allies can keep her economic distress from becoming unbearable, Italy will remain oriented toward the West.

(i) *Iceland*. An extreme sense of national independence governs Iceland's political conduct. Although very young as an independent nation, her whole history bespeaks independence of thought and spirit. Culturally, ideologically, and economically, Iceland is closely attached to Denmark, the other Scandinavian countries, and the United Kingdom. Commercial contacts with the USSR have proved highly profitable to Iceland, but the conduct of commercial negotiations was very evidently governed by political and strategic considerations. Iceland's understanding of the purposes and methods of the USSR have prompted her to join in the Atlantic Pact as the surest means of maintaining her independence. She can be expected to cooperate within the Pact to any extent short of compromising her sovereignty.

(j) *Portugal*. The basic aims of Portuguese foreign policy presently are to ensure the territorial integrity of the motherland and the empire, to maintain the economic stability on which the political stability of the regime depends, and to align Portugal with the Western powers. Realization on the part of the governing classes that Portugal's territorial integrity and economic stability depend on foreign military and political support probably is the basis of the country's signature of the Atlantic Pact. This departure from the traditional Portuguese policy of neutrality apparently was prompted by fears of an advance into Western Europe by the USSR.

(k) *Denmark*. The ratification by Denmark of the Atlantic Pact marks a significant change in foreign policy but no change in basic political objectives. Those objectives have been, and are, to maintain Danish independence and territorial integrity. For long, foreign policy in pursuit of the basic objectives has been one of strict neutrality and compromise to mutual benefit in relation to the contending great powers. Ratification of the Pact signalizes the realization by the Danes that neutrality, and compromise or accommodation with the USSR, will be difficult. It constitutes a public statement that Denmark is determined to maintain both her political independence and her ideological, cultural, and economic freedom.

(l) *Norway*. The remarks in the preceding paragraph concerning Denmark apply also to Norway, with, if possible, even more emphasis on the determination to maintain independence and freedom. Since the experience of World War II, Norway has been a leader among the Scandinavian countries in urging and engineering a departure from the traditional policy of complete neutrality and of adopting a policy of formal alliance. The government of Norway is exceptionally stable and it is expected that its policies will remain firm.

2. Economic Factors

a. *Soviet and Satellite*
  (1) *Basic Resources*
      In the overall picture, the USSR has a wealth of raw materials: it has the largest iron-ore reserves in the world, it is second only to the United States in coal reserves, and in 1947 it had proven petroleum reserves of 8 billion barrels. It is self-sufficient in food and most textile raw materials. On the debit side, the Soviet Union and the satellite countries depend entirely or partially on foreign sources of supply for industrial diamonds, natural rubber, cobalt, tin, tungsten, and molybdenum. The satellites are deficient in high-grade ore. USSR steel production by 1957 may reach 32 million tons; the United States in 1947 produced 79.7 million tons.* Soviet coal production in 1957 may be 375 million tons, but the United States in 1945 produced 570 million tons. The Soviet petroleum production for 1957 is estimated at 360 million barrels as compared to the United States 1945 figure of 2 billion barrels. While some deficiencies in high-grade gasoline and lubricants may exist in the USSR during the period under consideration, it is unlikely that their war economy will be initially impaired. However, the USSR has a very limited high-octane refinery capacity, which is a significant weakness.

***Editor's Note:** This is a superficial assessment of the Soviet Union's industrial achievements, although to be fair there were, of course, more comprehensive surveys available to the planners if required. The fact is that Russia's industrial development is one of the most remarkable in history. When the Bolsheviks came to power in 1917, Russia was an overwhelmingly agricultural nation. Her economy was devastated by World War I and the subsequent civil war. Her economy was devastated for a second time by World War II, although to a lesser degree—and certainly less than that estimated by the Pentagon. However, while very rich in most raw materials, industrially, economically, financially, and agriculturally she was far less powerful than the United States in 1945. It will be noted that she was to pass the United States in crude-steel production in 1971 and 1972.

(2) *Industrial Development*

(a) Following on the present development of the basic heavy industries, it is expected that the fifth Five-Year Plan ending in 1955 will see a large expansion of the Soviet manufacturing industries with consequent increase in the capacity for armament manufacture. A brake on the speed of her development will remain the capacity of her transport system. In spite of the advances she will have made in all fields of industrial development, her industrial efficiency, technical ability, and productivity will still be considerably lower than that of the Allied nations. This disparity, however, may not prevent the USSR from creating conditions of war.

(b) All of the satellite countries have ambitious economic plans, but it is likely that by 1957 only Poland, Czechoslovakia, Hungary, and Romania will have developed sufficiently for their economic assistance to the Soviet Union to be a significant factor under war conditions.

(3) *Industrial Manpower*

(a) It is estimated that by 1957 the total population will have risen to 220 million, including a labor force of 90 million. This labor force will include 49 million agricultural workers and a nonagricultural force of 41 million.

(b) The present drive to improve technical education will have begun to show results, and the shortage of skilled workers is likely to be less acute, with the result that an extensive call-up of industrial workers in 1957 would have less effect on industrial productivity than would be the case in 1949. The supply of unskilled workers will remain sufficient.

(4) *Dependence on Foreign Sources for Key Commodities*

It is considered that by 1957 the Soviet Union will not be critically deficient in any of the more important strategic materials. In cases such as natural rubber and industrial diamonds, where her productive capacity may fall short of her requirements, she will have made every effort to build up stockpiles, but her success in doing so will be to some extent dependent on the willingness of countries outside the Soviet orbit to meet her requirements in the interim period. The Soviet Union has had good success in importing strategic materials, with the exception of tin. The satellites will continue to require high-grade iron ore from Sweden, but if this were denied to them, the Soviet Union would be able to make good this deficiency, provided the necessary transportation could be made available.

(5) *Transport Capabilities*

(a) *Railroads.* It is considered that the railway mileage will have been considerably increased by 1957 and that the system will be more flexible and adaptable to war needs. Nevertheless it will still be insufficient to meet the needs of the greatly increased traffic and there will continue to be a shortage of locomotives and freight cars. The general standard of efficiency will remain low by Western standards.

(b) *Motor Transport*. Development of long-distance routes is at present concentrated on five main roads radiating from Moscow and on two lateral routes. Progress is slow but by 1957 these routes are likely to have approached Western European standards, and long-distance haulage will afford some relief to rail transport in the west of the Soviet Union. Development of the local road system is likely to have been considerable.

(c) *Civil Air Transport*. In spite of the improvement in other means of internal transport, it is considered the present reliance on civil air transport is likely to continue.

(d) *Inland Waterways*. Rehabilitation will have been completed, together with the reconstruction and enlargement of some canals and the completion of new projects. These factors, together with the mass production of metal and concrete barges and the increasing mechanization of cargo-handling facilities, will allow the inland waterways to take an increased percentage of total traffic and afford some further relief to the railways.

(e) *Coastal Shipping*. In 1957 the internal transport system of the Soviet Union is likely to remain a comparative weakness in [the] Soviet economy, though in a lesser degree than in 1949. The degree of reliance on coastal shipping in certain areas is therefore likely to persist, and an overall increase in coastal tonnage is foreseen in the existing Five-Year Plan.

(f) *Strategic Significance of Communications*. The main strategic strength of the Soviet Union and satellite countries will lie in their possession of interior lines of communications and on their ability to move economic and military traffic without resort to open sea routes. Although great efforts will be made to improve these communications and to overcome some of the gauge-change difficulties, the capacity of the Soviet railway system will continue to be inadequate and to be one of the Soviet Union's major economic problems.

(6) *Vulnerability of Soviet Industry*. Of great strategic importance is the fact that in 1945 nearly 70 percent of USSR petroleum needs were supplied by the vulnerable Caucasus region. New plants being built will reduce this concentration as well as that of the chemical, electric-power, and antifriction-bearing industries, but plants for manufacture of instruments and oil-producing equipment are still located almost exclusively in Moscow and the Transcaucasus complex, respectively. No reliable evidence exists to indicate the development of USSR underground industry. It may be expected, however, that some vital processes relating to jet engines, guided missiles, [and] atomic and biological weapons will be placed underground in small and scattered plants, but such procedures will increase needs for skilled labor and machinery and put greatly increased burdens on the already overtaxed transportation system.

(7) *Summary.* The industrial capacity of the Soviet Union will have advanced to a considerable degree beyond the 1949 level, and this will be particularly so in the manufacturing industries and hence in her ability to produce large quantities of armaments. Most of the strategic deficiencies prevalent in 1949 will have been overcome, and where productive capacity still lags behind war requirements, stockpiles will have been accumulated. It is in consequence considered that by 1957 the economy of the Soviet Union will be adequate to support her in a major war for a prolonged period.

b. *Allied Nations*

(1) *General.* The overall economic potential of the Allies in 1957 will be greater in almost every respect than that of the USSR and her satellites, with productive capacity of essential war industries of the United States and British Commonwealth alone at least twice as great. On the other hand, the occupation of Western and Northern Europe by Soviet forces could yield to the USSR a number of great long-range economic advantages. The principal gains would accrue to the USSR, however, only after the Soviet Union and the entire area under its control were relatively free from damaging attack and if commercial intercourse were possible with other areas.

(2) *United States.* The increasing dependence of the United States on foreign sources of strategic and critical materials will probably be the most significant factor influencing the economic position of the United States in the event of war in 1957. This dependence will require consideration of the security of certain overseas sources of supply and of sea and air LOCs [lines of communication] thereto. Our estimated position relative to dependence on foreign sources for strategic and critical materials in 1957 is discussed in the succeeding paragraphs; because of the special importance of oil and the tremendous quantities involved, it is treated separately.

(a) *Oil*

i. The oil position of the United States has changed from one of abundance to one of critical supply. This position is caused by two principal factors: first, the greatly increased civilian consumption, and second, the diminishing volume of new discoveries and the consequent lag in production sufficient to make up for the increase in consumption. As a result, the United States, for the first time in history, now imports more oil than it exports. Present demand in the United States now exceeds 6 million barrels a day, with production in the United States slightly in excess of 5.75 million barrels a day. Every indication is that United States consumption will continue to mount, with indigenous production unable to keep apace.

ii. In the event of war against the USSR in 1957, the skyrocketing demands of the armed forces will require a production far exceeding the estimated capabilities of the United States at that time. Although it has been difficult to estimate accurately our total requirements—both civilian and military—for a lengthy war beginning in

1957, the best information available indicates that those requirements may reach a maximum of 8 million barrels a day. A factor in such a tremendous increase will be the jet fuel requirements.

iii. In order to meet the greatly increased wartime requirements, the Allies must have access to all Western Hamisphere and Far Eastern sources of petroleum. It probably will be necessary to have access to some, if not all, Near and Middle East oil throughout a lengthy war.

iv. Within the framework of a national petroleum program, measures are being considered with the objective of meeting Allied war requirements without dependence on Middle East supply. These measures include the development of additional sources of natural crude oil, development of synthetics, construction of refineries, substitution of natural gas for nonmobile oil consumers, and stockpiling to an appropriate degree. The degree of implementation of these measures and the results which may be accomplished have not been determined at this time.

v. As an essential step in mobilization, a stringent rationing program and a maximum petroleum-production effort would necessarily have to be instituted. Nevertheless, without successful implementation of the national petroleum program, supplies would be inadequate from the beginning of war if Middle East sources were denied. In summary, adequate supplies for a prolonged war without some Middle East oil are by no means assured, and access to some, if not all, Middle East oil becomes a matter of primary consideration.

(b) *Other Strategic and Critical Materials*

i. The growing dependence of the United States on foreign sources for strategic and critical materials is the result of two significant factors: the first is the greatly increasing demand for these materials as a result of accelerated technological advances in industry; the second is the depletion of mineral reserves and the declining rate of discoveries of new sources of supply in the United States.

ii. During World War II approximately 60 percent, on a volume basis, of our total requirements for strategic and critical materials came from domestic production and 40 percent from imports. On the other hand, for a war beginning in 1957 it is estimated that for the first three years only about 40 percent of our total requirements can be met from United States production, while 60 percent must come from imports and stockpile withdrawals.

iii. Although the United States is currently engaged in a program for stockpiling up to five years' wartime requirements, originally slated for completion in 1951–1952 (minimum stockpile objectives), this program is now several years behind schedule. In addition the current stockpile is considerably unbalanced in that there are little or no stockpiles of some materials and large quantities of others. Nevertheless, by 1957 it is estimated that for many strategic materials, although not all, there will be stockpile supplies for up to five years' wartime requirements.* Unless the United States is cut off from access to foreign raw-material sources, it is unlikely, however, that great quantities will be withdrawn from the strategic stockpile during wartime. This is because a very heavy dependence on the stockpile would be a security risk in the event of a lengthy war, and any major discontinuance of imports would cause serious economic dislocations in the countries comprising our normal sources of supply, which in turn might induce these countries to turn against the United States.

iv. In view of the above considerations and assuming that normal import channels would be kept open, it is estimated that stockpile withdrawals for the first three years of a war beginning in 1957 would average 20 percent of our total requirements.

v. The estimated volume requirements for three years of war beginning in 1957—showing the relative quantities which would be obtained from domestic production, stockpile withdrawals, and imports—is shown in Table 1 below. Table 2 shows the quantities which would be required from each of the various world areas. . . .

vi. The volume figures and percentages shown in Tables 1 and 2 [below] do not present the entire picture as to the actual value of the different areas as sources of supply. Certain strategic and critical materials, while having a low volume figure, have an importance out of all proportion to their actual volume. Based upon a consideration of the actual importance of the principal strategic and critical materials, Table 3 below shows the relative importance of the world areas as sources of these materials during three years of war beginning in 1957. . . .

vii. Withdrawals from stockpiles naturally reduce the requirements of import volumes from the various world areas indicated on the map. Nevertheless, since this estimate is based on the premise that in the event of war, imports will continue, the relative importance of the world areas as sources of supply remains the same whether stockpiles be taken into account or not. For this reason, no separate column has been made for stockpiling in the square representing total U.S. supply in [the] map diagram.

(3) *United Kingdom*

(a) The United Kingdom is presently in a period of transition from war to peace. She is struggling under a burden of international financial

---

* Although not considered in this estimate, the condition of the stockpile could be further improved by 1957 by several factors, the principal of which would be the occurrence of a depression or the imposition of mandatory controls on industry.

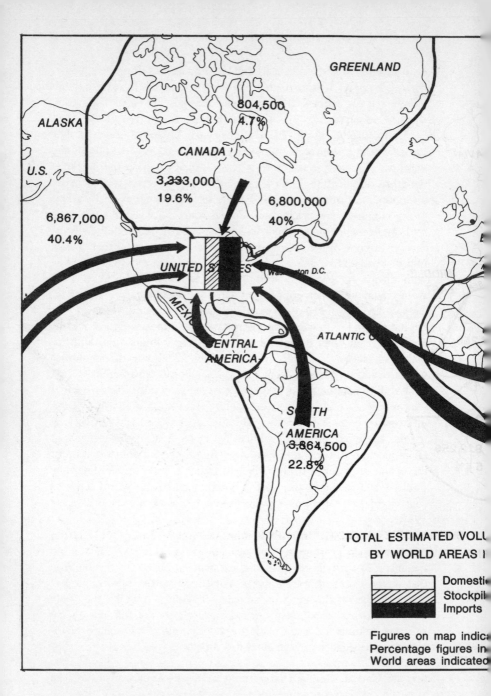

GREENLAND

ALASKA

U.S.

CANADA

804,500
4.7%

3,333,000
19.6%

6,800,000
40%

6,867,000
40.4%

UNITED STATES

Washington D.C.

MEXICO

CENTRAL
AMERICA

ATLANTIC OCEAN

SOUTH
AMERICA
3,864,500
22.8%

TOTAL ESTIMATED VOLU
BY WORLD AREAS I

Domesti
Stockpil
Imports

Figures on map indic
Percentage figures in
World areas indicated

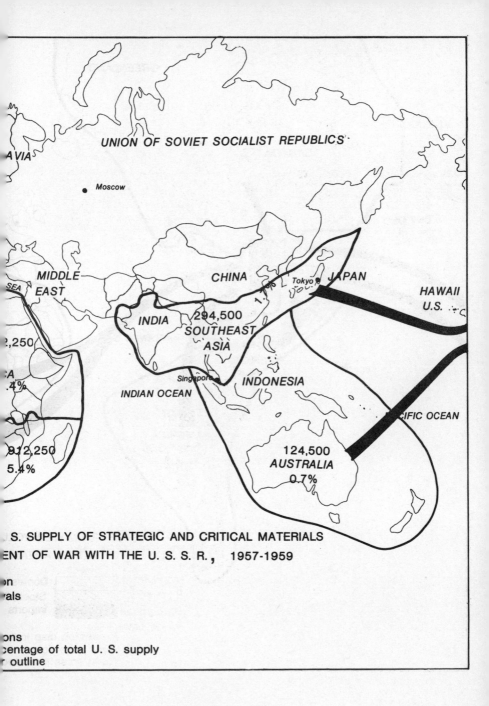

UNION OF SOVIET SOCIALIST REPUBLICS

• Moscow

MIDDLE
EAST

CHINA   Tokyo • JAPAN

HAWAII
U.S.

INDIA   294,500
SOUTHEAST
ASIA

1.7%

SEA

2,250

A
.4%

Singapore

INDONESIA

INDIAN OCEAN

CIFIC OCEAN

9,2,250
5.4%

124,500
AUSTRALIA
0.7%

S. SUPPLY OF STRATEGIC AND CRITICAL MATERIALS
ENT OF WAR WITH THE U. S. S. R., 1957-1959

n
als

ons
centage of total U. S. supply
outline

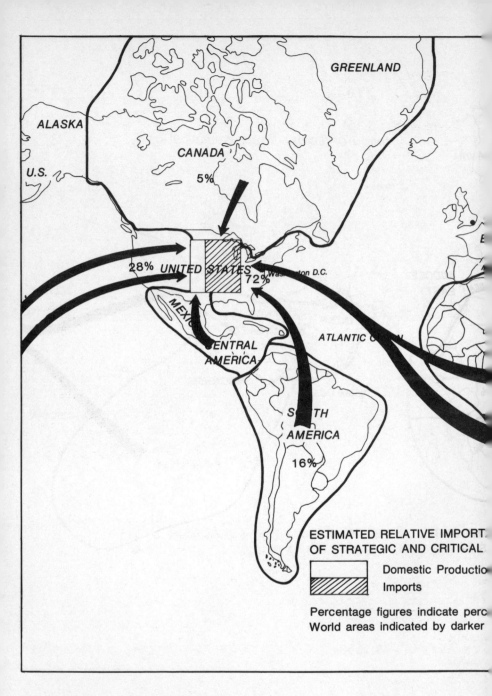

GREENLAND

ALASKA

U.S.

CANADA

5%

28% UNITED STATES

72%

Washington D.C.

MEXICO

CENTRAL
AMERICA

ATLANTIC OCEAN

SOUTH
AMERICA

16%

ESTIMATED RELATIVE IMPORT.
OF STRATEGIC AND CRITICAL

Domestic Productio
Imports

Percentage figures indicate perc
World areas indicated by darker

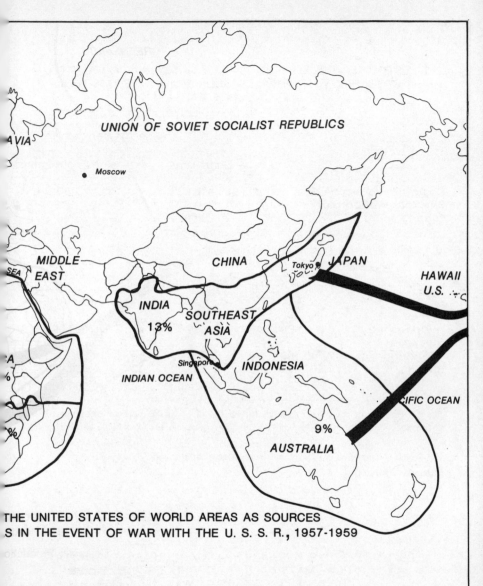

UNION OF SOVIET SOCIALIST REPUBLICS

• Moscow

AVIA

MIDDLE
EAST

SEA

CHINA

Tokyo JAPAN

HAWAII
U.S.

INDIA

13%

SOUTHEAST
ASIA

Singapore

INDIAN OCEAN

INDONESIA

CIFIC OCEAN

9%

AUSTRALIA

THE UNITED STATES OF WORLD AREAS AS SOURCES
S IN THE EVENT OF WAR WITH THE U. S. S. R., 1957-1959

U. S. sources of supply

TABLE 1
ESTIMATED RELATIVE VOLUME OF DOMESTIC PRODUCTION, STOCKPILE WITHDRAWALS, AND IMPORTS OF STRATEGIC AND CRITICAL MATERIALS DURING THREE YEARS OF WAR, 1957–1959

	Total 1957–1959	
	Short Tons	% of Total Supply‡
Domestic Production	20,400,000	40
Stockpile Withdrawals	10,000,000	20
Imports	20,600,000	40
	51,000,000*	100

	1957		1958		1959	
	ST	%TS†	ST	%TS	ST	%TS
Domestic Production	6,800,000	49	6,800,000	40	6,800,000	34
Stockpile Withdrawals	2,700,000	19	3,000,000	18	4,300,000	22
Imports	4,500,000	32	7,200,000	42	8,900,000	44
Totals	14,000,000	100	17,000,000	100	20,000,000	100

*Except for bauxite and cobalt, minerals included in this estimate represent metal content in ore. Minerals comprise about 84 percent of total supply requirements of strategic and critical materials.

†ST means "short tons"; %TS means "percentage of total supply."

‡Rounded figures.

TABLE 2
ESTIMATE OF U.S. AVERAGE YEARLY VOLUME OF STRATEGIC AND CRITICAL MATERIALS FROM VARIOUS WORLD AREAS DURING THREE YEARS OF WAR, 1957–1959

World Area	Average Yearly Volume Short Tons	% of Total U.S. Supply	% of Total Imports
South America	3,864,500	22.8	56
Africa	1,484,500	8.8	22
Canada	804,500	4.7	12
Mexico–Caribbean	294,500	1.7	4
Southeast Asia	294,500	1.7	4
Australia–Oceania	124,500	0.7	2
Totals	6,867,000	40.4	100

TABLE 3
ESTIMATED RELATIVE IMPORTANCE TO THE U.S. OF WORLD AREAS
AS SOURCES OF STRATEGIC AND CRITICAL MATERIALS
DURING THREE YEARS OF WAR, 1957–1959

World Areas	Percentage of Total Contribution to the U.S.
United States, domestic production	28
Imports, by world areas	72
South America	16
Africa	16
Mexico–Caribbean Area	13
Southeast Asia	13
Australia–Oceania	9
Canada	5
Total	100
Western Hemisphere	62
Eastern Hemisphere	38

and domestic economic problems, a serious manpower shortage, and political instability in the empire. It is unlikely that the United Kingdom will be able to finance another war effort as great as the last one.

(b) Overall industrial output of the United Kingdom is, however, substantially above prewar levels. Failure to modernize industrial equipment and improve production methods has been a limiting factor to increased output. The postwar level of coal production is less than prewar, largely due to shortage of manpower rather than obsolescent equipment. Nevertheless by 1957 the level of British industrial production will undoubtedly exceed 1949 levels. Britain's primary objective at the present time is to expand her foreign trade. An increase of 75 percent over the prewar volume is required to compensate for losses in income from overseas investments and shipping. Consequently Britain's exports will have to be maintained at a very high level in order to finance a major part of her food and raw-materials requirements for the next few years. By 1957 the merchant marine will equal or exceed present size and will consist largely of modern ships.

(c) Economic support for the British armed forces depends on the importation of large quantities of raw materials. Assuming that raw materials are acquired, British industry is capable of supporting her armed forces. However, the availability of materials abroad, the slowness of sea transport, and the time required to fill supply pipelines are factors which adversely affect procurement. The establishment of an effective British wartime economy would require rapid assistance from the United States. In a short war, consumer items such as food will be a more important factor than strategic industrial materials. In an extended war, the petroleum-refining industry will be able to meet only a small fraction of the needs of the armed forces, and industry in general will be heavily dependent upon imports.

(4) *Canada.* It is expected that in the next few years Canada will see a growth of all types of manufacturing, along with new discoveries and development of resources, e.g., iron and coal in Quebec, oil and natural gas in Alberta, and radioactive elements in Ontario and the Northwest Territories. Her capacity for surplus-food production will be greatly increased. By 1957 Canada's economic contribution to a war effort would be substantially greater than in World War II.

(5) *Australia and New Zealand.* Australia and New Zealand may be expected to increase output of manufactured products, especially in the aircraft and shipping industries. They could also make an important contribution of basic products.

(6) *The Union of South Africa.* The Union's contribution to the industrial potential of the empire consists primarily of the following minerals: gold, industrial diamonds, coal, manganese, chrome, asbestos, wool, copper, and iron. With the exception of ISCOR (Iron and Steel Industrial Corporation), where a great variety of steel products are made on an increasing scale, South Africa's manufacturing industry is negligible.

(7) *France*

(a) Postwar recovery efforts in France are directed toward the rehabilitation and expansion of capital equipment to overcome the physical damage and capital deterioration caused by the war and thereby to restore the framework of the prewar economy. For the six basic industries—coal, power, steel, cement, agricultural machinery, and transport—the 1950 target for industrial production is 160 percent of the 1930 level. Efforts are being made to modernize both agricultural and industrial production methods to raise output despite continuing labor shortages.

(b) By 1957 France may be expected to be virtually self-sufficient in all major food categories except fats and oils, the domestic production of which will probably supply less than half the country's requirements. France's most extensive indigenous raw materials are iron ore, bauxite, cement, and potash, in all of which the country is on an export basis. On balance, however, France is a heavy net importer of industrial raw materials, coal and oil being major import items. French coal production should increase substantially by 1957. Imports of at least 30 million tons or about one-third of total requirements will still be required. The dependence of the French iron and steel industry on raw materials from the Ruhr is such that France is expected to receive 30 percent of the total Ruhr exports of coal and coke.

(c) The Saar, now in economic union with France, is a highly industrialized area with important coal mines and steel mills and substantial production in chemicals and glass. The Saar is important to Western

Europe, especially to France, as an exporter of coal and finished steel. By 1957 annual exports from the Saar of 10 million metric tons of hard coal and 1.5 million tons of finished steel may be expected.

(d) Whereas France's imports normally consist predominantly of raw materials, exports are chiefly manufactured goods—textiles, vehicles, chemicals, and iron and steel. Industrial production has already exceeded the prewar rate by 17 percent. The acute postwar limitation of food, transportation, and labor are being overcome; continuation of the upward trend of production will hinge on the availability of coal, particularly from the Ruhr.

(8) *Belgium*

(a) Belgium is largely an industrial processing country. The principal products which Belgium produces in excess of its domestic requirements are iron and steel, textiles, cut diamonds, glass, cement, certain nonferrous metals, railroad cars, and some types of heavy machinery. Most raw materials required in the manufacture of the above products, however, are largely imported. The only industrial raw material available in large quantities in Belgium is coal, but even this material must be supplemented to some extent by imports. Belgium also is dependent upon outside sources for a considerable portion of its foodstuffs.

(b) In addition to the export of the products mentioned above, German transit trade through Antwerp was an important source of foreign exchange before the war. At present this trade is only a fractional part of its prewar level. It is expected that it will be much larger in 1957, although even then it may be less than prewar.

(c) It does not appear likely that there will be any great shift in the character of Belgian industry and trade during the next few years. A most likely development is an intensification of the industrial characteristics of the country that existed before the war, with the most important development between 1948 and 1957 probably being a considerable increase in production of iron and steel products.

(d) There are important respects in which trade between Belgium, Luxembourg, and the Netherlands is complementary. By 1957 it is likely that considerable progress will have been made toward a complete economic union of the three countries, and a combined strength of the Benelux economic union when fully implemented will be a strong economic bargaining unit in international economic relations.

(9) *Netherlands*

(a) The effects of the war are relatively greater in the Netherlands than in any Allied country in Western Europe. Economic recovery in the Netherlands consequently has been more difficult and is not as far advanced as in other Western European countries. Nevertheless manufacturing production in the Netherlands by the middle of 1948 had returned approximately to prewar levels.

(b) The long-range economic outlook in the Netherlands is not particularly promising. For many years the value of merchandise imports into the Netherlands was 40–50 percent more than merchandise exports. This commodity trade deficit was offset by income from overseas investments, from shipping, and from German transit trade. The principal commodities in which the Netherlands showed a net export were foodstuffs. Principal imports are iron and steel from Germany, Belgium, and Luxembourg. The United Kingdom, because of its increasing self-sufficiency, will not provide as good a market for Netherlands foodstuffs in the future as it did in the past. By 1957 Netherlands shipping may yield larger returns than in prewar years. Income from investments in the Netherlands Indies and returns from German transit trade, however, are not likely to equal prewar levels at any time in the foreseeable future. Moderate improvement in total industrial production over present levels should be attained by 1957, with a tendency toward production for an increased self-sufficiency. It is not likely, however, that the expected increases in industrial production by 1957 will more than offset the declines in visible income earned by the Netherlands before the war.

(10) *Luxembourg*. Luxembourg has developed within the last fifty years an iron and steel industry of international importance. The iron and steel industry, suffering only moderate damage during the war but in need of considerable modernization, has made rapid advances since the war. Luxembourg is now producing pig iron at the annual rate of 2.6 million metric tons, or approximately 10 percent of the total production of Western Europe, and crude steel at the annual rate of 2.2 million metric tons, or approximately 7 percent of the total production of Western Europe. The principal vulnerability of Luxembourg's production is its dependency on imports for high-grade ores and for coking coal. Given adequate imports of coking coal, increases of perhaps 50 percent from these record levels and substantial exports of crude and semifinished steel to other countries in Western Europe may be expected by 1957.

(11) *The Ruhr*

(a) Industrial expansion in France and the Benelux countries depends heavily on the coal industry of the Ruhr, and in the future Ruhr coal is likely to play an equally important part in the industrial activity of Western Europe. Assuming fairly stable peacetime conditions, the possibilities of stepping up Ruhr coal shipments to the West appear to be good. At present about 20 percent of the coal produced in the Ruhr is exported, of which about one-half goes to France and Benelux. The volume of future deliveries will be largely controlled by two factors: the amount of coal produced in the Ruhr and the amount of steel produced in Germany. Coal production is expected to rise to a level of at least 150 million tons by 1957, as compared to a current level of about 95 million tons and a prewar level of 135 million tons. The Western Allies have established a goal for Germany's steel production of 10.7 million metric tons, which is somewhat more than half of prewar output. This goal can probably be attained by 1952 but will not be exceeded in later years.

(b) The dependence of France and Benelux on Ruhr steel is much less important than their dependence on Ruhr coal, because of their current and projected expansion of their own steel and steel-products industries, including those of the Saar. In addition, for the next few years much, if not most, of the Ruhr steel products will of necessity be consumed at home in reconstructing Germany. After 1950, however, increasing quantities of Ruhr steel products will probably be imported by Western European countries.

(c) Ruhr coal and steel production is obviously providing a powerful stimulus to industrial growth in France and Benelux; loss of Ruhr production during the next few years, therefore, would be expected to cripple their industries in comparable proportions.

(12) *Italy*. Because Italy is heavily overpopulated in comparison to the extent and productivity of the land, she must remain dependent on outside areas for a large share of her food and other agricultural requirements. Industrially Italy has two distinct assets but has a liability which, under certain circumstances, would cripple industrial production. She has in existence a considerable industrial plan supported by a large reservoir of trained manpower, and she has a considerable hydroelectric plant backed by available water resources for a large expansion. She is, however, so deficient in natural resources that her industrial potential is almost entirely dependent on imports of raw materials and fuels. Nonavailability of these commodities, through interruption of lines of supply at any time, would destroy Italy's industrial usefulness.

(13) *Iceland*. Economically Iceland is important as a source of fish and fish products but otherwise has slight economic assets. Other than fish it has almost no natural resources, and its extremely limited manufacturing, mining, and agriculture are not sufficient to supply even its own small population.

(14) *Portugal*. The Portuguese economy is not self-sufficient in that it requires large imports of many necessities. Although Portugal's economy is based on agriculture and fishing, it is not self-supporting in foods. In the raw-material field, Portugal is the world's most important source of cork [and] has important quantities of tungsten, and there are extensive deposits of low-quality tin. Other minerals—largely undeveloped and some not even fully explored—include coal, iron, pyrites, sulfur, manganese, zinc, lead, and titanium. Production of these latter minerals is not sufficient even for local requirements, and very extensive development would be necessary before any of them could become important exports. Portuguese manufacturing industries are extremely limited and technically very backward.

(15) *Denmark*. Except for agricultural land and the fish-producing waters

around the peninsula, Denmark has few natural resources of consequence. Its economy is, therefore, largely agricultural. It is an important source of foods, its principal exports being meats and dairy and poultry products. It is, however, to a considerable degree dependent on imports of fertilizers and feed concentrates. Industrially Denmark has significant capabilities in food processing, farm machinery, diesel engines, shipbuilding, machine tools, construction-engineering equipment, railway rolling stock, cement, and clay processing but is dependent on imports of raw materials and fuels. The Danish labor force is not large but is highly skilled.

(16) *Norway.* The Norwegian economy is largely dependent on foreign trade. Normally only about one-half of the total food requirements are domestically produced, and in some essential items, notably bread and feed grains and protein concentrates, domestic production is only one-fourth of requirements. Most important among the physical resources are minerals, waterpower, forests, and fish. An almost complete lack of fuel is the most serious deficit.

Commercial shipping is Norway's most extensive and most important industry. The Norwegian commercial fleet is presently the third largest in the world and is expanding. Norway has well-developed industries in the fields of electrochemistry, electrometallurgy, fish, pulp and paper, and mining which produce significant surpluses for export. Pyrites and iron ore are the chief products of the mining industry, but copper, titanium, nickel, zinc, lead, molybdenum, magnesite, mica, tin, tungsten, cadmium, and chromite are also mined. Norway's shipbuilding capacity is quite limited, though a significant expansion is planned.

3. Relative Combat Power

a. *Soviet and Satellite Armed Forces*
   (1) *Strengths and Dispositions*
      (a) *Ground Forces*
         i. It is estimated that in 1957* the Soviet armed forces will have a strength of about 3.8 million men. In the Soviet army there will probably be some 2.2 million troops. A vast program of reorganization and reequipment is in progress throughout the Soviet army with the object of bringing a large proportion of its divisions up to Western standards and, in particular, of increasing the strength of the armored element and converting most of the horse-drawn formations to a motorized basis.

*Editor's Note: The Institute for Strategic Studies in 1959 began to publish an estimate of *The Military Balance*—the pamphlet enjoyed that name—between Russia and the NATO powers. While the editor acknowledges that in two years Russia could do a great deal for her armed forces, the fact is that Russia watching is almost always a retrospective game; an estimate made in 1959 is usually influenced by the events of 1957. Thus the use of a 1959 appreciation is valid. In any event, before 1959 there was nothing in the public sector to compare with *The Military Balance*. In the military sector there were, of course, extensive and frequent assessments. As of this editing, however, they had not been declassified. For the ISS study, which shows that the Dropshot assessment was both surprisingly accurate (who can be a prophet?) and grossly inaccurate (especially in the area of the development of Russian military technology), see Appendix D.

ii. By relating the estimate of the manpower available in 1957 to a conjecture as to the makeup of balanced forces, it is believed that the Soviet standing army may then comprise 12 rifle divisions, 60 motorized rifle divisions, 30 mechanized divisions, 24 tank divisions, 9 cavalry divisions, and 20 artillery and antiaircraft divisions, or a total of 155 divisions of all categories (total of 135 line divisions).

iii. It is considered that by 1957 the armies of the Soviet European satellite states combined will probably total some 115 divisions.* Of these, about 40 percent might be used in offensive ground operations. In addition, in the Far East the Outer Mongolian forces would number 80,000 and Chinese Communist forces would number approximately 1.45 million troops.

iv. On D-Day in 1957, disposition of Soviet line divisions might be as follows:

Area	Line Divisions
Western USSR	70
Occupied Western Europe	15
Southern USSR (Caucasus)	15
Central USSR (Urals to Lake Baikal)	10
South-central USSR (Tashkent)	5
Far East USSR (east of Lake Baikal)	20
TOTAL USSR	135

v. The disposition of the satellite forces on D-Day would be such that each country's forces, while located within its own borders, would be concentrated near nonfriendly borders.

* The USSR probably would call upon the satellites to ready forces of smaller proportions than their capacity due to the following considerations: an unusual buildup in the satellite areas would imperil the security of the impending attack, which the USSR would attempt to keep secret from the West as long as possible, and the Soviets would call for only such forces from the satellite countries as they believe would loyally fight or participate in occupation duties.

vi. Estimated Soviet–European satellite strengths:

Country	D-Day DIVS	D + 30 DIVS	D + 365 DIVS
USSR (a)	155*	248*	over 500*
Poland (b) (c) (e)	22	33	50
Czechoslovakia (b) (e)	15	37	50
Finland (b)	3	15	15
Soviet zone of Germany (d) (e)	—	—	25
Bulgaria (e)	12	15	25
Hungary (e)	5	5	8
Romania (e)	11	15	30
Yugoslavia (f)	43	50	65
Albania (e)	4	5	6

*Includes artillery and antiaircraft divisions.

(a) Excludes MVD (Ministry for Internal Affairs) troops and static air-defense forces. The D + 365 capabilities are in excess of any anticipated requirements for ground forces and probably will not be exercised.

(b) It is considered that Poland and Finland will not be able to equip an army larger than that of their D-Day strength. Czechoslovakia will not be able to equip an army larger than that of her D + 30 strength. The remainder of the equipment necessary to equip the "D + 365" armies must be furnished by the USSR. Although Finland is included as a Soviet satellite, it is by no means certain that Finnish troops would fight against the Allies.

(c) In the case of the eight satellites, Mobilization-Day and D-Day are assumed to be synonymous.

(d) The Soviets would have to equip any German forces recruited from the Soviet zone of Germany.

(e) Organization, equipment, training, and tactics would be based on Soviet doctrines. Expansion would be predicated on the USSR's ability to supply necessary equipment.

(f) If the present defection of Yugoslavia from the Soviet satellite orbit should continue to 1957, it is not likely that Yugoslavia would ally with the Soviet Union but would attempt to remain neutral and would be committed to resist Soviet and/or satellite attack.

vii. The Soviet army is in the process of a fundamental reorganization of its ground units. Three types of divisions—rifle, mechanized, and tank—are expected to evolve as the basic combat units. Their estimated strengths are as follows:

Type	Personnel	Tanks	SP Guns*
Rifle	11,000	52	34
Tank	10,300	250	21
Mechanized	12,850	160	44

* Self-propelled guns

viii. There is no indicated change in the organization of airborne units. The basic airborne unit is believed to be the brigade of 4,200 men (with combat strength of four battalions at 699 each).

(b) *Naval Forces*

i. The Soviet Union is expected to make a considerable effort in the development of her navies in the north, west, the Black Sea, and the Far East. The greatest menace is expected to be the submarine fleet, which will include high-submerged-speed types.

ii. It is known that the Soviet Union is taking great interest in the building of midget submarines and fast coastal craft of all types, and it is estimated that they will have large numbers of these by 1957.

iii. In the absence of firm intelligence the following is the best estimate which can be arrived at for the Soviet naval forces in 1957.

(i) *Battleships*. The hull of a 45,000-ton battleship remains undamaged in the slips at Leningrad, but there are indications that she is being dismantled. It is reasonably certain that no other ships of this category are under construction at the moment, and it is unlikely that the Russians have yet made up their minds as to what is required for the future.

(ii) *Aircraft carriers*. There is no credible evidence of aircraft-carrier construction in the Soviet Union. There is no evidence so far that aircraft suitable for operation from carriers are being built or even designed or that training of personnel for this work has been contemplated. However, even though the Soviet navy may decide that an aircraft-carrier force is necessary for the future, in view of their total lack of experience in this field, it seems unlikely that they can develop such a force by 1957. Furthermore, they cannot call upon German experience to help them in this.

(iii) *Monitor-type vessels*. The first unit of this type is the *Viborg* (ex-Finnish), with a life expectancy through 1959. New units may be added starting in 1955.

(iv) *Cruisers*. About thirty, the majority of which will be heavy, and of these about seven to ten will be about twenty years old.

(v) *Destroyers*. About 120, approximately 40 percent of which may be of a large type of 4,500 tons.

(vi) *Escort destroyers*. About 140.

(vii) *Submarines*. About 300–350 ocean-type, of which about 50 percent are expected to be high-submerged-speed type. About 200–300 coastal-defense type may also be in operation.

(viii) *Minor combatant types and landing craft*. Large numbers of all types, including motor torpedo boats, midgets, radio-controlled explosive motorboats, minesweepers, etc.

iv. The Soviet navy possesses its own air force, which is divided between the various fleets and flotillas of the navy. The present total strength is estimated to be about 3,100 aircraft, probably disposed as shown in subparagraph (c) below. Although little is known of the postwar developments of the Soviet naval air force, there is no sign of any contemplated carrier construction, and it is probable, therefore, that in 1957 the role of the naval air force will be that of a coastal air force. Its activities will probably be confined primarily to the defense of port areas, the support of land operations in coastal belts, amphibious operations, the protection of shipping, and attacks on Allied sea communications as opportunity offers. There is no evidence to suggest that the size of the force will be markedly different in 1957.

v. There are indications that the Soviet naval authorities are taking steps to intensify the training of personnel to suit the expansion of the fleet which is envisaged. The mobilization strength is expected to be 865,000, including marines, coast defense, and naval air personnel.

vi. The estimated total of operational naval forces of the Balkan satellite countries in 1957 is four destroyers; two corvettes; three submarines; fifty midget submarines; fifty motor gunboats. Of the other European satellites, Czechoslovakia may be expected to operate a Danube flotilla of fast armed craft, and Poland and Finland a total naval force of two destroyers, four submarines, and considerable numbers of small craft of all types. It is not expected that the Far Eastern satellites will possess naval forces of any consequence.

(c) *Air Forces*

i. . . . Numbers of combat aircraft set forth are estimated to be those in operational units. While it is believed that the Soviet Union possesses vast numbers of reserve combat aircraft at the present time, no firm estimate of reserves in 1957 can be made. A considerable number of stored aircraft will probably be available, however, and it is likely that reasonable losses can be replaced fairly rapidly.

ii. It is estimated that the Soviet Union has seventeen thousand aircraft in operational units at the present time. This force includes at least fifteen tactical air armies, a long-range force, a fighter defense force, and a naval air force.

iii. Distribution by aircraft by type of command is believed to be as follows: military (tactical) air force, 10,000; long-range force, 1,800; fighter defense force, 2,100; naval air force, 3,100.

iv. A responsible forecast of the composition and strength of the Soviet air force in 1957 cannot be made before 1952 at the earliest. Nevertheless, it seems reasonable to assume for planning purposes that the organization and size of the various arms in 1957 will not differ greatly from the organization and size at the present time. Therefore, utilizing similar strength figures, it is estimated that on any D-Day in 1957 the allocation of tactical aircraft of the Soviet air forces, including naval but not including the fighter defense force (PVO) and the long-range force, might be as follows:

	Western Europe	Middle East	Far East	Interior USSR	Totals
Fighters	2,600	1,000	1,400	400	5,400*
Ground Attack	1,600	700	700	300	3,300
Light Bombers	1,200	500	700	400	2,800
Miscellaneous Reconnaissance, etc.	600	400	400	200	1,600
	6,000†	2,600	3,200	1,300	13,100

*A proportion of the fighter aircraft in the tactical air armies would be responsible for the defense of the lines of communication—i.e., the interception of enemy reconnaissance and bomber missions passing over the area—and might consequently not be available for offensive tactical operations. This proportion might normally be up to 25 percent of the total fighter strength but would depend on the threat to be met and might on occasions be very much higher.

†Any aircraft required for operations in Norway and Sweden would be taken from the total of those allotted to the Western European theater.

v. Protection of political and industrial centers of the Soviet Union is the responsibility of the antiaircraft defense force, which includes antiaircraft units and early-warning systems in addition to an estimated 2,100 interceptor aircraft in the fighter defense force (PVO). The fighter defense force is responsible for the home defense of the Soviet Union and is divided into a number of air armies, each of which is responsible for the defense of a fixed area. Assuming present strength figures would obtain in 1957, it is estimated that its deployment on D-Day would probably be:

For the defense of the Soviet Union behind the Western European front	600
For the defense of northern Russia	300
For the defense of the Soviet Union behind the Near and Middle East front	700
For the defense of the Soviet Union behind the Far East front	500
Total	2,100

vi. The long-range air force currently contains an estimated 1,800 operational aircraft. Although no information is available as to the number of B-29-type aircraft in operational units, it is considered that the 150 B-29s estimated to be available for operational usage are assigned to this force. Other types assigned to the long-range air force include 1,400 light bombers and 250 transports. It is subject to centralized control and its objectives might differ widely geographically from day to day. Therefore, any percentage estimate of the proportion which might be devoted to any particular target area probably would be misleading and at best of doubtful value. The strategic bomber and transport aircraft, therefore, represent a force which might be used to attack targets in Western Europe, the United Kingdom, Scandinavia, or the Near and Middle East and the Far East. Aircraft of the force could also be used for attacks against Alaska, Canada, and the United States. With the introduction of Soviet superfortresses, IL-18 and TU-70 heavy transports, and later heavy jet bombers and possibly a conventional-engined aircraft comparable to the U.S. B-36, the effectiveness of the long-range force should be substantially increased, but more skilled manpower will be required.

vii. Current strength of Soviet naval air force is estimated at 3,100 aircraft of the same types used in the tactical air armies. It is organized into six fleet air forces designated by areas as the North and South Baltic, Black Sea, Arctic, North and South Pacific. The naval air force will probably be used primarily to protect the sea approaches to the Soviet Union and secondarily in support of the ground forces.

viii. In addition to the above Soviet air forces, the Soviet Union has a semimilitary air organization: the civil air fleet. By 1957 the medium transport aircraft of the civil air fleet and the long-range force will have been replaced by IL-12s, TU-70s, IL-18s, and other aircraft of increased performance. It is estimated that the total number of transports available for military operations would be at least 2,500 medium and heavy transports, of which at least 10 percent might be heavy transports. The reequipment should result in a greatly increased airlift potential. It is estimated that at any time up to 1957 the Soviet Union will have available more paratroops than her transport force will be able to carry in any single lift. The above transport force, however, should be able to lift as many as forty thousand to fifty thousand troops at one time.

ix. The satellites may be able to place a limited number of combat aircraft at the disposal of the Soviet Union by 1957.

(2) *Mobilization Capabilities*

(a) *Ground Forces.* It is estimated that there might be about 33 million males fit for military service in 1957 and that approximately 55 percent of these might be mobilized in the course of a protracted war. In the event of mobilization the evidence indicates that the peacetime army of about 135 line divisions of all categories could be increased by about 60 percent in thirty days, although the number of armored and mechanized divisions would probably not increase in the same proportion. It is estimated that by M plus twelve months the Soviets can build up to more than 500 divisions.*

---

* For mobilization capabilities of Soviet satellite ground forces see tabulation, page 98.

(b) *Naval Forces.* Since the Soviet navy does not maintain a reserve fleet except for minor craft, the mobilization of the navy would not be a major problem.

(c) *Air Forces.* A large proportion of the personnel inducted would have had three years of previous service, which would facilitate the rapid formation of new air-force units. There would be only a slight increase in the operational aircraft strength during the first ninety days of mobilization, since the first three months would be required for the formation, organization, and indoctrination training of new units. Based on current strength and known trends, the following estimate of mobilization capabilities by D + 180 for 1957 may reasonably be used for planning purposes:

	Fighters		Attack		Lt. Bombers		Long-Range Force	
TOTALS	Conv.	Jet	Conv.	Jet	Conv.	Jet	Conv.	Jet
20,000	3,000	7,000	3,000	1,000	3,000	1,000	1,600	400

(3) *Combat Efficiency*
  (a) *Soviet Armed Forces*
    i. *Army.* By 1957 it is estimated that a very small proportion of the Soviet army will be outside the borders of the Soviet Union, and the army will, therefore, be for the most part insulated from subversive influences. The standard of training should be satisfactory and the supply of specialists will probably be rather easier than in 1949. Although the extent of political control in 1957 cannot be assessed, it is likely that the Soviet army will be a more effective fighting force in 1957 than it is in 1949.

    ii. *Navy.* A significant increase in the Soviet maritime population has taken place since 1939. The effect of this will be a steady increase in the efficiency of the Soviet navy between now and 1957. In 1957 the most efficient arm of the navy will be the submarine force, although overall performance and attack techniques probably will be lower than our standards. Development in high-submerged-speed operations would present a serious threat. The small submarines, in which personal bravery is the predominant factor for success, will be a menace. Surface units will be inexperienced in modern warfare at sea. A policy of ocean raiding would not be suited to the Soviet technique, but individual commanders might be successful in this sphere. Advantage is being taken of German technique and experience in the development of surface-ship designs, and the Soviet surface fleet is expected to have much better oceangoing qualities than hitherto. Energetic steps have been taken to collect all available German knowledge, and therefore some improvement in staff work, technical efficiency, and sea sense as compared with the last war can be expected. It is therefore considered that although any Soviet ship would compare unfavorably in fighting efficiency with her counterpart in the British or United States navies, the Soviet navy, as a whole, could operate such numbers of fast modern surface ships and submarines at such widely scattered points as to present a serious menace to our sea communications.

iii. *Air Forces*. With the assistance of German aviation experts and the backing of the fast-developing Soviet aviation industry, it is reasonable to suppose that by 1957 the difference in efficiency between the Anglo-American and Soviet air forces will be less than it was during World War II.

(b) *Satellite Armed Forces*

i. *Armies*. The satellite armies are likely to increase in efficiency as a result of the training which they are being given by Soviet personnel and the Soviet equipment with which they are being supplied to varying extents. The armies of Finland, Hungary, Bulgaria, and Romania are limited by treaty and can therefore only be increased in size by covert means. In Bulgaria and Romania this has already been done. The Soviet Union will probably not connive at such a step in the case of Finland.

ii. *Navies*. The forces at present available to the satellite countries do not represent any considerable factor in overall Soviet maritime strength. Poland and Yugoslavia are, however, likely to increase the efficiency of their navies, possibly up to the prewar standard.

iii. *Air Forces*. The air forces of all the satellite nations are being developed on Soviet lines. However, it is doubtful if their combat effectiveness will have been developed substantially by 1957.

(4) *Defenses*

(a) *Fortifications*

i. It is not anticipated that between the present and 1957, Soviet fortification policy will undergo major changes. It is estimated that Soviet land-fortification activity will consist largely of improvements and expansions of existing installations.

ii. The satellite states and Soviet-occupied areas all have some remnants of World War II or earlier fortifications, especially in Poland, Finland, East Germany, and Czechoslovakia. These defense systems appear to have been expanded and modernized, and a line of light fortifications at the extreme limit of Soviet control may be expected in 1957.

(b) *Major Ports and Naval Bases*. Present plans for the defense of major ports and naval bases will probably have been carried out. Defense will probably include:

i. Antisubmarine measures (booms, nets, underwater detecting devices, controlled mines).

    ii. Coast-watching radar stations, with efficient personnel manning them.

    iii. Strong coast artillery with modern equipment, fire-control methods, and laying gear.

    iv. Beach defenses at suitable landing places near important objectives.

    v. Extensive use of camouflage.

Any additional bases acquired or developed in the interim period will be similarly defended. Inland defenses will be stiffened and possibly extended.

(c) *Airfield Defense*. There are some indications of a trend toward placing important airfield hangar and maintenance facilities underground in the Soviet Union and in satellite areas. By 1957, this measure for passive ground defense of aircraft may be extensively implemented.

(d) *Early Warning*

    i. In obtaining early warning of air attack against the USSR proper, Soviet defense forces are now and probably would be in 1957 aided by control or partial control in areas contiguous to her borders. The Soviet satellite countries and occupation zones provide roughly a five-hundred-mile-wide buffer between the USSR and the remainder of Europe. In a more narrow form, Finland extends this corridor northward to the Barents Sea. Sinkiang, Mongolia, Manchuria, and the Kuril Islands provide a buffer area in the Far East. Soviet vessels, including the Asiatic fishing fleets, further extend the possible warning zones.

    ii. By 1957 the Soviet Union could have developed a fairly efficient early-warning system for their important industrial areas and some of the likely approaches thereto.

    iii. By 1957, in the principal defense areas, it is possible that the Soviets could have an operating electronic-control system for interceptors and antiaircraft artillery. However, the problem of electronic control of interceptors, guided missiles, and antiaircraft artillery will be considerable; the entire system in any principal area will be subject to electronic countermeasures.

(5) *Weapons, New and Improved*

(a) *Atomic Weapons*. In 1956–1957 the Soviet stockpile may be expected to be something approximating 250 bombs at the most. The supply of uranium ore is the limiting factor. Uncertainty in this respect makes it impossible to forecast the stockpile of bombs with greater accuracy.

(b) *Aircraft*. Soviet aircraft performance will probably be somewhat below that of the United States and the United Kingdom but should show a degree of technical development comparable to that of the Allies. By 1957 the main equipment of the fighter regiments will probably be jet aircraft. Such aircraft may be supersonic but no firm estimate of performance can be given at present. Some ground-attack regiments may have been reequipped with a ground-attack jet aircraft. There is, however, no evidence as yet that the Soviet Union intends to dispense with the slower, very heavily armored reciprocating-engined aircraft for this purpose. Bomber aircraft of the tactical air armies will probably be comparable in type but inferior in performance to Anglo-American aircraft in 1957.

(c) *Antiaircraft*. Antiaircraft equipment available to the Soviets will include hypervelocity guns with calibers on the order of 120mm to 150mm, excellent directors for computing and transmitting firing data, satisfactory gun-laying radar, some type of proximity fuse, and ammunition improved in lethal radius. Use of this equipment, against aircraft flying near sonic speeds at altitudes up to forty thousand feet, would be limited to the tracking capability of the director and gun-laying radar. In addition, the equipping of gun-laying radar with some type of antijamming device may be attempted. With the acquisition of German blueprints and German scientists, Soviet fire-control equipment will improve rapidly, and by 1957 Soviet antiaircraft fire-control equipment should be at least as good as present-day U.K. and U.S. equipment.

(d) *Biological Warfare (BW)*. There is no evidence available of the Soviet Union's present ability to wage biological warfare, but it must be assumed that she possesses now the requisite basic knowledge. It is not possible, therefore, to assess her present or future biological-warfare potential, but it must be assumed that by 1957 the Soviet Union's capability of waging biological warfare will be limited only by the material effort diverted into this channel and by the availability of the requisite means of delivery. The use of biological warfare as a sabotage instrument is a capability and a distinct threat.

(e) *Chemical Warfare*. By 1957, in addition to considerable stocks of already well-known gases, the Soviet Union will be able to produce in quantity the most potent nerve gases at present known and possibly others even more poisonous and should have developed means of dissemination.

(f) *Guided Missiles*

   i. *Surface-to-Air:* In 1957 the USSR probably will have adequate quantities of surface-to-air missiles available for the defense of important targets. It is expected that the standard Soviet surface-to-air missile will be based on the German missile Wasserfall. This missile probably will reach a maximum altitude of sixty thousand feet, a horizontal range of approximately thirty miles, carry a warhead of approximately six hundred pounds, and will attain supersonic speed shortly after launching. Since this missile probably will be launched vertically, precluding control until approximately five seconds of flight have elapsed, another weapon will be employed to engage targets below an altitude of around five thousand feet. This missile will be most likely an improved model of the German Schmetterling or Rheintochter missiles or both. These missiles will attain an altitude of thirty thousand feet at a horizontal range of approximately thirty miles and carry a warhead of fifty to one hundred pounds. The control of all surface-to-air missiles probably will be by radar.

ii. *Surface-to-Surface*. The surface-to-surface missiles which can be available in operational quantities in 1957 include V-1 and V-2 types copied from the original German missiles as well as V-2 types with wings. These Soviet missiles may be expected to have improved operational characteristics. Ranges of six hundred nautical miles for V-1 types and four hundred nautical miles for V-2 types are within the Soviet capability.

iii. *Submarine-Launched*. There are indications that the Soviets are attempting to extend the areas of possible employment of the V-1-type missile by equipping submarines for missile launchings. Limited employment of submarine-launched missiles against areas beyond ground-launched missile ranges may be expected by 1957.

iv. *Air-to-Surface*. By 1957 the Soviets should have operational quantities of slightly improved German types of air-to-surface missiles. These include the Hs-293 and the Hs-294, the latter an air-to-underwater missile. The quantities will probably be such that only high-priority targets will merit their use. Ranges of these missiles will be approximately eight nautical miles at subsonic speeds, carrying warheads up to three thousand pounds. Improvement over German types will include homing devices and control during final trajectory.

v. *Air-to-Air*. Development of air-to-air missiles has been given a rather low priority according to current intelligence. Preliminary studies are apparently in progress, but the program is not as extensive as in other types of missiles. Little improvement is anticipated in the German types Hs-117-H, Hs-298, and the X-4 by 1957. Small quantities of similar missiles should be available.

(g) *Proximity Fuses*. It is considered that by 1957 the Soviet Union will have developed proximity fuses for AA and field artillery, and the scale of issue will depend upon the type selected for production and the effort put into it.

(h) *Naval*. The [Walther]*-type submarine, still in the development stage, may appear in appreciable numbers after 1954. Between 1950 and 1957 the Soviet navy may develop and put into general use antiaircraft rockets, guided missiles launched from aircraft, radio-controlled explosive motorboats, high-speed homing torpedoes designed for pattern running, and influence mines of all types used or projected by the Germans.

---

*Editor's Note: The German Walther U-boat was designed to operate more or less permanently underwater. Instead of an electric motor, its main underwater propulsion was an engine taking its oxygen from fuel in the form of high-strength hydrogen peroxide. Installed in a revolutionary new streamlined hull, this engine enabled medium-sized Walther boats to make twenty-four knots underwater for six hours—a breathtaking leap forward in submarine performance by the standards of the times. In the opinion of Grand Admiral Karl Doenitz, the German U-boat force commander and Hitler's successor, the Walther boat was the sort of weapon that would, he wrote, "decide the whole issue of the war." So it might have done had the Allied air forces permitted it to come into service at the right time and in the right numbers. But they did not permit this, and so only seven were operational at the end of the war. The Russians captured some, and so did the British.

b. *Allied Armed Forces**

*****Editor's Note:** See Appendix E for the 1959 Institute for Strategic Studies estimate of NATO forces.

(1) *United States*
(a) In view of the fact that a major purpose of this study is to develop force requirements for a war in 1957, no statement with respect to available U.S. forces is made at this time.
(b) *New and Improved Weapons*. Listed below is a summary of the most significant developments in new and improved weapons which it is estimated will be available operationally in 1957, unless otherwise indicated. . . .

(i) *Heavy Bombers*
B-52: A 330,000-lb. heavy bomber powered by eight turbojet engines; maximum speed 522 knots, combat radius 2,660 nautical miles at 453 knots with 10,000 lb. of bombs.†

(ii) *Medium Bombers*
B-47: A 185,000-lb. medium bomber with six turbojet engines; maximum speed over 500 knots, combat radius 2,400 nautical miles at 460 knots with 10,000 lb. of bombs.
A medium land-based bomber weighing 175,000 lb. capable of a maximum speed of 600 knots. Combat radius 2,000 nautical miles at 520 knots with 10,000 lb. of bombs. (As first experimental flight date is 1955, this aircraft may not be operationally available in quantity before mid-1957.)

(iii) *Attack Bombers* (Carrier)
XVA(H-1): An unarmed turbojet carrier-based plane having a maximum speed of 520 knots, a maximum takeoff weight of 75,000 lb., and a combat radius of 1,500 nautical miles at 485 knots with a 10,000-lb. bomb load.

---

† This estimate is for 1951. An air-force projected model of the B-52 equipped with four turbojet engines would by 1956 have a combat radius of 3,750 nautical miles with the same speeds and bomb loadings but would weigh up to 360,000 lb. at takeoff.

XA2J-1: A carrier-based plane powered by two turboprop engines, having a maximum takeoff weight of 71,000 lb. and a maximum speed of 420 knots. Combat radius 1,220 nautical miles at 370 knots with a 10,500-lb. bomb load.

AJ-1: A carrier-based plane powered by two reciprocating and one turbojet engine, having a maximum takeoff weight of 51,000 lb. and a maximum speed of 417 knots. Combat radius 770 nautical miles at 220 knots with a 10,500-lb. bomb load.

(iv) *Light Bomber*

B-51: A 56,500-lb. light bomber with three turbojet engines; maximum speed 500 knots at sea level, combat radius 378 nautical miles at 463 knots with 4,000 lb. of bombs.

(v) *Interceptors*

XF10F-1: A 26,700-lb. carrier-based interceptor, maximum speed 565 knots at 50,000 ft. Rate of climb 35,000 ft. in 3.5 minutes; combat radius 575 nautical miles. Armament: four 20mm guns.

XF3H-1: An 18,200-lb. carrier-based interceptor, maximum speed 562 knots at 53,000 ft. Rate of climb 50,000 ft. in 5.5 minutes; endurance, 70 minutes. Armament: twenty-four 2.75-inch rockets.

Land-based interceptor, weighing 15,000 lb., capable of a maximum speed of 690 knots at 50,000 ft. Rate of climb 45,000 ft. in 5 minutes, endurance 3 hours. Armament includes two guided missiles.

XF4D-X: A 17,000-lb. carrier-based interceptor, capable of a maximum speed of 850 knots at 58,000 ft. Rate of climb 50,000 ft. in 4 minutes, endurance 1 hour. Armament: rockets or guided missiles.

XF91: A land-based interceptor weighing 28,300 lb. (with assist rockets) capable of a maximum speed of 855 knots at 47,500 ft. Rate of climb 2.5 minutes to 47,500 ft. Endurance 25 minutes. Armament: four 20mm guns.

(vi) *Tactical Aircraft*

F-90: A 33,500 lb. single-place fighter with two turbojet engines; maximum speed 552 knots, combat radius 476 nautical miles at 473 knots. Armament: six 20mm guns, eight rockets, two 1,000-lb. bombs.

F-93A: A 26,500-lb. land-based fighter with one turbojet engine and a maximum speed of 540 knots at 35,000 ft. Combat radius 700 nautical miles at 465 knots. Armament: six 20mm guns, sixteen 5-inch rockets, two 1,000-lb. bombs.

Ground support: A land-based 20,000-lb. aircraft with reciprocating or turboprop engines, capable of a maximum speed of

500 knots at 12,000 ft. Combat radius 500 nautical miles. Armament: guns, rockets, and bombs.

(vii) *Reconnaissance*

Heavy, medium, and light bomber types described above would also be available for performance of the reconnaissance mission and would have slightly superior speed and altitude performance compared with the combat versions.

(viii) *Auxiliary Developments*

Efforts to overcome deficiencies in the above aircraft are resulting in development of in-flight refueling techniques for range extension of land-based and carrier-based aircraft,* afterburning or JATO for decreasing the lengths of runways required for jet aircraft takeoffs, and track-landing gear to eliminate elaborate runways for large bombers and transports. One-man radar and optical computing bomb sights, improved bomb-release mechanisms, and new bomb designs will solve problems associated with high bomber speeds and high-altitude bombing. Fighters will continue to experience difficulty in maneuvering near sonic speeds.

iii. *Guided Missiles*

(i) *Surface-to-Surface*

Navaho: A North American-built 44,000-lb. missile of speed Mach 2.8 carrying a 3,000-lb. warhead 868 nautical miles. Vertical launching. Accuracy 50 percent within 500 feet.

Snark: A Northrop-built missile of speed Mach .9, weighing 28,000 lb., and carrying a 5,000-lb. or special warhead a distance of 4,342 nautical miles. Uses rocket car on ramp for takeoff, then gasoline-powered turbojet for flight; accuracy, 50 percent within 500 feet with target seeker, otherwise 50 percent within 1 mile.

Boojum: Similar to Snark but weighing 90,000 lb. and having a speed of Mach 1.7.

Rigel and Regulus: Missiles designed for ship launching which can carry 3,000–4,000-lb. payload to a range of 400–500 nautical miles. Maximum speed Mach 2.0 and Mach .9, respectively. Accuracy, 50 percent within 3,000 ft., launching weights 19,000 and 11,600 lb., respectively.

Grebe II: A ship-launched 2,700-lb. antisubmarine surface-to-underwater missile which can carry a torpedo to a range of 20 miles at a speed of 350 knots. Accuracy, 40 percent hits against submerged submarines.

Hermes A-3: A 12,000-lb. tactical missile with a 1,000-lb.

---

* Estimated range extensions of bombers using tankers having the same characteristics of bombers are as follows: one tanker, 38 percent; two tankers, 75 percent; three tankers, 95 percent.

warhead for use at ranges up to 150 miles. Speed Mach 5.0; accuracy, 50 percent within 210 ft. Similar to German V-2 but lighter in weight.

(ii) *Air-to-Surface*

Rascal: A 12,000-lb. missile with a 3,000-lb. warhead capable of reaching targets 90 nautical miles from control aircraft. Rocket-propelled at speed Mach 1.6; accuracy, 50 percent within 300 ft. on land, 75 percent hits against water targets.

Tarzan: A 13,000-lb. free-fall missile carrying a 12,000-lb. warhead. Guidance by command control in aircraft, based on visual information or radar presentation. Accuracy, 100 percent within 100 ft. from 20,000 ft.

Dove: A 1,300-lb. free-fall missile carrying a 1,000-lb. warhead but using a passive infrafed homing-guidance system. Accuracy, 80 percent hits against destroyer or larger vessels.

Petrel: A 3,300-lb. torpedo-carrying missile with radar homing. Torpedo enters water 1,000 yd. from target and uses acoustic homing. Range, 20 miles at 350 knots. Accuracy, 50 percent hits.

Diver: Similar to Petrel but weighing 1,500 lb. and carrying a smaller warhead. Uses air- and water-reactive jet engine. Accuracy, 80 percent hits.

Puffin: A 1,250-lb. missile with a 500-lb. plunge bomb. Radar homing. Range 35 miles at 450 knots. Accuracy, 30 percent hits against destroyer or larger.

(iii) *Surface-to-Air*

Nike: A 2,600-lb. missile with a 325-lb. warhead and a range of 18 miles or 60,000 ft. altitude at a speed of Mach 2.5. Accuracy, 50 percent within 80 ft. against conventional bomber aircraft with speeds up to 525 knots.

Terrier: A ship-launched missile for use against fighters, weighing 2,600 lb. and carrying a 150-lb. warhead to a range of 9 miles or 40,000 ft. at a speed of Mach 1.8; accuracy, 50 percent within 45 ft.

Talos: Similar to Terrier but weighing 5,900 lb. and carrying a 300-lb. warhead 20 miles or 60,000 ft.

Zeus: A rocket missile weighing 110 lb. with a 60-lb. warhead, launched from rebored 8-inch naval guns. Speed Mach 5.0, range 7.5 miles or 40,000 ft. Accuracy, 50 percent within 180 ft.

Gapa: A 5,000-lb. missile with a 300-lb. warhead and a range of 30 miles or 60,000 ft. at a speed of Mach 2.0. Accuracy, 50 percent within 40 ft. against bombers.

(iv) *Air-to-Air*

MX-904: An internally stowed 77-lb. missile with a 5-lb. warhead, capable of omnidirectional coverage from bombers and forward launching from fighters. Speed Mach 1.5–3.0; accuracy, 50 percent within 10 ft. Target illumination to be from launching aircraft.

Meteor: A fighter-launched missile weighing 510 lb., carrying a 30-lb. warhead a distance of 10 nautical miles at a speed of Mach 2.0–2.6. Accuracy, 50 percent within 30 ft. Target illumination from launching aircraft, other aircraft, or ship.

Sparrow: Similar to above but weighing 275 lb. Target must be tracked and missile guided from launching aircraft.

iv. *Surface Vessels*

Antisubmarine warfare (ASW) vessels: Two new types of antisubmarine surface vessels are being provided in 1950 or earlier programs. These comprise a killer cruiser (5,500 tons) and four 3,650-ton destroyers specially designed for minimum noise to facilitate sonar operations.

v. *Submarines*

(i) The emphasis on future submarines is on high speeds and increased concealment, principally by completely submerged operation. Future submarines will be redesigned to withstand depths up to one thousand feet with excellent promise of greatly increased submerged range and speed. Using the closed-cycle, internal-combustion principle, a prototype combat submarine should be available by 1956, having a top submerged speed of twenty-five knots (twelve hours' endurance) and a submerged cruising endurance of over two days.

(ii) Submarine Weapons: The following torpedo developments are scheduled:

A 20,000-yard, pattern-running, 60-knot torpedo with an impact/influence fuse to be tested in 1954.

A 5,000-yard, 25-knot, antiescort torpedo with three-dimensional active or passive homing, or gyro control, using an impact fuse, to be tested in 1952.

A wire-guided torpedo, 30-knot speed, transmitting acoustic information to the launching vessel up to a 10,000-yard range, to be tested in 1952.

vi. *Antisubmarine Warfare*

(i) Sonar: No development promises to supplant sonar as the primary surface-vessel detection equipment. Reliability, accuracy of bearings, and depth determination of sonar (sound and ranging) will be improved, but range will not be increased significantly. Passive listening by deep submarines (SSK) hovering or at creeping speeds (low-level listening) provides detection and some bearing information to about twenty miles against snorkeling subs. Airborne sonar is limited to use by slow-moving blimps or helicopters.

(ii) Magnetic detectors* have been improved, but they are still of severely limited range, approximately 1,000 feet. Increases to 1,200 to 1,500 feet can be expected.

*Editor's Note: An interesting if (then) somewhat impracticable antisubmarine warfare device called MAD. Short for "magnetic anomaly detection," the idea was to locate the minute changes in the earth's magnetic field produced by a submerged submarine. As late as 1971 the reports were that the technique was unreliable and in any case worked only at very short ranges. Again as late as 1971 the most reliable ASW device was the old World War II sonar. A sniffing device called Autolycus would, it was hoped in 1957, enable ASW craft to detect submarines by their diesel fumes. But in practice it worked only at short ranges, and when nuclear powered submarines came in, it would not work at all.

(iii) Weapon "A" is a 12.75-inch ahead-thrown influence-fused rocket bomb with a 250-lb. HBX warhead. It will be fired at a rate of twelve a minute to a range of 800 yards.

(iv) Torpedoes: The Mark 35 torpedo will be tested in 1952. This will be a submarine-launched, 15,000-yard-range, 30-knot, active or passive homing torpedo. Its air-launched parallel will have a 10,000-yard range. A wire-guided torpedo (Mark 41), providing attack information to the firing vessel, will be in prototype form in 1952.

(v) Radar: The AN/APS-20 program will detect snorkel for a sweep width of twenty miles in a calm sea but is of little value in heavier seas. It is planned to test in 1951 an antisubmarine radar (AN/APS-44) providing two optional frequencies, choice of radiation polarization and combining IFF with the search radar.

(vi) Project General 2: A plan for protecting ships to a depth of fifty feet by streaming explosive charges alongside from paravanes, which gives some hope of destroying a considerable fraction of the torpedoes fired at a ship.

vii. *Electronics*

(i) Radar early warning: Line-of-sight limitations will continue to affect employment of radar, but improved ground or shipborne equipment will detect targets of one-square-meter equivalent area at ranges up to five hundred miles (target must be twenty-five miles high) and indicate ranges, altitudes, and azimuth with great accuracy over a 360-degree area. Airborne early-warning equipment will supplement the fixed type and will extend low-angle coverage out to 150 miles to detect the approach of low-flying aircraft. Outpost alerting radars, unattended in remote forward areas, arranged in a fencelike disposition, will transmit automatic warning signals when a target appears for the purpose of alerting the accurate tracking devices.

(ii) Navigational aids: Long-range systems dependent on ground stations should provide day and night coverage over land and water, undisturbed by Arctic effects, at ranges up to 3,000 miles with accuracies of up to plus or minus seven miles. These systems can be used by aircraft, surface vessels, and even land vehicles. Automatic-inertial, automatic-celestial, and radar-doppler dead-reckoning systems independent of ground stations will provide automatic ground-position indicators for carrier-based and land-based aircraft. Interceptor aircraft will be provided with automatic air-intercept control systems, probably linked to automatic pilots for ground control to the point of target acquisition by the fighter. Landing aids for use by aircraft during low-visibility conditions will be improved and information relayed to pilots by means of voice, radio, or pictorial radar.

(iii) Countermeasures: Equipment will be available for intercepting and jamming enemy radio, radar, and infrared transmissions within certain ranges, but knowledge will be required of specific enemy frequencies for 100 percent effectiveness. Confusion devices such as reflection material can be ejected from aircraft, ground vehicles, and even submerged submarines. False signals on the same frequency as enemy detection radar will be possible and further improvements in radar camouflage coating material are expected.

viii. *Chemical and Biological Warfare*

(i) Chemical: By 1951 at least one of the nonpersistent nerve gases (GB) along with the persistent agent mustard (HD) will be operationally available, with no problems of production, storage, handling, or dissemination. While no immunization or preventive drug against CW [chemical warfare] agents appears likely, considerable limitations on their effectiveness will be achieved through automatic alarms, improved protective clothing, decontaminating chemicals for food and water, and medical counteraction of CW poisoning. Chemicals now being developed may make possible by 1957 airborne means of interfering with jet and internal-combustion motors. Other projects by 1957 will assure more efficient fire bombs, new cluster bombs, and improved chemical warheads.

(ii) Biological: By 1953 several antipersonnel, antianimal, and anticrop organisms or chemicals should be available, and there will be acceptable solutions for the problems of storage, temperature and pressure sensitivity, and dissemination. However, employment of such agents is dependent on a period of up to eighteen months required to attain quantity production of these weapons. Effective defensive measures should also be available, although methods of rapid detection may still be under development. . . .

ix. *Antiaircraft* (other than guided missiles)

(i) Guns: Radar-controlled large-caliber guns (90mm, 120mm, 5-inch) firing proximity-fused projectiles at higher velocities, [at] higher rates of fire, and with automatic ammunition-handling. Will be able to engage aircraft at speeds up to 800 knots and at altitudes up to 50,000 feet.

(ii) Rockets: Liquid-fueled rocket, Loki, capable of carrying a 5½-lb. warhead to a height of 60,000 feet at a horizontal range of 24,000 yd. with a 30-second time of flight. Fires salvos of 60–100 rounds from a single multiple launcher. Is expected to provide an economical weapon for combating aircraft at speeds up to 1,000 mph.

(iii) Automatic weapons: Medium-caliber (75mm, 3-inch) guns with high rates of fire (45–90 rounds per minute), automatic loading, on-carriage or on-mount fire control, capable of engaging aircraft with speeds up to 900 mph and at altitudes up to 19,000 ft.

(2) *Allies*

(a) *Ground Forces* . . .

ii. In 1957, practically all Allied troops except those of Spain and France can be expected to be within the borders of their respective countries. Minor elements of the Belgian and Netherlands armies will be on colonial duty.

iii. The United Kingdom will have 200,000 troops in the British Isles, of which fourteen antiaircraft and two infantry brigades will be the only major tactical combat units located there. Three divisions will be overseas; one each in Germany, Cyrenaica, and Malaya.

iv. Spanish forces in Spanish Morocco will total 70,000 in four divisions; in addition, there will be 30,000 troops but no tactical units in other Spanish possessions.

v. French troops outside metropolitan France will include 130,000 men in three divisions in North Africa, 40,000 men and one division in French Indochina, and 50,000 men but no major units in other possessions.

DIVISIONS (Unless Otherwise Shown)*						
COUNTRY	D-day†	D + 30	D + 60	D + 90	D + 180	D + 365
United Kingdom (a)	3 (7)†	7	16	18	22	30
France (b)	15	20	20	25	25	30
Belgium (b)	2	3	4	4	4	4
Netherlands (b)	2	3	4	4	4	4
Luxembourg	0	0	0	0	0	0
Sweden (c)	0	0	12	18	20	20
Norway (d)	1 brig.	1 div.	1	2	2	2
Spain (e)	22 (23)†	24	27	29	30	33

DIVISIONS (Unless Otherwise Shown)*

COUNTRY	D-day†	D + 30	D + 60	D + 90	D + 180	D + 365
Italy (f)	9	9	9	10	12	14
Switzerland	0 (25)†	25	25	25	25	25
Austria (g)	0	0	0	0	0	0
West Germany (h)	Constabulary forces only					
Portugal (i)	0 (1)†	2	3	3	4	4
Turkey (j)	25	25	30	36	40	42
Greece	12	12	14	14	16	16
Arab League states (k)	4	4	5	7	9	11
Pakistan	4		Not estimated			16
Australia	1 brig.	1 brig.	1 div.	3	5	7
New Zealand	1 brig.	1 brig.	1 brig.	1 div.	1	2
South Africa	1 brig.	1 div.	2	2	2	2
Canada	1 brig.	1 div.	3	4	5	8
Argentina (l)	13		Not estimated			30
Brazil (l)	13		Not estimated			40
Mexico (l)	3		Not estimated			10
Total of other Latin American countries (l)	6		Not estimated			20
China	Unpredictable at this time					
Japan (m)	5	5	5	5	5	5

*Estimated numbers, not necessarily U.S. equivalent, of the types employed by the indicated country without a U.S. military-aid program.

† By the first 7 to 10 days after D-Day the following countries can have mobilized the divisions shown below additional to those shown on D-Day: United Kingdom, 4; Spain, 1; Switzerland, 25; Portugal, 1.

(a) ‡*United Kingdom:* Based on planned actual strength for 1957 and actual mobilization accomplishment in World War II, modified by estimated state of munitions stocks, industry, and trained reserves in 1957.

(b) *Belgium, Netherlands, France:* Based on assumption that industrial recovery and financial stabilization will have progressed to a point where these countries will have developed moderate stockpiles of munitions, either by domestic production or by foreign purchase, and will be able to convert considerable capacity to munitions production after mobilization, though somewhat less than in 1939–1940.

(c) *Sweden:* Twelve divisions would be formed immediately upon mobilization but would be undergoing unit training until after M + 30. Additional divisions could be formed later by intensifying munitions production and completion of refresher training programs.

(d) *Norway:* While six skeletonized divisions will exist on paper supposedly for full organization on mobilization, current economies and prospects for their continuance make it doubtful that Norway can actually mobilize more than two.

(e) *Spain:* Based on a considerable economic recovery of Spain despite its present exclusion from ERP.

‡ Letters in parenthesis refer to corresponding items on previous page.

(f) *Italy:* It is assumed that the main provisions of the peace treaty will still be in force but that substantial economic recovery and political stabilization will have been achieved.

(g) *Austria:* The position of Austria will be such that opposition to the Soviets, other than by underground warfare, will be impossible.

(h) *West Germany:* Some degree of assistance to the Allied war effort may be provided in terms of constabulary units and manpower only. Except for underground warfare, no other significant contribution can be made unless large-scale pre-D-Day military aid is provided, which is unlikely in view of the overriding priority of aid to Western Union nations and the almost certain negative reaction of the French to any appreciable rearming of West Germany.

(i) *Portugal:* Based on Western Allied encouragement of Portuguese military preparedness.

(j) *Turkey and Greece:* Based on a peacetime army considerably below present strength but able to effect a limited expansion.

(k) *Arab League states:* The major part of the forces of the Arab League states would be loosely organized, ill-equipped tribesmen. The force in Transjordan would probably be the most effective, provided that the British continue to support this force. The effectiveness of the Egyptian, Iraqi, and Syrian armies would depend upon Allied aid in arming and training these forces. The forces of Lebanon and Yemen, in all probability, would be negative factors. The army of Saudi Arabia would have limited capabilities, unless there is a considerable step-up in the present United States training activity.

(l) *Latin American countries:* Every Latin American country will require foreign aid to attain its mobilization potential and to maintain its forces equipped and at peak strength and efficiency.

(m) *Japan:* Defense of the home islands by Japanese military forces would constitute a contribution of considerable importance to the Allied war effort. Although modification of the present policy toward Japan to permit pre-D-Day provision of military equipment and organization of Japanese military forces would probably be opposed by some of the Allies of the U.S., it is considered that such opposition could be overcome if the Japanese military organization is limited to defense forces only.

(b) Naval Forces

i. It is estimated that the maximum strength (both active and reserve) of Allies and possible Allies on D-Day in 1957 will be as follows:

	CV	CVL	CVE	BB	OBB	CA–CL	OCA	DD	SS	DE	M*
U.K.	8	10	—	5	—	23	—	123	65	175	2
France	1	2	1	2	—	10	—	25	25	50	—
Netherlands	—	2	—	—	—	4	—	7	9	6	—
Belgium	Belgium will have only 6 minesweepers										
Spain	—	—	—	—	—	1	4	20	8	15	—
Portugal	—	—	—	—	—	—	—	5	3	10	—
Italy	—	—	—	—	2	3	1	4	—	35	—
Greece	—	—	—	—	—	1	—	—	6	15	—
Turkey	—	—	—	—	—	—	—	6	10	20	—
Argentina	—	1	—	—	2	3	—	15	5	15	—

	CV	CVL	CVE	BB	OBB	CA–CL	OCA	DD	SS	DE	M*
Brazil	—	—	1	—	—	2	—	15	5	10	—
Chile	—	—	—	—	1	1	—	10	5	10	—
Mexico	—	—	—	—	—	—	—	5	—	5	—
Peru	—	—	—	—	—	1	—	5	5	5	—
Australia	—	2	—	—	—	4	—	12	—	15	—
Canada	—	1	—	—	—	2	—	10	—	15	—
New Zealand	—	—	—	—	—	2	—	—	—	6	—
China	Unpredictable at this time										

Note: See Glossary for explanation of abbreviations.

*Monitor.

ii. According to British sources, the following ships will be in commission on M-Day in 1957:

	CV	CVL	BB	CA–CL	DD	SS	Frigates(DE)	AM
U.K.	3	7	3	17	57	40	49	20
Canada	—	1	—	1	6	—	2	2
Australia	—	2	—	2	8	—	11	16
N. Zealand	—	—	—	1	—	—	6	—
S. Africa	—	—	—	—	—	—	2	1

iii. It is not possible to determine the percentage of ships of countries other than the above which will be in commission on M-Day.

(c) *Air Forces.* The following estimates of 1957 combat strengths are considered to be optimum strengths, commensurate with the various countries' financial, logistic, and training capabilities. With the exception of the United Kingdom, Sweden, Switzerland, and to a great extent France, all countries must obtain a majority of their aircraft elsewhere. Other countries—namely, Argentina, Canada, Australia, and the Netherlands—should be able to manufacture some of their own aircraft by 1957. Unless considerable impetus is given to expanding production in the United States, this country will be unable to furnish the newest types of aircraft to others in 1957. Consequently the air forces of the Allies may consist, in the major part, of types which by 1957 will be obsolescent or obsolete.

i. It is probable that by 1957 the Royal Air Force (RAF) will be equipped with high-speed, high-altitude, jet-propelled bombers and with jet-propelled fighters.

ii. Sweden is constantly increasing the strength of its air force by purchasing aircraft from Britain and is now planning to manufacture its own jet fighters. It is anticipated that Sweden will have, from the standpoint of quality, one of the best air forces in Western Europe.

iii. It is assumed that, although the French aircraft industry will be able to supply a substantial portion of French aircraft requirements by 1957, the French air force will continue to be dependent on Great Britain and the United States for at least part of its needs. Efforts are being devoted largely to replacing present obsolete aircraft.

iv. It is presumed that the increasingly conciliatory attitude of the Spanish government,* as well as the desire of the Western democracies to consolidate the defense of Western Europe, will result in the rehabilitation of the Spanish air force, which is presently at a low level of operational efficiency.

*Editor's Note: At this time Spain was the outcast of the Western world. The UN, refusing to recognize the constitutionality of the Franco regime, urged its members in 1946 to break diplomatic relations with Spain. This resolution was not rescinded until 1950. Spain did not enter the UN until 1955. But the U.S. did manage to overcome its scruples concerning Franco, and in 1953 Franco was offered military and economic assistance in return for SAC bases. Franco accepted quickly and gladly. However, these bases were not quite as secure as SAC hoped. In the 1950s and 1960s there was considerable if muffled political unrest, which the Soviets sought to inflame by relentless agitprop and clandestine supplies of arms to the survivors of the old Spanish Republican Army of civil war days. To make SAC's tenure of its bases in Spain somewhat more tenuous, two B-52s collided and dropped their H-bombs on Spanish soil. The weapons were of megaton range, but mercifully they did not fuse.

v. By terms of the Peace Treaty, the Italian air force is limited to 350 aircraft, of which no more than 200 may be combat types.

vi. The figures for Argentina include purchases in Britain and Canada; however, the bulk of future purchases will likely come from the United States and from Argentine manufacture.

vii. The tables below indicate the estimated totals of combat aircraft of the British Commonwealth, France, Sweden, and Switzerland which would be in operational units in 1957 (backed up by a reserve of aircraft sufficient to replace reasonable losses from those shown during a limited period). Figures for all other Allied nations represent estimated total inventory.

i. British Commonwealth				
	Total	M/B*	L/B*	FTR/FTR Bombers
United Kingdom	1,804	400	144	1,260
(Naval Air Arm)	(300)†	—	—	(300)†
Canada	228	8	24	196
(Naval Air Arm)	(60)†	—	—	(60)†

i. British Commonwealth

	Total	M/B*	L/B*	FTR/FTR Bombers
Australia	251	59	—	192
(Naval Air Arm)	(60)†	—	—	(60)†
New Zealand	84	—	42	42
S. Africa	90	—	45	45
Middle East	120	—	24	96

ii. Western Europe

	Total Combat	Light Bomber	Attack	Fighter
Sweden	1,300	100	400	800
Norway	100	—	—	100
Belgium	155	—	30	125
France	500	—	—	500
(Naval Air Arm)	(150)†	—	—	(150)†
Netherlands	300	50	—	250
(Naval Air Arm)	100	—	—	(100)†
Switzerland	400	—	—	400
Spain	350	50	50	250
Portugal	100	—	—	100
Italy	200	—	—	200

iii. Near East

	Total Combat	Light Bomber	Attack	Fighter
Turkey	880	280	—	600
Greece	200	20	—	180
Egypt	98	18	—	80
Saudi Arabia	44	12	—	32
Syria	40	—	—	40
Iraq	72	24	—	48

*U.S. classifications

†Naval-air-arm aircraft shown in parentheses are also included in totals.

iv. *Middle and Far East.* It is believed that Pakistan can reach and support their planned strength of ninety-six fighter-bombers by 1957.

The critical nature of the situation in China makes it unprofitable to attempt to estimate the 1957 strengths of the Chinese non-Communist air forces. In any event, neither the non-Communist nor Communist air forces will have aircraft except from outside sources.

v. *Latin America.* Assuming implementation of the Western

Hemisphere defense program, the Latin American countries would have air-force combat strengths by 1957 as follows:

	Total	M/B	L/B	Attack	Fighter
Argentina	580	80	125	75	300
(Naval Air Arm)	—	—	(25)*	(25)*	(50)*
Brazil	655	125	150	80	300
Mexico	305	40	70	70	125
(Naval Air Arm)	—	—	(20)*	(20)*	(25)*
Remaining countries	800	100	200	200	400

* Naval aircraft in parenthesis are included in totals.

vi. *Mobilization Capabilities.* Consideration of mobilization capabilities was included in estimates of Allied air-force strengths as given above. It is unlikely that D-Day strengths will approach the optimum figures shown unless mobilization is initiated several months before D-Day.

c. *Logistics*
   (1) *Soviet and Satellite*
   (a) *Land Transport*
      i. *Soviet Union.* It is estimated that by 1957 the USSR will have adequate logistical facilities to support operations for the overrunning of wide areas of Eurasia and the launching of bombing and airborne attacks against Canada and the United States, although the capability for support of airborne attacks would be extremely limited. The railway system of the USSR should be in a position to meet most of the essential industrial and military requirements, although in a war of attrition the inadequate reserve capacity would constitute a vulnerable sector of the Soviet military economy. However, for at least the first phase of operations, Soviet domestic rail transport, supplemented by satellite increments and captured rolling stock of invaded countries, would be sufficient to furnish the main logistical support for operations in Europe and the Far East, and to a lesser extent in the Near and Middle East.

      ii. *Europe.* Rail-transport capacity would be complemented substantially by the inland waterway, motor, and horse transport of the USSR. Satellite and enemy (after invasion) inland-waterway, motor, and horse-transport facilities would be used to their full capacities as adjuncts to rail transport. Transshipping points between Soviet broad-gauge railroads and the narrow- and standard-gauge railroads of European countries would create great logistical difficulties in the transshipment of a minimum of sixty thousand short tons of maintenance supplies (less food) required per day per one hundred divisions on the western front. The requirements for air support will represent additional tonnages. The Rhine River bridges, if destroyed or seriously damaged, would also result in serious bottlenecks. If the Soviets attempted to invade the Iberian peninsula, the logistical problems involved would be of considerable magnitude because of the mountanous terrain and the lack of adequate roads and railroads. Of particular significance would be the few LOCs [lines of communication] through the Pyrenees and the ease with which they could be blocked.

iii. *Near and Middle East.* Soviet operations in the mountainous and desert areas of the Near and Middle East would be tremendously complicated because of the inadequacy of suitable railroads, roads, the shortages of truck transportation and the extreme vulnerability of the numerous bridges and tunnels throughout the area. . . . Operations in Turkey, Iraq, Iran, and Saudi Arabia would be extremely difficult to support logistically. The Tigris and Euphrates Rivers offer little relief because of their shallow depth and the lack of shipping facilities. Utilization of the oil resources of the Near and Middle East for Soviet operations in that area would reduce their logistical problem considerably, if the oil facilities could be captured undamaged. . . . If extensive damage has occurred to the oil facilities from air attacks or demolition, it is doubtful that the Soviets could effect repairs for even partial operation in less than six to twelve months, and continued Allied air attacks or guerrilla warfare could probably delay reconstruction indefinitely.

The usefulness of captured Near and Middle East oil to the Soviets, except for operations in the Near and Middle East, would depend on their ability to transport crude oil or refined products to the USSR. As noted above, LOCs through the Near and Middle East are easily disrupted. The principal feasible means of transporting Near and Middle East oil to the Soviet Union is by sea. Considering the limited number of tankers available to the Soviets and that control of the eastern Mediterranean and the maintenance of oil pipelines thereto would be essential, transportation of Near and Middle East oil by sea appears most unlikely.

(b) *Sea Transport*

i. It is estimated that at present the combined Soviet and satellite merchant fleets (cargo ships, tankers, combination tanker–cargo, and miscellaneous) total approximately 573 ships of over 1,000 gross tonnage (g.t.) with a total of roughly 2,036,827 g.t. This does not include Finland and Yugoslavia, nor does it include an estimated 119 ships employed in the Caspian Sea. About one-fourth of this tonnage belongs to the satellites. The total is about equally divided between the Pacific and Atlantic Ocean areas (the latter including the Black and

Baltic Seas). The troop lift in any area is considered adequate for coastal amphibious operations or movements within contiguous sea areas. In the event of war, all satellite shipping would presumably become available to the Soviets for troop and cargo lift in operations in the Baltic, Atlantic, Black Sea, and possibly in the Mediterranean.

ii. By 1951 the Soviet merchant fleet, assuming a normal building and maintenance program, would be able to lift sufficient troops for short-range operations and amphibious operations as indicated above. By 1957 it is not likely that the Soviet merchant fleet could be greatly increased, as most of the new production would be required to replace obsolete vessels. Even with other shipping which might be seized soon after the outbreak of war, the Soviet merchant fleet is not likely to be able to provide continuing support for a large, long-distance overseas operation. Large numbers of troops could, however, be moved in short-haul operations.

(c) *Air Facilities*

i. Existing airfield facilities in the USSR and the satellites would be adequate to support first-phase air operations. Required logistic support for extensive air operations probably would not be a serious problem in Europe but might become a critical factor in the Near, Middle, and Far East.

ii. The Soviets probably will not have stockpiled sufficient quantities of aircraft material and supply in the Far East to make them independent of the limited capacity of the Trans-Siberian Railway and Arctic waters. By 1957 the situation will have improved if the rail line now under construction north of, and parallel to, the Trans-Siberian Railway is completed.

(d) *Ports*. Soviet, satellite, and captured port facilities and capacities would be more than adequate to handle the naval ships and merchant vessels of the USSR. Therefore, naval strength and troop-lift capacity, rather than port capacities, would be the limiting factors in the scale of Soviet naval warfare and amphibious warfare.

(e) *Stockpiles*. It is reasonable to assume that adequate stockpiles of most essential war materials and supply would be accumulated prior to D-Day. On the basis of evidence now available it is considered that POL [petroleum, oil, lubricants] would be in shortest supply but that stockpiles plus normal production would be sufficient for all first-phase operations in Eurasia and against Alaska, Canada, and the United States.

II.PROBABLE SOVIET STRATEGIC OBJECTIVES

1. *General Objectives*. It is estimated that in 1957 the ultimate objective of the Soviets will be the defeat of the United States, which would permit them to realize their goal of world domination. Contributing to the attainment of this ultimate objective will be a number of interim objectives which will be integral parts of a plan progressively directed toward the neutralization or destruction of the United States and Allied potential for war. Attainment of these interim objectives and their exploitation would establish the USSR as the dominant world power, and the attainment of their ultimate objective would be materially advanced.

2. *Interim Objectives*. In order to achieve the ultimate objective, the Soviet leaders would probably consider that the successful outcome of as many as possible of the following campaigns would be strategically desirable and that certain of them would be essential steps.

a. *A Western European campaign to gain the Atlantic seaboard for the purposes of achieving three aims: first, to provide base facilities for conducting intensive warfare against Anglo-American sea communications; second, to achieve the most advantageous positions from which to mount a subsequent campaign against the British Isles; and third, to exploit the economic potential of Western Europe. Simultaneous attacks would be expected on Italy and Sicily for the purpose of controlling the central Mediterranean, if the control of Italy has not already been achieved by a Communist coup.

b. *An intensive air and sea offensive against the British Isles, with the initial objective of neutralizing Great Britain as a serious military factor and of preventing the use of the British Isles as a base by United States forces, and with the possible later aim of invasion and complete occupation.

c. An invasion of Scandinavia with the object of:

(1) Securing complete control of the Baltic.
(2) Providing naval and air bases for operations against the trade routes and Allied bases in the North Atlantic.
(3) Providing early-warning and interception facilities against possible British and U.S. bomber attack against western Russia.
(4) Denying the use of air and naval bases to the Anglo-American powers.

d. Operations to occupy or neutralize North Atlantic islands with the object of denying the use of air and naval bases to the Anglo-American powers

---

* Considered essential in achieving the ultimate objective.

and advancing Soviet bases closer to the northeast approaches to the Western Hemisphere.

e. An invasion of Spain and Portugal with the object of providing naval and air bases for operations against Atlantic trade routes, sealing the Strait of Gibraltar, providing access to northwest Africa, and denying the use of air bases to the Anglo-American powers.

f. *A campaign in the Middle East, including Greece and Turkey, with the primary objects of denying the Middle East oil resources and the Suez Canal area to the Anglo-American powers and of adding depth to the air defenses of south Russia.

g. Attacks on Pakistan to deny the use of its bases to the Anglo-American powers.

h. *A campaign to dominate the northern seaboard of the western Pacific coupled with an attack on Alaska and air and sea offensives against U.S. bases, including those in Japan, with the object of neutralizing them as bases for attacks on the Soviet maritime provinces and Manchuria and of containing the greatest number of United States forces in the Pacific.

i. *Air attacks against the United States and Canada.

j. *A sea and air offensive against Anglo-American sea communications.

k. *Subversive activities and sabotage against Anglo-American interests in all parts of the world.

3. The Soviet leaders might wish to avoid launching full-scale offensives in a number of areas simultaneously. However, they would realize that the Anglo-American powers would not permit the different areas to be overrun singly. Realizing that the Allies would attack the Soviet Union from any direction which was possible, the Soviet leaders would probably decide to launch a full-scale offensive in a number of areas. Such a plan would also make the best use of the overwhelming superiority of the Soviet Union in land and tactical air forces and would enable her to retain the initiative.

4. Upon successful completion of these campaigns, and after a period to consolidate the economic and political resources gained, the USSR would be in a most favorable position to attain their goal of world domination.

III. SOVIET CAPABILITIES

1. Eurasia

Against the maximum defensive forces that could be provided by the Western European nations from their own resources without military aid from the United States, and not considering the as yet unevaluated effect of the air offensive, it is estimated that the Soviets could occupy all of Continental Europe (except the

---

*Considered essential in achieving the ultimate objective.

Iberian peninsula) in two and a half to three and a half months*; invade the
Near and Middle East and seize the oil-producing areas of Saudi Arabia, Iraq,
and Iran within three months; in six months virtually complete the conquest of
Turkey; in twelve months seize the Suez Canal area; establish, as necessary,
operational bases in areas of China held by Chinese Communist forces; and occupy southern Korea and seize Hokkaido in less than one month. In the following discussions the strengths of forces are approximations only, and directions
of attack are schematic. Timing would vary, depending upon such factors as
the degree of Soviet D-Day preparedness and the circumstances of combat as
well as the size and D-Day dispositions of the defensive forces.

a. Western Europe (less the Iberian Peninsula)

(1) If the European Recovery Program achieves its objectives and a coordinated
defensive system in Western Europe is developed to the extent possible without
significant military aid, the initial Soviet attack against France and the Low
Countries is likely to be held temporarily on the Rhine. Soviet forces could
then build up to a strength of at least 100 line divisions within the first month,
supported by about 5,000 combat tactical aircraft, units of the long-range air
force (total in USSR: 1,800), and elements of the air-transport fleet (total in
USSR: 2,500). These forces could probably overcome Allied defenses on the
Rhine, overrun France and the Low Countries, and reach the line of the
Pyrenees by about $D + 2\frac{1}{2}$–3 months.

(2) It is estimated that the Soviets probably would use a force of about 5 line
divisions and 400 combat aircraft, initially (additional forces would be available if required), in attacks from the vicinity of Stettin through Hamburg and
Lübeck to the Danish border, then north along the Danish peninsula, seizing all
important ports and major cities of Denmark. This force could consolidate
along the Danish border by $D + 5$, seize Copenhagen and major ports by
$D + 10$, and consolidate the entire peninsula and Zeeland by $D + 15$. Thereafter
the force could be built up as necessary for a subsequent attack against southern
Sweden.

(3) An attack on Scandinavia probably would not be undertaken until Denmark had been overrun and the required buildup of forces completed. The Soviets could begin the Scandinavian campaign about $D + 1\frac{1}{2}$ months, employing
initially approximately 13 line divisions and 600–900 tactical aircraft, all from
the total available for the campaign in Western Europe, supported by elements
of the northern and Baltic fleets. Developing the attack from four thrusts, two
from the south and two smaller ones from the north, the Soviets could capture
Tromsö, Narvik, and Luleå and complete the landing in south Sweden by $D + 2$

---

* If the present defection of Yugoslavia from the Soviet satellite orbit should continue to 1957, it is
not likely that Yugoslavia would ally with the Soviet Union but would attempt to remain neutral,
and would be committed to resist Soviet and/or satellite attack. If such should eventuate, the Soviet
campaign against Italy and Greece would be slowed down from 1 to 3 months.

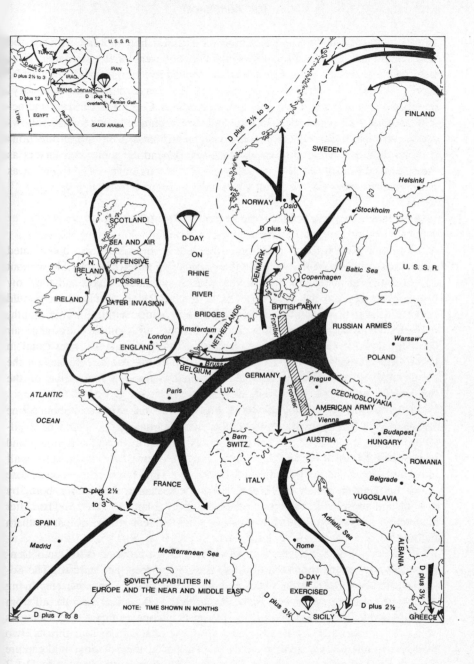

SOVIET CAPABILITIES IN
EUROPE AND THE NEAR AND MIDDLE EAST

NOTE: TIME SHOWN IN MONTHS

months; capture the Narvik–Luleå railway and the Stockholm–Oslo areas by D + 2½ months; and complete the occupation of south Sweden and south Norway, in particular the areas Christiansand, Stavanger, Bergen, and Trondheim, shortly after D + 2½ months. If necessary, initial Soviet attacking forces could readily be reinforced from air and ground reserves within the USSR to the extent necessary to overcome Swedish and Norwegian resistance. The Soviets could triple the initial number of line divisions and build up to more than 2,000 combat aircraft if required to overcome Scandinavian resistance or to expedite the occupation of this area.

(4) Austria and southern Germany could be completely occupied by D + 10 days.

(5) Against Italy the Soviets could employ 10–15 Yugoslav* line divisions supported by at least 600 combat aircraft (two-thirds Yugoslav). Later in the campaign the ground forces could be reinforced by perhaps 10 Soviet divisions. This force could probably complete the occupation of Italy by D + 2½ months and of Sicily by about D + 3½ months. The Soviets would have a D-Day airborne capability against Sicily, but it is doubtful if it would be exercised because of logistic difficulties involved in supply and resupply.

(6) In a campaign against Greece the Soviets, employing approximately 5 Soviet and 15 satellite divisions supported by at least 700 combat aircraft (two-thirds Yugoslav) could overrun all of Greece by not later than D + 3½ months.† After consolidation of Greece, operations could be mounted to secure the Aegean islands and Crete. The Soviets would have a D-Day airborne capability against Crete, but it is doubtful that they would exercise it because of logistic difficulties involved in its supply and resupply.

b. Iberian Peninsula

A full-scale Soviet attack against the Iberian peninsula could not be undertaken until after a successful completion of the main offensive in France and the Low Countries. An Iberian campaign probably could be carried on simultaneously with an air and sea offensive against the British Isles, but with difficulty. It is believed that logistic considerations would preclude an Iberian campaign simultaneously with an invasion of the British Isles. Assuming that there is no simultaneous invasion of the British Isles and that the Spanish receive no appreciable amount of military assistance from the United States, the Soviets probably could complete the occupation of the Iberian peninsula by D + 7–8 months.

---

* If the present defection of Yugoslavia from the Soviet satellite orbit should continue to 1957, it is not likely that Yugoslavia would ally with the Soviet Union but would attempt to remain neutral and would be committed to resist Soviet and/or satellite attack. In any event, the Soviet Union should be able to deal with the situation effectively and complete the Italian campaign with a delay of one to three months. Additional Soviet forces required should not materially detract from capabilities in other areas.

† See footnote to preceding paragraph. Assuming that reliable Yugoslav forces would not be available, Soviet forces could make up the deficit along with other Balkan satellites.

c. Turkey and the Near and Middle East

(1) In an attack against Turkey the Soviet Union would probably employ initially a total of 33 line divisions, supported by 1,400 combat aircraft and the Black Sea fleet. The attack could be developed in three thrusts: one (25 line divisions, 900 aircraft) starting from Bulgaria against Turkey in Europe and crossing the Bosporus and Dardanelles; a second (5 line divisions, 300 a/c) landing on the Black Sea coast at Samsum, Zonguldak, and Trabzon and driving inland; and a third (3 line divisions, 200 a/c) starting from the Soviet Caucasus and advancing along the line Kars–Erzurum. If Turkey did not receive early outside assistance, mobile elements of the first and second forces could reach the Iskenderun area in about D + 5 months. Winter weather and effective demolition of road and rail lines at strategic points would create great logistic problems and would delay Soviet advances. In the event that demolitions of the magnitude of those now being planned for the Iran–Iraq area in a study* on "Special Operations Against Selected Middle East Lines of Communication," made by the working staff of the Joint Strategic Plans Committee, were undertaken in Turkey and were 50 percent effective against the Soviet lines of communication, it is considered that not more than 4 to 5 Soviet divisions could reach the Iskenderun area by overland routes prior to D + 12 months. If such demolitions were made, logistical supply through Turkey to Soviet forces attacking toward the Cairo–Suez area would be drastically limited.

(2) In a campaign for Near and Middle East oil and control of the Cairo–Suez area, the Soviets could launch simultaneous attacks by four forces to overrun Iran, Iraq, Syria, and North Palestine, seizing all major airfields, oil fields, and refineries. These forces initially would probably total about 16 line divisions, supported by about 600 combat aircraft. One force of 5 divisions and 200 combat aircraft could, operating via Tabriz–Mosul, consolidate in the Kirkuk–Mosul area by D + 1½ months. A second force of 6 line divisions and 200 combat aircraft, operating Resht–Hamadan–Baghdad, could consolidate in the Baghdad area by D + 1½ months. A third force of 4 line divisions and 150 combat aircraft, operating Tehran–Basra, could consolidate in the Basra–Abadan area by D + 1½ months, while a fourth force of 1 line division and 50 combat aircraft could consolidate in the Bandar Abbas area by D + 2 months. One line division and about 50 aircraft from the Basra–Abadan area could consolidate in the Bahrein–Dhahran area shortly after D + 3 months.

(3) Small advance-guard elements of forces in the Tigris–Euphrates valley could arrive at the Levant coast prior to D + 3 months. Between D + 3 and D + 8 months the Soviets could build up their strength in the Levant to 9 divisions and about 400 aircraft. The delay in buildup would be caused by logistic considerations, principally the time required to reopen and repair the Mosul–Aleppo railroad, and by the necessity for synchronizing further opera-

* On file in JCS Secretariat.

tions with forces arriving from Turkey and with the opening of the LOCs through Turkey. Thereafter, they could reach the Suez Canal, capturing and securing Cairo and Alexandria by D + 12 months. The Soviets would have the additional capability of employing 3–4 airborne brigades against the Basra–Abadan and Bahrein–Dhahran areas on D-Day.

(4) In the event that demolitions now being planned for the Iran–Iraq area in a study on "Special Operations Against Selected Middle East Lines of Communication," made by the working staff of the Joint Strategic Plans Committee, were even 50 percent effective, it is estimated that the Soviet tonnage capacity into the Tigris–Euphrates valley would be reduced to about 1,000 tons daily, a tonnage considered to be insufficient to support more than 5–6 divisions. Further, it is believed that it would require not less than six months for the Soviets to repair the lines of communication sufficiently to get a force of even this size into the area.

(5) With this limitation on supplies and assuming no water transportation in the Mediterranean, the Soviet operations would be restricted to raiding parties based in the Tigris–Euphrates valley, which might be capable of reaching the eastern Mediterranean coast. If water transportation could be made available by the Soviets in the eastern Mediterranean, it would be possible that a force not in excess of 1 division could be landed along the eastern coast, and this force might be augmented by not more than 2 divisions from the Tigris–Euphrates valley. Supplied from the USSR by water transportation, this force of only 3 divisions could attack the Cairo–Suez area not earlier than D + 12 months.

(6) A possible line of action of the Soviets is to make an attack into India and Pakistan through Afghanistan. It is considered, however, that the Soviets would have a very limited capability in this area because of logistic difficulties due to the nature of the terrain. Air attacks by the long-range force would probably be the chief threat to these countries.

d. Far East

(1) Assisted by Chinese Communist forces, the Soviet forces in the Far East (estimated as 20 line divisions and 2,800 combat aircraft), together with available elements of the long-range air force, could readily establish bases in China as required by Soviet plans.

(2) Soviet control of the coast of China, Korea, Sakhalin, and the Kurils would facilitate air and amphibious attacks against Japan and other Pacific Islands. Although an invasion of the main islands of Japan would be handicapped during the initial stages of the war by shortages of airlift, shipping, and naval support due to higher-priority requirements in other theaters, the Soviet forces could seize Hokkaido with an estimated 2–3 divisions and air support from Sakhalin and the Kurils. Unless Japanese defense forces were organized, trained, and equipped or the Allied occupation forces augmented beyond the four divisions now present, a major air-amphibious assault against Honshu and Kyushu could be undertaken with reasonable chances of success.

2. British Isles

The initial attack against the British Isles, probably commencing on D-Day, would be an aerial bombardment by the Soviet long-range air force, possibly employing weapons of mass destruction. Concurrently an offensive against British ports and against sea communications with the British Isles could be launched by aircraft and submarines. A strong sabotage effort may be expected. These attacks could be carried on concurrently with the campaign against Western and Northern Europe, the successful completion of which would permit increasing the tempo of the air and sea offensive against the British Isles, utilizing captured air and naval bases. Upon successful completion of this offensive, the Soviets would have the capability of invading the British Isles.

3. Canada and the United States

Soviet estimates of their offensive capabilities against the United States and Canada in 1957 will probably lead them to launch attacks against those countries with the objective of seriously reducing their military potential. Such action would be timed with the major Soviet operations in Europe, the Near and Middle East, and the Far East.

a. It is considered that attacks against Canada and the United States would include an air attack, or closely coordinated series of air attacks, with the probable employment of atomic bombs and biological and chemical agents. A surprise attack might be attempted initially from eastern Siberian and northern Soviet and European bases.

b. The clandestine use of biological and chemical agents in the United States by subversive groups is an important capability. There is also a possibility of Soviet employment of cargo vessels as atomic-bomb carriers.

c. Concurrently with an initial offensive operation against Canada and the United States, the Soviets could seize undefended bases in the Atlantic approach areas and in Alaska for intermediate staging purposes.

d. It is considered unlikely that the USSR could mount a large-scale amphibious*–airborne expedition against critical areas in the United States with any prospect of success. The Soviets are not given the capability of reducing the United States war potential, including forces in being, by preliminary air, submarine, and sabotage attacks to a point where such an invasion would be successful. However, numerous sabotage and demolition parties could be landed for special operations.

e. Soviet apparatus for espionage, subversion, and sabotage constitutes a serious threat to the United States war potential. The USSR will continue to improve that apparatus.

---

* It is realized that a considerable amount of naval and commercial shipping would accrue to the USSR in the overrunning of Western Europe.

f. Sabotage is one of the most important and effective weapons in the Communist arsenal and will be employed by the Soviets immediately preceding armed conflict. It is estimated that the Soviets have the capability of causing a serious initial interruption of the United States war production. In this connection it should be noted that the highly integrated but decentralized industries of the United States are acutely vulnerable to sabotage if left unprotected.

4. North Atlantic Islands

By 1957 in surprise attacks, simultaneously with attacks on Canada and the United States, any or all the principal bases in the North Atlantic approach area, if undefended, could be sabotaged or seized by the USSR. Although the forces so used could not expect long survival in the face of strong United States counteraction, the securing of these areas for even a few days might contribute greatly to the initial all-out Soviet effort against the United States by denying use of these facilities to the United States and by forcing dispersal of our limited means for their recapture and/or reconstruction.

5. Alaska, the Aleutians, and the North Pacific

a. Neutralization of United States bases in Alaska and the Aleutians may become increasingly important to the Soviets after they have atomic bombs available. To secure their northeast Siberian bases and prevent interception of their long-range bombers, the Soviets would make serious efforts to neutralize United States air strength in the Alaska–Aleutian area.

b. A Soviet attack against Alaska and the Aleutians probably would be accompanied by air attacks against western Canada and the northwestern United States. Bombing and limited airborne attacks could be initiated from bases in northeast Siberia, while naval forces could carry out small-scale raids against outlying bases known to be inadequately defended.

c. Intensive antishipping submarine raids, involving as many as fifty long-range, high-submerged-speed submarines and approximately sixty long-range conventional submarines could be carried out throughout the Pacific north of the equator.

d. Assuming minimum initial United States resistance, the Soviets probably would have the capabilities of securing or destroying the principal objectives in Alaska and the Aleutians, seriously delaying United States use of the area for bases, and utilizing these bases to a limited extent for operations against the continental United States.

6. Caribbean Area

a. The major Soviet objectives in the Caribbean area would be interference with the Panama Canal and the all-important United States coastal sea lines of communication, over which many strategic materials are carried, and interruption of oil supplies from Venezuela.

b. The greatest Soviet capability against the Canal and other objectives, such as the oil installations of Venezuela and refineries located on the Dutch islands of Aruba and Curaçao, is sabotage by pro-Soviet or Soviet agents. There is also the possibility of detonating an atomic bomb concealed in the cargo of a ship within the locks. Soviet submarines could seriously interfere with United States shipping in this area.

7. Allied Sea Communications

a. The main attack on sea communications would probably take the form of attacks on shipping and ports and their approaches by torpedo attacks, mining, bombing, and sabotage. Such attacks would be carried out mainly by aircraft and submarines.

b. In 1957 Soviet long-range submarines on normal patrol missions will have a radius of action of six thousand nautical miles, provided the greater part of the transit from base to operating area can be made on the surface. However, Soviet submarines would be able to conduct limited operations beyond a six-thousand-mile radius by supplementary refueling. Submarine operations would be expected against sea lines of communication in the Atlantic, Pacific, Mediterranean, the Alaskan and Caribbean areas, the approaches to the Panama Canal, and the coastal waters of the United States and Canada. Limited operations could also be conducted in the Indian Ocean.

c. Intensive attacks could be expected on ports and on concentrations of shipping within range of fast coastal craft, submarines, and aircraft. Except for raiders, major surface units of the Baltic, northern, and Far Eastern fleets would constitute a definite threat to Allied sea lines of communication only in limited areas.

d. Aircraft of the Soviet naval air forces would be available for attacks on sea communications within range of their bases and could be supplemented by units from the tactical air forces insofar as this does not interfere with the requirements of the land campaigns. Aircraft of the long-range force might be employed concurrently in attacks on ports and their approaches.

e. Naval forces available against sea communications will vary with the progress of hostilities. As long as campaigns are in progress which involve one or both flanks of the Soviet army resting on the sea, a proportion of the Soviet navy, especially the major surface units, would be required in support.

f. The threat against allied sea LOCs would increase considerably if the Soviets acquire naval and air bases on the European–Atlantic seaboard. The greatest concentrations of all forms of attack would probably be in the North Sea, in the western and southwestern approaches to the British Isles, and in the approaches to and in the Mediterranean.

g. The principal bases from which the Soviet fleet could operate at the outset are set forth below. (Except where otherwise stated, all would be capable of being used as operational bases for ships of all categories likely to use them, and all could be kept open in winter by icebreakers):

North Atlantic
Petsamo
Kola Inlet (including Murmansk, Rosta, Polyarnoe, and Vaenga Bay)
White Sea ports (including Molotovsk and Archangel)

Baltic
Kronstadt, Tallinn, Paldiski, Libau, Memel, Danzig, Gdynia, and Swinemunde

Central Mediterranean
In Yugoslavia: Pola, Split, Gulf of Kotor, and many small ports and bays
  which might be used as advanced bases for limited numbers of small craft
In Albania: Valona Bay (including Durazzo, Valona, and Saseno Island), Porto
  Palermo

Black Sea
Sevastopol, Novorossisk, Poti, and Batumi
In Romania: Constanta

Pacific
Dairen and Port Arthur
Vladivostok, Nakhodka, and anchorages in the vicinity
Sovetskaya Gavan
Nikolaevsk (cannot be kept open by icebreakers between late October and late
  May)
Otomari in south Sakhalin
Petropavlovsk in Kamchatka
Nagaevo (cannot be kept open by icebreakers between November and May)
Dekastri (being developed and may possibly replace Nikolaevsk; icebound from
  mid-November to early May)

IV. PROBABLE SOVIET COURSES OF ACTION

1. Summary of Strategic Considerations

a. The Soviet leaders would wish to complete their campaign against France and the Low Countries as early as possible and will give it a high priority, realizing that on its progress would hinge the execution, timing, and effectiveness of their campaigns against the United Kingdom and Spain and that its completion would be essential for the attainment of their ultimate objective.

b. The Soviet leaders would probably estimate that the invasion of the British Isles would be extremely difficult even after the successful conclusion of their campaign in Western Europe and that it would be of the greatest importance that they make every effort to achieve complete success before the United States and the Dominions could reinforce the British Isles. Their initial objective, therefore, would be neutralization of the British Isles, and they would probably combine heavy aerial-bombardment, mine-laying, and submarine operations against the British Isles concurrently with their drive in Western Europe.

c. The Soviet leaders would probably estimate that the Near and Middle East oil resources are a very valuable part of the Allied war potential. Moreover, they would appreciate that their own oil areas in the Caucasus and Romania, as well as a large part of their other industries, would be vulnerable to attack from air bases in the Near and Middle East. They would therefore probably conclude that in the absence of effective opposition by the Arab countries and of adequate Anglo-American forces in the Near and Middle East, a campaign there would be successful and would give them a great strategic gain at relatively small cost.

d. The execution of a Scandinavian campaign would depend upon the actions, after the outbreak of war, of Sweden and the Allies and might be undertaken to deepen Soviet defense against Allied air attacks and to forestall Allied use of the Scandinavian peninsula. It would also depend upon the degree of success achieved by the Soviet Union in its campaign in Western Europe and against the British Isles and therefore cannot be assessed accurately at this time. This campaign would be subsidiary to and without prejudice to that in Western Europe.

e. Occupation of Spain, Portugal, and Gibraltar would close the Mediterranean in the west; would provide air and naval bases for operations against Allied LOCs; would provide a key to northwest Africa; and would protect the Soviet southwestern flank. This campaign would be most difficult and would be undertaken only if practicable without prejudice to the Soviet offensive against the United Kingdom.

f. An attack on Pakistan would be of a purely preventive nature; would be for the purpose of denying Allied use of air bases there; and would probably be limited to air attacks on those bases.

g. The Soviet Union would probably utilize its forces in the Far East to attempt to neutralize U.S. advance bases, to dominate China as far south as necessary, and to contain the maximum Allied force in the Far East theater. The Soviet Union would be unlikely, however, to allocate any additional forces to the Far East, although bases in this theater might be used on occasion by the long-range air force.

h. Soviet estimates of their offensive capabilities against the United States and Canada in 1957 would probably lead them to launch attacks by air with the objective of seriously reducing the military potential of Canada and the United States, particularly during the critical period of their mobilization. Such action would be timed with the major Soviet operations in Europe, the Near and Middle East, and the Far East.

2. Initial Courses of Action

The foregoing consideration of Soviet strategic objectives and capabilities leads to the conclusion that the Soviets would probably adopt simultaneous or staggered courses of action as follows:

a. Campaigns in Western Europe (including Denmark, Italy, and Sicily) to reach the Atlantic seaboard and secure base facilities for operations against Allied sea and air communications and for a possible subsequent invasion of the United Kingdom. Seizure of Italy and Sicily would aid in the closing of the Mediterranean, and Denmark could be used as a base for attack against Norway and Sweden.
b. Operations to gain control of Norway and Sweden for security, denial, or offensive purposes.
c. Air attacks and submarine operations designed to neutralize the United Kingdom.
d. An offensive against Greece to help close the Mediterranean and to flank Turkey.
e. Sea and air offensives against Allied sea communications.
f. A campaign to seize control of the Near and Middle East, including Turkey and the Cairo–Suez area.
g. The occupation of Korea; a campaign to seize control of Hokkaido; establishment of base areas in China; and air attacks against Allied base areas in the Far East generally.
h. Air, naval, limited airborne, and, possibly, guided-missile attacks to neutralize or occupy base areas in Alaska, the Aleutians, and the North Atlantic islands.

i. Operations to seize or neutralize such other Allied base areas and to destroy or contain such naval forces as might be used for launching air attacks with atomic weapons.
j. Air attacks, with the probable employment of atomic bombs and biological and chemical agents, against Canada and the United States.
k. Subversive activities and sabotage against the United States, Canada, and other Allied powers.

3. Subsequent Courses of Action

Depending upon the success of their initial courses of action, and while continuing those considered essential, the Soviet powers may be expected to initiate the following additional campaigns:

a. Airborne–amphibious invasion of the United Kingdom, forces available and weakness of opposition permitting.
b. Operations against Switzerland if such operations become imperative for security or denial purposes.
c. A possible campaign in the Iberian peninsula in order to deny it as a base for the Allies and to close the Mediterranean in the west. This operation would follow the general campaign in other areas of Western Europe and probably would be undertaken only if it would not seriously prejudice the success of other operations.
d. Invasion of the Japanese main islands to extend the Soviet defensive zone and for possible use as bases of operations.

V. ALLIED COURSES OF ACTION

1. General Considerations

a. Military courses of action pursued by the Allies upon the outbreak of war with the Soviets must be in consonance with the national objectives of the United States, which have been stated as follows:

(1) "To reduce the power and influence of the USSR to limits which no longer constitute a threat to the peace, national independence, and stability of the world family of nations."
(2) "To bring about a basic change in the conduct of international relations by the government in power in Russia, to conform with the purposes and principles set forth in the United Nations charter."

b. The primary tasks of our military forces will be to take such offensive action as would eliminate the will and capacity of the Soviet Union to wage aggressive war and to destroy the machinery whereby the USSR is able to dominate areas outside of traditional Russian territory. However, Allied operations toward these objectives will initially be conditioned by the situation existing at the beginning of the war, since the Soviets will have in being greatly superior ground and tactical air forces and will possess the initiative and the initial capabilities for overrunning large areas of Eruasia, for imposing a serious threat to our lines of communication, and for destructive air attacks against the United States. These capabilities would initially place the Allies generally on the defensive for the purpose of protecting their war-making potential, generating sufficient forces to stabilize the Soviet offensive, protecting their lines of communication, and projecting their offensive strength overseas. While the British will have some offensive power in bombers and naval vessels, only the United States will have any major initial offensive capability.

c. Our principal initial capability will lie in our ability to initiate an air offensive with atomic bombs against the USSR. In addition, our naval forces will be able to project their strength against Soviet naval and other forces within range from the sea. On the one hand, by the degree of opposition to Soviet advances in certain areas which can be exerted by the regenerating military forces of the Allies and, on the other, by the reduction in the Soviet capacity, as the result of our air offensive, to power and sustain those advances, a stabilization of the initially adverse military situation would sooner or later be obtained. The initiative and advantages of the general offensive would at that time pass to the Allies.

d. From the military standpoint, our strategy overseas should be based on a consideration of the following principles, from which, however, temporary deviations may have to be made because of overriding economic and political considerations:

(1) To seek action with Soviet forces only in those areas and under those circumstances where the bulk of their elements of superiority cannot be brought to bear against us and where our elements of superiority can be exploited to advantage.
(2) To conduct only those operations which contribute directly to the overall strategic concept or which are essential to the security of our positions in support thereof.

e. The military strength of the Allies in 1957 will be in proportion to the extent of pre-D-Day preparation. It must be recognized that serious shortages in reserves of Allied aircraft, ships, ground-force equipment, and POL supplies for military operations may result in some of the most desirable courses of action being completely infeasible unless the existing deficiencies are remedied.

f. The . . . courses of action . . . discussed in subsequent paragraphs are open to the Allies. . . .

2. Western Hemisphere: Secure the Western Hemisphere

a. Consideration of Soviet capabilities and recognition of the fact that the Soviets probably will strike with little or no warning leads to the inescapable conclusion that the United States will be in grave danger in the event of war in 1957. The possibility of an initial catastrophe in the continental United States far exceeding that of Pearl Harbor is real. Destructive blows involving atomic and other weapons of mass destruction against selected vital industrial and administrative centers could so cripple us that our powers of retaliation would be either temporarily paralyzed or greatly retarded. Consequently the protection of the war-making potential of the United States must receive first priority in all considerations of strategy. The protection of this war-making potential should be achieved not only by defensive measures but also by means of a strong Allied counter-air-offensive with atomic and conventional bombs against Soviet facilities for assembly and delivery of weapons of mass destruction. Requirements for this offensive are discussed on pages 159–161. Defensive measures would of necessity involve a defense, in varying degrees, of the continental United States, Hawaii, Alaska, Canada, the northeast approaches (Greenland, Newfoundland, and Labrador), Bermuda, Latin America, and the Caribbean area. This defense must be, for the most part, in being on D-Day. It will have to consist of an adequate early-warning network; air and antiaircraft defense; defense of outlying areas, sea approaches, coastwise and intercoastal shipping; and defense against internal sabotage and the possibility of limited airborne attacks. All of these measures will constitute a severe drain on our resources but will be vitally necessary in order to avoid disaster and to be able to retaliate rapidly and effectively as well as to generate forces and materiel for later operations. [See force-requirement chart.] . . .

3. North Atlantic Approaches: Secure the North Atlantic Islands

a. Of the North Atlantic islands (Iceland, the Azores, Jan Mayen, Spitzbergen, Bear Island), Iceland, if available, would be of the greatest value to the Soviets. It could be utilized as a bomber staging base and for reconnaissance and early warning.

b. Of the group of islands mentioned above, Iceland and the Azores are of considerable importance to the Allies because of their potential use as air and naval bases and their strategic location with respect to sea and air LOCs. Iceland, in particular, could become a major naval base for support of Allied submarine operations, ASW operations, and carrier-replenishment groups. Other northern islands, such as Jan Mayen, Spitzbergen, and Bear Island, lie far within the Arctic Circle but would be of value to either side as outpost early-warning stations and weather reporting posts and, in the case of Spitzbergen, a source of coal. Neutralization by bombing would be feasible. The Azores are geographically located so as to be relatively immune from Soviet seizure but would still require defenses—estimated at one battalion of ground forces, one squadron of all-weather fighters, and adequate radar coverage— against air raids and sabotage.

c. Iceland is a most probable objective of the Soviets and in any event should be secured by the Allies as soon as possible. If this occupation could be effected before the arrival of Soviet forces, one Rejuvenated Combat Team [RCT] and one fighter group including all-weather fighters should be sufficient for initial defense. If the island had been seized by the Soviets prior to the arrival of U.S. forces, an amphibious assault by at least one division would be necessary to retake it.

d. The defense of Spitzbergen and Bear Island does not appear to be necessary or feasible and is therefore rejected. The retention of Jan Mayen is desirable and would appear feasible with small forces except against appreciable Soviet effort. However, the limited value of Jan Mayen to the Allies and its vulnerability to attack, particularly if Norway is overrun by the Soviets, would probably not justify its retention. The defense of Iceland and the Azores is retained; therefore, this task is reworded to read: "Secure Iceland and the Azores."

4. Western Europe

a. Hold the United Kingdom

(1) The United Kingdom has great strategic significance because of its manpower and industrial potential [and] its suitability as a base for air operations against the USSR, as a base for naval operations, and as a base for mounting major operations to seize other strategic areas in Western or Northern Europe when such operations become necessary and feasible. Loss of the United Kingdom would be a serious blow to Allied industrial capabilities, with a possible consequent increase in Soviet capabilities. Further, the psychological effect on the other Allies and potential Allies would be considerable. These factors make the holding of the United Kingdom mandatory. Soviet capabilities will be such that the United Kingdom will be in grave danger from air, guided-missile, and airborne attacks, especially if Western Continental Europe is overrun. Contributing greatly to the effective defense of the United Kingdom would be the holding of Western Europe as far east as possible. The security of the United Kingdom must of necessity be primarily a British responsibility. The British should be able to provide the ground defense and to control the adjacent sea areas.

(2) It is difficult to determine the number of Allied aircraft required for air protection of the United Kingdom alone since the division of Soviet air effort between attacks on Western Europe and the expected air offensive against the United Kingdom cannot be accurately estimated. The British have estimated

that with eight hundred to nine hundred fighters [see the study of the Institute for Strategic Studies in appendices] and supporting antiaircraft units in the United Kingdom the RAF should be able to inflict at least 10 percent losses on the maximum scale of Soviet long-range bomber attack expected during the initial phase. This aircraft requirement should be within British capabilities, although a considerable buildup of antiaircraft may be required.

(3) The initial requirement for combat aircraft for defense of Western Europe including the United Kingdom (but excluding Italy) is estimated to be approximately 4,000 aircraft. Present estimates indicate that U.S. and Western Union air forces available on D-Day in the U.K. and Western Europe (excluding Italy) will total approximately 2,550 combat aircraft.* Therefore, as many as 1,450 additional aircraft, in combat units, will have to be provided for the defense of the Western Union, including the United Kingdom, either by a program of military aid or by immediate reinforcement with combat aircraft from the United States. In the event of the loss of Western Europe further reinforcement of the fighter defense of the United Kingdom will be required. This course of action is retained.

b. Hold maximum areas in Western Europe

(1) Hold Western Germany

In the areas east of the Rhine there are only two geographical features that may be considered as major obstacles to which a defense could be anchored. These are that portion of the Elbe River lying in the British zone and the Black Forest rising eastward from the upper Rhine in the French zone. Between these two areas there is no natural defense line. Allied defense of any general line including these two features would retain the Ruhr but would be infeasible because of the prohibitive requirements in forces and the inability of the Allies to deploy forces to such advanced positions in time to meet the initial Soviet assault. This course of action is therefore rejected.

(2) Hold the Rhine–Alps–Piave Line

(a) This line is the best natural defense line in Western Europe and the most easterly line feasible of defense. Its successful defense would retain the bulk of the manpower and industrial potential of Western Europe, including Italy and

---

* U.S.	150
U.K.	1,500 (excludes naval air arm)
France	450 (includes all but 50 naval air arm a/c)
Belgium	150
Netherlands	300 (includes naval air arm)
	2,550

Sicily, in Allied hands. Retention of Italy and Sicily would contribute to control of the central Mediterranean and would permit Allied use of air bases in Italy for air operations against targets in the Balkans. Defense of this line would greatly contribute to the defense of the United Kingdom and would secure major base areas on the Continent for later offensive operations against the Soviets. It has the disadvantage of giving up two-thirds of the Netherlands and the entire Ruhr industrial area.

(b) It is estimated that to hold the general line of the Rhine from Switzerland to the North Sea would require approximately 60* U.S. equivalent divisions and 4,000 combat aircraft. Present estimates indicate that without a military-aid program U.S. and Western Union forces available by D + 30 days for defense of the Rhine will total approximately 26 divisions† of varying degrees of combat efficiency and 2,550 combat aircraft. The difference between the above estimated requirements and availabilities would have to be made up primarily by a program of military aid to Western Union. The problem of such an aid program is considered in a later course of action. There also exists the possibility of assistance by Spanish forces shortly after D-Day in the defense of the Rhine line. This possibility should be developed thoroughly, both politically and psychologically, since it could cut down considerably the requirements imposed on Western Union and indirectly, to some extent, the requirements of a U.S. military-aid program.

* Editor's Note: At this time a U.S. division "slice" consisted of about 25,000 men. Thus 1.5 million men would be required to hold this line. In 1957 actual forces existing consisted of about 20 divisions or 0.5 million men. It is doubtful whether this force could have held the line. On the other hand, the reality in terms of air power exceeded the projection. Excluding strategic bombers, the Allied commander-in-chief could dispose some 5,000 tactical aircraft and a large and varied force of missiles.

(c) The defense of Italy from the junction of the Swiss, Austrian, [and] Italian borders, thence along the Piave River to the Adriatic would probably require an estimated 16 U.S. equivalent divisions and 500 combat aircraft. These forces are beyond the estimated Italian availability of 9 divisions and 200 combat aircraft, which are their maximum capabilities under the restrictions of the Italian Peace Treaty. Modification of the peace treaty and U.S. military aid would permit rearming the Italians to the extent [that] they could make up the difference themselves. There exists the possibility of keeping Yugoslavia neu-

---

† U.S.   2
  U.K.   5
  France   13
  Belgium   3
  Netherlands _3_
              26

tral.* If the latter could be done, it would reduce considerably the Soviet threat against Italy and the requirements for its defense. This possibility should be developed politically and psychologically.

(d) A preliminary estimate of the requirements for defense of Western Europe along the general line of the Rhine–Alps–Piave total about 76 U.S. equivalent divisions† and 4,500 combat aircraft. Part of these divisions—to counter the Soviet air-drop threat against vital portions of the Rhine defensive positions and to meet the immediate Yugoslav threat against the Piave—must be in position on D-Day. It is estimated that a minimum of 9 Italian divisions would be required to meet the initial Yugoslav effort and not less than 4 divisions in position to counter the Soviet air-drop capabilities against the Rhine. The remainder of the estimated 76 divisions would have to be available, approximately as shown in the table below, in order to meet the Soviet buildup.

† **Editor's Note:** A U.S. division as visualized at this time consisted of 25,000 men. Thus 1.9 million men would be required to hold this line, if the Dropshot projection is correct. The reality was that in the arc from Norway to Turkey the Allied supreme commander in 1957 disposed about 45 divisions or 1.125 million men.

(e) The following table shows the estimated probable Soviet buildup on this line in the first thirty days, the estimated Allied requirements to meet the Soviet threat, and the estimated Allied buildup capability (without a U.S. military-aid program).

	LINE DIVISIONS						
	D-Day	D + 5	D + 10	D + 15	D + 20	D + 25	D + 30
Soviet Buildup	12	30	45	70	85	100	115
Allied Requirements‡ (1949 U.S. equivalents)	13	17	30	45	55	65	76
Allied Capability (w/o U.S. aid; not U.S. equivalents)	20	27	27	31	31	31	35

‡ To hold the line for approximately six months.

A buildup of additional Allied forces behind this line would have to begin in the first months following D-Day in order to block Soviet capabilities beyond the first six months and to prepare for later offensive operations. The total

* If the present defection of Yugoslavia from the Soviet satellite orbit should continue to 1957, it is not likely that Yugoslavia would ally with the Soviet Union but would attempt to remain neutral and would be committed to resist Soviet and/or satellite attack.

requirements of forces beyond the first six months are difficult of determination at this time without an assessment of the results of the air offensive.

(f) Although the requirements for defense of this line as estimated above are large, they do not appear beyond the capabilities of the nations concerned, providing the necessary program of U.S. military aid is furnished. Therefore, this course of action is retained for further consideration.

(3) Hold the Rhine–French–Italian Border Line

(a) This course of action differs from the preceding course of holding the Rhine–Alps–Piave line in that it gives up all of Italy and Sicily. It would result in the loss of the industrial and manpower potential of Italy and Sicily and the loss of air bases for operations against targets in the Balkans. In addition, any significant measure of control over the central Mediterranean would be lost unless special operations were undertaken either to retain, neutralize, or retake Sicily. Retention of Sicily, under this course of action, would require 2 U.S. equivalent divisions and 300 combat aircraft.

(b) The requirements for holding that portion of the line from Switzerland to the North Sea are the same as in the preceding course of action, i.e., 60 U.S. equivalent divisions and 4,000 combat aircraft. It is estimated that it would take approximately 10 U.S. equivalent divisions and 400 combat aircraft to hold the French–Italian border against maximum Soviet and satellite capabilities.

(c) The requirements for defense of this line also appear to be within the capabilities of the nations concerned, providing the necessary program of U.S. military aid is furnished. Therefore, this course of action is retained for further consideration.

(4) Hold the Cotentin Peninsula

(a) This course of action would be considered only if Allied forces were unable to hold positions along the general line of the Rhine. Its purpose would be to retain a bridgehead on the Continent for a possible later buildup and subsequent operations against the Soviets on the Continent. The most feasible line for defense of the Cotentin Peninsula would be along the general line Isigny–Carentan–Lessay. This line, approximately twenty-five miles long, cannot be considered a natural defense line, although some small rivers, canals, and marsh areas would be of some defense value. Depth to the line would be lacking, as it is only about thirty miles to Cherbourg on the north coast. It is estimated that it would require approximately 10 U.S. equivalent divisions to hold this line. For any protracted defense these forces would require air support on a basis of at least air equality. There are only two inadequate airfields available on the Cotentin Peninsula, which together with the small size of the peninsula would make it infeasible to base air there. Consequently air support would have to come from the south of England, approximately one hundred miles away. Although such support would be possible, Soviet air superiority by this time could be increasing to such an extent that it would require a major Allied air effort to oppose it. The number of Allied aircraft necessary to oppose the Soviets might be on the order of 4,000, since the division of Soviet air effort between the attacks on the Cotentin Peninsula and the expected air offensive against the United Kingdom cannot be determined.

(b) Although the port capacity of Cherbourg, the only major port on the Cotentin Peninsula, and the capacities of the LOCs are ample to support the defense force required, it is considered that Soviet air power could destroy or damage the port of Cherbourg, sink shipping in the harbor, and attack the LOCs, supply dumps, and forces to such an extent that logistical support of the peninsula would be extremely difficult. In addition, the Cotentin Peninsula is not considered suitable for the debouchment of large forces because of its narrowness and consequent lack of maneuver room. This course of action is considered to be unprofitable and infeasible and is rejected.

(5) Hold the Brittany Peninsula

(a) A withdrawal to and a holding of the Brittany peninsula would be considered with the principal objective of holding a major bridgehead on the Continent for later buildup of Allied forces and subsequent operations against the Soviets. Initially, it could be used as a base for air operations and to some extent as a naval base. There are three major ports on the peninsula: Brest, Lorient, and Saint-Nazaire. Adequate lines of communication exist. There are approximately fourteen airfields of various types on the peninsula, few of which would be adequate for Allied use.

(b) There is no natural defense line on the peninsula. The most suitable line would probably be generally across the base of the peninsula extending for approximately 100 miles along the general line Saint-Nazaire–Rennes–Mont-Saint-Michel. Defense of this line would give maximum depth to the bridgehead, approximately 140 miles, thus giving better protection to the port areas. The port of Saint-Nazaire, however, would probably be rendered unusable because of its proximity to the front lines. It is estimated that approximately 20 U.S. equivalent divisions as a minimum would be required to hold this line. Air support could be based on the peninsula, providing considerable airfield reconstruction were undertaken. Support could be furnished from the south of England approximately 175 miles away. Soviet air superiority, by this time, however, could be increasing to such an extent that it would require a major Allied air effort to oppose it. The number of Allied aircraft necessary to oppose the Soviets might be on the order of 4,000, since the division of Soviet air effort between the attacks on the Brittany peninsula and the expected air offensive against the United Kingdom cannot be determined.

(c) Notwithstanding the probable ability of the Allied forces to hold the peninsula, it is believed the gradually increasing Soviet air attacks on the two major port areas would eventually make logistical support of the peninsula extremely difficult. This course of action is rejected as being unprofitable and infeasible.

(6) Hold the Pyrenees Line

(a) The Iberian peninsula is strategically important chiefly because control of it would permit control of the Strait of Gibraltar and the western Mediterranean. In addition, the peninsula could provide air bases for air operations against the Soviets, although the number of first-class all-weather airfields in the peninsula is small and considerable construction would be required. Also the Iberian peninsula is not particularly well suited for strategic air attacks against the USSR.

(b) The Iberian peninsula has some further strategic significance as a bridgehead on the Continent for subsequent major land operations against the Soviets. Port capacity on the Iberian peninsula is ample, although the best ports on the northern coast and the Mediterranean coast lie relatively close to the Pyrenees, which would make them vulnerable to Soviet air attacks. Ports farther south and west would still be adequate; however, the lines of communication leading from them to the Pyrenees are vulnerable [and] inferior and are inadequate for sustained heavy military traffic without a large-scale program of reconstruction.

(c) Egress of large Allied forces from the Iberian peninsula into France in major operations against Soviet opposition would be extremely difficult from both a tactical and logistical standpoint. Amphibious operations around each end of the Pyrenees in order to flank Soviet positions would probably be necessary.

(d) Large-scale Allied utilization of the Iberian peninsula would be a drain on U.S. resources because of the economic poverty of Spain. Extensive rehabilitation of Spanish airfields and LOCs would be required.

(e) The best defense line on the Iberian peninsula is formed by the Pyrenees. It extends for approximately 260 miles and has only four main passes through it. The two major routes through the Pyrenees are at its extremities. The successful defense of this line would keep airfields suitable to the Soviets approximately 575 miles from the Strait of Gibraltar, a distance which would make effective interdiction difficult by air action against lines of communication through them. It is estimated that it would require approximately 34 U.S. equivalent divisions and 800 combat aircraft to defend Iberia from maximum Soviet capabilities against the Pyrenees for an indefinite period. Assistance by carrier air from the Mediterranean or the Bay of Biscay would be possible.

(f) Present estimates indicate that Spanish forces available for defense of Iberia will total 22 divisions and 350 combat aircraft. Portuguese forces could contribute only about 3 divisions and 100 combat aircraft. The balance of the forces required would have to be provided by the Allies.

(g) In summary, the Iberian peninsula is not particularly suitable as a base for air operations against the Soviets, is not a desirable bridgehead from which to extend subsequent major land operations against the USSR, but does have strategic significance through its control over the Strait of Gibraltar and the western Mediterranean and because it is a key to northwest Africa. These latter factors, and the fact that the estimate of forces required for its defense appear to be reasonable, warrants retention of this course of action for further consideration.

(7) Hold the Apennines Line

(a) This course of action should be considered either in conjunction with holding the Rhine–French–Italian border line or by itself, on the strength of its affording a bridgehead in Continental Europe and control of the central Mediterranean. A successful defense along this line would retain the bulk of Italy in Allied hands with its ample system of air bases, especially those in the Foggia region. It has the disadvantage of giving up the great industrial region of northern Italy, especially the armament industry, the major portion of which is located in the Turin–Genoa–Milan triangle. The remainder of Italy, largely agrarian in economy, would thus be heavily dependent on the Allies for economic support, and continued operations of Italian armed forces would depend on Allied military aid.

(b) Retention of all or any part of Italy would not provide a good bridgehead for subsequent land operations into the Continent. While operations into northern Italy from the line of the Apennines would be feasible, egress from the northeastern borders of Italy into central Europe would be difficult both tactically and logistically for Allied forces on a major scale. Routes of advance and lines of communication would be limited to the two major passes through the Alps, the Brenner Pass [and] Tarvisio Pass, and a gateway across the rugged plateau east of Trieste at Postumia.

(c) Although there is an ample number of airfields, it is not considered that they would be utilized extensively for strategic bombing against the USSR until Soviet air power had been materially reduced. There is the possibility, however, that those airfields could be used as mounting areas for airborne operations into central Europe at such time as such operations become feasible.

(d) The line of the Apennines south of Bologna is a strong natural defense line. Extending for approximately 125 miles from Rimini on the Adriatic to just south of La Spezia it has only eight or nine passes through it. It is estimated that it would require approximately 20 U.S. equivalent divisions and 500 combat aircraft for a defense of this line. Maximum Italian capabilities would be approximately 9 divisions and 200 combat aircraft, assuming that all Italian forces have been able to retire intact behind this line. The balance of the forces required would have to be furnished by the Allies. Port capacities and LOCs on the peninsula would be adequate for support of the required forces.

(e) In summary, it is considered that Italy south of the Apennines is not of sufficient importance to require its retention by the Allies because of its limited value either as a bridgehead for subsequent operations against the Soviets or as a base for strategic air operations. It has great significance, however, because it can contribute greatly to the control of the central Mediterranean. For this reason it is retained for further consideration.

(8) Hold the Mediterranean Islands

(a) Sicily, Crete, and Cyprus are of strategic importance to the Allies because of their commanding position with respect to control of the Mediterranean and the sea lines of communication therein. In addition, the retention of Crete and Cyprus by the Allies would also contribute to the defense of the Cairo–Suez area.

(b) If Italy is overrun by the Soviets, it is estimated that Sicily could be defended by Italian forces withdrawn from Italy augmented by 2 Allied divisions and 300 combat aircraft. Retention of Sicily would also make Malta secure. If Sicily is seized by the Soviets, the Allied position in Malta would be precarious and its usefulness as a base would be limited by the extent that combat aircraft reinforcements could be provided.

(c) If Greece is overrun by the Soviets, the Greeks should withdraw to Crete in the maximum strength practicable. This would require the influencing of Greek strategic planning to bring it into consonance with Allied plans in the eastern Mediterranean region. If the Greeks were to base their main defenses in the north, the Soviets could concentrate sufficient force in that area to destroy the Greek army and thereby facilitate their subsequent overrunning of Greece. On the other hand, the terrain and the few and poor lines of communication to the south are such that if the Greeks were to avoid a major action in the north and were instead to withdraw to the south, while employing maximum delaying action and carefully planned demolition of transportation systems on withdrawal, the Soviet campaign could be prolonged. Such a course of action by the Greeks, in addition to helping Allied operations in the overall, would avoid the destruction of the Greek army in the north; would offer a hope to the Greeks of holding on the mainland; and would give them reasonable assurance of preserving at least part of Greek territory (namely Crete) under Greek control. It is estimated that about two Greek divisions and one fighter group could hold Crete. Adequate shipping to transport these forces to Crete should be available in Greek waters from the sizable Greek merchant fleet. Protection for the crossing to Crete could be furnished by Allied naval forces which would be in the eastern Mediterranean, supplemented by Allied air forces in the Cairo–Suez and Cyrenaica areas. The above factors make a withdrawal of Greek forces to Crete appear to be feasible. If seized by the Soviets, which is unlikely because of supply difficulties, Crete could be neutralized by Allied forces in the Cairo–Suez and Cyrenaica areas.

(d) If Turkey is overrun by the Soviets, the Allied position in Cyprus would be untenable unless the Cairo–Suez area is retained by the Allies, thereby permitting reinforcement of Cyprus. If Soviet seizure of Cyprus occurred, which is unlikely, it could be neutralized by Allied forces in the eastern Mediterranean area.

(e) The Balearics, Corsica, and Sardinia, while of less importance, must also be considered. If Spain is held by the Allies, it is highly improbable that the Soviets would attempt to seize the Balearics because of the impossibility of supplying them. If Spain is occupied by the Soviets, retention of the islands by the Allies would be neither feasible nor desirable. It is considered, therefore, that no Allied forces should be allocated for the defense of the Balearics and that Spanish forces only should be responsible for their defense.

(f) Corsica occupies a similar strategic position with respect to Italy as do the Balearic Islands to Spain. No Allied forces, therefore, should be allocated for the defense of Corsica, which should be a responsibility of French forces.

(g) Sardinia, although of more strategic importance than the Balearic Islands or Corsica, would be of little value to the Soviets if the Allies hold Sicily. Soviet capabilities against Sardinia are insignificant unless they occupy Italy, and even then logistical problems would be most difficult if Sicily is held by the Allies. On the other hand, if the Allies cannot hold Sicily, there would be little to gain by attempting to defend Sardinia. Italian forces, therefore, should be responsible for its defense.

(h) This course of action is reworded as follows and retained: "Hold the Mediterranean islands of Sicily, Malta, Cyprus, and Crete."

5. Northern Europe

a. General

(1) The courses of action open to the Allies in the Scandinavian area of Northern Europe—i.e., "Hold Norway and Sweden" and "Hold Denmark"—and the treatment accorded them in paragraphs b and c below are predicated on the special assumption to this plan which states that Sweden "will attempt to remain neutral but will join the Allies if attacked or seriously threatened." As a consequence of this assumption, Allied dependence upon a combined defense of Scandinavian territory by the three Scandinavian countries is precluded. If, however, Sweden were at some time in the future to signify its adherence to a pact for the common defense of Scandinavian territory, courses of action open to the Allies in that area would have to be reassessed.

(2) In anticipation of such a possible realignment on the part of Sweden, a preliminary examination indicates that it would appear feasible to retain at least a part of Scandinavia with Scandinavian forces, provided some military aid is furnished. It is estimated that defense of Zealand and southern Norway and Sweden, at least as far north as a line running generally east from Trondheim,

could be effected with approximately 16 U.S. equivalent divisions and 1,400 combat aircraft. With a program of military aid it is considered that the combined Scandinavian forces could meet the above requirements.

(3) Since the assumption referred to in paragraph (1) above remains, however, a limiting factor as regards the participation of Sweden, both in mutual planning for defense and at the outbreak of war, it is considered that analysis of courses of action open to the Allies should at this time be limited to those in paragraphs *b* and *c* below.

b. Hold Norway and Sweden

(1) Norway and Sweden would be strategically significant to the Allies from both an offensive and a defensive standpoint. Offensively these countries could provide air bases for bombing the USSR. These bases would be five hundred to seven hundred miles closer to the northern industrial regions of the USSR than would be bases in the British Isles. Allied forces based in Norway and Sweden would be in a position to deny free use of the Baltic Sea by Soviet shipping and submarines and would threaten the northern flank of Soviet forces operating in Western Eruope. In addition, they could subsequently launch a feint or secondary attack through Finland to sever the Murmansk–Kola Peninsula area, establishing bases therein to further threaten Soviet shipping and bases in the White Sea area. The avenue of approach from Norway and Sweden through Finland is not suitable, however, for major Allied operations into the heart of the USSR because of the poor lines of communication, limited port capacities, weather, and terrain.

(2) Defensively Allied retention of Norway and Sweden would deny them to the Soviets as a base area for air and naval operations and would permit the Allies to prevent Soviet shipping from utilizing the Skagerrak entrance to the North Sea.

(3) Soviet control of Norway and Sweden would provide a considerable expansion of their early-warning system against the Allied air threat from the north and west and would permit establishing bases for projecting air and naval operations (especially submarine) against the British Isles and against Allied sea lines of communication in the North Atlantic. In addition, it would ensure continued supplies of Swedish uranium, industrial products, and iron ore.

(4) Soviet attacks by air, airborne, and amphibious forces against Norway and Sweden from bases in Germany, Denmark, the Baltic States, and the Murmansk–Finland areas, beginning about D + 1½ months, would be opposed by Scandinavian forces estimated at 12 divisions and 1,300 aircraft for the Swedes and 1 division and 100 combat aircraft for the Norwegians. To meet the Soviet threat in the north, it is estimated that at least 1 U.S. equivalent division and 100 combat aircraft would be required in the Narvik area of Norway and 5 U.S. equivalent divisions and 400 combat aircraft in northern Sweden. To meet the Soviet threat from Denmark, it is estimated that 10 U.S. equivalent divisions

and 1,000 combat aircraft would be required in south Sweden opposite Denmark, and 2 U.S. equivalent divisions and 100 combat aircraft in southern Norway. An estimated 2 additional divisions and 200 combat aircraft would be required in central Sweden to include the Stockholm area. These requirements total 20 U.S. equivalent divisions and 1,800 combat aircraft and are estimated to be the absolute minimum necessary to hold the Scandinavian peninsula. It is apparent from the above estimates that Swedish and Norwegian forces estimated to be available would be inadequate to repel the Soviets. Furthermore the Allies could not reinforce Norway or Sweden subsequent to D-Day in sufficient strength in time to block the Soviets. Assuming that pre-D-Day reinforcement by the Allies would be politically unacceptable and in view of the scale of the requirement for such reinforcement (estimated to be about 7 U.S. equivalent divisions and 400 combat aircraft, assuming the 13 available divisions were also made U.S. equivalent), the only other alternative would be to establish a program of U.S. military aid sufficient to provide the required Swedish and Norwegian forces.

(5) However, based on the advantages accruing to the Allies of retaining Norway and Sweden and on the possibility that with sufficient U.S. military aid those countries could successfully defend themselves, this course of action is retained for further consideration.

c. Hold Denmark

(1) The principal strategic importance of Denmark lies in its position with relation to the sea exits from the Baltic through the Kattegat to the North Sea (the Sound, Great Belt, and Little Belt). Secondarily Denmark is strategically significant because of its potentiality as a base for air operations.

(2) The topographic features of Denmark render the country virtually indefensible against attack from the south and east, and its proximity to the USSR makes it particularly vulnerable to air attack. Southern Jutland, while only about thirty miles in width at its narrowest point, has no natural defense line. The eastern coast of Jutland and the coasts of the principal islands of Zealand and Fyn are vulnerable to amphibious and other seaborne landings.

(3) Denmark has extensive road and railroad systems and ample port capacities, all of which are adequate to support considerable Allied forces. Airfields are neither extensive nor adequate, but potentially the area could be developed as an air base, provided considerable airfield reconstruction were undertaken.

(4) Although the Soviets would probably use, initially, about 5 line divisions and 400 combat aircraft against Danish resistance in attacks by land through Jutland, they could employ considerable additional forces if required by the presence of other Allied forces. Therefore it is estimated that at least 10 U.S. equivalent divisions and 600 combat aircraft would be required to hold Jutland and the two principal islands of Zealand and Fyn. These requirements are well beyond the capabilities of the Danes to meet. By 1957, even with a consider-

able program of military aid, Danish forces could total only a maximum of approximately 5 divisions and an insignificant number of combat aircraft. Consequently, in order to ensure the holding of Denmark, the Allies would have to reinforce it to the required strength immediately after D-Day. Such reinforcement would clearly be beyond their capabilities. Therefore, in spite of the advantages to be gained by holding Denmark, this course of action is rejected as being infeasible of accomplishment.

6. Near and Middle East

a. Hold Turkey or Portions Thereof

(1) Control of Turkey would be of great importance to the USSR, since it would provide them a base for air and ground operations against the Cairo–Suez area and the Persian Gulf while denying the same to the Allies. Soviet possession of Turkey could also eliminate a major threat to Black Sea shipping and would permit submarine operations into the Mediterranean via the Turkish straits. Conversely, Allied possession of Turkey would give them a base area for projecting operations against vital areas of the USSR and would contribute to the security of the Cairo–Suez and Middle East oil areas.

(2) As a base of operations, however, Turkey has several disadvantages. Its roads, railroads, and air-transport systems are very poor; there are few adequate ports; and the greater portion of Turkish terrain is very rugged. Air attacks against LOCs by either side would make logistic support of major operations most difficult.

(3) Soviet capabilities against Turkey would be such that Turkish resistance might be continued for about five months, depending upon the season of the year. Allied aid prior to and during the campaign in the form of the provision of equipment and air support from carrier and land-based air in the eastern Mediterranean region could prolong this resistance.

(4) Allied requirements for holding all of Turkey are estimated as about 12 British or U.S. divisions in addition to Turkish forces, plus about 10 U.S. fighter groups. Some of these forces would have to be in place and operational on D-Day.

(5) It is concluded that because of the scale and timing of forces required and the excessive logistic effort that would be necessary, the holding of all of Turkey would not be possible.

(6) There appear to be two alternatives, however, that should be considered: the holding of a maximum portion of southeastern Turkey and the holding of the Iskenderun "pocket" area (Silifke–Cilician Gates–Maras–Aleppo). In consequence of the rejection of the holding of all of Turkey and a consideration of the two alternatives discussed below, it follows that Turkish strategic planning should be influenced to the extent necessary to bring it into consonance with

Allied plans in this area. Specifically, and in either of the above alternatives, Turkish plans should provide for maximum possible delaying action in European Turkey and in other areas of northern and eastern Turkey consistent with the capability of withdrawing intact the greatest possible forces to the south and southeastward. Any all-out stand in the northern area of Turkey would only lead to the encirclement and destruction of Turkish forces. Considering the superiority of the Soviet forces and the extreme difficulty of withdrawal over the poor LOCs in Turkey, it is reasonable to assume for planning purposes that the Turks could probably withdraw the equivalent of approximately eleven divisions to the south and southeast. It does not appear sound, however, to assume that any more than a negligible portion of their air force could withdraw.

(7) Retention of southeastern Turkey generally along the line Silifke–Cilician Gates–Malatya–Van Golu to the junction of the Turkish–Iraq–Iran borders would be an important political and psychological asset leading to the maximum use of Turkish forces; would secure the important Iskenderun 'pocket" area; would secure the only railroad linking the Tigris Valley and the eastern Mediterranean; and would simultaneously secure both the oil-bearing areas and the Cairo–Suez area from Soviet threats developing through Turkey. Because of the rugged, mountainous terrain and the generally poor LOCs, this area of Turkey should be relatively easy to defend. Assuming that approximately 11 Turkish divisions have been able to withdraw to participate in the defense of this area, it is estimated that additionally about 4 divisions, 5 fighter groups, 1 light-bomber group, and 1 tactical reconnaissance group, either U.S. or British, would be required. The air forces would have to be in place and operational by about D + 4 months and the ground force by about D + 6 months.

(8) An Allied defense of the Iskenderun "pocket" in itself would be insufficient, as the flank and rear of this area would be exposed to Soviet threats developing through both Turkey and Iran, with the result that this area would become a pocket in reality, accessible only by sea and air. Consequently its defense should be coupled with that of a line running south along the Jordan rift toward the Gulf of Aqaba. The defense of this combined area would preserve a foothold in Turkey, thus permitting utilization of Turkish forces, and would secure the Cairo–Suez area from Soviet threats developing from Turkey and Iran.

(9) An Allied defense of the Iskenderun "pocket"–Jordan rift line would require approximately 7 U.S. or British divisions and 6 fighter groups, 1 light-bomber group, and 1 tactical-reconnaissance group, assuming that approximately 11 Turkish divisions have been able to withdraw to participate in the defense of this area. Two divisions and two fighter groups would have to be deployed along the Jordan rift by D + 3 months, with a buildup to a total of 4 divisions and 3 fighter groups by not later than D + 7 months. The remaining 3 fighter groups, 1 light-bomber group, and 1 tactical-reconnaissance group would have to be in position in the Iskenderun "pocket" by D + 4 months, while the remaining 3 divisions would have to be there by D + 6 months. An

early and intensive interdiction and demolition effort would be required against Soviet LOCs. Maximum use should be made of planned demolitions by Turkish forces, augmented as necessary by Allied air interdiction.

(10) Since both of the above two alternate courses of action are considered feasible and advantageous to the Allies, they are retained for further consideration and are worded as follows:

(a) "Hold southeastern Turkey."
(b) "Hold the Iskenderun 'pocket'–Jordan rift line."

b. Hold the Cairo–Suez Area

(1) The Cairo–Suez area is a most important strategic area because of its numerous airfields and base facilities, ports, manpower and industrial potential its communications network, and the Suez Canal. Bases in this area would not only facilitate attacks against the vulnerable southern flank of the USSR but could support operations to aid the Turks, to retain or regain Middle East oil and to project subsequent advances toward the heart of the USSR.

(2) Since bases in the Cairo–Suez–Aden area will probably be in British hands on D-Day, Allied bombers should be able to launch attacks on Soviet targets from these bases on D-Day if necessary prestocked supplies and prepared facilities can be made available.

(3) The British naval bases in the eastern Mediterranean at Alexandria and Port Said could be utilized. Port facilities in the Red Sea at Suez, Port Sudan, Massawa, and Aden could also be expanded for support of forces in the Cairo–Suez–Aden area.

(4) D-Day requirements for defense of this area against Soviet attack are estimated to be 1 division and 1 fighter group increasing to a maximum of 5 divisions, 4 fighter groups, and 1 light-bomber group by D + 7 months. Egyptian forces available would probably not exceed the equivalent of 1 division, 80 fighters, and 18 light bombers. The Egyptian division, however, could probably not be counted on for more than internal security. Early assistance to ground and air forces could be provided by a carrier task force which will probably be in the Mediterranean and which could, in addition to other operations, attack Soviet LOCs in Iran, Iraq, and Turkey and otherwise assist in the defense of the Cairo–Suez area.

(5) This course of action is retained.

c. Hold the Oil-Bearing Areas

(1) The oil resources of the Near and Middle East (Bahrein–Saudi Arabia, Kuwait–Iran, and Mosul–Kirkuk) estimated to have a daily production of about 2.3 million barrels by 1957 (approximately 25 percent of worldwide) are of great importance to the Allies and consequently of great interest to the USSR.

refineries located in these areas will probably have a total capacity slightly less than 1 million barrels a day, with the Abadan refinery, largest in the world, alone handling 500,000 barrels a day.

(2) While the Soviets would not require the petroleum of the Persian Gulf for initial operations, they would probably attempt to seize the area immediately to deny its use to the Allies as a source of oil and as a base for air operations, as well as to add depth to the defenses of their own southern border and oil-producing area.

(3) Allied requirements for holding the above areas against Soviet D-Day airborne capabilities of 3–4 airborne brigades against Basra–Abadan and Bahrein–Dhahran would be about 1 division and 3 fighter groups at Abadan and 1 Rejuvenated Combat Team [RCT] plus 1 fighter group at Dhahran. Indigenous forces in these areas will be loosely organized and ill-equipped and would be of little value unless a substantial Allied aid program is in effect. There are currently and will probably continue to be employed by the Arabian-American Oil Company in the Bahrein–Dhahran area about 4,000 American men who are, for the most part, of military age and physically well conditioned. With military equipment stocked in the area for the purpose, with limited training and organization, and with a nucleus of regular troops, this labor force could be of great assistance in defending the airfield and the oil installations on an emergency basis against Soviet airborne capabilities on D-Day and until reinforced or relieved by regular forces.

(4) An early and intensive interdiction and demolition effort will be required against Soviet LOCs. Maximum use should be made of planned demolitions by indigenous forces, augmented as necessary by Allied air interdiction. In addition to long-range air interdiction provided by Allied naval and land-based air listed under other courses of action, at least one light-bomber group would also be required in the Abadan–Mosul area from D-Day onward. Additional Allied forces of two divisions should be deployed not later than D + 1 month for defense of the Tigris Valley in order to protect the oil-bearing areas against Soviet forces attempting to advance through the mountain passes of Iran and Iraq.

(5) Political and economic considerations in the stationing of U.S. or British forces of the size required in the Near and Middle East prior to D-Day may present considerable difficulty. Politically such action during peacetime might be regarded by the USSR as an overt act and in any event would require diplomatic negotiations. The above course of action is retained for further consideration due to the grave importance of the availability of Near and Middle East oil resources to the Allied war effort.

d. Retake the Oil-Bearing Areas Immediately

(1) In the event of early Soviet seizure of Near and Middle East oil areas, the oil position of the United States and its allies would be such that immediate retaking of these areas would be necessary in order to ensure adequate supplies of

POL [petroleum, oil, lubricants] to the Allied powers. It is unlikely that the refineries, storage facilities, wells, and pipelines could be recaptured before being partially destroyed by USSR troops if not already destroyed prior to the initial withdrawal of the Allies, but the need for crude oil would necessitate operations to retake the area and reactivate production.

(2) If Allied demolition and bombing attacks on LOCs from carriers of Cairo–Suez have successfully reduced Soviet capabilities, an attack by one airborne RCT, a 1-division amphibious assault force, and a fast carrier task force should be sufficient to recapture the Bahrein–Dhahran area, provided it were launched not later than D + 2½ months.* A 20-knot amphibious assault force could reach the Bahrein area twenty-five days after departure from the east coast by way of the Cape of Good Hope and in seventeen days if the Mediterranean route could be used. Two fighter groups would have to be established ashore prior to the departure of the carrier task force.

(3) After recapture of Bahrein–Dhahran, a buildup for an assault on the Basra–Abadan area should be undertaken. An estimated 5 divisions (3 infantry 1 armored, and 1 airborne), and 5 fighter groups and 1 light-bomber group might be required to retake the area. Initial landings would probably be made in the Kuwait area by a 1-division amphibious assault force and would include a 1-airborne-division assault on the Abadan refinery and other key facilities. The above operations would ensure access to the bulk of the Middle East oil areas. Subsequent offensives should then reduce Soviet forces remaining in the Kirkuk–Mosul area. This course of action is retained for consideration in the event the retention of these areas is infeasible.

e. Retake the Oil-Bearing Areas Subsequently

(1) If the Near and Middle East oil areas are not retained, or retaken in the early phases of the war, the oil position of the Allies would necessitate subsequent operations to retake it. After gaining access to Near and Middle East oil, it would require at least six months, and probably longer, to reactivate production after recapture of the areas.

(2) Soviet buildup in the three major oil-producing areas would depend on Allied action and on their estimate of our intentions. Requirements for Allied operations to retake the Persian Gulf area are therefore difficult to determine. If the Soviets are permitted to consolidate and strengthen their positions, an Allied amphibious assault may be extremely costly. Forces required would at least be on the order of those listed in the preceding task and might be considerably larger. If the Allies still held the Cairo–Suez area and in addition had reduced Soviet capabilities by the air offensive and combined offensives on other fronts, a feasible approach to the oil-bearing areas would be an advance from Cairo–

---

* It would be desirable to retake this area as rapidly as possible in order to prevent Soviet consolidation.

Suez eastward, combined with an amphibious operation similar to that outlined in paragraph *d* above. Requirements for this course of action cannot be estimated until such time as an evaluation of the then-current strategic position of the Soviets and the Allies can be made.

(3) The above course of action does not appear beyond Allied capabilities and is therefore retained for further consideration in the event either retention or early recapture of these oil-bearing areas has proved infeasible.

f. Hold Maximum Areas of the Middle East

(1) It is assumed that the principal countries of the Middle East (Iran, Afghanistan, Pakistan, and India) would attempt to remain neutral and that in view of their geographic positions and probable economic, political, and military situations, only Pakistan probably would join the Allies if she were attacked or seriously threatened, while the others would probably submit to adequate armed occupation by either side rather than fight.

(2) The northern frontier of India and Pakistan is the lofty and militarily impassable Himalaya mountain range. Afghanistan presents a formidable terrain obstacle to invasion, with practically no feasible north–south lines of communication. Only in Iran are there feasible avenues of invasion, and these are tenuous and incapable of supporting sizable military forces, particularly if subjected to interdiction operations by air. There would appear little to be gained by the USSR by an invasion of India, Pakistan, or Afghanistan which could not be accomplished by political and subversive means, and the military effort required would be disproportionate to the gains. On the other hand, invasion of Iran as a part of the campaign to seize control of the oil-bearing areas of the Near and Middle East is a probability and is treated with elsewhere in this estimate, including the proposed means of its containment.

(3) It is concluded, therefore, that except for possible air action by the Soviets against Allied use of air bases (not initially envisaged) in India or Pakistan, the military threat to the Middle East countries other than Iran is negligible. The Allied counter to the threat through Iran to the oil-bearing areas is covered elsewhere in this estimate.

(4) Accordingly, this course of action is retained but is reworded as follows: "Hold maximum areas of the Middle East consistent with indigenous capabilities, supported by other Allied courses of action."

7. Far East

a. General

Analysis of possible Allied courses of action in the Far East necessitates consideration of the following factors:

(1) All of the areas of the Far East, including the Far Eastern USSR, are remote from those areas of the USSR which are vital to the Soviet war-making capability. This factor, together with the meager lines of communication, eliminates the area as a profitable avenue of land approach to the heartland of the USSR.

(2) The degree of industrial development within the area is such that it would contribute little to the support of a Soviet or an Allied war effort within the first three or four years of war.

(3) The area does not contain substantial amounts of available strategic raw materials vital to an Allied war effort, except in areas adjacent to the South China Sea.

(4) Soviet conquest of much of this area, except for Southeast Asia and the East Indies, would provide few military advantages and would not substantially increase their overall military capacity.

(5) Any major operations in this area by Allied forces would constitute an unprofitable diversion of Allied resources.

(6) It would be desirable to limit the advance of Soviet forces in the Far East and to prevent their acquiring the resources of Southeast Asia and the East Indies.

(7) Realization of long-term Allied objectives in the Far East requires that the Allies be in a position at the conclusion of the war to ensure the alignment of the countries of the Far East as members of the friendly family of nations.

b. Hold Japan

(1) Retention of Japan would assist in blocking Soviet expansion in the Far East and would strengthen our position in that area. In addition, it would contribute to the security of Okinawa. It is estimated that at least 2 U.S. divisions and 3 fighter groups will be actually in or will be available for D-Day deployment in Japan on D-Day. Present surplus equipment in Japan, if properly maintained, would be sufficient to fully equip 2 Japanese divisions, 3 on a substitute basis, and 5 on a strict austerity basis. The latter 5 would be capable of internal-security duties only. Two U.S. divisions and about 3⅔ U.S. fighter groups—together with the 10 Japanese divisions, if equipped as indicated above, with the support of a U.S. carrier task group which it is estimated will be in the Pacific on M-Day—should be adequate for the defense of Japan except Hokkaido.

(2) This course of action is retained and is reworded as follows: "Hold Japan less Hokkaido."

c. Hold Okinawa

Okinawa—because of its present facilities, location, and its relative security from Soviet attacks—is the most suitable base for strategic air operations in the

Far East. Initial defense requirements are estimated at 1 RCT, and 1⅓ fighter groups. This course of action is retained.

d. Hold Maximum Areas of Southeast Asia

(1) The retention of maximum areas of Southeast Asia, to include the East Indies and as much as possible of China, would ensure the availability of their economic resources, provide additional security for our bases and lines of communication in the western Pacific and Indian Ocean areas, provide advanced air and naval bases, encourage dissension as well as underground and guerrilla resistance within Communist-controlled areas, and strengthen our position relative to our long-term objectives in the Far East. However, to provide effective opposition to major Soviet advances over a wide area would require the introduction of Allied forces onto the mainland of Asia on a scale out of all proportion to the results that could be obtained. Except for about one infantry division and one-third fighter group for the security of the natural rubber-producing areas in Malaya, it would therefore not be feasible to undertake major offensive or defensive operations on the mainland of Southeast Asia. Our assistance should consist mainly of psychological- and underground-warfare measures, along with a judicious U.S. aid program and air and naval attacks on enemy bases and lines of communication.

(2) This course of action is retained but is reworded to read: "Hold maximum areas of Southeast Asia consistent with non-Communist capabilities supported by other Allied courses of action."

8. General Courses of Action

a. Conduct an Air Offensive Against the Soviet Powers

(1) The most powerful immediately available weapon the Allies will possess in 1957 which can be applied against the USSR will be the A-bomb. A strategic air offensive against the USSR utilizing the A-bomb supplemented with conventional bombs should be instituted immediately after the outbreak of hostilities. This offensive—directed against facilities for production of weapons of mass destruction, key government and control facilities, major industrial areas, and POL facilities—would accomplish great disruption of the Soviet war potential. Particular emphasis should be placed on blunting Soviet offensive capabilities. Accordingly attacks against atomic-bomb production and storage facilities and important air bases from which atomic-bomb attacks are most likely to be launched should be given high priority. Attacks should also begin immediately against Soviet and satellite LOCs, supply bases, and troop concentrations. Attacks with bombs and mines should be undertaken against submarine-operating

bases, channels [and] construction and repair yards to assist Allied naval forces engaged in the destruction of these facilities as discussed under the task "Conduct Offensive Operations to Destroy Enemy Naval Forces, etc.," page 163. Attacks against important targets in the petroleum-refining, electric-power, and iron and steel industries must also be initiated at the earliest practicable date. This offensive, of necessity, would have to begin from bases initially available. These will consist of bases in the United Kingdom, the Cairo–Suez–Aden area, Okinawa, Alaska, and the United States, utilizing the closer as long as tenable, and aircraft carriers, if available from other tasks. If the United Kingdom becomes untenable, bases in Iceland might be required. As soon as possible and in order to permit an intensified and sustained attack, additional bases closer to the USSR should be established. Utilization of bases in the above areas would complete a ring of bases around the USSR and would permit continuing attacks into the heart of the Soviet citadel.

(2) Guided missiles in significant numbers for strategic bombardment will probably not be available by 1957 but when available could become valuable adjuncts to the air offensive, providing their capabilities warrant their relative economic cost.

(3) To achieve maximum effectiveness, the atomic attacks should be launched with optimum force at the earliest possible date after D-Day and should be completed in the minimum practicable time consistent with the availability of bombs, the effectiveness of delivery, and the scope of the target program. It is estimated that U.S. and British forces required would be approximately 5 groups of heavy bombers, 21 groups of medium bombers, and 6 groups of long-range reconnaissance and weather aircraft. These would be assisted by carrier task groups when available from other tasks. . . .

(4) It is estimated that an initial deployment of the above air forces should be as follows:

	D-Day	D + 1
U.S.		
Heavy Bomb. Gp.	4(120)	4
Alaska		
Med. Bomb. Gp.	1(30)	1
Str. Recon. and Wea. Gp.	2/3(24)	2/3
U.K.		
Heavy Bomb. Gp.	1(30)	1
Med. Bomb. Gp.	15(550)*	15*
Str. Recon. Gp.	3(108)†	3
Okinawa		
Med. Bomb. Gp.	2(60)	2
Str. Recon. and Wea. Gp.	2/3(24)	2/3
Cairo–Suez–Aden		
Med. Bomb. Gp.	3(90)	3
Str. Recon. and Wea. Gp.	2/3(24)	2/3

	D-Day	D + 1
Labrador–Iceland–Azores–Bermuda–Guam		
Str. Wea. Gp.	1(36)	1
Summary		
Heavy Bomb. Gp.	5	5
Med. Bomb. Gp.	21*	21*
Str. Recon. and Wea. Gp.	6†	6†

*7 equivalent groups (210 a/c initially) to be provided by the British.

†1 equivalent group (36 a/c initially) to be provided by the British.

(5) An initial air offensive as outlined above would materially reduce the war potential of the USSR, disrupt political and military control centers, interfere with communications, slow down Soviet advances, seriously hamper Soviet ability to replace initial stockpiles, and thereby shorten the war. It might cause the Soviet government to capitulate; but if not, the offensive should be continued from bases progressively advanced with the object of completely destroying the Soviet war potential and capacity to resist.

(6) This course of action is retained.

b. Secure Sea and Air Lines of Communication

(1) Sea Lines of Communication

(a) General

i. Sea lines of communication to Newfoundland, Iceland, the United Kingdom, Africa, South America, the eastern Mediterranean, the Persian Gulf, Western Europe, and within the Pacific Ocean areas will probably be essential for deployment and support of forces overseas, support of the U.S. war economy, and aid to allies.

ii. Preliminary analysis of surface escort requirements, giving due consideration to the capabilities of modern submarines employing long-range torpedoes and the number of Soviet submarines, indicates that escort requirements may be considerably higher than those necessary in World War II. Antisubmarine escorts may be required in all ocean waters. The density of escorts required will depend on the strategy of the Soviet submarine campaign and on the effectiveness of the Allied antisubmarine campaign.

iii. Convoys within range of Allied air bases should be provided with air cover. Escort carriers for air defense of convoys would be necessary when convoys are within range of Soviet air attack and air cover cannot be provided by Allied land-based aircraft.

iv. Hunter–killer groups would be required in the Atlantic and Pacific

Oceans and in the Mediterranean Sea. It is estimated that on D-Day one group would be required in the Atlantic, one in the Pacific, and one in the Mediterranean. Minesweepers, patrol craft, harbor-defense nets, and detection devices would be required at all bases necessary for support of sea lines of communication.

(b) Mediterranean

i. The significance of the Mediterranean Sea LOC will depend in part on Allied strategy in the Near and Middle East. Use of this LOC to support operations in the Near and Middle East would make possible a more rapid buildup of forces and a large reduction in shipping requirements.

ii. Control of the Strait of Gibraltar would make possible use of the western Mediterranean. The central Mediterranean could be used if Sicily and southern Italy were neutralized or denied to the Soviets. Use of the eastern Mediterranean would require neutralization or denial of Crete and retention of the Cairo–Suez–Palestine area. Air and naval bases along the North African coast would also be necessary. Determination of whether or not the Mediterranean Sea LOC should or could be maintained cannot be made until selection of Allied courses of action is completed.

iii. If the Mediterranean Sea LOC cannot be maintained, the necessity for reopening it and the scale and nature of operations required therefor cannot be estimated until an evaluation of the Soviet and Allied strategic positions at the time is made.

(2) Air Lines of Communication

(a) Air LOCs to areas outside the United States must be built up to accommodate the traffic envisaged in deployment and support of overseas forces, airlift of special missions and strategic and critical materials, and overall aid to Allies.

(b) The following air LOCs should be established and maintained:

i. *North Pacific:* U.S.–northwest Canada–Alaska–Aleutians and U.S.–Alaska.

ii. *Central Pacific:* U.S.–Hawaii–Johnston–Kwajalein–Marianas–Okinawa, Marianas–Japan, and Marianas–Philippines.

iii. *South Pacific:* Hawaii–Line Islands–Phoenix Islands–Fiji Islands–New Caledonia–New Zealand and Australia.

iv. *North Atlantic:* U.S.–Newfoundland–Azores–U.K.–Western Europe, U.S.–Labrador–Iceland–U.K.–Western Europe, U.S.–Bermuda–Azores, and Azores–North Africa–Cairo.

v. *South Atlantic:* U.S.–Trinidad–British Guiana–Brazil–Ascension–Liberia–Gold Coast–Nigeria–Khartoum–Cairo (or Aden–Oman area) and possibly Karachi.

vi. *Far East-India:* Philippines–French Indochina–Siam–Burma–Calcutta–New Delhi–Karachi. (Alternate: Philippines–Singapore–Ceylon–Oman.)

(3) This course of action is retained but is reworded as follows: "Secure sea and air lines of communication essential to the accomplishment of the overall strategic concept."

c. Conduct Offensive Operations to Destroy Enemy Naval Forces, Shipping, Naval Bases, and Supporting Facilities

(1) *General.* The North Atlantic and North Pacific form the shortest sea and air approaches to the Western Hemisphere, flank the LOCs to the United Kingdom and Japan, contain the strategic North Atlantic islands and the Aleutians, and must be under control of the Allies. While Soviet naval forces based in the White Sea–Murmansk–Baltic area and in the western Pacific would probably not be of sufficient strength to challenge openly Allied control of the sea, they would be capable of harassing attacks and of serious interference with sea LOCs in limited areas. Unless destroyed or contained, the existence of these forces would require uneconomical diversion of heavy units to convoy duty. Offensive operations against the source of this threat are considered the most effective and least expensive means of obtaining desired results and at the same time of providing a means of counteraction against Soviet air capabilities from these areas and of disrupting Soviet coastal shipping. Allied control of the Mediterranean would be an important contribution to operations in the Near and Middle East and would probably be contested strongly by Soviet air and submarine action from progressively advanced bases. The operations required to control these vital sea areas would be conducted primarily by carrier task forces and submarines, assisted by land-based aviation. . . .

(a) *Barents–Norwegian Sea Area.* Missions in this area would include destruction of the Baltic, Barents, and White Sea naval forces, bases, shipping, [and] port facilities and interdiction of the Baltic–White Sea canal. Such areas as the Murmansk approaches, Naryan-Mar, the White Sea entrance, and Kara Strait, among others, should be mined. The Kiel Canal and the entrances to the Baltic should also be mined, but this task should be accomplished initially by Allied forces in Germany and Scandinavia and thereafter primarily by aircraft based in the United Kingdom. Carriers performing the above primary missions would assist in the air offensive. It is estimated that two carrier task groups—one of which might be British—reinforced by U.S. and British submarines and British fleet air squadrons would be required on D-Day or as soon thereafter as possible.

(b) *Mediterranean Sea*

i. Missions in this area would be destruction of the Black Sea naval forces, shipping, naval bases, and port facilities and mining of the Bosporus. In addition, carrier task forces would interdict Soviet advances in the Near and Middle East and would assist in the air offensive.

ii. The ability of a carrier task force to remain in the Mediterranean, in view of Soviet air capabilities, will depend on its strength, on the extent of the Soviet advances into both Western Europe and the Near and Middle East, and on the amount of Allied land-based air that can be allocated to Near and Middle East and North African bases. It is estimated that three carrier task groups, one of which might be British, probably would be required on D-Day or shortly thereafter, in addition to submarines and fleet air squadrons, probably based in North Africa.

(c) *Western Pacific*. Missions in this area would include destruction of naval bases, shipping, and port facilities. Such areas as the approaches to Vladivostok, Sovetskaya Gavan, Nikolaevsk, Petropavlovsk, Port Arthur, [and] Dairen, among others, should be mined. Naval forces in this area could also assist in the defense of Japan; D-Day requirements probably would be one carrier task group, reinforced by a cruiser task group, submarines, and fleet air squadrons.

(d) *Arabian Sea*. Any requirement for carrier forces in this area in connection with possible operations in the Persian Gulf or for participation in the air offensive must be provided from forces indicated above as being required in the Mediterranean.

(2) This course of action is retained.

d. Expand the Overall Power of the Armed Forces for Later Offensive Operations Against the Soviet Powers

(1) To provide for the contingency that the air offensive is not decisive, the Allies must implement the buildup of strong, mobile, balanced military forces for later major offensive operations. The necessary basis for this buildup must be in existence on D-Day, and the necessary expansion must be set in motion with the outbreak of war. It cannot be postponed until results of the initial air offensive have been determined. A phased mobilization of manpower for the military forces in consonance with their planned employment and consistent with the manpower requirements of war industry should be initiated, coincident with maximum industrial mobilization based upon the requirements for a lengthy war.

(2) The training of forces must be commenced and plans must be made for their transportation to staging areas in or near contemplated theaters of employment in accordance with strategic plans and phased schedules of employment. Equipment and supplies for prolonged operations must be stockpiled both at home and in the overseas staging areas. Ultimate operations may include the clearing of the major Soviet armed forces from Western Europe, and it may be necessary to occupy selected areas of the USSR proper in order to terminate hostilities.

(3) This course of action is retained.

e. Initiate Major Offensive Land Operations Against the USSR as Required

(1) Although initial Allied strategy against the USSR should emphasize the application of heavy atomic and conventional bombing attacks against selected critical targets and a continuation of the air offensive until the capitulation of the Soviets, it is imprudent to assume that complete victory can be won by the air offensive alone. Achievement of our war objectives will undoubtedly require occupation of certain strategic areas by major Allied land forces and may require a major land campaign.

(2) The lessons of history, the vastness of the USSR, and the magnitude of the effort required, both manpower and logistical, all point up the tremendous difficulties involved in major land operations in the USSR. If, however, the initial air offensive is not decisive, the air offensive should be continued, unremitting pressure maintained against the Soviet citadel, and appropriate major offensive land operations initiated as required. These operations would be initiated when required and as conditions permit. They should not be developed on a major scale until the Soviet logistic capabilities have been reduced to a point where the Soviets no longer have the capability of supplying and rapidly reconcentrating their forces in the campaign area. The prerequisite conditions to such operations would be that the bulk of Soviet war industries and communications systems have been destroyed and their oil production reduced to such a level that for all practical purposes their air forces have been grounded and their naval and ground forces have been rendered relatively immobile. Only when the above conditions have obtained is it considered feasible to initiate major offensive land operations. No accurate estimate can be made at this point of the time when such operations could be initiated since they would be dependent upon the timing and degree of success of the air offensive and the capabilities of the Allies to mobilize, equip, transport to the theater of operations, and logistically support the large forces required.

(3) The only suitable major base areas which may be available to the Allies and from which large-scale operations could be launched against the USSR would be the British Isles, Western Europe, and the North African–Near Eastern area.

(4) Avenues of approach into the USSR from the British Isles could be through:

(a) the Arctic Ocean and the Murmansk–Kola peninsula area.
(b) Norway, Sweden, and Finland.
(c) The Baltic Sea.
(d) Western Europe.

(5) The avenue of approach through the Murmansk–Kola peninsula area would not be feasible for large-scale offensive operations because of poor lines

of communication, limited port capacities, weather, and terrain. Logistic considerations would also preclude the employment of large forces in the avenue of approach through Norway, Sweden, and Finland. These two avenues should be used only in connection with feints or secondary attacks.

(6) The avenue of approach through the Baltic would be directly into the USSR. It would require, however, certain preliminary operations, namely, control of the Danish peninsula and northern Germany, at least neutralization of Soviet forces in southern Norway and southern Sweden, or neutrality of Sweden. Utilization of this avenue would also require large amphibious forces. Consequently it is considered that this avenue would be used only in conjunction with the avenue through Western Europe.

(7) The avenue through Western Europe would require a large amphibious expedition to gain a lodgement on the Continent, unless suitable areas thereof were retained by the Allies. It also would have the disadvantage of long routes of advance with the bulk of Soviet forces in opposition until the USSR is reached. On the other hand, it would have the advantage of the best land lines of communication into the USSR. This avenue, in spite of its major disadvantage, would be the best approach. It would probably be advantageous to utilize the sea route through the Baltic in conjunction with this avenue of approach.

(8) From a base area in Western Europe, excluding Spain, the most favorable avenue of approach would be through the north German plain into Poland, the Baltic states, and northern USSR if necessary. This avenue would support all the Allied forces that could be made available for such an operation. Its major advantage and disadvantage are as stated in the preceding paragraph.

(9) The development of the Iberian peninsula as a base area from which to launch major land operations would constitute a serious drain on Allied economic resources. Its use for such a purpose would involve the acceptance of ancillary amphibious operations into western and southern France in order to assure debouchment through the Pyrenees. These operations would then join up in France to proceed along the avenue as outlined in the previous paragraph. It is therefore considered that Spain would not provide a desirable base area from which to launch major land operations.

(10) Avenues of approach from the North African–Near Eastern area could be through:

(a) Southern France.
(b) Italy.
(c) The Balkans.
(d) The Aegean Sea, Turkish straits, and the Black Sea to the Ukraine.
(e) Caucasus and Turkistan.

(11) An approach through southern France, while suitable for large-scale amphibious operations to gain a lodgement on the Continent, would initially present restricted avenues of advance and would entail the longest land routes of advance into the USSR.

(12) Italy does not provide a suitable bridgehead for launching large-scale operations into the Continent. Routes of advance and lines of communication from northern Italy into central Europe are extremely limited and would not support a major operation either tactically or logistically.

(13) Consideration of terrain and logistical factors indicates that the avenue of approach through the Balkans would present major difficulties.

(14) The avenue through the Aegean Sea, Turkish straits, and the Black Sea to the Ukraine would have the disadvantages of a long sea route and the requirement for a large amphibious landing. Lines of communication leading north through the Ukraine would not be especially good for large-scale operations and would require a considerable engineering effort. In addition, certain preliminary operations would be required. Operations to neutralize any Soviet forces in western Turkey [and] to secure Crete, the Athens area, eastern Macedonia, Thrace, and the Turkish straits would be the minimum requirements. This avenue of approach, however, would be the most suitable for launching land operations directly against the heart of the USSR.

(15) Avenues of approach through the Caucasus and Turkistan are not considered feasible. The Caucasus presents some of the most formidable terrain in the world. The lines of communication through the rugged terrain of eastern Turkey and Iran would be extremely vulnerable and could not support a major operation into the USSR. In Turkistan there would be an almost total lack of north–south lines of communication.

(16) A consideration of the major advantages and disadvantages of the base areas and avenues of approach discussed in the preceding paragraphs leads to the following conclusions:

(a) It is most desirable to retain a major base area in Western Europe. If this area could be retained, the principal avenue of approach should be through the north German plain into Poland, the Baltic states, and northern USSR, if necessary.

(b) If a major base area cannot be retained in Western Europe but the British Isles remain tenable, it would be desirable to develop the British Isles as a major base area and to launch attacks therefrom into Western Europe and thence into the USSR.

(c) If a base area in neither Western Europe nor the British Isles can be maintained, then major land operations should be launched from the North African–Near Eastern area, after undertaking preliminary operations to gain control of the Aegean Sea–Turkish straits region through the Black Sea to the Ukraine. Such a course of action, however, presents so many major difficulties that it should be followed only as a last resort as the major effort.

(17) The extent of and the forces required for such major land operations as envisaged above cannot be foreseen clearly at this time. The probable magnitude of such operations would undoubtedly constitute a severe drain on Allied resources and might even prove unsupportable. Further studies of major land operations against the USSR will be undertaken later in this study.

(18) This course of action is retained.

f. Establish Control and Enforce Surrender Terms in the USSR and Satellite Countries.

(1) *Following Early Capitulation*

(a) Early capitulation of the USSR might possibly result from an atomic-bombing campaign of such staggering effectiveness that it has paralyzed the entire nation. In the event this occurs, steps should be taken to receive surrender of Soviet troops, disarm them, and inaugurate some system of control before the country has had time to recover from the shock. In the event of capitulation within the first few months, the Allies would not have the strength in troops nor the available resources to proceed with a full-scale occupation in the conventional manner. Also, Soviet troops would remain in many portions of Europe.

(b) The following methods of control of the USSR and enforcement of surrender terms after an early capitulation are open to consideration:

i. The concentration of available Allied forces in countries around the periphery of the USSR.

ii. The occupation of selected bridgeheads within the USSR by available Allied forces.

iii. The occupation of key points and areas within the USSR by available Allied forces.

iv. Combinations of the above.

(c) Because of the limited Allied forces available at this time, maximum use of all available means for control and enforcement of surrender terms with the USSR would be required. Maximum use of remaining Soviet channels of authority would be obligatory. A concentration of available Allied forces in countries around the periphery of the USSR (*i* above), while taking maximum advantage of the initial location of Allied forces, would place the occupation burden and its attendant problems upon the peripheral countries. It would also present many difficulties in control of the USSR and enforcement of surrender terms. The occupation of selected bridgeheads within the USSR (*ii* above) would relieve peripheral countries of the occupation burden but, except for the bridgehead areas, would present the same difficulties of control within the vast areas of the USSR. The occupation of key points and areas within the USSR (*iii* above) would provide the most certain means of control and enforcement of surrender terms, but the limited availability of Allied forces would require a modification of this course of action if necessary control is to be established and maintained.

(d) Key urban areas selected as bases for projection of control should be of strategic importance because they perform one or more of the following functions: political and administrative center, industrial center, communication center, major seaport or naval base, oil-producing or -refining center. The occupation of a sufficient number of such key centers should permit adequate control over the country.

(e) Since an early capitulation would probably find Soviet forces occupying much of Europe, Allied forces must be prepared to establish temporary control in satellite and certain of the liberated countries. This control, as in the USSR, would have to be skeletonized, with major forces centered principally in the various capitals and certain key seaports and urban areas. The principal mission of these forces would be the establishment of control, enforcement of surrender terms, disarmament of Soviet and satellite forces, and return of disarmed Soviet forces to the USSR.

(f) It is considered that indigenous policy and armed forces in partially over-run countries should be capable of disarming and exercising control over Soviet forces that have surrendered within these countries. If they are unable to do so, and if requested by these countries, additional Allied forces would have to be made available. It is obvious that these occupation forces cannot all be trained units, and many would have to be hastily assembled and transported to the countries of occupation.

(g) It is estimated that the total requirement for Allied occupation forces would be 23 divisions in the USSR proper and 15 divisions in the satellite areas. Air support for these forces should consist of about 5 reinforced tactical air forces totaling approximately 30–35 groups. These requirements would be well within Allied capabilities from D-Day onward.

(h) A combination of courses *ii* and *iii* above—i.e., occupation of selected bridgehead areas within the USSR by available major forces, while occupying selected key areas within the USSR by skeleton forces—is considered the best use of available Allied forces and is selected for further development in the outline plan.

(2) *Following Later Capitulation*

(a) If an early capitulation of the USSR as a result of the initial atomic-bomb attacks has not occurred, preparations for the control of the USSR and her satellites must continue and take into consideration the following conditions:

i. Capitulation as the result of an extension of the initial air offensive and prior to the initiation of a major land operation.

ii. Capitulation or disintegration following the initiation of land operations against the USSR.

(b) In either condition *i* or *ii* above, the problem of establishing control in the USSR or her satellites for the purpose of ensuring compliance with our national war objectives will be less difficult than the problem facing the Allies after an early capitulation. As the war progresses, the Allies will generate increasing numbers of forces which can be made available for control purposes in the event of capitulation. If capitulation occurs at the end of a lengthy air offensive or after a land offensive has been initiated, adequate control forces would be available from those forces engaged in or preparing for those offensives.

(c) This course of action is retained.

g. Initiate or Intensify Psychological, Economic, and Underground Warfare

(1) Psychological, economic, and underground warfare is an essential adjunct to military operations in the accomplishment of national and military aims. The vast improvements in the fields of communications have been an important factor in this development. This type of warfare, if properly employed, can play an important role in overcoming an enemy's will to fight, in harassing his operations, and in sustaining the morale of friendly groups in occupied territories.

(2) Psychological and economic measures directed at our allies and neutral nations can be of comparable importance to those measures directed at our enemies. From the military standpoint such measures—carefully integrated with military policies, plans, and operations—can facilitate the military prosecution of the war.

(3) In general, objectives of this type of warfare should be as follows:

(a) To assist in overcoming an enemy's will to fight.

(b) To sustain the morale of friendly groups in enemy territory.

(c) To improve the morale of friendly countries and the attitude of neutral countries toward the Allies.

(4) This course of action is retained.

h. Provide Aid to Allies

(1) Military aid can be divided into two categories: that provided prior to D-Day and that provided subsequent to D-Day. A matter of significant importance to Allied military planning is the extent to which military aid can be furnished to the Atlantic Pact nations, and especially the Western Union nations, prior to D-Day. Prewar military aid should be furnished on the largest possible scale consistent with the maintenance of sound economics and a satisfactory state of U.S. and British military preparedness. Aid should also be provided to other countries, including Sweden, the Arab League, Turkey, Greece, Latin America, and China. Aid furnished should be based on a long-range program in accordance with the overall strategic concept and plan of operations.

(2) Military aid subsequent to D-Day will constitute a substantial demand on industry at a time when industry will be strained to the utmost to meet mobilization requirements. The requirement for aid subsequent to D-Day will depend in large measure on the amount provided prior to D-Day.

(3) This course of action is retained but is reworded to read: "Provide essential aid to our allies in support of efforts contributing directly to the overall strategic concept."

VI. SELECTION OF ALLIED COURSES OF ACTION

1. Basic Undertakings

a. Examination and analysis of those courses of action retained for further consideration reveal that certain of them require no further analysis or comparison and are so necessary to a successful prosecution of the war as to be basic undertakings and thus become a first charge against our resources. These are as follows:

(1) Secure the Western Hemisphere.
(2) Conduct an air offensive against the Soviet powers.
(3) Hold the United Kingdom.
(4) Expand the overall power of the armed forces for later offensive operations against the Soviet powers.
(5) Conduct offensive operations to destroy enemy naval forces, shipping, naval bases, and supporting facilities.
(6) Secure sea and air lines of communication essential to the accomplishment of the overall strategic concept.
(7) Provide essential aid to our allies in support of efforts contributing directly to the overall strategic concept.

b. It is also apparent from the analyses of the several alternatives under the course of action "Hold maximum areas in Western Europe" that this course of action should be considered essential to the attainment of our war objectives and therefore should be accepted as a basic undertaking. The selection of the areas to be held is made in paragraph 4 below.

2. Other General Courses of Action

In addition to the foregoing there are certain other broad courses of action which, although their details cannot be determined at this time, will be necessary to any strategic concept for successful prosecution of the war leading to a peace which would be in consonance with our national aims and objectives. In this category are the following courses of action which are therefore selected:

a. Initiate or intensify psychological, economic, and underground warfare.
b. Initiate major offensive land operations against the USSR as required.
c. Establish control and enforce surrender terms in the USSR and satellite countries. . . .

. . . There are two clearly dominant issues which must be faced by the Allies, i.e., the holding of maximum areas in Western Europe and access to the oil-bearing areas of the Near and Middle East.

4. Western Europe

a. Suitability of Courses of Action

(1) A comparison of the remaining courses of action in Western Europe indicates that the successful defense of the Rhine–Alps–Piave line will achieve the greatest results since it would retain in Allied hands the bulk of the manpower and industrial potential of Western Europe and would contribute greatly to the defense of the United Kingdom. The defense of the Rhine–French–Italian border line will achieve the next greatest results, differing from the former in that it gives up all of Italy. The defense of Sicily would assume increasing importance if this course of action were adopted. Of the two remaining courses of action—that is, holding the Pyrenees line and the Apennines line—it is apparent that combining them would be the next most suitable course of action. A comparison of the latter two courses of action indicates the following factors: although neither of the two areas, Iberia and the Italian peninsula, is particularly suitable or feasible as a bridgehead for subsequent major operations into the Continent, Iberia would be of greater value because of its size, its availability as an area to which Allied forces could retreat if withdrawal from Rhine positions were forced, its lesser vulnerability, and because its retention would permit the use of shorter and more easily defended sea lines of communication; the Italian peninsula would be more suitable for air operations against the Soviets because of its strategic location, but its relative advantage here would be somewhat canceled out by its much greater vulnerability; although both Iberia and the Italian peninsula have strategic significance because of their control over the western and central Mediterranean, respectively, the control over the western Mediterranean and the Atlantic approaches thereto would be more important to the Allies than control of the central Mediterranean. From the above factors it is concluded that holding the Pyrenees line would be more suitable than holding the Apennines line.

(2) Retention of the Mediterranean islands of Sicily, Malta, Cyprus, and Crete would contribute to the security of the Cairo–Suez area and North Africa and to the control of the eastern and central Mediterranean. In the event Spain were overrun, however, the usefulness of Sicily in this connection would be measurably decreased and the difficulty of its retention increased. It is apparent, therefore, that the suitability of holding Sicily is largely dependent upon the holding of Spain. The same is not entirely true of the islands of Malta, Crete, and Cyprus, the holding of which should therefore be treated as a separate possible course of action.

(3) In summary, from the standpoint of suitability only, courses of action in Western Continental Europe would be of relative value to the Allies in the following order:

a) Hold the Rhine–Alps–Piave line.

b) Hold the Rhine–French–Italian border line.

c) Hold the Pyrenees and Apennines lines.

d) Hold the Pyrenees line and Sicily.

e) Hold the Pyrenees line.

f) Hold the Apennines line.

g) Hold the Mediterranean islands of Malta, Crete, and Cyprus.

b. Feasibility of Courses of Action

(1) Examination of the above courses of action from the standpoint of their feasibility indicates that implementation of either of the first two courses of action would be dependent upon an adequate program of U.S. military aid. Forces required for defense of the Rhine–Alps–Piave line for the first six months of combat are estimated at 76 United States equivalent divisions and 4,500 combat aircraft. Estimated Allied capabilities in the absence of a United States military-aid program would be approximately 35 divisions of varying degrees of combat efficiency by $D+30$ days and 2,750 combat aircraft. Assuming that the 35 available divisions were made United States equivalent, a deficit would still remain which by $D+30$ days would be on the order of 41 United States equivalent divisions and 1,750 combat aircraft. With a United States military-aid program on the necessary scale, Allied ground-force capabilities are estimated at 76 divisions, which could hold this line for approximately $D+6$ months.

(2) Defense of the Rhine–French–Italian border line is estimated to require 70 United States equivalent divisions and 4,400 combat aircraft, on the same basis indicated above. However, since it would probably be unrealistic to assume that any Italian forces would be available for the defense of the French–Italian border, the deficit for this course of action would be 44 United States equivalent divisions and 1,850 combat aircraft, assuming that the available 26 divisions were also made United States equivalent. From the standpoint of terrain and forces required, the defense of the French–Italian border line would be less difficult than defense of Italy along the Alps–Piave line. On the other hand, the probable unavailability of any Italian forces for defense of the French–Italian border would actually create a greater overall deficit of forces required for defense of the entire Rhine–French–Italian border line than for defense of the Rhine–Alps–Piave line, i.e., 3 divisions and 100 combat aircraft plus 2 divisions and 300 aircraft required if Sicily were to be held.

(3) From the above calculations it is concluded that from the overall standpoint it would be slightly more difficult to generate the additional forces required for defense of the Rhine–French–Italian border line than for the

Rhine–Alps–Piave line; consequently, it would be comparatively more feasible to defend the latter.

(4) An analysis of the requirements for the simultaneous defense of both the Pyrenees line and the Apennines indicates that the Spanish would have a deficit of 12 United States equivalent divisions and 450 combat aircraft for the Pyrenees and the Italians a deficit of 11 United States equivalent divisions and 300 combat aircraft for the Apennines; these deficits total 23 divisions and 750 combat aircraft, assuming that the available divisions were also made United States equivalent. It is therefore apparent that these lines could be defended together only by the introduction of Allied forces in the above totals into Spain and Italy unless a prior program of military aid is furnished to those countries in order to reduce Allied requirements. It is obvious that the retention of these two lines would be considerably more feasible than those in the first two courses of action.

(5) In the event the Apennines cannot be held in conjunction with the retention of Spain, holding the Pyrenees and Sicily would make possible a large measure of control over the western and central Mediterranean and could be accomplished with considerably less force. Holding Sicily would permit the exercise of some control over the central Mediterranean although not to the degree obtained by holding the Apennines. Defense forces of two United States or British divisions and 300 combat aircraft would be required in additon to the Italian forces which could be withdrawn and would have to be deployed there probably not later than $D+3$ months. The requirements of forces and their timing appear to be feasible.

(6) The additional Allied forces required for the defense of Iberia would not have to be deployed in position as rapidly as would be required for defense of the Apennines. Soviet forces would be unable to assault the Pyrenees earlier than $D+3$ months, whereas Soviet and satellite forces might be able to assault the Apennines line as early as $D+1$ month. Logistic problems involved in defense of the Apennines would render that course of action infeasible in event the western Mediterranean LOC were closed by loss of the Iberian peninsula. Therefore it can be concluded that not only would it be more feasible to defend the Pyrenees line than the Apennines line, but the defense of the latter would be infeasible after loss of the Iberian peninsula.

(7) Requirements for defense of Malta, Crete, and Cyprus, in addition to Greek forces that could be withdrawn to Crete, would be less than 1 United States or British division and 1 fighter group supported by land-based combat aircraft in the Cairo–Suez area and carrier-based aircraft. It is unlikely that Soviet forces could assault the islands until after $D+3$ months. Considering these factors, therefore, it is concluded that defense of the above islands would be the most feasible of all Western Europe courses of action considered.

(8) In summary, it appears that from the standpoint of relative feasibility the feasible courses of action in Western Europe should be arranged in the following order:

(a) Hold the Mediterranean islands of Malta, Crete, and Cyprus.
(b) Hold the Pyrenees line.
(c) Hold the Pyrenees line and Sicily.
(d) Hold the Pyrenees and Apennines lines.
(e) Hold the Rhine–Alps–Piave line.
(f) Hold the Rhine–French–Italian border line.

c. Acceptability of Courses of Action.

(1) The above courses should next be considered from the standpoint of their acceptability, i.e., the possibility of success or failure, the consequences of failure, and the expected gains as compared to the requirements in forces. The successful defense of the Rhine–Alps–Piave line while achieving maximum results would require the generation of the largest numbers of Allied forces. These forces could only be generated by an adequate program of United States military aid over a period of years. Such a program, if carried out, would permit the requirements of forces for the initial defense of this line—estimated at 76 divisions and 4,500 combat aircraft—to be realized. Failure to hold this line would not be disastrous to the Allies, since if at any time it became apparent that this line could not be held, a planned withdrawal could be effected to one or more of the alternate positions discussed herein. Such a withdrawal would have a reasonable chance of extricating the bulk of the Allied forces to alternative positions. Therefore it is considered that, balancing the chances of success and the results to be achieved from such success against the possibility of failure, this course of action would be most desirable and would be acceptable providing the above-mentioned United States military-aid program could be implemented.

(2) The defense of the Rhine–French–Italian border line accepts approximately the same degree of risk as the defense of the Rhine–Alps–Piave line. This is because the principal threat will likewise be to the northern portion of the line, that lying along the Rhine, and the greatest problem will be that of reenforcing this line during the first few weeks sufficiently to block the probably increasing Soviet capabilities. However, the Allied capability of executing a planned withdrawal from this line, if forced by the Soviets, would be slightly greater than in the previous course of action, chiefly because any withdrawal from the French–Italian border would be easier than from the Alps–Piave line. It is concluded that the consequences in case of failure in this course of action would not be quite as serious as in the preceding case. On the other hand, defense of the Rhine–French–Italian border line would not achieve nearly the gains of the preceding course of action although the cost would be approximately the same. Therefore, weighing the comparative possibility of success and failure, the consequences of failure, and the objectives to be gained, this course of action is considered to be less acceptable than the preceding course of

action. (The same provisions concerning military aid apply in this course of action.)

(3) The combined course of action of holding both the Pyrenees and the Apennines is the most suitable alternative to holding the Rhine–Alps–Piave line or the Rhine–French–Italian border line. Forces required, in addition to Spanish and Italian forces, are estimated to be 23 divisions and 750 aircraft. Total forces required are estimated as 54 United States equivalent divisions and 1,300 combat aircraft to hold indefinitely, as compared to 76 United States equivalent divisions and 4,500 aircraft required to hold the Rhine–Alps–Piave line for six months.

(4) The results to be gained are considerably less than could be attained by holding the Rhine River line in that France and Benelux and, accordingly, a major bridgehead on the Continent are abandoned and the threat to the United Kingdom greatly increased. The major advantages of this course of action are that, if successful, it would stabilize the Soviet advance, assure retention of the Mediterranean Sea LOC, and therefore contribute in large measure to the feasibility and success of operations in the vital Near and Middle East area.

(5) If the Pyrenees–Apennines line is the initial defense line, part of the Allied forces required in Spain would have to be deployed by $D + 3$ and the major part of the forces required in Italy by $D + 1$. The latter would be extremely difficult of accomplishment, unless United States and British forces required could be greatly reduced by a United States military-aid program or deployment of United States or British forces to Italy commenced prior to D-Day.

(6) If the Pyrenees–Apennines line is defended as a result of planned withdrawal from the general line of the Rhine River, the chances of success would depend on the length of delay possible along the latter line and the amount of Allied forces that could be withdrawn to the Pyrenees–Apennines line. It is believed that this course of action should be acceptable to the Allies as an alternative course.

(7) As previously stated, holding the Pyrenees line and Sicily would contribute to the control of the western and central Mediterranean and could be achieved with relatively smaller forces. This course of action would be acceptable to the Allies as an alternate course of action.

(8) The holding of the Pyrenees line alone would present no great risk to the Allies; its chances of success are excellent and it would make secure the best major area to which large Allied forces could withdraw without disastrous loss of men and equipment. Since the additional forces required for this course of action could probably be furnished from those forces withdrawing from more easterly positions, the gains of this course appear to be commensurate with the expected costs. Therefore it is believed that this course of action could be acceptable to the Allies as an alternative course of action in the event that more easterly lines in Western Europe become untenable.

(9) The course of action to hold the Mediterranean islands of Malta, Crete, and Cyprus would have a high probability of success. Failure to hold these

islands would not be disastrous to the Allied position because the Allies would retain a considerable capability of neutralizing them. Gains to be expected as compared to the small requirements in forces would appear to make this course of action acceptable to the Allies in the event that more advanced positions could not be held.

(10) Summarizing, it is concluded that from the standpoint of acceptability alone the acceptable courses of action in Western Europe should be arranged in the following order:

(a) Hold the Rhine–Alps–Piave line.*
(b) Hold the Rhine–French–Italian border line.*
(c) Hold the Pyrenees and Apennines line.†
(d) Hold the Pyrenees line and Sicily.
(e) Hold the Pyrenees.
(f) Hold the Mediterranean islands of Malta, Crete, and Cyprus.

(11) A further scrutiny of the courses of action in Western Europe reveals a possible alternative which should be given additional consideration; this course would be to hold the Pyrenees and a defensive position farther south in Italy. The only position farther south in Italy which could be considered would be the line approximately thirty-five miles northwest of the line Naples–Foggia. This line, approximately eighty miles in length across the narrowest part of the Italian peninsula, is mountainous, rugged, and ideally suited for defense. A successful defense of this line would permit a degree of control over the central Mediterranean somewhat less than by holding the Apennines. Defense of this line would probably require a minimum of 14 United States equivalent divisions and 400 combat aircraft. The probable inability of the Italians, withdrawing down the peninsula, to get all of their forces intact on this line would require the augmentation by considerable additional forces, probably on the order of 7–8 United States equivalent divisions and 300–400 aircraft. These forces would have to be deployed in position probably not later than $D + 2$ months. It is doubtful that such a deployment would be feasible.

(12) Considering the forces required in addition to those required for holding the Pyrenees and the gains to be expected, it is considered that this course of action would not be acceptable to the Allies.

d. Selected Course of Action

(1) In summary, a consideration of all the factors of suitability, feasibility, and acceptability indicates that Allied courses of action in Western Europe should be arranged in the order of priority indicated below. It should be noted that

---

* Providing the previously mentioned United States military-aid program could be implemented in full.

† Providing a substantial United States military-aid program could be implemented.

each course of action listed after the first would be an alternative to each preceding course in case of failure of the preceding course.

(a) Hold the Rhine–Alps–Piave line.
(b) Hold the Rhine–French–Italian border line.
(c) Hold the Pyrenees–Apennines line.
(d) Hold the Pyrenees line and Sicily.
(e) Hold the Pyrenees line.
(f) Hold the Mediterranean islands of Malta, Crete, and Cyprus.

(2) The implementation of either of the first two courses of action would depend upon the adequate program of United States military aid previously indicated. Based on the assumption that such a program has a reasonable possibility of being carried out, the course of action listed in subparagraph (1) (a) above—i.e., "Hold the Rhine–Alps–Piave line"—is selected as the course of action.

5. Near and Middle East

a. Since it appears at this time the Allies will require access to the oil areas in the Near and Middle East beginning with D-Day, it is readily apparent that the holding or very early retaking of some of the Near and Middle East oil will be essential and may even become a basic undertaking.

b. It is reasonable to consider that between now and 1957 certain measures could be instituted to assure the presence of Allied forces in or close to the oil-bearing areas on D-Day which, together with air interdiction of Soviet LOCs leading to them, would be sufficient to hold those areas against initial Soviet attacks.

c. It is obvious, therefore, that the most desirable course of action would be to hold the oil-bearing areas since it would obviate the necessity for their recapture and the 3⅓ divisions, 4 fighter groups, and 1 light-bomber group required would be considerably less than would be required to retake them either immediately or subsequently. Immediate retaking of the oil areas as far north as the Iranian areas at the head of the Gulf would require a total of approximately 5 divisions, 5 fighter groups, and 1 light-bomber group. Additional operations to retake the Kirkuk–Mosul areas would undoubtedly require increased forces. The greater the delay in retaking the oil areas, the more time would be available to the Soviets for consolidation of their positions, and consequently subsequent retaking would be even more costly to the Allies.

d. Since the forces for holding, as outlined above, would be sufficient only to protect the oil areas from Soviet airborne attacks and overland advances through Iran, it would be necessary to provide additional forces to protect their flank and rear from the Soviet threat through Turkey which may be developing soon after D + 5 months. This could best be accomplished by holding southeastern Turkey. It is apparent that holding the oil areas and southeastern Turkey would greatly reduce the threat to the Cairo–Suez area and the forces required therein for its retention.

e. Comparing the forces required for holding either the Cairo–Suez area (5 divisions, 4 fighter groups, and 1 light-bomber group by D + 7) or the Iskenderun pocket–Jordan rift line (7 divisions, 6 fighter groups, 1 light-bomber group, and 1 tactical reconnaissance group by D + 7) reveals that holding the Cairo–Suez area would be more feasible but the gains would be considerably less.

f. On the other hand, the combination of holding the oil areas and southeastern Turkey would require a total of 7⅓ divisions, 9 fighter groups, 2 light-bomber groups, and 1 tactical reconnaissance group by D + 6 months. Therefore, considering that this latter course would achieve the threefold objective of holding the oil areas and a portion of Turkey and would secure the Cairo–Suez area with only a moderately greater expenditure of forces, that course would be the most acceptable in the Near and Middle east.

g. The above requirements, however, will compete with those required for defense of maximum areas in Western Europe. Also, in both areas the requirements develop immediately upon the outbreak of war. If the implementation of the national petroleum program has not met the early deficiencies, the retaking of the Middle East oil cannot be deferred. Operations to assure access to the oil must commence on D-Day or immediately thereafter. Since the difference between the forces required for retention of Cairo–Suez and those for retention of the oil areas would be relatively small (2⅓ divisions, 5 fighter groups, 1 light-bomber group, and 1 tactical reconnaissance group), this difference would be all that would accrue to Western Europe by virtue of deferment of access to the oil areas.

h. A consideration of the above factors leads to the conclusion that forces should be allocated for the retention of the oil-bearing areas and the holding of southeastern Turkey. This conclusion is arrived at with a clear understanding that this course of action would reduce the forces available for other areas.

i. The remaining course of action in the Middle East ("Hold maximum areas of the Middle East," etc.) requires no further consideration beyond the previous discussion, since Allied forces other than indigenous will not be specifically provided therefor.

j. The following courses of action are, therefore, selected in the Near and Middle East:

(1) Hold the area: southeastern Turkey–Tigris Valley–Persian Gulf.
(2) Hold maximum areas of the Middle East consistent with indigenous capabilities, supported by other Allied courses of action.

6. Northern Europe

a. Although the advantages of Allied retention of Norway and Sweden would be significant, such retention would not be vital to Allied prosecution of the war. It is evident that it would require a large-scale United States aid program to build up the armed forces of those countries, particularly Norway, to give reasonable assurance of their retention. Such an aid program would be either in addition to that already envisaged or would have to be compensated by a reduction in military aid afforded other countries, notably those of the Western Union, Italy, and the Near and Middle East. The provision of the required aid would be justified only in the event it develops that there is a reasonable assurance that Sweden would join with Norway and Denmark in a concerted defense of Scandinavia in the event the Soviets elect to exercise their capabilities against any of the three Scandinavian countries.

b. The holding of maximum areas in Western Europe, with its greater military potential, would achieve far greater results than retention of Norway and Sweden. The retention of at least a part of the oil-bearing areas of the Near and Middle East is essential. Both should have a higher priority than Norway and Sweden.

c. Although it is considered unacceptable to divert sufficient means to ensure defense of Norway and Sweden, unless the latter would join with Norway and Denmark in a concerted defense of Scandinavia, the advantages of delaying Soviet advances in this area warrant token military aid to encourage their resistance against Soviet political and military advances.

d. Based upon the above considerations, the course of action "Hold Norway and Sweden" is rejected.

7. North Atlantic Approaches

a. The value of Iceland to the Allies, both offensively and defensively, is sufficient to warrant its occupation as soon as possible. The forces required—i.e., ⅓ division and 1 fighter group—are sufficiently small in proportion to the results to be gained that such employment of available forces is justified. If Iceland, however, were to be seized by the Soviets first, which is a possibility, its immediate recapture by an amphibious operation involving 1 division would be necessary to ensure its use as an air and naval base in support of the basic undertakings.

b. A consideration of the value of the Azores to the Allies and the small forces required for their defense—1 battalion and 1 fighter squadron—justify early action to secure it. The following course of action is therefore selected: "Secure Iceland and the Azores."

8. Far East

a. Although Allied objectives in the Far East require some military action to block Soviet expansion, reduce their offensive capabilities, and to ensure the postwar position of the Allies in that area, this action must be kept to an absolute minimum in light of the requirements for major Allied efforts in the European and Near Eastern theaters. The estimate of United States forces required for the defense of Japan and Okinawa would total 2⅓ divisions and 5 fighter groups if adequate Japanese forces were to be provided. These forces are small in relation to the gains that can be expected.

b. The retention of maximum areas in Southeast Asia would be a responsibility of the non-Communist indigenous forces (except in Malaya), with air and naval support by Allied forces in the Far East from bases outside these areas.

c. The following courses of action in the Far East are therefore selected:

(1) Hold Japan, less Hokkaido.
(2) Hold Okinawa.
(3) Hold maximum areas of Southeast Asia consistent with non-Communist capabilities supported by other Allied courses of action.

9. Consolidation of Certain Selected Courses of Action

a. A further examination of the two selected courses of action pertaining to the holding of maximum areas of the Middle East and of Southeast Asia indicates that, because of their contiguity as to area and the similarity of treatment accorded them, those two courses of action may be advantageously combined into one. Therefore the following course of action is substituted: "Hold maximum areas of the Middle East and Southeast Asia consistent with indigenous capabilities supported by other Allied courses of action."

b. In addition, it appears that the two courses of action pertaining to the security of Iceland and the Azores and of Okinawa—together with those courses which will be developed subsequently involving the securing of other overseas base areas required behind or adjacent to the main defensive areas as offensive or supporting bases, or as necessary to the security of sea and air lines of communications—can be conveniently grouped into a single course of action. Accordingly, the following combined course of action is substituted and added to the list of basic undertakings already selected: "Secure overseas bases essential to the accomplishment of the overall strategic concept."

10. Summary of Selected Courses of Action

Each of the selected courses of action should contribute to or be required by the national objectives, both for peace and war. Certain of the selected courses of action—namely, the "Basic Undertakings" . . . and "Other General Courses of Action" . . .—are of such a nature as to be essential to the maintenance of an adequate military posture to assure the successful prosecution of the war. These, together with the balance of the selected courses of action, are considered to be in furtherance of and in consonance with the ultimate fulfillment of the Allied objectives and would therefore serve to generate the initial tasks of which the Allied "concept of operations" should consist. Not listed in priority, these selected courses of action are:

a. Secure the Western Hemisphere.
b. Conduct an air offensive against the Soviet powers.
c. Conduct offensive operations to destroy enemy naval forces, shipping, naval bases, and supporting facilities.
d. Hold the United Kingdom.
e. Hold the Rhine–Alps–Piave line.
f. Hold the area: southeastern Turkey–Tigris Valley–Persian Gulf.
g. Hold maximum areas of the Middle East and Southeast Asia consistent with indigenous capabilities supported by other Allied courses of action.
h. Hold Japan, less Hokkaido.
i. Secure sea and air lines of communication essential to the accomplishment of the overall strategic concept.
j. Secure overseas bases essential to the accomplishment of the overall strategic concept.
k. Expand the overall power of the armed forces for later offensive operations against the Soviet powers.
l. Provide essential aid to our allies in support of efforts contributing directly to the overall strategic concept.
m. Initiate or intensify psychological, economic, and underground warfare.
n. Initiate major offensive land operations against the USSR as required.
o. Establish control and enforce surrender terms in the USSR and satellite countries.

VOLUME 3

THE STRATEGIC COUNTER-OFFENSIVE AND THE DEFEAT AND OCCUPATION OF THE USSR.

CONTENTS

Phase I. Development of tasks and force requirements
General / 186
Relative importance of courses of action / 186
Secure the Western Hemisphere / 186
Conduct an air offensive against the Soviet powers / 194
Conduct offensive operations to destroy enemy naval forces, shipping, naval bases, and supporting facilities / 206
Hold the United Kingdom / 207
Hold the Rhine–Alps–Piave Line / 214
Hold the area southeastern Turkey–Tigris Valley–Persian Gulf / 218
Hold maximum areas of the Middle East and southeast Asia consistent with indigenous capabilities supported by other allied courses of action / 221
Hold Japan less Hokkaido / 224
Secure sea and air lines of communications essential to the accomplishment of the overall strategic concept / 225
Secure overseas bases essential to the accomplishment of the overall strategic concept
Immediately after D-Day provide forces by air and sea transport to occupy or recapture Iceland and the Azores and establish necessary air and naval bases thereon / 229
Establish or expand and defend allied bases as required in NW Africa and North Africa / 231
Ensure the availability of suitable bases required in the Cairo–Suez–Aden area prior to D-Day / 236
Have forces in being on D-Day in Okinawa for the security of that island / 238
Provide necessary minimum protection for other overseas bases essential to the maintenance of sea and air lines of communications / 238
Expand the overall power of the armed forces for later operations against the Soviet powers / 240

Phase II / 240

Phase III
Provide essential aid to our allies in support of efforts contributing directly to the overall strategic concept / 241
Initiate or intensify psychological, economic, and underground warfare / 242
Establish control and enforce surrender terms in the USSR and satellite countries / 242

(PHASE I) DEVELOPMENT OF TASKS AND FORCE REQUIREMENTS

1. General

The purpose of this [section] is to develop further the courses of action selected in the strategic estimate. . . .

For planning purposes only, Phase I is considered as covering the period from D-Day to D + 6 months. Although the end of Phase I may occur either earlier or later, the adoption of a different period for planning purposes would not affect the requirements for D-Day forces which are developed herein.

2. Relative Importance of Courses of Action

There is no element of priority indicated in the order of listing of courses of action. It is considered that in a plan of this scope and magnitude no 1-2-3 order of priority can be stated, since many courses of action are of equal importance in different spheres of action and/or at different times chronologically. A general measure of the importance of each course of action will be found in the analysis in each case, by the manner it is weighed against enemy capabilities, and in some cases through the expression of its effect on or relationship to other courses of action. While these courses are, in general, so interrelated that the accomplishment of any one is dependent on or greatly influenced by the accomplishment of others, it is considered that the holding of maximum areas in Western Europe and the holding of the United Kingdom are essential to the attainment of our national war objectives.

3. Secure the Western Hemisphere

a. Analysis

The bulk of the war-making capacity of the Western Hemisphere lies within the borders of the United States. The vital, critical, and most important installations of the United States . . . are highly concentrated and hence extremely vulnerable to successful attack by air or sabotage. Their location develops the most important areas of the United States and indicates the areas for which defenses must be considered. These areas contain the majority of our government and control facilities, industrial and population centers, major ports, communications systems, and most of our atomic-energy installations. Destruction or neutralization of certain vital installations could seriously handicap the abil-

:y of the United States to mobilize promptly for maximum war effort and delay
r weaken the initial offensive and defensive measures required. While a de-
ree of passive defense may be achieved by future dispersion and underground
onstruction, no great change in the relative concentration of industry in these
ıreas is expected by 1957.

Initial enemy capabilities against the Western Hemisphere in 1957 included
ırganized sabotage, air attacks against the most important areas with atomic
ınd conventional weapons, limited guided-missile attacks from surface or sub-
surface vessels, limited "commando"-type attacks against installations ad-
acent to the coasts, submarine and mining attacks against shipping, and
ıossible clandestine cargo-ship-borne atomic attacks against important ports
ınd the Panama Canal. Soviet seizure or neutralization of bases in Alaska or in
he North Atlantic would greatly increase the threat to vital areas of the Western Hemisphere and limit Allied defensive and offensive capabilities.

Full and complete protection against these enemy capabilities would be
ırohibitive. A reduction in these capabilities and a consequent reduction in
defensive measures required could be effected by a strong Allied counter-air-of-
`ensive with atomic and conventional weapons against Soviet facilities for the
assembly and delivery of weapons of mass destruction. However, reasonable
objectives to provide an appropriate measure of defense would still require:

(1) An adequate early-warning and control network to cover the most important
   areas and approaches thereto against air attack.*

Editor's Note: When Dropshot was written in 1949, U.S. air defenses were
ın a lamentable state and certainly did not compare with those of England
and Germany during World War II. In a letter to W. Stuart Symington, the
U.S. Secretary of the Air Force, on 11 April 1950, Major General S. E. Anderson, USAF director of plans and operations, stated that the USAF could *not*
guarantee the defense of the continental United States. The quantitative
deficiency in aircraft was estimated at 12⅓ fighter groups, 81 basic radars,
and 4 control centers. The qualitative deficit was much greater, since only 2
of the 10 fighter groups available had the ability to fly in all weathers. Moreover the 28 radars and 7 control centers already deployed were poorly located and inadequately manned, and the manpower available was only
partially trained. Under the circumstances Soviet one-way suicide attacks—
for the range of bombers then existing made it impossible for the Red air
force to make round-trip attacks—were almost bound to have succeeded.
However, in 1950 the Russians did not have an air-portable atomic weapon,
or at least they did not have air-portable weapons in quantity. On the other
hand, it is possible to state that they would at least have tried to atom-bomb
New York, Chicago, San Francisco, Seattle, or other such targets, if only for
political warfare objectives. Fatefully Dewline—the radar, computer, and
communications network intended to provide tactical warning of impending
penetrations of the North American air space from Russia—did not become
operational until 1957, the year the projected war was supposed to break

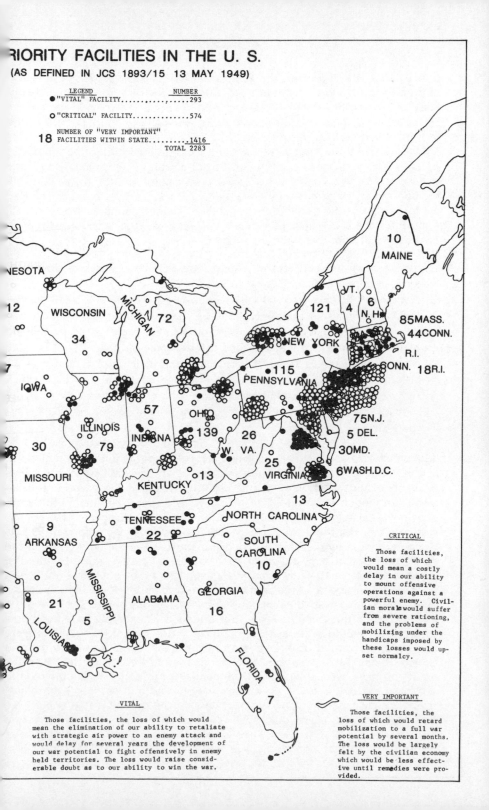

out. By that time, however, the Russian "Bear" Tu-95 very-long-range turboprop was in service. It could fly 7,800 miles with a 25,000-pound bombload and, given the state of Dewline in 1957, could have made dangerous penetrations of American air space. Moreover, in 1956 the Soviets had the four-jet Bison coming into service. This aircraft had a range of 6,050 miles (7,000 miles with in-flight refueling) and an ordnance load of about 20,000 pounds. The main hopeful factor in Soviet strategic air capability was this question: At that time were the Soviet crews good enough to get through the sort of very determined defense the USAF was likely to put up? The Red air force had no long-range air capability of significance in World War II, and unlike the USAF and the Royal Air Force, no large reservoir of trained crews or heavy-bomber doctrine existed.

(2) Sufficient all-weather fighters disposed for defense of the most important areas to impose a distinct threat to an attacking force.
(3) Antiaircraft defense forces disposed primarily for defense of vital installations. Antiaircraft defense forces must be composed mainly of local nonmilitary personnel, assisted by the necessary cadres, and must be trained and used as both antiaircraft and ground-defense forces.
(4) Static defense forces located to provide instant defense of certain vital installations against strongly organized sabotage efforts or "suicide" attack by airborne or commando-type landing forces,* together with a highly mobile reserve centrally located to provide prompt reinforcement of minimum static defense forces.

*Editor's Note: The planners' alarms concerning parachute and commando troops landing in the United States was not misplaced, although it was probably exaggerated. In 1949 and 1957 the Russians did have large paratroop formations in being—nine divisions of about 7,500 men each were known to exist in Eastern Europe. Moreover, the Russians had a large marine force. But the limiting factor where paratroops were concerned was troop-carrying aircraft. All their troop transports were medium-range of the DC-3 and DC-4 variety, and while they had an estimated twelve hundred of these in service in 1949 their range was such that they could not engage in operations outside a range of twelve hundred miles from their airfields. They could have invaded Alaska and in an emergency could have found the means to drop three and possibly four brigades. They might have been able to drop on Seattle and cause great havoc. But if such expeditions were launched, they could only have been of nuisance value, assuming that the United States Army was available for immediate contest. The Russians could not have been resupplied, their casualties in both aircraft and men to and from the target would have been very heavy (and perhaps even disastrously heavy), and ultimately the survivors on the ground would either have been wiped out or they would have been forced to surrender—for the Red air force would probably not have been able to resupply the drop zones. Supply would have been the duty of the Red navy, and the Red navy, given the strength of the United States Navy at that time, would have been wiped off the face of the sea. Britain was the most vulnerable point for airborne landings. Submarines could have landed small parties of commandos along the eastern seaboard of the U.S., but again, while causing havoc locally, at best they could have had only a nuisance value—except, possibly, in the Washington area. What would have happened had a hundred or two well-trained and determined commandos got into the Pentagon or the White House? And what was there to stop them?

(5) Naval surface and air forces to extend and reinforce the early-warning net and to provide protection for coastwise and intercoastal shipping and for major ports and naval bases.
(6) A civil-defense organization to provide optimum protection against disaster, panic, and sabotage and to furnish air-warning service. The civil-defense organization, together with other existing organizations (Department of Justice, Federal Bureau of Investigation, Secret Service, state and local police, Immigration Service), must be organized and prepared to relieve the armed forces of all primary responsibility in these defense fields.

As the threat of Soviet A-bomb attack increases, heavy pressure on the Department of Defense for maximum protection against air attack of all large populated areas may be expected, regardless of their military importance. Complete protection is not practicable, and attempts to provide it could consume an undue proportion of our available resources without commensurate increase in the degree of protection afforded. In order not to weaken dangerously our offensive capabilities by maintaining a vast defensive organization, a carefully calculated measure of defense should be provided for the most important areas, and except for incidental protection afforded by this defense, a calculated risk must be accepted for other less important areas and installations. Dispersion or duplication of facilities in many cases would be cheaper than provision of complete protection. SUFFICIENT DISPERSION OR DUPLICATION OF VITAL INSTALLATIONS TO ENSURE THAT AN UNACCEPTABLE LOSS IS NOT OCCASIONED BY THE DESTRUCTION OF ANY ONE INSTALLATION MUST BE ACCOMPLISHED BEFORE THE SOVIETS HAVE THE ESTIMATED CAPABILITY OF SUCCESSFUL ATTACK AGAINST THE CONTINENTAL UNITED STATES WITH ATOMIC WEAPONS.

Calculation of the fighter and AA defense for the continental United States requires a consideration of the degree of protection to be obtained, together with an estimate of the intensity and duration of the attack. Similarly the degree of protection that may be expected from a given allocation of fighters and AAA [Anti-Aircraft Artillery] to the air-defense mission will depend on the duration and intensity of the attack. Experience during World War II demonstrated that 100-percent protection against determined air attack cannot reasonably be expected and indicated that complete protection could not be achieved without destruction of the enemy capability to launch an air attack. An undue proportion of the national resources could be devoted to purely defensive measures without achieving complete protection. While it has been stated that the Battle of Britain indicated that a determined air defense could make a continuing air offensive too costly for the attacker to maintain, the use of weapons of mass destruction will tremendously increase the effects of air attack when measured in terms of the expected attrition of attacking forces and emphasizes the necessity for stopping such attack at its source.

The foregoing considerations indicate that the allocation of fighters and AAA to defensive tasks should be held to the minimum so as not to commit an undue proportion of the national resources to the impossible task of providing complete protection. It should be possible to reduce initial fighter defenses by the end of Phase I—because of the anticipated reduction in the Soviet air threat—in order to permit their redeployment overseas. On the other hand, since AAA battalions in defense of the most vital installations in the United States would be composed mainly of civilian personnel, no redeployment overseas would be feasible and therefore no reduction during Phase I should be contemplated. A carefully calculated risk must be accepted in the computation of air-defense forces, and the appropriate means must be devoted to counter-air-force measures designed to reduce at its source the enemy capability to launch an air attack. These offensive forces are developed under: "Conduct an Air Offensive Against the Soviet Powers."

In summary the analysis of the problem of air defense of the United States leads to the conclusions that:

(1) The minimum air defense worthy of consideration is that defense in being that will serve as a continuing threat to an attacking force and will cause enemy airplanes to carry protective equipment at the expense of offensive payload. This defense may be expected to reduce the enemy offensive payload capability by about 50 percent* but cannot be expected to provide a high degree of protection nor of attrition of enemy forces. It would, however, contribute measurably to civilian morale and serve to avert pressure for provision of disproportionately large defensive forces.

(2) Beyond the minimum defense defined in (1) above, the added protection that may be expected from additional resources devoted to purely defensive measures must be balanced against that to be gained by offensive counter-air action. Beyond the degree of minimum defense set forth in (1) above, a point is rapidly reached where resources are more profitably applied in offensive counter-air-force action than in defensive measures.

(3) The optimum air defense of the United States may be obtained by dispos

---

* The necessity for defense against enemy attack requires that a large proportion of the combat payload of bombers be devoted to defensive equipment. As a current example a B-36 bomber on a combat mission, carrying ten thousand pounds of bombs, would also carry over thirteen thousand pounds of defensive armament. Thus a defense system in being reduces the bomb-carrying capability of an enemy bomber by approximately 50 percent before actual combat is joined.

ing available fighters for area defense, augmented by antiaircraft artillery and/or guided missiles disposed to protect the most vital installations.

A combination of fighter and antiaircraft defenses has therefore been developed . . . which is considered to be as strong as our economy could reasonably be expected to support in the light of overall military requirements. The effectiveness of this air defense will be in direct proportion to the extent and effectiveness of the control and early-warning system provided.

In addition to the above fighter and AA defenses for the continental United States, certain other ground, air, and naval forces would be required. Ground forces in the United States could probably be limited initially to one airborne division prepared to move to any part of the Western Hemisphere and other defense forces equivalent to 2⅓ infantry divisions for defense of our most vital installations. Of the 2⅓ infantry divisions, ⅓ would be required in the Seattle area, ⅓ in the San Francisco–Los Angeles–San Diego area, ⅔ in the Boston–New York–Washington area, and the remaining 1 division for defense of the Soo locks and certain atomic installations. In the event of emergency, divisions in training could also be utilized. In support of these ground forces, only one tactical reconnaissance group would be required, since other tactical-air-force requirements can be met by the use of U.S. fighter defenses and other air units in training. For protection of coastal shipping and important ports and harbors, escort forces, fleet air squadrons, and naval local-defense forces would be necessary. Requirements for naval forces, unlike those for fighter defenses, would require some increases in the months immediately after D-Day and could probably not be reduced at all during first-phase operations because of increases in the number of convoys to support overseas operations and the continuance of the submarine threat. Outside of the continental United States the peripheral areas and bases necessary to our defense would require one or more of the following: ground forces, air forces, naval local-defense forces, fleet air squadrons, and antiaircraft defenses. These areas and bases include Alaska, Canada, Greenland, Labrador, Newfoundland, Bermuda, the Caribbean area (including Puerto Rico, Cuba, Trinidad, Curaçao, Aruba, and Panama), Brazil, and Hawaii.

Alaska is a highly important defense area in the Western Hemisphere. Ground forces required for the defense of Alaska should be limited to those necessary for defense of the airfields in the Fairbanks and Anchorage areas and for defense of the naval base at Kodiak. Fighter and AA protection for these areas should also be included. AA protection for naval and air installations on Adak would be required. Fighters will also be required for intercept missions and for opposing any attempted Soviet lodgements in Alaska or the Aleutians. Naval-fleet air squadrons and naval local-defense forces will also be required.

Ground-force and naval-force requirements for peripheral areas and bases other than Alaska are not developed in detail herein but are listed in the tables following this discussion. Ground forces, in general, are principally for defense against Soviet lodgements and sabotage. Naval forces defending bases from submarine attacks would include several patrol craft and minesweepers per base for harbor defense, while one or more heavy or medium patrol squadrons, aided in some cases by blimp squadrons, would be stationed within supporting distance to provide surveillance of areas to seaward.

In Newfoundland, Labrador, and Greenland the greatest threat would exist on D-Day or shortly thereafter from surprise Soviet airborne and seaborne landings. It is considered that ground forces and accompanying tactical reconnaissance air groups could be reduced progressively beginning at about D + 3 months as the Soviet threats diminish.

Except as required for defense of U.S. bases and for the security of Curaçao, Aruba, Trinidad, and the Venezuelan oil fields, defense of other Western Hemisphere nations and their possessions should be the primary responsibility of indigenous forces. [See relevant map.] . . .

b. Tasks

(1) Maintain surveillance of the approaches to the North American continent.
(2) Provide an area air defense of the most important areas of the United States.
(3) Provide the antiaircraft defense of the most vital installations of the United States.
(4) Provide for the protection of Western Hemisphere coastal and intercoastal shipping and of important ports and harbors in the continental United States.
(5) Ensure the security of the refineries on the islands of Curaçao, Aruba, and Trinidad and of associated sources of oil.
(6) Provide the optimum defense against sabotage, subversion, and espionage.
(7) Establish or secure and defend the following peripheral areas and bases necessary to the defense of the continental United States: Alaska, Canada, Greenland, Labrador, Newfoundland, Bermuda, the Caribbean, northeastern Brazil, and Hawaii.
(8) Defend the sea approaches to the North American continent and to its peripheral bases.
(9) Provide the optimum ground-force defense of the most important areas of the continental United States, including a mobile striking force. [See force-requirement chart.] . . .

4. Conduct an Air Offensive Against the Soviet Powers*

a. Analysis

(1) *General Considerations:* U.S. national policy envisages that "in the event of war with the USSR we" would "create conditions" to attain "U.S. objectives," "ensuring," among others, that "if any Bolshevik regime is left in any

part of the Soviet Union," it would "not control enough of the military–industrial potential of the Soviet Union to enable it to wage war on comparable terms with any other regime or regimes which may exist on traditional Russian territory." And further, we should seek "to create postwar conditions which will: Prevent the development of power relationships dangerous to the security of the United States and international peace." Disruption of centralized Communist control and of the integrated industrial economy which lends it power is an essential step in obtaining those objectives.

*Editor's Note: For a fuller assessment of SAC's capabilities in a war with Russia than is contained in the editor's introduction, see appendix for "Summary of Conclusions."

Soviet capabilities which pose serious initial threats to the Allied war effort include attacks with weapons of mass destruction on the United States, Canada, and the United Kingdom; conquest of Western Europe, the Near and Middle East, and probably the Scandinavian peninsula; and interruption of sea lines of communication by submarine warfare.

It is considered that the most powerful immediately available means of blunting initial Soviet land, sea, and air offensive capabilities, of destroying sufficient of their integrated military–industrial economy to render them unable to wage war successfully, and of weakening centralized Communist control in the USSR and its satellites would be an air offensive with atomic and conventional bombs initiated immediately after D-Day. It is recognized, however, that the scope of attacks of the air offensive must be carefully calculated to obtain only that destruction essential to the fulfillment of the national war objectives.

In addition to the defensive measures developed under "Secure the Western Hemisphere," "Hold the United Kingdom," and other courses of action, protection of Allied war potential against the Soviet air-offensive threat will require an immediate Allied offensive effort to destroy or neutralize the bases and facilities from which the Soviet air offensive with weapons of mass destruction would be launched. This task should be given first priority, providing sufficiently accurate intelligence is available to enable our immediate attack and destruction of these targets. Blunting of Soviet land and sea offensives by air attack against LOCs, supply bases, and troop concentrations directly supporting initial Soviet advances and against naval bases capable of supporting the initial Soviet submarine campaign should also receive a high priority.

The Soviet threat to the Allied air offensive would consist of both offensive and defensive measures. Offensively the Soviets would attack atomic installations in the United States; air bases in the United States, United Kingdom, Cairo–Suez–Aden area, Okinawa, and Alaska which they would consider likely to be used for launching atomic-bomb attacks; and aircraft carriers which they believed capable of performing similar missions. They would probably employ air attacks, sabotage, and airborne troops where practicable. Defensively their capabilities would include a defense-in-depth early-warning network embody-

U.S.-CANADIAN FIGHTER INTERCEPT CAPABILITIES
(SHOWING COVERAGE OF MOST IMPORTANT AREA OF THE U.S.)
INTENSITY OF CONCENTRATIONS INDICATED BY DEGREES OF SHADING

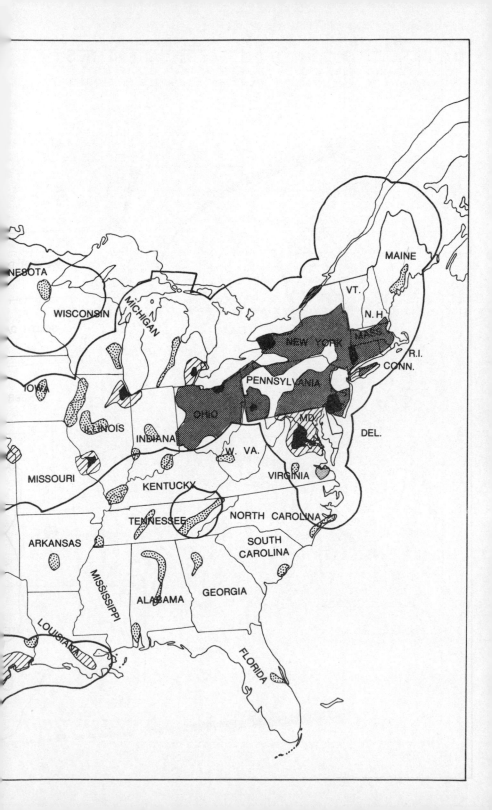

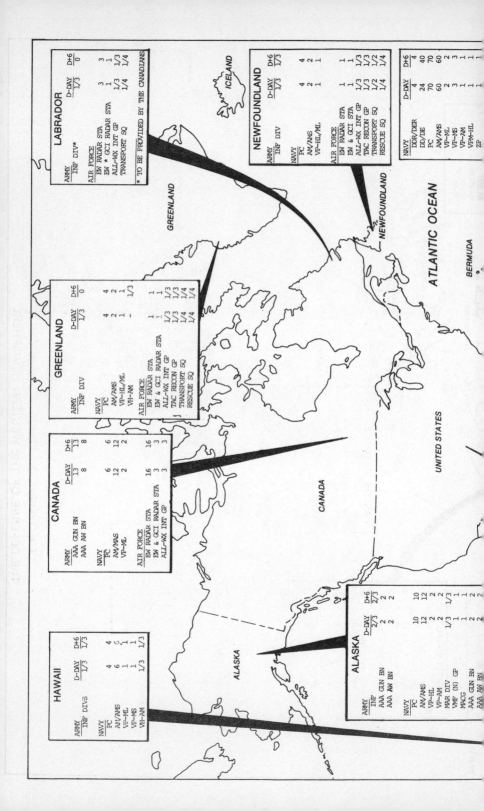

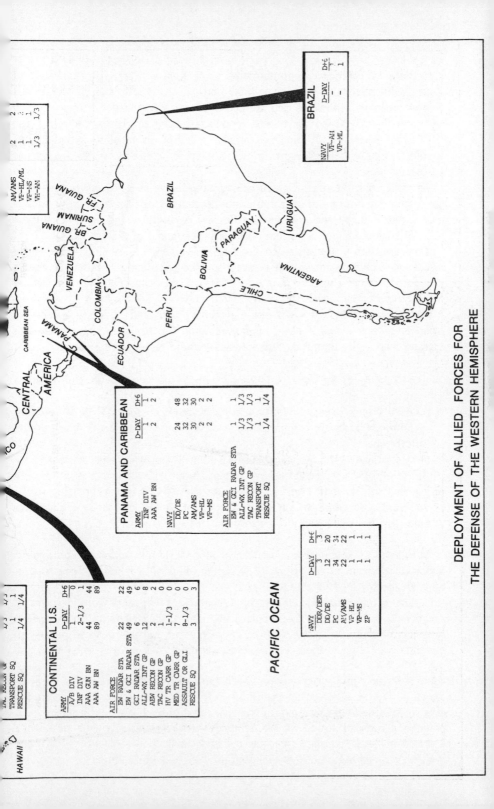

DEPLOYMENT OF ALLIED FORCES FOR
THE DEFENSE OF THE WESTERN HEMISPHERE

ing radar and electronics countermeasures, a fighter defense force (PVO) of some 2,100 interceptors which will be mainly jet aircraft, and an antiaircraft defense utilizing both guns and surface-to-air guided missiles. Properly timed and coordinated Allied air attacks conducted from air bases encircling the USSR and from aircraft carriers engaged primarily in attacking naval targets should in a large measure minimize the Soviet air defensive system against our air offensive.

As visualized, the overall air offensive would have as its objectives two separate but related series of operations, not necessarily distinct in point of time—those to abort or blunt Soviet initial offensive capabilities and those to collapse to a calculated degree the military–industrial economy of the USSR.

The campaign to blunt Soviet naval offensive capabilities with Allied naval forces, to include a mining offensive, is discussed, analyzed, and the forces therefore developed under: "Conduct Offensive Operations to Destroy Enemy Naval Forces," etc., page 206.

(2) *Target Systems:* The blunting of Soviet air, land, and sea offensives against the Allied war-making capacity should be the initial mission of our striking forces. Simultaneous air offensives would be required against:

i. Soviet facilities for the assembly and delivery of weapons of mass destruction.
ii. LOCs, supply bases, and troop concentrations in the USSR, in satellite countries, and in overrun areas, the destruction of which would blunt Soviet offensives.
iii. Naval targets of the Soviet powers, to blunt Soviet sea offensives by the destruction of enemy naval and merchant shipping, submarine assembly and repair facilities, naval bases, and the air defenses of such supporting facilities and with emphasis on the reduction of Soviet submarine capabilities and the offensive mining of enemy waters.

At the earliest practicable moment, air attacks should be undertaken against important elements of the Soviet and satellite industrial economy. These operations are further analyzed as follows:

(a) *Strategic air attacks against Soviet facilities for assembly and delivery of weapons of mass destruction.* Present intelligence is inadequate to provide a firm determination as to the requirements for attack on facilities for the assembly and delivery of weapons of mass destruction. However, it is considered that this deficiency will probably be remedied by 1957. The importance of our being fully prepared for this operation cannot be overemphasized. Its immediate and effective accomplishment upon the outset of hostilities would have not only a stunning effect on Soviet offensive capabilities but would progressively reduce the forces required for the defense of the Western Hemisphere and the United Kingdom. In point of fact the calculated risks which have been accepted in these two defensive tasks in this plan for 1957 would no longer be acceptable were not this attack made the first charge on the operations of our strategic air forces.

In spite of the inadequacy of present intelligence it is considered that a reasonable requirement for attacks on atomic-assembly facilities, storage points, and heavy-bomber airfields considered likely to be used for launching atomic attacks might be on the order of seventy-five to one hundred atomic bombs on target. In order to achieve maximum effectiveness, this campaign should be completed at the earliest possible date. Since it is envisaged that during this campaign each bomb carrier would have four accompanying aircraft to provide electronics countermeasures and other defensive coverage as well as to increase the probability of successful delivery of the A-bombs, about eleven heavy and medium groups would be required to conduct this offensive.

(b) *Strategic air attacks against LOCs, supply bases, and troop concentrations.* An important element in blunting Soviet offensives would be the use of atomic weapons and conventional bombs against LOCs, supply bases, and troop concentrations in the USSR, in the satellites, and in overrun countries which directly support Soviet advances. The use of atomic bombs against satellite and overrun areas, however, should be confined as far as possible to those targets the destruction of which would not involve large masses of population. These attacks, beginning immediately after D-Day, should be carried out in coordination with and supplemental to the operations of the tactical air and naval air elements which are developed under other tasks. Studies are currently under way to establish firm requirements for this campaign. However, as a result of preliminary examinations of the problem, it is considered that a reasonable requirement for atomic bombs on target for this purpose might be on the order of an additional one hundred atomic bombs of a type not now available but which are considered capable of development and production in sufficient quantity by 1957. This number includes the atomic bombs which might be required in the attack against Soviet naval capabilities.

The forces required for attacking those targets located in Western Europe—in addition to those established in the courses of action "Hold the Rhine–Alps–Piave line" and "Conduct offensive operations to destroy enemy naval forces," etc.—would be on the order of about twelve medium bomb groups based in the United Kingdom.*

The forces required for attacking those targets located in the Middle East—in addition to those developed under the courses of action "Hold the area: southeastern Turkey," etc., and "Conduct offensive operations to destroy enemy naval forces," etc.—would be on the order of about three medium bomb groups based in the Cairo–Suez–Aden area.

(c) *Air attacks against naval targets of the Soviet powers* to blunt Soviet sea offensives, including offensive mining, is discussed and the requirements there-

---

* Of this total, the equivalent of seven groups (210 a/c) should be provided by the British Commonwealth.

for developed under "Conduct offensive operations to destroy enemy naval forces," etc., page 206.

(d) *Strategic air attacks on important elements of Soviet and satellite military–industrial economy.* In a campaign employing atomic and conventional bombs against Soviet and satellite industry, the latest available air-force intelligence studies have concluded that the greatest overall effects can be achieved by attacking the petroleum industry, the electric power system, and the iron and steel industry. Destruction of 75–85 percent of [the] petroleum industry, including storage facilities, would reduce offensive capabilities of all Soviet forces and seriously affect agriculture, industry, transportation, and shipping; destruction of 60–70 percent of the important electric-power-grid systems would paralyze the Soviet industrial economy, since modern industry requires a continuous supply of electric power, which cannot be stockpiled; elimination of 75–85 percent of [the] iron- and steel-producing facilities would prevent recovery of industrial capacity for two to three years. Important by-products of attacks on these systems would be destruction of political and administrative centers and internal communication systems; in addition there would probably be an extreme psychological effect, which if exploited might induce early capitulation.

In initiating the air offensive against the above target systems, it is considered that attacks should first be directed against those in the USSR itself in order that we might strike at the heart of Soviet industrial power and exploit to full advantage the psychological effects of this campaign. Upon completion of this offensive, attacks should be shifted to key satellite industries whenever it is determined that they are making a significant contribution to the Soviet war effort.

. . . Additional intelligence of the Soviet economy may indicate revisions in this program as time goes on. It is considered, however, that this program is adequate for the present purpose of providing a basis for the establishment of force requirements for 1957. Accomplishment of these operations . . . would serve to fulfill the objective of disrupting the Soviet and, if necessary, the satellite economies for two to three years. It is envisaged that initial attacks would be in maximum force on USSR targets alone, to be followed by progressively widening attacks on elements in the program as destructive and psychological results were evaluated. Seven heavy- and medium-bomber groups would be required to provide the optimum capability for this task.

Air assistance would be provided by Allied naval forces when available from primary tasks.

(3) *Summary.* The separate force requirements developed above, if added together, would be on the order of 33 heavy and medium bomb groups. It is considered, however, that in view of the flexibility inherent in the strategic air operations envisaged with regard to selection of targets and time phasing of attacks, and having due regard for the logistics involved, the attack on Soviet industry could be initiated and conducted by the same groups which conduct the

attacks on Soviet offensive capabilities. The optimum U.S. force requirements for the performance of these tasks could therefore be reduced to nineteen heavy and medium bomb groups on D-Day. The RAF requirement would be seven medium bomb groups. It would be highly desirable if these groups could be provided with a reserve of aircraft for replacing combat losses during the first six months. However, preliminary cost estimates have shown that a pre-D-Day program of this magnitude would increase the military budget to an unacceptable degree. An alternative would be to reduce the number of combat groups in order to provide a reserve of planes for replacement of combat losses. This, however, would also reduce the magnitude of the initial air attacks against the USSR. It is therefore concluded that greater returns could be expected, commensurate with the cost factor, if the strategic air offensive were initiated with the maximum possible number of combat groups, accepting attrition with only partial replacement, as opposed to initiating the strategic air offensive with a smaller number of combat groups backed up by an adequate reserve for replacing combat losses. It is estimated that the operational strength of the nineteen U.S. groups conducting the above campaigns would probably not fall below 50 percent of total initial strength during the first phase.* A similar loss rate would probably be applicable to British Commonwealth air units required above.

*Editor's Note: In the light of information contained in the editor's introduction, and considering the facts contained in the "Summary of Conclusions" concerning SAC's effectiveness (see appendix), this seems overoptimistic. Neither does this assessment take into consideration the inevitable loss of morale that would follow such casualties. It will be recalled that in the final stages of the air campaign against Hanoi, SAC began to take severe casualties from SAM missiles. While no doubt the lack of motivation implicit in the closing stages of the Vietnam war played its part in the decline of SAC's morale, the effect of severe casualties on the air-crew morale caused by heavy casualties was a sobering by-product of the fighting. According to World War II studies (when the Germans began to use air-to-air missiles in the closing stages) air-crew morale tended to remain relatively high when the crews were engaged by fighters. It tended to decline when the crews were attacked by missile, simply because there was so little that the crew could do to avoid or prevent its own destruction.

Supporting reconnaissance groups for the bomber forces listed above would be on the order of about four strategic reconnaissance groups—one of which should be British—and two strategic weather groups. Attrition for reconnaissance aircraft would be about 50 percent of initial strength during the first-phase operations, but these losses should be replaced in all areas except the United Kingdom. Strategic weather aircraft would not be exposed to enemy attacks and would suffer only operational losses. [See relevant map.] . . .

CENTERS OF CONTRO[L]

BARENTS SEA

KARA SEA

PETSAMO

KOLA INLET

KARA STRAIT

WHITE SEA ENTRANCE

YUGORSKI STRAIT

PYECHORA BAY

MURMANSK

NARYAN MAR

MOLOTOVSK

WHITE SEA CANEL

UNION O[F]

THE SOUND

LENINGRAD

TALLINN

GREAT BELT

RIGA

GORKI

SVERDLOVSK

LITTLE BELT

KAUNAS

CHELYABINSK

OMSK

KIEL CANEL

DANZIG

MINSK

MOSCOW

HAMBURG

WARSAW

KUIBISHEV

BERLIN

KIEV

KHARKOV

PRAGUE

BUDAPEST

ROSTOV

ZAGREB

ODESSA

BELGRADE

NOVOROSSISK

CASPIAN SEA

TASHKENT

SPALATO

SEVASTOPOL

TIRANA

SOFIA

BATUMI

BAKU

BOSPORUS

CONSTANTA

MEDITERRANEAN SEA

BUCHAREST

ATLANTIC OCEAN

EUROPE

AFRICA

D MINING TARGETS

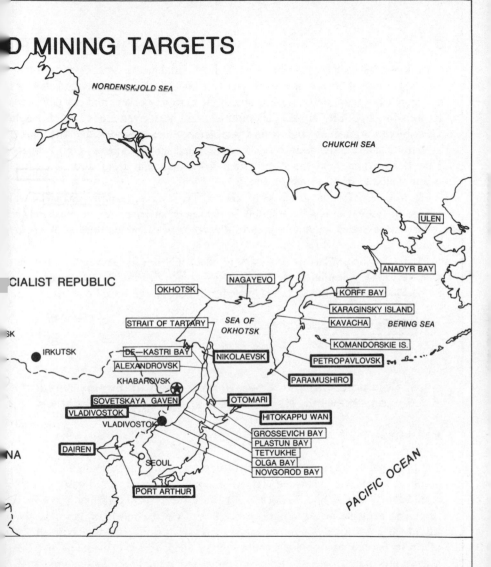

NORDENSKJOLD SEA

CHUKCHI SEA

ULEN

ANADYR BAY

CIALIST REPUBLIC

OKHOTSK

NAGAYEVO

KORFF BAY

KARAGINSKY ISLAND

KAVACHA   BERING SEA

STRAIT OF TARTARY

SEA OF
OKHOTSK

SK

IRKUTSK

KOMANDORSKIE IS.

DE—KASTRI BAY

NIKOLAEVSK

PETROPAVLOVSK

ALEXANDROVSK

KHABAROVSK

PARAMUSHIRO

SOVETSKAYA GAVEN

OTOMARI

VLADIVOSTOK

VLADIVOSTOK

HITOKAPPU WAN

GROSSEVICH BAY

NA

DAIREN

PLASTUN BAY

TETYUKHE

SEOUL

OLGA BAY

NOVGOROD BAY

PACIFIC OCEAN

PORT ARTHUR

MINING TARGETS

PRIMARY TARGETS

SECONDARY TARGETS

Soviet submarine fleet estimated to
consist in 1957 of 300-350 ocean type
and between 200 and 300 of the coastal
defense type.

Allied mining of primary targets
upon outbreak of war and of such
secondary targets as then current intelligence indicates to be necessary would
be an important offensive measure to
destroy enemy subs or to contain them.

Mines to be laid by submarines and
aircraft. Total mine requirements
(primary and secondary targets) 40,000
mines for first 6 months.

b. Tasks

(1) Initiate, as soon as possible after D-Day, strategic air attacks with atomic and conventional bombs against Soviet facilities for the assembly and delivery of weapons of mass destruction against LOCs, supply bases, and troop concentrations in the USSR, in satellite countries, and in overrun areas, which would blunt Soviet offensives, and against petroleum, electric power, and steel target systems in the USSR, from bases in the United States, Alaska, Okinawa, the United Kingdom, and the Cairo–Suez–Aden area and from aircraft carriers when available from primary tasks.

(2) Initiate, as soon as possible after D-Day, air operations against naval targets of the Soviet powers to blunt Soviet sea offensives with emphasis on the reduction of Soviet submarine capabilities and the offensive mining of enemy waters.

(3) Extend operations as necessary to additional targets both within and outside the USSR essential to the war-making capacity of the Soviet powers.

(4) Maintain policing of target systems reduced in the initial campaigns.

c. Requirements. [See map.] . . .

5. Conduct Offensive Operations to Destroy Enemy Naval Forces, Shipping, Naval Bases, and Supporting Facilities

a. Analysis

The principal threat from Soviet naval forces would lie in their submarine capabilities, which are analyzed under "Secure sea and air lines of communication," etc. While Soviet naval surface forces would probably not be of sufficient strength to challenge openly [the] Allied control of the sea, they would be capable of harassing attacks and of serious interference with sea LOCs in limited areas, which could require uneconomical diversion of Allied heavy units to convoy duty. Enemy shore-based aircraft would constitute an effective threat against Allied shipping, ports, and their approaches within range. Soviet merchant shipping would be an appreciable adjunct to their transportation system, as well as affording troop lift and auxiliary means of supply in the execution of their campaigns.

Offensive operations against the source of these threats are considered the most effective and least expensive means of neutralizing them. These operations would have as their primary objectives the destruction of enemy naval and merchant shipping, submarine assembly and repair facilities, naval bases, and the air defenses of such supporting facilities. For location of these targets, see map. Included also would be offensive mining of sea approaches to enemy ports and bases, hunter–killer operations, antisubmarine submarine operations, and the destruction of enemy naval surface forces which get to sea. . . .

Operations against those targets constituting the source of Soviet naval strength would be conducted principally by fast carrier task forces, hunter–killer groups, and submarines, assisted by land-based air. In view of the extensive area to be controlled in the western Pacific and as an economical means of providing naval surface support to the theaters concerned where and when needed or to reinforce the carrier task group, a small cruiser task group is required in addition to the fast carrier task group.

The air elements of the forces generated by this course of action would participate in the air offensive, in coordination with the Allied air forces, when available from primary tasks. Air assistance in mining and other appropriate tasks would be provided by Allied air forces shown under "Conduct an air offensive," etc.

Disposition of forces for conducting offensive operations to destroy enemy naval forces, etc., is shown on the map.

Forces for this course of action—together with forces shown under "Secure sea and air LOCs," etc. . . .—are also shown on the maps. . . .

b. Tasks

(1) Destroy Soviet naval forces, shipping, naval bases, supporting facilities and their air defenses. .

(2) Mine important enemy ports, and focal sea approaches thereto, in the Baltic–Barents–White Sea area, northeast Asia, the Black Sea, the Adriatic, and the Turkish straits.

(3) Establish a sea blockade of the Soviet powers.

c. Requirements.

(1) Army. None.

6. Hold the United Kingdom.

a. Analysis

Defense of the United Kingdom would retain for the Allies a wealth of manpower and industrial potential; a major base for air, naval, and ground operations against Western and Northern Europe (including the western USSR); and an incalculable political and psychological asset with respect to other allies and potential allies. Loss of the United Kingdom would not only deny these advantages to the Allies but in addition would greatly augment the military and possibly the industrial potential available to the Soviets.

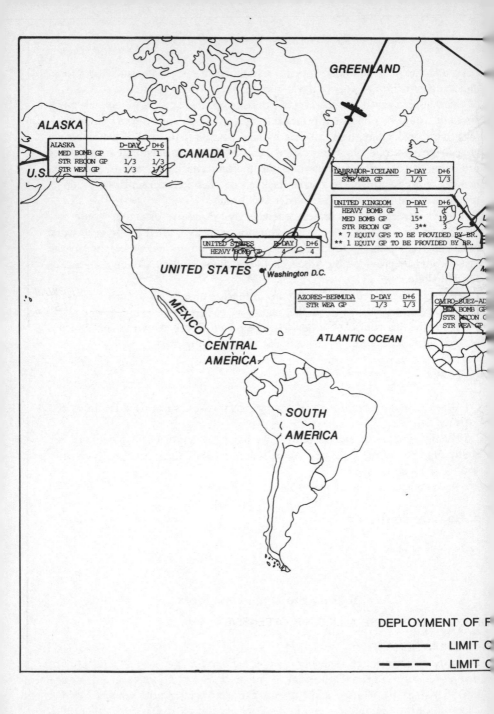

ALASKA

ALASKA	D-DAY	D+6
MED BOMB GP	1	1
STR RECON GP	1/3	1/3
STR WEA GP	1/3	1/3

CANADA

GREENLAND

LABRADOR-ICELAND	D-DAY	D+6
STR WEA GP	1/3	1/3

UNITED KINGDOM	D-DAY	D+6
HEAVY BOMB GP	1	2
MED BOMB GP	15**	19
STR RECON GP	3**	3
* 7 EQUIV GPS TO BE PROVIDED BY BR.
** 1 EQUIV GP TO BE PROVIDED BY BR.

U.S.

UNITED STATES	D-DAY	D+6
HEAVY BOMB GP	4	4

UNITED STATES • Washington D.C.

AZORES-BERMUDA	D-DAY	D+6
STR WEA GP	1/3	1/3

CAIRO-SUEZ-AD...	
MED BOMB GP	
STR RECON G...	
STR WEA GP	

MEXICO

CENTRAL
AMERICA

ATLANTIC OCEAN

SOUTH
AMERICA

DEPLOYMENT OF F

———— LIMIT O

– – – – LIMIT O

SUMMARY	D-DAY	D+6
HEAVY BOMB GP	5	5
MED BOMB GP	21*	21
STR RECON GP	4**	4
STR WEA GP	2	2
* 7 EQUIV GPS TO BE PROVIDED BY BR.		
** 1 EQUIV GP TO BE PROVIDED BY BR.		

OKINAWA	D-DAY	D+6
MED BOMB GP	2	2
STR RECON GP	1/3	1/3
STR WEA GP	1/3	1/3

GUAM	D-DAY	D+6
STR WEA GP	1/3	1/3

OR CONDUCTING THE ALLIED AIR OFFENSIVE

S - MEDIUM BOMBER

S - HEAVY BOMBER

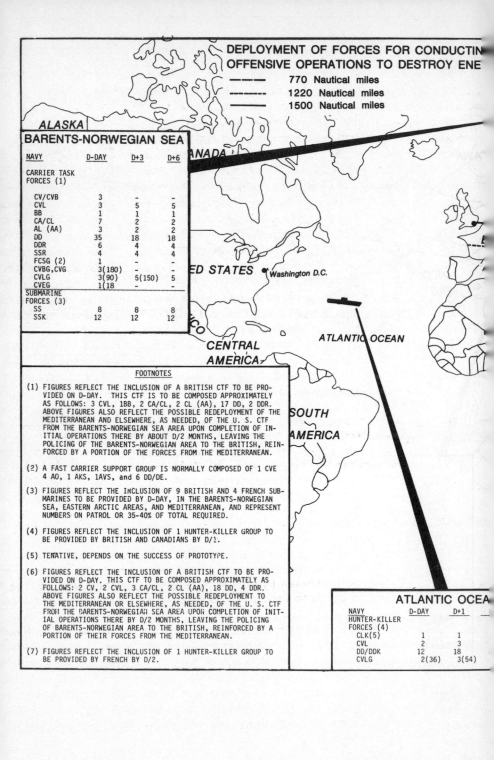

DEPLOYMENT OF FORCES FOR CONDUCTIN...
OFFENSIVE OPERATIONS TO DESTROY ENE...

------- 770 Nautical miles
-·-·-·- 1220 Nautical miles
——— 1500 Nautical miles

ALASKA

BARENTS-NORWEGIAN SEA

NAVY	D-DAY	D+3	D+6
CARRIER TASK FORCES (1)			
CV/CVB	3	-	-
CVL	3	5	5
BB	1	1	1
CA/CL	7	2	2
AL (AA)	3	2	2
DD	35	18	18
DDR	6	4	4
SSR	4	4	4
FCSG (2)	1	-	-
CVBG,CVG	3(180)	-	-
CVLG	3(90)	5(150)	5
CVEG	1(18	-	-
SUBMARINE FORCES (3)			
SS	8	8	8
SSK	12	12	12

Washington D.C.

ATLANTIC OCEAN

CENTRAL AMERICA

SOUTH AMERICA

FOOTNOTES

(1) FIGURES REFLECT THE INCLUSION OF A BRITISH CTF TO BE PRO-
VIDED ON D-DAY. THIS CTF IS TO BE COMPOSED APPROXIMATELY
AS FOLLOWS: 3 CVL, 1BB, 2 CA/CL, 2 CL (AA), 17 DD, 2 DDR.
ABOVE FIGURES ALSO REFLECT THE POSSIBLE REDEPLOYMENT OF THE
MEDITERRANEAN AND ELSEWHERE, AS NEEDED, OF THE U. S. CTF
FROM THE BARENTS-NORWEGIAN SEA AREA UPON COMPLETION OF IN-
ITIAL OPERATIONS THERE BY ABOUT D/2 MONTHS, LEAVING THE
POLICING OF THE BARENTS-NORWEGIAN AREA TO THE BRITISH, REIN-
FORCED BY A PORTION OF THE FORCES FROM THE MEDITERRANEAN.

(2) A FAST CARRIER SUPPORT GROUP IS NORMALLY COMPOSED OF 1 CVE
4 AO, 1 AKS, 1AVS, and 6 DD/DE.

(3) FIGURES REFLECT THE INCLUSION OF 9 BRITISH AND 4 FRENCH SUB-
MARINES TO BE PROVIDED BY D-DAY, IN THE BARENTS-NORWEGIAN
SEA, EASTERN ARCTIC AREAS, AND MEDITERRANEAN, AND REPRESENT
NUMBERS ON PATROL OR 35-40% OF TOTAL REQUIRED.

(4) FIGURES REFLECT THE INCLUSION OF 1 HUNTER-KILLER GROUP TO
BE PROVIDED BY BRITISH AND CANADIANS BY D/1.

(5) TENTATIVE, DEPENDS ON THE SUCCESS OF PROTOTYPE.

(6) FIGURES REFLECT THE INCLUSION OF A BRITISH CTF TO BE PRO-
VIDED ON D-DAY. THIS CTF TO BE COMPOSED APPROXIMATELY AS
FOLLOWS: 2 CV, 2 CVL, 3 CA/CL, 2 CL (AA), 18 DD, 4 DDR.
ABOVE FIGURES ALSO REFLECT THE POSSIBLE REDEPLOYMENT TO
THE MEDITERRANEAN OR ELSEWHERE, AS NEEDED, OF THE U. S. CTF
FROM THE BARENTS-NORWEGIAN SEA AREA UPON COMPLETION OF INIT-
IAL OPERATIONS THERE BY D/2 MONTHS, LEAVING THE POLICING
OF BARENTS-NORWEGIAN AREA TO THE BRITISH, REINFORCED BY A
PORTION OF THEIR FORCES FROM THE MEDITERRANEAN.

(7) FIGURES REFLECT THE INCLUSION OF 1 HUNTER-KILLER GROUP TO
BE PROVIDED BY FRENCH BY D/2.

ATLANTIC OCEA...

NAVY	D-DAY	D+1
HUNTER-KILLER FORCES (4)		
CLK(5)	1	1
CVL	2	3
DD/DDK	12	18
CVLG	2(36)	3(54)

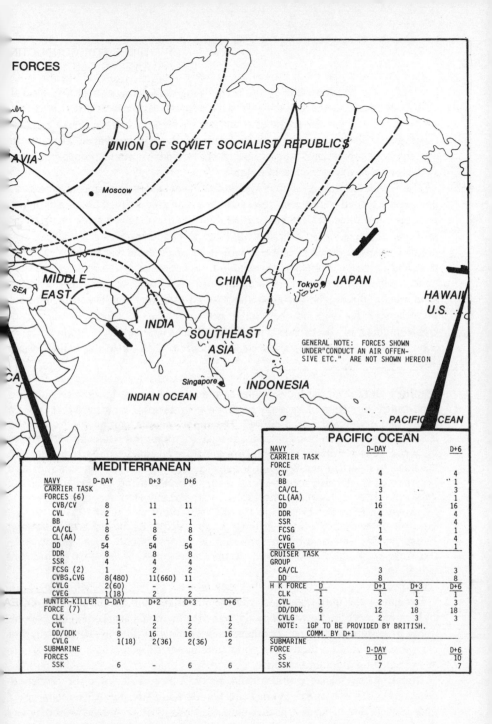

FORCES

UNION OF SOVIET SOCIALIST REPUBLICS

• Moscow

AVIA

MIDDLE EAST

SEA

INDIA

CHINA   Tokyo •   JAPAN

HAWAII U.S.

SOUTHEAST ASIA

INDONESIA

Singapore

INDIAN OCEAN

PACIFIC OCEAN

CA

GENERAL NOTE: FORCES SHOWN UNDER "CONDUCT AN AIR OFFENSIVE ETC." ARE NOT SHOWN HEREON

MEDITERRANEAN

NAVY	D-DAY	D+3	D+6	
CARRIER TASK FORCES (6)				
CVB/CV	8	11	11	
CVL	2	-	-	
BB	1	1	1	
CA/CL	8	8	8	
CL(AA)	6	6	6	
DD	54	54	54	
DDR	8	8	8	
SSR	4	4	4	
FCSG (2)	1	2	2	
CVBG,CVG	8(480)	11(660)	11	
CVLG	2(60)	-	-	
CVEG	1(18)	2	2	
HUNTER-KILLER	D-DAY	D+2	D+3	D+6
FORCE (7)				
CLK	1	1	1	1
CVL	1	2	2	2
DD/DDK	8	16	16	16
CVLG	1(18)	2(36)	2(36)	2
SUBMARINE FORCES				
SSK	6	-	6	6

PACIFIC OCEAN

NAVY	D-DAY	D+6		
CARRIER TASK FORCE				
CV	4	4		
BB	1	1		
CA/CL	3	3		
CL(AA)	1	1		
DD	16	16		
DDR	4	4		
SSR	4	4		
FCSG	1	1		
CVG	4	4		
CVEG	1	1		
CRUISER TASK GROUP				
CA/CL	3	3		
DD	8	8		
H K FORCE	D	D+1	D+3	D+6
CLK	1	1	1	1
CVL	1	2	3	3
DD/DDK	6	12	18	18
CVLG	1	2	3	3

NOTE: 1GP TO BE PROVIDED BY BRITISH. COMM. BY D+1

SUBMARINE FORCE	D-DAY	D+6
SS	10	10
SSK	7	7

It is estimated that the principal threat to the United Kingdom, beginning or D-Day, would be an assault by the Soviet long-range air force (D-Day total in USSR: eighteen hundred), probably with weapons of mass destruction. Some of the five thousand Soviet tactical aircraft in Western Europe could assist in this task and also support the expected submarine offensive against British ports and sea communications. In addition, Soviet saboteurs would probably make a strong effort to assist the overall plan.

The Soviet long-range air force would be faced with two major tasks: attacks against the United States and attacks against the United Kingdom. Since its objectives might differ widely geographically from day to day, any estimate of the proportion of this force which would be devoted to a particular target area might be misleading and, at best, would be of doubtful value. However, for planning purposes it appears reasonable to assume that of the total of eighteen hundred* long-range bombers available to the Soviets, as many as one thousand might initially be assigned the task of attacking the United Kingdom. Fighter escort for these bombers might not be significant initially, but a considerable number of these escorts could be expected about D + 1 month, or as soon as the Soviets had established fighter airfields closer to the United Kingdom.

*Editor's Note: The planners' belief that the Russians had eighteen hundred long-range bombers may well have been a serious exaggeration due to faulty or nonexistent intelligence. The most reliable estimate—that of the ISS military-balance study—shows that in 1959 the Russians had two hundred "Bear" turboprop long-range bombers and perhaps five hundred "Bison" four-jet bombers. Even these figures may have been exaggerated because of Soviet deception—they were forever playing games to lead the Western order of battle experts to overestimate Red air-force strength. Moreover, it is useful to note in the ISS statement that until 1951 all Soviet long-range bombers were piston-engined and of the World War II variety. These figures are for aircraft available on all fronts and for all purposes— the Atlantic, Pacific, and Arctic; attack, reconnaissance, weather, in-flight refueling, etc.

Except for the initial attacks on D-Day the maximum scale of Soviet air attack would probably be considerably less than the totals available, since operational availability of Soviet bombers may become as low as 50 percent. For planning purposes no more than about five hundred bombers per attack would be expected on a continuing basis.

British planners have estimated that in 1957 they could force the Soviets to cease sustained operations against the United Kingdom if RAF fighters could intercept maximum Soviet attacks on a ratio of one RAF fighter to two Soviet bombers. Assuming a fighter operational availability of 75 percent, the RAF has estimated that it would need about 350 fighters if all fighters were in a position to intercept. Since fighters based in the south of England would probably be unable to intercept Soviet bombers attacking targets in the north of England and vice versa, the requirement for fighters would have to be doubled. The initial aircraft requirement for defense against bombers would therefore become about 700 fighters. As soon as the Soviets provide fighter escort, an increased requirement would develop. This might be as much as 200 additional fighters. The total requirement for air defense of the United Kingdom would then increase to about 900* fighters, all of which should be high-performance all-weather interceptors. In addition to these there would be a need for AA defenses and control and warning squadrons. Since it is considered unlikely that Soviet airborne attacks would be made against the United Kingdom as long as the line of the Rhine was held by the Allies, it is believed that home-guard units and other forces in training would be sufficient for ground defense and protection against saboteurs.

*Editor's Note: The actual figure of RAF aircraft available in 1949 is not given, probably for security reasons. For the same reason the 1957 postulation is not revealed. It is certain that the RAF did not have 900 such fighters available in 1949, and if it did, then not all would have been available for the defense of the home islands—Britain then had worldwide commitments. By 1957 the defense position would have improved somewhat, but the RAF could not have had 900 fighters for service by that date.

It is believed that the United Kingdom would not be initially subjected to serious harassing attacks by short-range Soviet tactical aircraft since most of these aircraft will be required in support of Soviet operations against the Rhine–Alps–Piave line.

The conduct of the air offensive will require the availability of selected air bases in the United Kingdom which could be operational on or immediately after D-Day. The requirements for this course of action are covered under: "Conduct an air offensive," etc.

Defense against the submarine offensive against sea communications to the United Kingdom would require a major effort by Allied naval forces. This task is covered under "Secure sea and air lines of communication," etc., and "Conduct offensive operations to destroy enemy naval forces," etc.

b. Tasks

(1) Maintain surveillance of the approaches to the United Kingdom.
(2) Provide the air defense of the most critical areas of the United Kingdom.
(3) Provide the anticaircraft defense of the most critical areas of the United Kingdom.
(4) Provide for the protection of United Kingdom coastal shipping and of important ports and harbors in the United Kingdom.
(5) Provide the optimum defense against sabotage, subversion, and espionage.

(6) Provide the optimum ground-force defense of the most critical areas of the United Kingdom.

7. Hold the Rhine–Alps–Piave Line

a. Analysis

Defense of the line Rhine–Alps–Piave River retains in Allied hands the bulk of the manpower and industrial resources of Western Europe, takes advantage of the terrain most favorable to the defense, and lends depth to the defense of bases in the United Kingdom and in Western Europe. The Soviets will appreciate that Allied retention of this line would greatly facilitate the overall Allied strategy and will endeavor to seize critical points along this line before they can be defended in sufficient force by the Allies. The advantages to the Allies of holding on the Rhine–Alps–Piave River line, as compared to any position west of that line, are so great as to warrant maximum effort to hold on this line from D-Day onward.

The Soviet threat to the Rhine River line would probably materialize on D-Day with airdrops on selected Rhine River bridges. Airborne units allocated for these missions might total the equivalent of two divisions. Within five days the Soviets could probably have fifteen divisions at the Rhine River line with a buildup to a maximum of one hundred divisions in thirty days. Both during this period and thereafter the Soviet buildup would be limited by logistic considerations. It is considered, however, that the execution of planned demolitions and air interdiction of LOCs as envisaged in this plan would limit Soviet capabilities, during the first six months, to logistic support of a maximum of one hundred divisions and accompanying air units on the Rhine line. (See the interdiction task as covered under "Conduct an air offensive," etc., page 194).

The threat to the Alps–Piave River line would come initially from the Yugoslavs, who would probably have available upwards of fifteen divisions. These would probably be supported by about six hundred combat tactical aircraft, two-thirds of which would be Yugoslav. The Soviets could reinforce the above forces with about ten divisions, if necessary, early in the campaign.*

The Rhine River portion of this line extends for approximately five hundred miles from the Zuider Zee to the Swiss border. Its principal topographical features, from north to south, are as follows:

---

* If the present defection of Yugoslavia from the Soviet satellite orbit should continue to 1957, it is not likely that Yugoslavia would ally with the Soviet Union but would attempt to remain neutral and would be committed to resist Soviet and/or satellite attack. In any event, the Soviet Union should be able to deal with the situation effectively and complete the Italian campaign with a delay of one to three months. Additional Soviet forces required should not materially detract from capabilities in other areas.

(1) The Dutch lowlands and Cologne plain, extending about two hundred miles inland from the Zuider Zee and containing the majority of the LOCs and Rhine bridges.
(2) The Rhine highlands, with elevations up to three thousand feet, extending about 175 miles south from Bonn.
(3) The Vosges Mountains, with maximum elevations of four thousand feet, extending for approximately 125 miles to the south from the area opposite Karlsruhe.
(4) The Belfort Gap.

Ground-force requirements for defense of the Rhine River line are esimated at 60 divisions (including 12 armored divisions).* An estimated 20 divisions would be required for defense of the Dutch lowlands and Cologne plain, 12 divisions for the Rhine highlands, 5 divisions for the Vosges, and 3 divisions for the Belfort Gap. An estimated 20 divisions would be required for general reserve.

Editor's Note: No doubt large-scale mobilization would have taken place by D-Day—provided the West received some foreknowledge of Russia's plans. Even so it is difficult to see how the West would have been able to get 80 divisions of trained men together. As we have seen in the ISS 1959 study, NATO disposed only 21⅓ divisions for the defense of this sector. There was virtually no reserve, and two of these divisions—French—would have been on active service in Algiers.

Initial requirements for the tactical air support of the Rhine River defenses would be approximately 26 groups of fighters, 6 groups of light bombers, and 6 groups of tactical reconnaissance aircraft. About 7 additional groups of all-weather interceptor aircraft would be required for defense of Allied areas west of the Rhine River defenses. The above requirements total 45 groups or approximately 3,100 aircraft. Attacks against Soviet bases and LOCs in eastern Germany and Poland would require medium bombers, the requirements for which are established under "Conduct an air offensive," etc.

The principal topographical features along the Alps–Piave River line are:

(1) The Alps—about 150 miles of extremely rugged mountainous terrain, with few routes of approach and relatively easy to defend.
(2) The Dolomites—approximately 95 miles along the Piave River through the rugged Dolomite Alps to the Venetian lowlands.
(3) The lowlands—approximately 50 miles of line behind the Piave River through the lowlands to the Adriatic.

Defense requirements for the Alps–Piave line are estimated at 3 (mountain) divisions each for the Alps and the Dolomites, with 7 divisions (including

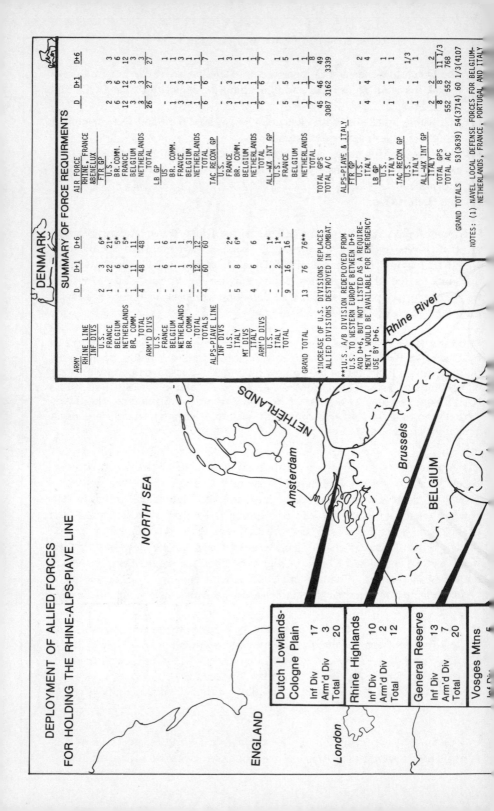

DEPLOYMENT OF ALLIED FORCES
FOR HOLDING THE RHINE-ALPS-PIAVE LINE

Map labels: ENGLAND · London · DENMARK · NORTH SEA · NETHERLANDS · Amsterdam · Rhine River · Brussels · BELGIUM

Dutch Lowlands-Cologne Plain

Inf Div	17
Arm'd Div	3
Total	20

Rhine Highlands

Inf Div	10
Arm'd Div	2
Total	12

General Reserve

Inf Div	13
Arm'd Div	7
Total	20

Vosges Mtns

Inf Div	5

SUMMARY OF FORCE REQUIREMENTS

ARMY	D	D+1	D+6
RHINE LINE			
INF DIVS			
U.S.	2	3	6*
FRANCE	1	22	21*
BELGIUM	-	6	5*
NETHERLANDS	-	6	5*
BR. COMM.	1	11	11
TOTAL	4	48	48
ARM'D DIVS			
U.S.	-	1	1
FRANCE	-	6	6
BELGIUM	-	1	1
NETHERLANDS	-	1	1
BR. COMM.	-	3	3
TOTAL	-	12	12
TOTALS	4	60	60
ALPS-PIAVE LINE			
INF DIVS			
U.S.	-	-	2*
ITALY	5	8	6*
MT DIVS			
ITALY	4	6	6
ARM'D DIVS			
U.S.	-	-	1*
ITALY	-	2	1*
TOTAL	9	16	16
GRAND TOTAL	13	76	76**

*INCREASE OF U.S. DIVISIONS REPLACES ALLIED DIVISIONS DESTROYED IN COMBAT.

**1 U.S. A/B DIVISION REDEPLOYED FROM U.S. TO WESTERN EUROPE BETWEEN D+5 AND D+6, BUT NOT LISTED AS A REQUIREMENT, WOULD BE AVAILABLE FOR EMERGENCY USE BY D-6.

AIR FORCE	D	D+1	D+6
RHINE, FRANCE & BENELUX			
FTR GP			
U.S.	2	3	3
BR. COMM.	6	6	6
FRANCE	12	12	12
BELGIUM	3	3	3
NETHERLANDS	3	3	3
TOTAL	26	27	27
LB GP			
US	-	1	1
BR. COMM.	3	3	3
FRANCE	1	1	1
BELGIUM	1	1	1
NETHERLANDS	1	1	1
TOTAL	6	6	7
TAC RECON GP			
FRANCE	3	3	3
BR. COMM.	1	1	1
BELGIUM	1	1	1
NETHERLANDS	1	1	1
TOTAL	6	6	7
ALL-WX INT GP			
U.S.	-	-	1
FRANCE	5	5	5
BELGIUM	1	1	1
NETHERLANDS	1	1	1
TOTAL	7	7	8
TOTAL GPS	45	46	49
TOTAL A/C	3087	3162	3339
ALPS-PIAVE & ITALY			
FTR GP			
U.S.	-	-	2
ITALY	4	4	4
LB GP			
U.S.	-	-	1
ITALY	1	1	1
TAC RECON GP			
ITALY	1	1	1
ALL-WX INT GP			
ITALY	-	-	1/3
U.S. ITALY	1	1	1
TOTAL GPS	2	2	2
TOTAL GPS	8	8	11 1/3
TOTAL AC	552	552	768
GRAND TOTALS	53(3714)	54(3639)	60 1/3(4107)

NOTES: (1) NAVEL LOCAL DEFENSE FORCES FOR BELGIUM-NETHERLANDS, FRANCE, PORTUGAL AND ITALY

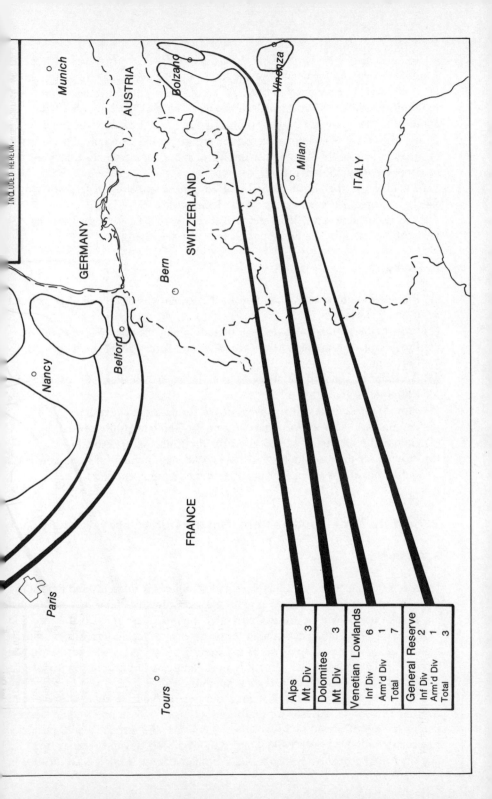

INCLUDED HEREUN.

Munich

AUSTRIA

Bolzano

Vicenza

Milan

ITALY

GERMANY

SWITZERLAND

Bern

Nancy

Belford

FRANCE

Paris

Tours

Alps	
Mt Div	3

Dolomites	
Mt Div	3

Venetian Lowlands	
Inf Div	6
Arm'd Div	1
Total	7

General Reserve	
Inf Div	2
Arm'd Div	1
Total	3

1 armored division) for defense of the lowlands. An additional 3 divisions, one of which should be an armored division, would be required in general reserve.

Initial requirements for tactical air support of the Alps–Piave line would be about 4 fighter groups, 1 light-bomber group, and 1 tactical reconnaissance group. At least 2 all-weather interceptor groups would be required for defense of areas in rear of the Alps–Piave line. The above requirements total 8 groups or approximately 550 aircraft.

In addition to the above ground and air forces, antiaircraft defenses would also be required for areas in rear of the Rhine–Alps–Piave line. . . .

. . . Escort and naval local defense forces would be necessary for the defense of coastal shipping and focal ports in Western Europe.

b. Tasks

(1) Provide the ground-force defense of the Rhine River line from Switzerland to the Zuider Zee.
(2) Provide the ground-force defense of Italy along the Alps–Piave River line.
(3) Provide tactical air support of Allied ground forces along the Rhine–Alps–Piave line.
(4) Accomplish planned demolitions and interdict Soviet LOCs east of the Rhine–Alps–Piave line.
(5) Provide air defense of areas west of the Rhine–Alps–Piave line.
(6) Provide AA defenses for areas west of the Rhine–Alps–Piave line.
(7) Gain and maintain air superiority over the Rhine–Alps–Piave line.
(8) Provide for the protection of Allied coastal shipping and of important ports and harbors in Western Europe. [See force-requirement chart.] . . .

8. Hold the Area Southeastern Turkey–Tigris Valley–Persian Gulf

a. Analysis

Defense of this area protects the Near and Middle East oil fields and the Cairo–Suez–Aden area from overland assault and lends depth to their defense against air attack. It secures the Suez Canal and important air and naval bases and LOCs in the area and lends strength to the defense of the eastern Mediterranean area. Making all practicable use of available Turkish forces and of the rugged terrain and vulnerable LOCs generally north and east of the area, it provides an integrated defense of the area at minimum cost.

The Soviet threat to this area stems from two probable campaigns: the one to overrun Turkey and the other through Iran to seize the Near and Middle East oil fields. A total of about 33 Soviet divisions and 1,400 aircraft would probably be utilized initially in the Turkish campaign, and 16 Soviet divisions and 600 aircraft would probably be used initially in the Near and Middle East thrusts. In ddition the Soviets would have the capability of employing 3–4 airborne rigades against the Basra–Abadan and Bahrein–Dhahran areas on D-Day. The ifficult and most vulnerable aspects of these campaigns are the mountainous errain and the long, tenuous, and easily blocked LOCs required. It is estimated hat Soviet forces, operating against indigenous resistance only, could reach the skenderun area by D+5 months and the Iran–Iraq passes before D+1 month.

In the Bahrein–Dhahran area there are several facilities which should be given protection on D-Day. These are the airfields, principally the U.S.-built airfield at Dhahran; the refinery on Bahrein Island, which is approximately thirty-five miles southeast of Dhahran; the refinery at Ras Tanura about thirty miles north of Dhahran; and the associated installations.

It is estimated that one RCT should be sufficient to provide the ground defense of these areas. This requirement could be somewhat reduced by organizing and arming the American civilians in the above areas. Since Soviet initial threats would be confined to limited bombing and airborne attacks, air defenses required should not exceed one fighter group and a small amount of antiaircraft. It is unlikely that bombing of the refinery areas could be completely prevented, but damage could be minimized and severe losses probably could be inflicted on the attacking forces. Soviet airborne attacks, unless heavily escorted, would also be extremely vulnerable to fighter attacks, and any attempted air resupply could be seriously interfered with.

In the Basra–Abadan area the principal facilities requiring protection on D-Day will be the Abadan refinery, its associated installations, and the oil fields 30–130 miles to the north and east. In addition the key communication and port facilities should be defended.

It is estimated that one U.S. or British infantry division in addition to indigenous forces would be required to ensure the defense of this area against Soviet D-Day airborne capabilities. Allied combat aircraft requirements on D-Day in the Basra–Abadan area would be three fighter groups to maintain air superiority and to furnish protection against airborne or bombing attacks. Antiaircraft defense would also be required to protect the most important facilities in this area.

The optimum means of providing the defense of the foregoing installations would be through arrangements with Iraq, Iran, Bahrein, and Saudi Arabia whereby the required forces could be in place prior to D-Day. Arrangements should be concluded whereby the nucleus of such forces could be in the Basra–Abadan and Bahrein–Dhahran areas on a continuing basis, ostensibly for other purposes such as the training of indigenous forces. In this respect the British would seem to be in the best position under current treaty provisions with Iraq, and accordingly the initial defense of the Basra–Abadan installations should be a British responsibility. Through an extension of the Dhahran air-base arrangement with Saudi Arabia, provision should be made for the introduction of U.S. ground forces into that area prior to D-Day. The rapid introduction of air units would present less difficulty in an emergency. Failing arrangements for pre-D-

Day introduction of the necessary ground forces for defense, the initial groun
defense could be provided from marine forces afloat in the Mediterranean
which in any case should be available for emergency use in the area.

In order to prevent Soviet advances through the mountains of Iran into Ira
and the Iranian oil areas, Allied planned ground demolition and air interdictio
of LOCs to those areas would be required, and Allied ground forces woul
have to defend the mountain passes. There are three principal passes; they ar
on the Tehran–Hamadan–Abadan road, the Hamadan–Kermanshah–Baghda
road, and the Dzulfa–Mehabad–Mosul road. There is only one railroad tha
reaches the Iraq border from Iran (Bandar Shah–Tehran–Abadan), and it is ex
tremely vulnerable to demolition and air interdiction. Assuming effective im
plementation of planned ground demolitions followed by air interdictio
immediately after D-Day of the LOCs leading through Iran, it is believed tha
Allied ground forces would probably not have to be in position to defend thes
passes until about D + 1 month.

Two divisions, additional to the one already in the Basra–Abadan area woul
be required at about this time to block Soviet advances in these areas. Th
fighter groups already in the Basra–Abadan area should provide tactical air sup
port for Allied ground forces and assist in attacks against Soviet LOCs throug
Iran. About one additional light bomb group, however, should be provided fo
air interdiction and ground support. Further assistance to Allied ground force
would be furnished by carrier and land-based aircraft engaged in air interdictio
as covered in other courses of action. AA defenses would also be required a
Baghdad and Mosul.

Defense of southeastern Turkey could be conducted along the general lin
Silifke–Cilician Gates–Malatya–Van Golu to the junction of the Turkish–Iraq
Iran borders. The left anchor of this line would be in the generally high an
rugged Taurus Mountains. The right flank would be anchored in the even mor
mountainous regions north and east of Mosul. The regions between are onl
slightly less high and rugged. The few routes leading into this area from th
north are generally poor [and] extremely vulnerable and could be easil
blocked. The principal one of these routes would be through the Taurus Moun
tains (Cilician Gates) into the Iskenderun area, with a secondary route leadin
from the north into Malatya. Except for these two routes no others of any sig
nificance exist.

It is estimated that with proper advance planning approximately eleven Tur
kish divisions could be reasonably expected to be able to withdraw to thi
defense line. In addition to these Turkish divisions approximately four Allie
divisions (three infantry and one armored) would be required to bolster th
Turkish defenses; of these, two infantry and one armored should be provide
by the U.S. and one infantry by the British. These divisions would probabl
have to be in position by not later than D + 6 months.

Allied air forces assisting in defense of southeastern Turkey would b
required to maintain air superiority over the battle areas, interdict Soviet LOCs

and furnish support to ground forces as required. It is estimated that, in addition to the one Egyptian fighter group already in the Cairo–Suez area, one fighter group should be in the Mosul area by D + 4 months and four groups plus one light bomb group and one tactical reconnaissance group should be in the Iskenderun–Aleppo area by D + 4 months. The fighter group in the Mosul area should be British; those groups in the Iskenderun–Aleppo area would probably have to be supplied by the United States. These groups would be assisted by carrier and land-based aircraft engaged in air interdiction of Soviet LOC's. . . . AA protection for installations in the Iskenderun–Aleppo area and the LOCs southward would also be required at D + 4 months. [See relevant map.] . . .

b. Tasks

(1) Provide the ground, air, and AA defenses of the refineries and associated installations at Bahrein and Ras Tanura and the airfield at Dhahran.
(2) Provide the ground, air, and AA defenses of the Abadan refinery, its associated installations and oil fields, and the key communications and port facilities in that area.
(3) Accomplish planned demolitions and air interdiction of the Soviet LOCs leading through Iran and Turkey.
(4) Gain and maintain air superiority over the Iranian mountain passes and over the southeastern Turkey battle areas.
(5) Provide the ground-force defense of the mountain passes leading into Iraq and the Iranian oil areas.
(6) Provide the ground-force defense of southeastern Turkey.
(7) Provide tactical air support of Allied ground forces.
(8) Provide AA protection for Baghdad, Mosul, the Iskenderun–Aleppo area, and the LOCs southward from the latter.
(9) Provide naval local-defense forces in the Bahrein–Dhahran area.
(10) Provide a floating reserve of ground forces. [See force-requirement chart.] . . .

9. Hold Maximum Areas of the Middle East and Southeast Asia Consistent with Indigenous Capabilities Supported by Other Allied Courses of Action

a. Analysis

The principal Allied interests in the countries of the Middle East and Far East would be the retention of the oil-bearing areas of Iran and the economic resources of the Indian subcontinent, Southeast Asia, and the East Indies; their denial to the USSR; and the protection of our LOCs. Limitation of further

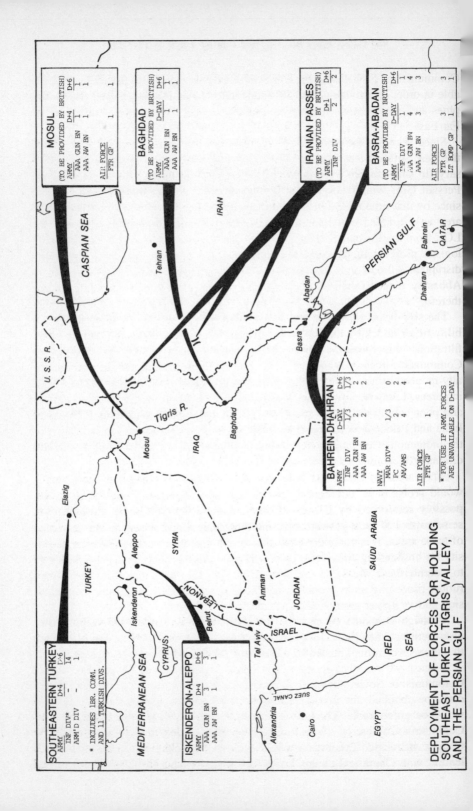

MOSUL
(TO BE PROVIDED BY BRITISH)

ARMY	D+6	D+4
	1	1
AAA GUN BN	1	1
AAA AW BN		1
AIR FORCE		
FTR GP		1

BAGHDAD
(TO BE PROVIDED BY BRITISH)

ARMY	D-6	D-DAY	D+6
	1		1
AAA GUN BN		1	1
AAA AW BN		1	

IRANIAN PASSES
(TO BE PROVIDED BY BRITISH)

ARMY	D-6	D-1	D+6
INF DIV	2	2	2

BASRA-ABADAN
(TO BE PROVIDED BY BRITISH)

ARMY	D-6	D-DAY	D+6
INF DIV	1	1	1
AAA GUN BN	4	4	4
AAA AW BN	3	3	3
AIR FORCE			
FTR GP	3	3	3
LT BOMB GP	1	1	

BAHREIN-DHAHRAN

ARMY	D-DAY	D+6
INF DIV	1/3	1/3
AAA GUN BN	2	2
AAA AW BN	2	2
NAVY		
MAR DIV*	1/3	0
PC	2	2
AM/AMS	4	4
AIR FORCE		
FTR GP	1	1

*FOR USE IF ARMY FORCES ARE UNAVAILABLE ON D-DAY

SOUTHEASTERN TURKEY

ARMY	D+6	D+4
INF DIV*	14	-
ARM'D DIV	1	-

*INCLUDES 1BR. COMM. AND 11 TURKISH DIVS.

ISKENDERON-ALEPPO

ARMY	D+6	D+4
	3	3
AAA GUN BN	1	1
AAA AW BN		

DEPLOYMENT OF FORCES FOR HOLDING
SOUTHEAST TURKEY, TIGRIS VALLEY,
AND THE PERSIAN GULF

Communist or Soviet advances in Southeast Asia would be particularly desirable in order to provide additional security for Japan, Okinawa, and the Philippines and to strengthen our position relative to our long-term objectives in the Far East.

Since securing the oil-bearing areas of Iran has been covered under "Hold the area: Southeastern Turkey," etc., no further discussion of this task is necessary. In southeastern Iran, however, a small Soviet threat to Allied use of the Persian Gulf would develop at Bandar Abbas . . . at about $D+2$ months, since by that time the Soviets would have the capability of consolidating in that area an estimated one line division and fifty combat aircraft. However, the LOC from the Caspian Sea area to Bandar Abbas would present a most difficult logistic problem to the Soviets, since it would be long, tenuous, and easily disrupted. Allied combat aircraft . . . could neutralize Soviet forces in Bandar Abbas by virtue of their ability to attack that area and interdict the LOC leading thereto.

The significant threats to the Indian subcontinent would be, first, the possibility of air attack by the Soviet long-range force and second, the danger of infiltration, underground action, and possibly open attack by indigenous Communist forces in Southeast Asia. The air threat would probably be materially reduced by the Allied air offensive and by other operations in the oil-bearing areas. Likewise any Soviet invasion would be confronted by difficult terrain and poor communications. Inasmuch as it is assumed that the armed forces of India and Pakistan would be able to defend those countries against the threat of the indigenous Communist forces in Southeast Asia, it is considered that no additional Allied forces are required in the Indian subcontinent.

Other areas of Southeast Asia—notably Malaya, Burma, and Indochina—would probably be threatened considerably by indigenous Communist forces, possibly reinforced by Chinese Communists, which would be attempting to seize control of local governments and thus deny Allied access to the resources of those areas. It is considered that this threat must be accepted since the necessity for husbanding Allied resources will preclude the allocation of major forces to defend these areas. In Malaya, however, the importance of the natural rubber-producing areas would justify a requirement for 1 British infantry division and ⅓ fighter group for their protection.

Although it should be possible to retain Formosa under Allied influence, elsewhere in China the Communist and Soviet freedom of action would be such that their forces could push as far into south China as required by Soviet plans.

Because of the disproportionately large forces required to oppose further Communist or Soviet advances into south China, with respect to the results that could be obtained, the introduction of Allied forces onto the mainland of China would be unprofitable. The most suitable alternative would be to assist the non-Communist Chinese by air and naval supporting action from bases outside the Chinese mainland. This action would consist of attacks on land and sea LOCs leading into China and enemy bases in China, by land-based air in Japan and

Okinawa and by carrier and cruiser task forces based in the western Pacific. Psychological, economic, and underground warfare measures should also be intensified. . . .

b. Tasks

(1) Conduct air attacks against Soviet forces which threaten Bandar Abbas and interdict the LOC leading thereto.
(2) Provide ground and air defenses against indigenous Communist forces in Malaya.
(3) Interdict Soviet land and sea LOCs leading into China and neutralize enemy bases in China. [See force-requirement chart.] . . .

10. Hold Japan less Hokkaido

a. Analysis

Seizure and control of Japan by the Soviets would add the Japanese industrial capacity and technical ability to the Soviet war potential, provide the Soviets with additional air and naval bases in the Pacific, and present a threat to the security of Okinawa. Soviet attacks on the Japanese Islands, unless resulting in the capture and holding of one or more of the main islands, present no serious threat to the Allied strategic concept, and Allied forces committed to the defense of Japan should be kept to the minimum necessary to prevent Soviet invasion and occupation.

The principal Soviet threat to Japan would be an amphibious assault accompanied by airborne landings prefaced and supported by strong air attacks.

The Soviets probably initially would have an estimated 20 line divisions and 2,800 combat aircraft—together with elements of the long-range air force—available for all operations in the Far East. Utilizing 2–3 divisions from this total and supported by aircraft based in Sakhalin and the Kurils, the Soviets could probably seize Hokkaido. Assault of the other main islands would depend upon the availability of the necessary airlift, shipping, and naval support, which might be required to satisfy higher-priority operations in other theaters. Amphibious attacks could develop from Korea against northern Kyushu and southern Honshu, and airborne landings could be made to seize the Kanto plain.

Because of the relative lack of importance of Hokkaido, the comparative ease with which the Soviets could seize it with forces based in Sakhalin and the Kurils, and the disproportionately large additional forces required for its defense, it is considered infeasible to provide ground and air forces on Hokkaido for its defense.

Organization, equipment, and training of Japanese forces would reduce the requirement for U.S. forces in defense of Japan. Five Japanese infantry divisions, fully armed and equipped, and five Japanese security divisions for guarding vital installations and lines of communication would reduce the requirement for U.S. ground forces to two infantry divisions. Unless the indicated Japanese infantry divisions are provided, at least two additional U.S. infantry divisions would be required for the defense of Japan. Provision of Japanese noncombat air units, naval local-defense forces, and logistic supporting units would reduce U.S. commitments.

To meet the above threats, forces estimated at 1 U.S. infantry division, 2 Japanese divisions, 1 fighter group, and ⅓ of an all-weather interceptor group would be required in the northern Kyushu–southern Honshu area, and 3 Japanese divisons, 1 fighter group, and ⅓ of an all-weather interceptor group in the extreme northern Honshu area. One U.S. infantry division and one all-weather interceptor group would be required in the Kanto plain to protect that area from airborne attacks and to serve as a general reserve. AA defenses would also be required. Five Japanese divisions equipped on an austerity basis should be sufficient for internal-security duties guarding vital installations and lines of communication. [See force-requirement chart.] . . .

11. Secure Sea and Air Lines of Communication Essential to the Accomplishment of the Overall Strategic Concept

a. Analysis

Planned Soviet aggression would include initial deployment of Soviet forces to interrupt critical Allied sea and air lines of communication. Allied plans for initial deployment must include adequate measures to prevent unacceptable losses during this period, particularly losses from submarine action. Until eliminated or greatly reduced, the Soviet submarine capability would present a serious threat to Allied sea communications.

While the enemy submarines would present the principal threat to Allied shipping, the Soviets would be capable of a considerable mining effort against Allied ports and their focal approaches. Enemy land-based air and surface naval forces would present a lesser threat to essential sea LOCs.

The Soviet capability to interrupt air LOCs would consist principally of the possible seizure or neutralization of certain air bases along such lines. A limited capability would exist in some areas for attack on aircraft en route. Although the North Atlantic and northwest Pacific would appear to be the only areas in which these capabilities could be exercised initially, Soviet seizure or neutralization of one or more bases in these areas would require an undesirable diversion of Allied means for their recapture and/or rehabilitation and might delay Allied deployment.

In 1957 it is estimated that the USSR will have between 300 and 350 ocean-

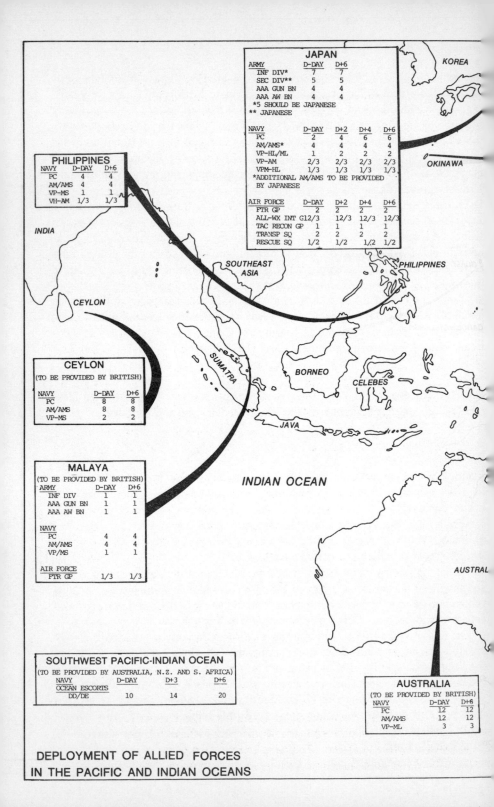

JAPAN

ARMY	D-DAY	D+6
INF DIV*	7	7
SEC DIV**	5	5
AAA GUN BN	4	4
AAA AW BN	4	4

*5 SHOULD BE JAPANESE
** JAPANESE

NAVY	D-DAY	D+2	D+4	D+6
PC	2	4	6	6
AM/AMS*	4	4	4	4
VP-HL/ML	1	2	2	2
VP-AM	2/3	2/3	2/3	2/3
VPM-HL	1/3	1/3	1/3	1/3

*ADDITIONAL AM/AMS TO BE PROVIDED
BY JAPANESE

AIR FORCE	D-DAY	D+2	D+4	D+6
FTR GP	2	2	2	2
ALL-WX INT GP	12/3	12/3	12/3	12/3
TAC RECON GP	1	1	1	1
TRANSP SQ	2	2	2	2
RESCUE SQ	1/2	1/2	1/2	1/2

PHILIPPINES

NAVY	D-DAY	D+6
PC	4	4
AM/AMS	4	4
VP-MS	1	1
VH-AM	1/3	1/3

CEYLON

(TO BE PROVIDED BY BRITISH)

NAVY	D-DAY	D+6
PC	8	8
AM/AMS	8	8
VP-MS	2	2

MALAYA

(TO BE PROVIDED BY BRITISH)

ARMY	D-DAY	D+6
INF DIV	1	1
AAA GUN BN	1	1
AAA AW BN	1	1

NAVY		
PC	4	4
AM/AMS	4	4
VP/MS	1	1

AIR FORCE		
FTR GP	1/3	1/3

INDIAN OCEAN

SOUTHWEST PACIFIC-INDIAN OCEAN

(TO BE PROVIDED BY AUSTRALIA, N.Z. AND S. AFRICA)

NAVY	D-DAY	D+3	D+6
OCEAN ESCORTS			
DD/DE	10	14	20

AUSTRALIA

(TO BE PROVIDED BY BRITISH)

NAVY	D-DAY	D+6
PC	12	12
AM/AMS	12	12
VP-ML	3	3

KOREA

OKINAWA

INDIA

CEYLON

SOUTHEAST
ASIA

PHILIPPINES

SUMATRA

BORNEO

CELEBES

JAVA

AUSTRAL

DEPLOYMENT OF ALLIED FORCES
IN THE PACIFIC AND INDIAN OCEANS

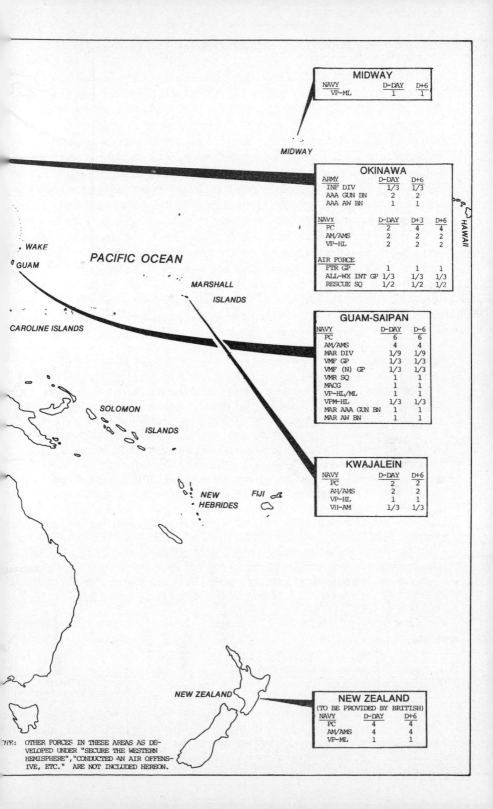

MIDWAY

NAVY	D-DAY	D+6
VP-ML	1	1

OKINAWA

ARMY	D-DAY	D+6	
INF DIV	1/3	1/3	
AAA GUN BN	2	2	
AAA AW BN	1	1	

NAVY	D-DAY	D+3	D+6
PC	2	4	4
AM/AMS	2	2	2
VP-HL	2	2	2

AIR FORCE			
FTR GP	1	1	1
ALL-WX INT GP	1/3	1/3	1/3
RESCUE SQ	1/2	1/2	1/2

GUAM-SAIPAN

NAVY	D-DAY	D-6
PC	6	6
AM/AMS	4	4
MAR DIV	1/9	1/9
VMF GP	1/3	1/3
VMF (N) GP	1/3	1/3
VMR SQ	1	1
MACG	1	1
VP-HL/ML	1	1
VPM-HL	1/3	1/3
MAR AAA GUN BN	1	1
MAR AW BN	1	1

KWAJALEIN

NAVY	D-DAY	D+6
PC	2	2
AM/AMS	2	2
VP-HL	1	1
VH-AM	1/3	1/3

NEW ZEALAND
(TO BE PROVIDED BY BRITISH)

NAVY	D-DAY	D+6
PC	4	4
AM/AMS	4	4
VP-ML	1	1

MIDWAY

HAWAII

WAKE

GUAM

PACIFIC OCEAN

MARSHALL ISLANDS

CAROLINE ISLANDS

SOLOMON ISLANDS

NEW HEBRIDES

FIJI

NEW ZEALAND

NOTE: OTHER FORCES IN THESE AREAS AS DE-
VELOPED UNDER "SECURE THE WESTERN
HEMISPHERE", "CONDUCTED AN AIR OFFENS-
IVE, ETC." ARE NOT INCLUDED HEREON.

type submarines,* of which about 50 percent are expected to be capable of high submerged speed, and between 200 and 300 submarines of the coastal-defense type. On the basis of an expected radius of action of about six thousand nautical miles for the ocean-going types, Soviet submarines could operate in the Atlantic, Pacific, Mediterranean, the Alaskan and Caribbean areas, and the coastal waters of the United States and Canada. It is possible (with refueling clandestinely or at sea) that limited operations could be conducted in the Indian Ocean. In general, the expected submarine density in any area (and hence the threat) would vary inversely as the distance from the submarines' bases, other factors being equal. It is possible that initially as many as 40–50 percent of the Soviet submarine fleet could be at sea; thereafter about ⅓–¼ on patrol might be a reasonable expectancy. Russian surface forces built around an estimated 30 cruisers (heavy and light) would constitute a potential but lesser threat to our LOC. It is not expected that their surface forces, except for raiders, would operate far beyond the umbrella of Soviet shore-based air. Unless they are contained or destroyed, however, the defense of convoys would have to include uneconomical use of heavy units.

*Editor's Note: Again Dropshot planners seem to have been suffering from a lack of reliable intelligence. By 1956 the Soviet submarine fleet more probably consisted of some 450 deep-water and coastal submarines. By 1959 the ISS military-balance study shows that the real total may have been 500–600. But it should not be imagined that all these vessels were of the deep-water type concentrated in the North Atlantic. Many of them were coastal, and a very large number of Soviet submarines would have been required for service in the Pacific, if only to guard the Soviet Asian coast. Nevertheless the number is extremely formidable—the more so when it is kept in mind that the German submarine fleet in World War II rarely exceeded 50 vessels at sea in all waters. Small as it was, however, it inflicted severe and sometimes almost catastrophic casualties upon the mercantile marines of England and America. Even with increased ASW [Anti-Submarine Warfare] capabilities Allied losses in any war around 1957 would perforce have been at least as serious—although, it should be remembered, Russian submarine capabilities have never been demonstrated against very experienced and resourceful enemies such as the U.S. Navy and the Royal Navy would be.

The three principal methods of controlling our lines of communication are through:

(1) Attack on enemy threat at source.
(2) Offensive control.
(3) Defensive control.

The attack at source includes destruction of enemy submarine production and repair facilities, operating bases, ships, and supporting facilities including defensive air. Offensive control includes offensive mining of approaches to enemy ports and bases, hunter–killer operations, antisubmarine submarine operations, and interception and destruction of enemy naval surface forces which get to sea. Defensive control includes convoy escort (both surface and air), defensive mining, and arming of merchant ships. All three methods will be required and are mutually supporting. The more effective the offensive methods, the less the need for the purely defensive and the less the forces required therefor. Further, the elusive qualities of the modern submarine and the effectiveness of the long-range, pattern-running torpedo emphasize the importance of the attack on this enemy threat at source.

Essential sea and air lines of communication and the Soviet submarine threat to them are shown on the map, page 232. . . .

It is considered that ground and air defenses of air LOC bases within effective range of Soviet air attack would be provided by Allied forces listed under other courses of action. At bases where no Allied defense forces are provided under other courses of action and which may be exposed to sporadic air or surface raids, sufficient qualified personnel should be provided to maintain defensive equipment and instruct the local base operating personnel in its use.

Fighter defense of convoys would be essential only in areas where enemy air attack would be a normal expectancy. Defense of convoys in areas where only sporadic air attacks could be expected should be limited to antiaircraft defense provided by convoy escorts. Forces provided under other courses of action are considered adequate to provide essential fighter protection for convoys except in the Mediterranean between Crete and Cyrenaica. It is estimated that ⅓ day fighter group and ⅓ night fighter group would be required to provide for this area. . . .

b. Tasks

(1) Establish a convoy system and control and routing of shipping.
(2) Provide convoy air and surface escorts.
(3) Provide air defense of convoys within effective range of enemy air. [See force-requirement chart.] . . .

12. Secure Overseas Bases Essential to the Accomplishment of the Overall Strategic Concept

a. Immediately After D-Day Provide Forces by Air and Sea Transport to Occupy or Recapture Iceland and the Azores and Establish Necessary Air and Naval Bases Thereon

(1) *Analysis*
  (a) *Iceland.* The security of Iceland should be assured by the Allies because of its strategic location with respect to offensive air and naval bases and sea and

air LOCs. While it may not be required for the strategic air offensive as long as the United Kingdom is held, it would be of great value to Allied forces as a base for staging aircraft, for support of submarine operations, ASW operations, and a fast-carrier support group. It should also be denied to the Soviets as a base for reconnaissance, early warning, and bomber staging.

Seizure or destruction of established or potential bases in Iceland by air, naval, and limited airborne attacks would be the principal Soviet threats requiring counteraction by U.S. forces. In addition sabotage could be employed against important facilities. In a surprise movement on D-Day, airborne and seaborne troops and supplies could be landed, but these units would ultimately be lost because of difficulties of resupply due to Allied counteraction.

In order to secure Iceland, one RCT and one composite fighter group— together with necessary AA protection—should be established in Iceland via airlift immediately after D-Day or before, if practicable. Naval forces for local defense would be required as soon afterward as possible. However, if Iceland were seized by the Soviets before U.S. forces had arrived, it is estimated that a 1 division amphibious assault would be necessary to retake it. The division thus required should be in being on D-Day. This division would be composed mainly of the RCT mentioned above and the $^4/_9$ division earmarked for operations in North Africa but not required until D + 3 months as set forth under "Establish or expand and defend Allied bases as required in northwest Africa and North Africa," page 231. Further protection against Soviet naval forces would be provided by Allied naval forces listed under "Conduct offensive operations to destroy enemy naval forces," etc., and "Secure sea and air lines of communication," etc.

(b) *Azores*. The Azores would have strategic importance in the maintenance of essential sea and air LOCs and as a necessary base area for ASW operations. They should also be denied to the Soviets as a base for bomber staging or submarine refueling.

Since the Azores are over two thousand nautical miles from any air or naval bases likely to be in possession of the Soviets on D-Day, the only significant threats to these islands would be sporadic bombing and submarine attacks and possible sabotage. These activities would probably be conducted only on a small scale as the Soviets will have far more lucrative targets closer to the USSR.

Security of the Azores as an important link in sea and air LOCs would require employment of one battalion of ground forces and one all-weather fighter squadron. Naval local-defense forces would also be required, with some buildup during the first three months as shipping through this area increases. Initial forces for defense of the Azores should be provided as soon after D-Day as possible.

Forces for this course of action together with forces shown under "Conduct offensive operations to destroy enemy naval forces," etc., and "Secure sea and air LOCs," etc., are also shown on the map. . . .

(2) *Tasks*

(a) Immediately after D-Day—or before, if practicable—provide ground, air, and antiaircraft forces to secure and defend Iceland, utilizing airlift as necessary.
(b) As soon as possible after D-Day provide ground and air units to secure and defend the Azores.
(c) Defend the sea approaches to Iceland and the Azores.
(d) Provide naval local-defense forces for Iceland and the Azores. [See force-requirement charts.] . . .

b. Establish or Expand and Defend Allied Bases as Required in Northwest Africa and North Africa

(1) *Analysis*

The maintenance of sea and air lines of communication in the Mediterranean for the furtherance of Allied operations in the Near and Middle East and the support and logistic supply for naval forces in the Mediterranean would require bases in the Port Lyautey–Casablanca, Oran–Algiers, Bizerte—Gabes Gulf areas, Tripoli, and Cyrenaica. Cognizance is taken that Malta would probably be used by U.S. forces, particularly submarines, and that Gibraltar and Alexandria could be used for some support of U.S. escort and ASW units.

Base requirements in North Africa would be as follows:

Port Lyautey	Air base.
Casablanca	Naval operating base.
	Escort terminal with facilities for limited ship repairs.
	Base on the air LOC.
Oran	Intermediate escort station for convoy assembly.
Algiers	Intermediate escort station for convoy assembly.
	Alternate base on the air LOC.
Bizerte	Escort terminal.
	Secondary naval air base.
	Advanced secondary operating base with facilities for emergency ship repairs.
Gabes Gulf	Major fleet anchorage with minimum facilities ashore.
Tripoli	Limited escort terminal.
	Base on the air LOC.
Cyrenaica	Fighter air base for protection of sea LOC between Crete and Cyrenaica.
	Alternate base on the air LOC.

The need for these bases would require that facilities at Port Lyautey, Casablanca, and the air LOC facilities at Tripoli be available on D-day. Bases at Bizerte, Gabes Gulf, and Cyrenaica would be required by D + 1 and those at Oran and Algiers by D + 3. Naval base facilities at Tripoli would also be

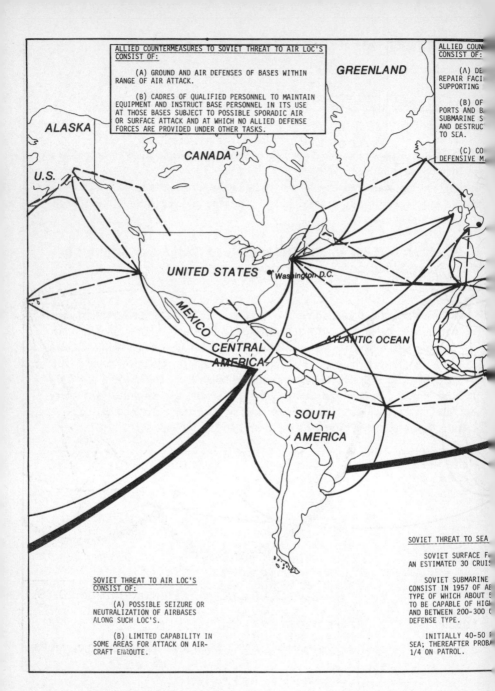

ALLIED COUNTERMEASURES TO SOVIET THREAT TO AIR LOC'S
CONSIST OF:

    (A) GROUND AND AIR DEFENSES OF BASES WITHIN
RANGE OF AIR ATTACK.

    (B) CADRES OF QUALIFIED PERSONNEL TO MAINTAIN
EQUIPMENT AND INSTRUCT BASE PERSONNEL IN ITS USE
AT THOSE BASES SUBJECT TO POSSIBLE SPORADIC AIR
OR SURFACE ATTACK AND AT WHICH NO ALLIED DEFENSE
FORCES ARE PROVIDED UNDER OTHER TASKS.

ALLIED COUN
CONSIST OF:

    (Λ) DE
REPAIR FACI
SUPPORTING

    (B) OF
PORTS AND B
SUBMARINE S
AND DESTRUC
TO SEA.

    (C) CO
DEFENSIVE M

GREENLAND

ALASKA

U.S.

CANADA

UNITED STATES   Washington D.C.

MEXICO

CENTRAL
AMERICA

ATLANTIC OCEAN

SOUTH
AMERICA

SOVIET THREAT TO AIR LOC'S
CONSIST OF:

    (A) POSSIBLE SEIZURE OR
NEUTRALIZATION OF AIRBASES
ALONG SUCH LOC'S.

    (B) LIMITED CAPABILITY IN
SOME AREAS FOR ATTACK ON AIR-
CRAFT ENROUTE.

SOVIET THREAT TO SEA

    SOVIET SURFACE F
AN ESTIMATED 30 CRUIS

    SOVIET SUBMARINE
CONSIST IN 1957 OF AE
TYPE OF WHICH ABOUT 5
TO BE CAPABLE OF HIGH
AND BETWEEN 200-300 C
DEFENSE TYPE.

    INITIALLY 40-50 F
SEA; THEREAFTER PROBA
1/4 ON PATROL.

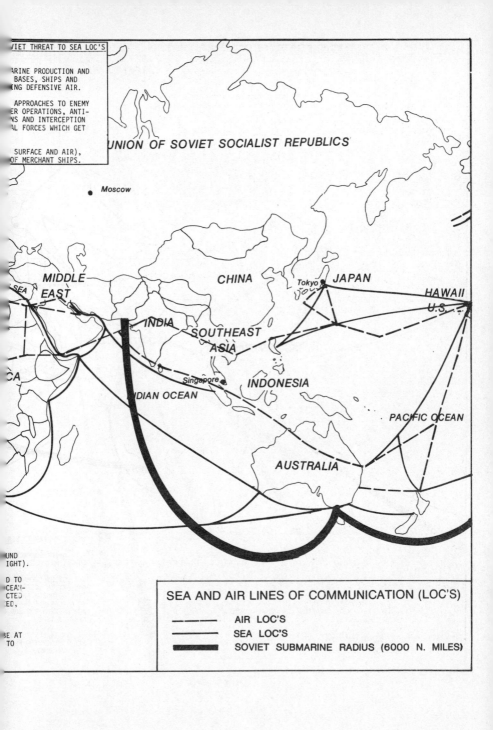

UNION OF SOVIET SOCIALIST REPUBLICS

Moscow

MIDDLE
EAST
SEA

CHINA

Tokyo JAPAN

HAWAII
U.S.

INDIA

SOUTHEAST
ASIA

CA

Singapore

INDONESIA

DIAN OCEAN

PACIFIC OCEAN

AUSTRALIA

UND
IGHT).

D TO
CEAN-
CTED
ED,

E AT
TO

SEA AND AIR LINES OF COMMUNICATION (LOC'S)

– – – –	AIR LOC'S
————	SEA LOC'S
██████	SOVIET SUBMARINE RADIUS (6000 N. MILES)

DEPLOYMENT OF ALLIED FORCES IN THE BARENTS-NORWEGIAN SEA, ATLAN...

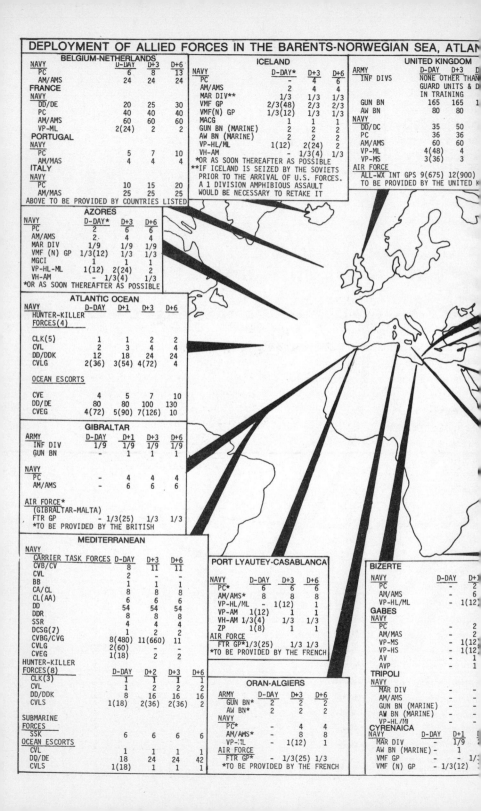

BELGIUM-NETHERLANDS

NAVY	D-DAY	D+3	D+6
PC	6	8	13
AM/AMS	24	24	24

FRANCE

NAVY			
DD/DE	20	25	30
PC	40	40	40
AM/AMS	60	60	60
VP-ML	2(24)	2	2

PORTUGAL

NAVY			
PC	5	7	10
AM/MAS	4	4	4

ITALY

NAVY			
PC	10	15	20
AM/MAS	25	25	25

ABOVE TO BE PROVIDED BY COUNTRIES LISTED

ICELAND

NAVY	D-DAY*	D+3	D+6
PC	-	4	6
AM/AMS	2	4	4
MAR DIV**	1/3	1/3	1/3
VMF GP	2/3(48)	2/3	2/3
VMF(N) GP	1/3(12)	1/3	1/3
MACG	1	1	1
GUN BN (MARINE)	2	2	2
AW BN (MARINE)	2	2	2
VP-HL/ML	1(12)	2(24)	2
VH-AM	-	1/3(4)	1/3

*OR AS SOON THEREAFTER AS POSSIBLE
**IF ICELAND IS SEIZED BY THE SOVIETS
PRIOR TO THE ARRIVAL OF U.S. FORCES.
A 1 DIVISION AMPHIBIOUS ASSAULT
WOULD BE NECESSARY TO RETAKE IT

UNITED KINGDOM

ARMY	D-DAY	D+3	D
INF DIVS	NONE OTHER THAN		
	GUARD UNITS & D		
	IN TRAINING		
GUN BN	165	165	1
AW BN	80	80	

NAVY			
DD/DC	35	50	
PC	36	36	
AM/AMS	60	60	
VP-ML	4(48)	4	
VP-MS	3(36)	3	

AIR FORCE
ALL-WX INT GPS 9(675) 12(900)
TO BE PROVIDED BY THE UNITED K

AZORES

NAVY	D-DAY*	D+3	D+6
PC	2	6	6
AM/AMS	2	4	4
MAR DIV	1/9	1/9	1/9
VMF (N) GP	1/3(12)	1/3	1/3
MGCI	1	1	1
VP-HL-ML	1(12)	2(24)	2
VH-AM	-	1/3(4)	1/3

*OR AS SOON THEREAFTER AS POSSIBLE

ATLANTIC OCEAN

NAVY	D-DAY	D+1	D+3	D+6
HUNTER-KILLER FORCES(4)				
CLK(5)	1	1	2	2
CVL	2	3	4	4
DD/DDK	12	18	24	24
CVLG	2(36)	3(54)	4(72)	4
OCEAN ESCORTS				
CVE	4	5	7	10
DD/DE	80	80	100	130
CVEG	4(72)	5(90)	7(126)	10

GIBRALTAR

ARMY	D-DAY	D+1	D+3	D+6
INF DIV	1/9	1/9	1/9	1/9
GUN BN	-	1	1	1
NAVY				
PC	-	4	4	4
AM/AMS	-	6	6	6
AIR FORCE* (GIBRALTAR-MALTA)				
FTR GP	-	1/3(25)	1/3	1/3

*TO BE PROVIDED BY THE BRITISH

MEDITERRANEAN

NAVY	D-DAY	D+3	D+6
CARRIER TASK FORCES			
CVB/CV	8	11	11
CVL	2	-	-
BB	1	1	1
CA/CL	8	8	8
CL(AA)	6	6	6
DD	54	54	54
DDR	8	8	8
SSR	4	4	4
DCSG(2)	1	2	2
CVBG/CVG	8(480)	11(660)	11
CVLG	2(60)	-	-
CVEG	1(18)	2	2

HUNTER-KILLER FORCES(8)	D-DAY	D+2	D+3	D+6
CLK(3)	1	1	1	1
CVL	1	2	2	2
DD/DDK	8	16	16	16
CVLS	1(18)	2(36)	2(36)	2

SUBMARINE FORCES				
SSK	6	6	6	6

OCEAN ESCORTS				
CVL	1	1	1	1
DD/DE	18	24	24	42
CVLS	1(18)	1	1	1

PORT LYAUTEY-CASABLANCA

NAVY	D-DAY	D+3	D+6
PC*	6	6	6
AM/AMS*	8	8	8
VP-HL/ML	-	1(12)	1
VP-AM	1(12)	1	1
VH-AM	1/3(4)	1/3	1/3
ZP	1(8)	1	1
AIR FORCE			
FTR GP*	1/3(25)	1/3	1/3

*TO BE PROVIDED BY THE FRENCH

ORAN-ALGIERS

ARMY	D-DAY	D+3	D+6
GUN BN*	2	2	2
AW BN*	2	2	2
NAVY			
PC*	-	4	4
AM/AMS*	-	8	8
VP-ML	-	1(12)	1
AIR FORCE			
FTR GP*	-	1/3(25)	1/3

*TO BE PROVIDED BY THE FRENCH

BIZERTE

NAVY	D-DAY	D+
PC	-	2
AM/AMS	-	6
VP-HL/ML	-	1(12)

GABES

NAVY		
PC	-	2
AM/MAS	-	2
VP-MS	-	1(12)
VP-HS	-	1(12)
AV	-	1
AVP	-	1

TRIPOLI

NAVY		
MAR DIV	-	-
AM/AMS	-	-
GUN BN (MARINE)	-	-
AW BN (MARINE)	-	-
VP-HL/MI	-	-

CYRENAICA

NAVY	D-DAY	D+1
MAR DIV	-	1/9
AW BN (MARINE)	-	1
VMF GP	-	1/
VMF (N) GP	-	1/3(12)

MEDITERRANEAN-ARABIAN SEA AREAS

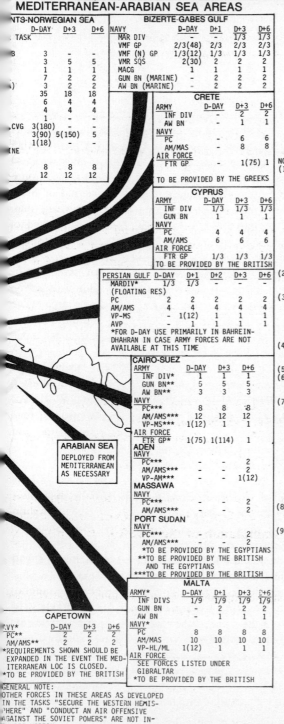

NTS-NORWEGIAN SEA

	D-DAY	D+3	D+6
TASK			
B	3	-	-
	3	5	5
	1	1	1
	7	2	2
A)	3	2	2
	35	18	18
	6	4	4
	4	4	4
	1	-	-
CVG	3(180)	-	-
	3(90)	5(150)	5
	1(18)	-	-
NE			
	8	8	8
	12	12	12

BIZERTE-GABES GULF

NAVY	D-DAY	D+1	D+3	D+6
MAR DIV	-	-	1/3	1/3
VMF GP	2/3(48)	2/3	2/3	2/3
VMF (N) GP	1/3(12)	1/3	1/3	1/3
VMR SQS	2(30)	2	2	2
MACG	1	1	1	1
GUN BN (MARINE)	-	2	2	2
AW BN (MARINE)	-	2	2	2

CRETE

ARMY	D-DAY	D+3	D+6
INF DIV	-	2	2
AW BN	-	1	1
NAVY			
PC	-	6	6
AM/MAS	-	8	8
AIR FORCE			
FTR GP	-	1(75)	1

TO BE PROVIDED BY THE GREEKS

CYPRUS

ARMY	D-DAY	D+3	D+6
INF DIV	1/3	1/3	1/3
GUN BN	1	1	1
NAVY			
PC	4	4	4
AM/AMS	6	6	6
AIR FORCE			
FTR GP	1/3	1/3	1/3

TO BE PROVIDED BY THE BRITISH

PERSIAN GULF

	D-DAY	D+1	D+2	D+3	D+6
MARDIV*	1/3	1/3	-	-	-
(FLOATING RES)					
PC	2	2	2	2	2
AM/AMS	4	4	4	4	4
VP-MS	-	1(12)	1	1	1
AVP	-	1	1	1	1

*FOR D-DAY USE PRIMARILY IN BAHREIN-DHAHRAN IN CASE ARMY FORCES ARE NOT AVAILABLE AT THIS TIME

CAIRO-SUEZ

ARMY	D-DAY	D+3	D+6
INF DIV*	1	1	1
GUN BN**	5	5	5
AW BN**	3	3	3
NAVY			
PC***	8	8	8
AM/AMS***	12	12	12
VP-MS***	1(12)	1	1
AIR FORCE			
FTR GP*	1(75)	1(114)	1

ADEN

NAVY	D-DAY	D+3	D+6
PC***	-	-	2
AM/AMS***	-	-	2
VP-AM***	-	-	1(12)

MASSAWA

NAVY	D-DAY	D+3	D+6
PC***	-	-	2
AM/AMS***	-	-	2

PORT SUDAN

NAVY	D-DAY	D+3	D+6
PC***	-	-	2
AM/AMS***	-	-	2

*TO BE PROVIDED BY THE EGYPTIANS
**TO BE PROVIDED BY THE BRITISH AND THE EGYPTIANS
***TO BE PROVIDED BY THE BRITISH

ARABIAN SEA

DEPLOYED FROM MEDITERRANEAN AS NECESSARY

MALTA

ARMY*	D-DAY	D+1	D+3	D+6
INF DIVS	1/9	1/9	1/9	1/9
GUN BN	-	2	2	2
AW BN	-	1	1	1
NAVY*				
PC	8	8	8	8
AM/MAS	10	10	10	10
VP-HL/ML	1(12)	1	1	1
AIR FORCE				

SEE FORCES LISTED UNDER GIBRALTAR
*TO BE PROVIDED BY THE BRITISH

CAPETOWN

	D-DAY	D+3	D+6
NAVY*			
PC**	2	2	2
AM/AMS**	2	2	2

*REQUIREMENTS SHOWN SHOULD BE EXPANDED IN THE EVENT THE MEDITERRANEAN LOC IS CLOSED.
**TO BE PROVIDED BY THE BRITISH

GENERAL NOTE:
OTHER FORCES IN THESE AREAS AS DEVELOPED IN THE TASKS "SECURE THE WESTERN HEMISPHERE" AND "CONDUCT AN AIR OFFENSIVE AGAINST THE SOVIET POWERS" ARE NOT INCLUDED HEREON.

NOTES:
(1) FIGURES REFLECT THE INCLUSION OF A BRITISH CTF TO BE PROVIDED ON D-DAY. THIS CTF TO BE COMPOSED APPROXIMATELY AS FOLLOWS: 3CVL, 1BB, 2CA/CL, 2CL(AA), 17DD, 2DDR. ABOVE FIGURES ALSO REFLECT THE POSSIBLE REDEPLOYMENT TO THE MEDITERRANEAN AND ELSEWHERE, AS NEEDED, OF THE U.S. CTF FROM THE BARENTS-NORWEGIAN SEA AREA UPON COMPLETION OF INITIAL OPERATIONS THERE BY ABOUT D+2 MONTHS, LEAVING THE POLICING OF BARENTS-NORWEGIAN AREA TO THE BRITISH, REINFORCED BY A PORTION OF THE FORCES FROM THE MEDITERRANEAN.
(2) A FAST CARRIER SUPPORT GROUP IS NORMALLY COMPOSED OF 1CVE, 4A), 1AE, 1ASK, 1AVS, AND 6DD/DE.
(3) FIGURES REFLECT THE INCLUSION OF 9 BRITISH AND 4 FRENCH SUBMARINES TO BE PROVIDED BY D-DAY, IN THE BARENTS-NORWEGIAN SEA, EASTERN ARCTIC AREAS, AND MEDITERRANEAN AND REPRESENT NUMBERS ON PATROL OR 35-45% OF TOTAL REQUIRED.
(4) FIGURES REFLECT THE INCLUSION OF 1 HUNTER-KILLER GROUP TO BE PROVIDED BY BRITISH AND CANADIANS BY D+1
(5) TENTATIVE, DEPENDS ON SUCCESS OF PROTOTYPE.
(6) FIGURES REFLECT THE INCLUSION OF 30 DD/DE TO BE PROVIDED BY BRITISH AND CANADIANS ON D-DAY WITH A BUILD-UP TO 50 DD/DE BY D+6.
(7) FIGURES REFLECT THE INCLUSION OF A BRITISH CTF TO BE PROVIDED ON D-DAY. THIS CTF TO BE COMPOSED APPROXIMATELY AS FOLLOWS: 2CV, 2CVL, 3CA/CL, 2C/L(AA), 18DD, 4DDR. ABOVE FIGURES ALSO REFLECT THE POSSIBLE REDEPLOYMENT TO THE MEDITERRANEAN OR ELSEWHERE, AS NEEDED, OF THE U.S. CTF FROM THE BARENTS-NORWEGIAN SEA AREA UPON COMPLETION OF INITIAL OPERATIONS THERE BY ABOUT D+2 MONTHS LEAVING THE POLICING OF BARENTS-NORWEGIAN AREA TO THE BRITISH, REINFORCED BY A PORTION OF THEIR FORCES FROM THE MEDITERRANEAN.
(8) FIGURES REFLECT THE INCLUSION OF 1 HUNTER-KILLER GROUP TO BE PROVIDED BY FRENCH BY D+2.
(9) FIGURES REFLECT THE INCLUSION OF 12 DD/DE TO BE PROVIDED BY BRITISH AND FRENCH ON D-DAY WITH A BUILD-UP TO 30 BY D+6.

required by $D+3$. An additional threat to these bases could exist from un-friendly native elements.

The principal Soviet threat to the foregoing bases would probably take the form of air and submarine attacks from progressively advanced bases in Greece and Turkey and would increase in intensity after $D+3$ months.

To counteract the Soviet threats, Allied forces would be required as follows: at Port Lyautey and Casablanca, a small number of fighters should be provided on D-day, together with naval local-defense forces; at Oran and Algiers a small number of fighters, antiaircraft defenses, and naval local-defense forces should be provided by $D+3$ months; at Gibraltar and Malta beginning on D-Day, minimum ground forces, fighter and antiaircraft defenses, and naval local-defense forces should be provided; in the Bizerte–Gabes Gulf–Tripoli–Cyrenaica area, between $D+1$ month and $D+3$ months, forces equivalent to a total of about ⅔ division, 1 fighter group, antiaircraft defenses, and naval local-defense forces should be provided. Alexandria is covered under subparagraph c of this course of action dealing with the Cairo–Suez area.

To counteract the threat from unfriendly natives, at least 1 additional Allied division would be required in North Africa from D-Day onward.

(2) *Tasks*

(a) Provide air defenses and naval local-defense forces for bases at Port Lyautey and Casablanca.
(b) Provide ground defenses, air defenses, antiaircraft defenses, and naval local-defense forces for Gibraltar, Malta, and Bizerte–Gabes Gulf.
(c) Provide air defenses, antiaircraft defenses, and naval local-defense forces for Oran and Algiers.
(d) Provide ground defense, antiaircraft defenses, and naval local-defense forces for Tripoli. [See force-requirement chart.] . . .

c. Ensure the Availability of Suitable Bases Required in the Cairo–Suez–Aden Area Prior to D-Day

(1) *Analysis*. Defense of the Cairo–Suez–Aden area would retain for the Allies strategic air bases for attacks against the vulnerable southern flank of the USSR and would provide the vital base area required to support operations for ensuring the availability of Near and Middle East oil. This area would also provide a base for projecting subsequent advances toward the heart of the USSR. The Cairo–Suez area contains airfields and base facilities, ports, important manpower and industrial potential including a communications network, and the Suez Canal. The holding of Crete and Cyprus would contribute considerably to the security of the Cairo–Suez and Iskenderun–Aleppo areas and the LOCs leading thereto. The Aden area would be important to the control of the Red Sea–Arabian Sea LOC and in addition contains British air bases and port facilities which should be available on D-Day.

As long as the Allies hold the area southeastern Turkey–Tigris Valley–Persian Gulf, the Soviet threat to the Cairo–Suez–Aden area would be reduced to air attack and air and sea interdiction of LOCs. The Cairo–Suez–Aden area would be within range of Soviet long-range bombers on D-Day, although the Aden area should be relatively safe from such attacks. Soviet submarines could attack sea communications to Alexandria and Port Said. Airborne attacks against the Cairo–Suez area would also be possible, but forces used would undoubtedly be sacrificed because of the difficulty of resupply.

By D + 3 months some increase in the air threat in the eastern Mediterranean might be expected since air bases in Greece and Turkey would probably be available to the Soviet air forces. However, this increased threat would not be too serious in the Cairo–Suez area since it would be counteracted by the buildup of Allied land-based air and carrier task forces in the eastern Mediterranean area as developed in other courses of action.

Allied D-Day requirements for the air defense of the Cairo–Suez area would be about one fighter group (75 a/c). The strength of this group would have to be increased to wartime strength (114 a/c) by D + 3 months to take care of the increased threat. Naval forces would also have to provide local defense for both Alexandria and Port Said. Ground-force requirements are estimated to be one U.S. equivalent division for defense against airborne attacks. AA defenses would be required at Alexandria, Cairo, Port Said, Ismalia, and Suez. The island of Crete should be secured by Greek forces withdrawing from Greece at about D + 3 months. These should consist of 2 divisions, 1 fighter group, and a small amount of AA protection and naval local-defense forces. Cyprus should be defended on D-Day by British forces consisting of ⅓ infantry division, 1 fighter squadron, and necessary AA protection and naval local-defense forces. Additional protection for the Cairo–Suez area and defense of sea approaches thereto would be provided by the naval forces required in the Mediterranean and discussed under "Conduct offensive operations to destroy enemy naval forces," etc.

Requirements for the defense of Aden and other Red Sea ports would not be significant unless the Cairo–Suez area becomes untenable. Necessary minimum forces should be provided for keeping the Red Sea LOC open and providing necessary protection for ports, airfields, and other installations. . . .

(2) *Tasks*

(a) Provide ground, air, and antiaircraft defenses of the Cairo–Suez area.

(b) Defend the sea approaches to the Cairo–Suez–Aden area.

(c) Provide naval local-defense forces for Alexandria, Port Said, Aden, Massawa, and Port Sudan.

(d) Provide ground, air, antiaircraft, and naval local-defense forces for Crete.

(e) Provide ground, air, antiaircraft, and naval local-defense forces for Cyprus. [See force-requirement chart.] . . .

d. Have Forces in Being on D-Day in Okinawa for the Security of that Island

(1) *Analysis*. Because of its existing facilities, location, and relative security from Soviet attacks, Okinawa would be the most suitable base for strategic air operations in the Far East.

The principal Soviet threat to Okinawa would probably be in the form of air attacks developing primarily from Korea and North and East China. The Soviets might have some additional capabilities for airborne and seaborne attacks, although logistic difficulties involved in supply and resupply would probably preclude any such attacks except on a minor scale. The defense of Okinawa should therefore be achieved primarily by air and naval forces developed under other tasks.

Since the holding of Japan would provide additional security for Okinawa, it is estimated that ground and air forces for the defense of Okinawa could be limited to 1 RCT, 1 fighter group, and ⅓ all-weather interceptor group and some AA protection.

The defense of the sea approaches to Okinawa should be provided by carrier and cruiser task groups and fleet air squadrons in the western Pacific. . . .

(2) *Tasks*

(a) Provide ground, air, and AA defenses of Okinawa.
(b) Defend the sea approaches to Okinawa.
(c) Provide naval local-defenses forces. [See force-requirement chart.] . . .

e. Provide Necessary Minimum Protection for Other Overseas Bases Essential to the Maintenance of Sea and Air Lines of Communication

(1) *Analysis*

. . . Guam would be required as a major naval supporting base in the Pacific. Other bases required for the sea LOCs in the Pacific would include Midway, Kwajalein, and the Philippines. Emergency repair and sea LOC bases at Singapore, Colombo, and Trincomalee in Ceylon—together with escort terminal bases in Australia and New Zealand—would be used. Facilities at Capetown should be expanded to provide escort terminal facilities in the event the Mediterranean lines of communication should be closed. In addition to the foregoing, air bases for servicing traffic on the air LOCs in the Pacific should be established and maintained in Hawaii, Johnston Island, Kwajalein, the Marianas, the Philippines, the Line Islands, the Fiji Islands, Canton Island, New Caledonia, Australia, and New Zealand. In Southeast Asia, air LOC bases would be required in French Indochina, Burma, Siam, India, Singapore, and Ceylon. Those in the South Atlantic–central Africa area would be in Trinidad, the Guianas, Brazil, Ascension Island, French West Africa, Liberia, the Gold Coast, Nigeria, and the Anglo-Egyptian Sudan:

The principal threat to bases in the central and south Pacific would probably be sporadic harassing raids by submarines. The importance of Guam as a base for U.S. naval units in the Pacific would make it an additional objective for Soviet long-range bombing attacks. Singapore, Ceylon, Australia, and New Zealand are within the radius of Soviet submarines. Bases in the Indian Ocean–Southeast Asia area could be attacked by Soviet long-range aircraft. The initial threat to the Philippines would probably consist of occasional air raids plus Soviet submarine activity in the approaches to Manila. As the Soviets advance south in Asia, increased bombing attacks on Allied bases in the Indian Ocean–Southeast Asia area and on Allied airfields and shipping facilities in the western Pacific could be expected.

The Soviet threat to bases on sea and air LOCs in the South American–South Atlantic–central Africa area would be negligible and would probably consist only of limited submarine and mining activity in some areas.

Requirements for defense of Pacific–Indian Ocean area bases would vary with their importance and their distance from Soviet bases. Air bases on Midway [and] Johnston Island and in the Line Islands, Canton Islands, the Fiji Islands, New Caledonia, Australia, New Zealand, Southeast Asia, and the Indian Ocean area would require no local defense forces except for base personnel. Kwajalein would require naval local-defense forces. Guam, being an important naval base, would require 1 BCT [Battalion Combat Team], ⅓ night fighter group, antiaircraft, and naval local–defense forces. Local naval and antiaircraft defenses for Singapore and local naval defenses for bases in Ceylon, Australia, and New Zealand should be provided. Local naval defense forces would be required at Subic Bay and Sangley Point. Finally, as a theater reserve for the entire western Pacific area, it is considered that one RCT should be available to the theater commander by about $D + 2$ months to counter possible Soviet lodgement which might pose a threat to the line Japan–Okinawa–Philippines. Additional protection would be furnished by fleet air squadrons based on Midway, Guam, Kwajalein, [and] Okinawa and in Japan and the Philippines as covered under "Secure sea and air lines of communication," etc.

Requirements for defense of bases in the South Atlantic–central Africa area would not be significant owing to their great distance from Soviet bases. Air LOC bases in Trinidad, the Guianas, Brazil, Ascension Island, French West Africa, Liberia, the Gold Coast, Nigeria, and the Anglo-Egyptian Sudan would require no protection beyond that furnished by base personnel.

At essential bases where no Allied defense forces are provided under other courses of action and which may be subject to sporadic air or surface raids, sufficient qualified personnel should be provided to maintain defensive equipment and instruct the local base operating personnel in its use.

(2) *Tasks*

(a) Provide ground, air, antiaircraft, and naval local-defense forces for Guam.

(b) Provide antiaircraft and naval local-defense forces for Singapore.

(c) Provide naval local-defense forces for bases in Kwajalein, the Philippines, Ceylon, Australia, New Zealand, and Capetown.

(d) Provide a theater reserve of ground forces for the western Pacific. [See force-requirement chart.] . . .

13. Expand the Overall Power of the Armed Forces for Later Operations Against the Soviet Powers

a. Analysis.

The Allies must provide at the earliest possible date additional balanced forces of all arms for major offensive operations. A phased mobilization of manpower for the military forces in consonance with their planned employment for Phases I, II, and III and consistent with the manpower requirements of war industry should be initiated as far in advance of D-Day as warranted by intelligence of heightened Soviet war preparation. Simultaneously, a maximum industrial mobilization for the requirements of a long war should also be set in motion.

It is probable that the personnel and materiel requirements of U.S. and Allied forces for implementing Phase I of the concept of operations will impose a heavy burden on our resources, since D-Day strength of the armed forces must provide for initial offensive and defensive dispositions, replacement of combat losses, and for the cadres necessary for activation and training of additional units required for later operations. Depending upon the type units required and upon prewar stocks of materiel available, and generally exclusive of national-guard units and of organized reserves, a period of twelve to eighteen months after the initiation of mobilization will be required before trained and equipped combat units, in addition to those in being on M-Day, will be available for combat deployment. . . .

PHASE II

(1) Continue the air offensive, to include the intensification of the air battle with the objective of obtaining air supremacy.

(2) Maintain our holding operations along the general line of discriminate containment, exploiting local opportunities for improving our position there and exerting unremitting pressure against the Soviet citadel.

(3) Maintain control of other essential land and sea areas and increase our measure of control of essential lines of communication.

(4) Reenforce our forces in the Far East as necessary to contain the Communist forces to the mainland of Asia and to defend the southern Malay Peninsula.

(5) Continue the provision of essential aid to Allies in support of efforts contributing directly to the overall strategic concept.

(6) Intensify psychological, economic, and underground warfare.

(7) Establish control and enforce surrender terms in the USSR and satellite countries in the event of capitulation during Phase II.

(8) Generate at the earliest possible date sufficient balanced forces, together with their shipping and logistic requirements, to achieve a decision in Europe.

PHASE III

(1) While continuing courses of action . . . of Phase II, initiate a major land offensive in Europe to cut off and destroy all or the major part of the Soviet forces in Europe.* [See force-requirement chart.] . . .

*Editor's Note: To accomplish Phase III, the Pentagon considered that in addition to those forces that were in existence during—and survived—Phase I, there would be required an extra 55 U.S. divisions (1,375,000 men); France, 18 divisions (450,000); Belgium, 4 divisions (100,000); British Commonwealth, 16 divisions (400,000); Holland, 3 divisions (75,000); Luxembourg, 1 division (25,000). There would also have to be correspondingly heavy manpower requirements for all other arms. In all, the Western powers, for the entire war, would have to find manpower for something of the order of 250 divisions or 6.25 million men. Air, naval, civil defense, antiaircraft (of 10 million men called to the colors in Germany in World War II, 1 million served in flak units), mercantile marine, and essential services combined would probably require a further 8 million men. Thus the West would be required to field something of the order of 20 million men during the entire span of the war. This was, probably, greater than could be found—especially if the manpower of all Europe fell under Russian rule. If Britain fell, then such figures would stretch American and Canadian manpower reserves to the maximum and perhaps beyond into economic chaos.

14. Provide Essential Aid to Our Allies in Support of Efforts Contributing Directly to the Overall Strategic Concept

The successful accomplishment of many of the courses of action . . . will depend fully as much upon timely provision of essential military aid to our allies as upon fulfillment of requirements for our own military forces. . . .

Further development of this course of action cannot be made prior to a revision of the program by the Joint Munitions Allocation Committee and its review by the Munitions Board.

15. Initiate or Intensify Psychological, Economic, and Underground Warfare

a. Analysis

The initiation or intensification of psychological, economic, and underground warfare directed at both friendly and enemy groups or countries would greatly enhance the chances of an early and successful conclusion of the war by assisting in overcoming the enemy's will to fight, sustaining the morale of friendly groups in enemy territory, and improving the morale of friendly countries and the attitude of neutral countries toward the Allies.

This type of warfare has a peacetime application against the Soviets and toward friendly nations as well, but it should be greatly stepped up upon the outbreak of war and should exploit to the maximum the psychological effects of the strategic air offensive. It would require participation of all services to assist other agencies in its execution.

It is considered that no force requirements additional to those developed by other courses of action are generated, although specially trained personnel, special types of equipment, some logistic support, and other facilities on a minor scale will be required within the military establishment.

b. Tasks

(1) Collaborate in the integration of psychological, economic, and underground warfare with plans for military operations.
(2) Provide assistance as necessary for the execution of psychological, economic, and underground warfare. . . .

16. Establish Control and Enforce Surrender Terms in the USSR and Satellite Countries (in the Event of a Possible Early Capitulation of the USSR During Phase I)

a. Analysis

In order to ensure compliance with our national objectives, the Allies would have to occupy selected areas of the USSR and her satellites and establish some form of Allied control in each of those countries.

A method of control under the conditions which would exist in the event of early capitulation, affording maximum control with minimum forces, might be to occupy selected bridgeheads in the USSR and other selected centers which would serve as bases for projection of control in both the USSR and her satellites. It is considered that the greater portion of control forces should be in bridgehead areas with minimum forces in the interior.

Areas selected as centers of control in the USSR should be urban areas which are of strategic importance such as the following: political and administrative centers, communication centers, major seaports or naval bases, oil-producing or refining centers. Areas selected in the satellites as centers of control should be the various capitals and certain key seaports and urban areas.

Centers of control in the USSR should be grouped into larger regions of responsibility. Regions of responsibility in the USSR with their respective control centers selected for this plan, are as follows: . . .

Regions of Responsibility	Main Control Centers	Subcenters of Control
Western USSR	Moscow	Moscow Leningrad Murmansk Minsk Gorki Kuibishev
Caucasus–Ukraine	Kiev	Kiev Kharkov Odessa Sevastopol Rostov Novorossisk Batumi Baku
Ural–West Siberia– Turkestan	Omsk	Omsk Sverdlovsk Chelyabinsk Novo Sibirsk Tashkent
East Siberia–Transbaikal– Maritime	Khabarovsk	Khabarovsk Irkutsk Vladivostok

[For] centers of control in the European satellites and Korea, as selected for this plan, [see relevant] map, page 204.

Except for Korea, which it is considered will be under the firm control of Soviet forces, no requirements for control forces for the possible Far Eastern satellites are developed. It is considered that Communist China and other areas of Southeast Asia controlled by indigenous Communists, unlike Korea and the European satellites, will not be under the complete domination of the Soviets and in the event of an early capitulation by the USSR will not necessarily also capitulate. Consequently the introduction of Allied control forces into those areas may be neither feasible nor desirable upon the capitulation of the USSR since full-scale operations against opposition may be required. Therefore appropriate action in those areas would have to be decided upon after a determination of the existing situation following the capitulation of the USSR. Cognizance should be taken of the possibility that the fulfillment of the national objectives of the United States may require major offensive operations in the Far East and Southeast Asia after the capitulation of the USSR.

It is considered that the basic element of control should be exercised by ground forces based in and operating from the control subcenters. The most suitable control unit readily available would be the division augmented by additional motor transport to give it increased mobility. On this basis, a total of thirty-eight divisions is estimated to be the minimum requirements for the control centers shown on the map referred to above.*

*Editor's Note: It is to be assumed that thirty-eight divisions would constitute about a million men. This seems to be on the low side if the Soviet partisan capability as demonstrated in World War II is recalled. The Ukraine provides an interesting case history. It began pro-German and anti-Russian and ended pro-Russian and anti-German. Nevertheless 220,000 partisans were known to be operating within German lines, and they are said to have killed 175,000 Germans. If the Western powers failed to gain the hearts and minds of the Greater Russian population, then there would have been severe guerrilla warfare. American capacities for this type of warfare have rarely been tested in recent history. Certainly American distaste for occupation duties has been amply demonstrated in both Germany and Japan. The bearing and conduct of the troops was not impressive, and there is no evidence that it would improve simply because they were on occupation duty in Russia—where the hardships and discomforts would have been immeasurably greater than they were in Germany and Japan.

Since the means of control envisaged would in reality be a skeleton occupation, it is considered that a high ratio of air-force units would be desirable in order to bring visible evidence of Allied strength before the Soviet and satellite people. These air-force units should be organized, disposed, and controlled on a broader regional concept than the ground forces in order to assure flexibility and maximum effectiveness with the minimum of forces in assisting and supporting the ground forces. On this basis five reinforced tactical air forces, each consisting of approximately five to six combat groups and one troop-carrier group with an attached assault or glider squadron, should be assigned the following regions of responsibility: western USSR, Caucasus–Ukraine, Urals–west Siberia–Turkestan, east Siberia–Transbaikal–maritime (including Korea) and the European satellite area.

Ground and air forces would be provided from forces released from other tasks and should be moved to selected centers of control by the most feasible and rapid means available in each case. Logistic support would be mainly by sea transport and railroad, augmented, especially in the initial stages, by air transport. It is recognized that tremendous logistic problems would exist in the supply of Allied control forces, particularly those destined for areas deep in the USSR. Allied troop-carrier and air-transport units would be strained to the utmost in providing airlift. A considerable period might elapse before full complements of Allied ground and air forces reached all control centers, but every effort should be made to reduce this time to the minimum, even though capitulation had already been obtained.

A carrier task force should be provided in each of the Baltic and Black seas to provide a reserve striking force and to serve as a psychological factor to impress the Soviet and satellite peoples.

A reserve of divisions, fighter and bomber groups, and troop-carrier units should be earmarked by the Allies when released from other tasks to be available for reenforcement of the control forces if required. The size and composition would be dependent upon the situation existing at the time.

The forces required for this course of action, with the possible exception of those required for airlift, could be made available from those which have been developed for the other courses of action in Phase I. The balance of forces then in existence should be retained operational in reserve until full control of the USSR and her satellites is established and until the situation in Southeast Asia and the Far East has been clarified.

b. Tasks

(1) Move control forces to selected centers in the USSR and in satellite countries.
(2) Establish some form of Allied control in the USSR and in satellite countries.
(3) Enforce surrender terms imposed upon the USSR and its satellites.
(4) Reestablish civil government in the USSR and satellite countries.

c. Requirements

The estimated Allied forces initially required for control of the USSR and satellite areas are set forth [below]. Subsequently these forces would be reduced as rapidly as possible, consistent with the degree and effectiveness of the accomplishment of their tasks.

(1) *Army. USSR*: Moscow (2 divisions); Leningrad (1); Minsk (1); Murmansk (1); Gorki (1); Kuibishev (1); Kiev (1); Kharkov (1); Odessa (1); Sevastopol (1); Rostov (1); Novorossisk (1); Batumi (1); Baku (1); Sverdlovsk (1); Chelyabinsk (1); Tashkent (1); Omsk (1); Novosibirsk (1); Irkutsk (1); Khabarovsk (1); Vladivostok (1); Total: 23 divisions.

(2) *Navy*. Port Detachments: *Black Sea*—1 carrier task group; *Baltic Sea*—1 carrier task group.

Satellite Areas	Location	Divisions
Germany	Berlin	1
	Hamburg	1
Poland	Danzig	1
	Warsaw	1
Czechoslovakia	Prague	1
Estonia	Talinn	1
Latvia	Riga	1
Lithuania	Kaunàs	1
Hungary	Budapest	1
Romania	Bucharest	1
	Constanta	1
Bulgaria	Sofia	1
Yugoslavia	Belgrade	1
	Zagreb	1 (-1RCT)
Albania	Tirana	1 RCT
Korea	Seoul	1
		15 Divs.

(3) *Air Force*

	Fighter Group	Tactical Recon. Group	Troop Carrier Group	Glider Squadron	Total Combat Groups
Western USSR	4	1	1	1	5
Caucasus–Ukraine	4	1	1	1	5
Urals–West Siberia–Turkestan	4	1	1	1	5
East Siberia–Transbaikal–Maritime (incl. Korea)	4	1	1	1	5
European Satellite Area	5	1	1	1	6
Totals	21	5	5	5	26

EDITOR'S EPILOGUE

What follows is a scenario for the opening stages of Dropshot.

METRIC TOP SECRET

From	SACEUR G2 Versailles. Operational Immediate (G2)
To	JIC Washington.
Info	NSC, Dir. Ops. CIA, Exec. Dir. NSA, Exec. Dir. DIA, G2, A2, ONI, Waroff London, Foroff Paris, Foroff Brussels, SecState Oslo, Waroff Copenhagen, CinC AG North, Center, South.
DTG	2359 31 Dec 56.

Daily sitsum. General sit. normal. Some evidence redisposition Sov. Third Shock Army near frontier Ludwislust sector. Source AI. Nineteenth Tank Army previously reported Brno Cz now located along line Erfurt–Plauen, reportedly for late winter maneuvers. 35 transports Seventh A/B (prev. located Torun, Poland, see Bulletin 49 '56) reported parked Magdeburg airfield. HQ Sov. Army Group Center still reported Plzen, Cz. Brit. Rhine Army HQ reports considerable flare activity across Sov. border near Wittenberg. CI authorities Wesel report CP officials examining three Rhine bridges. Some Sov a/c recce along line Frisian Islands.

Political sitsum: West German internal political situation normal but tense. General situation normal but tense.

Berlin sitsum: Informant previously reported as reliable states considerable CP discussion new directive exMoscow. Nature directive unknown but believed to concern strike power, telephones, railroad on May Day. Civsit. otherwise normal.

Ends msg.

0012Z SFH Ack.

0014Z PTG Ack.

Nite.

Nite, Sam.

Just after four o'clock in the morning of 1 January 1957 the Saladin 6-by-6 armored car of the Third Royal Dragoon Guards makes its way along the narrow roads past half-timbered and thatched-roof farmhouses of the Lüneburger Heide near Fallingsbostel. The corporal of horse calls the halt when he sees a red-over-green signal light arc over the dark woods that marks the edge of the Soviet zone. The red is followed by a yellow. Mystified, the corporal of horse clambers down onto the frozen earth and puts his ear to the ground. The corporal of horse had served in the western desert and recognizes the rumbling sound immediately. The sound is that of tank treads on hard ground. There is no doubt about it—a large number of tanks, possibly a regiment, is on the move beyond the woods.

The corporal of horse gets back onto the turret and picks up the hand mike. He calls the code word back to the squadron commander in the regimental laager on the western side of Fallingsbostel. The code word is *Grantham Three*. It means that a large force of Soviet armor can be heard moving—or their engines running—on the frontier. The squadron commander interrogates the corporal of horse. Is he sure? Sure he's sure, replies the corporal of horse. The squadron commander relays the code word to division; division sends it to British Army of the Rhine HQ near München-Gladbach. It reaches München-Gladbach G2, who passes the information on to Saceur G2 Versailles.

The warning is timely but useless. Out of the predawn twilight come the lead tank squadrons of the Third Shock Army.

TOP SECRET EYES ONLY (Note to secretary: present immediately)
From: **Howlett, duty G2 JIC**
To: **Exec. Sec. NSC**
DTG: **310405EST**

Sir: see attached messages. Disturbed night. (a) Coast Guard called re arrival suspicious Soviet freighters Boston, Port Elizabeth, New York, Baltimore, Washington, Mobile, New Orleans, Galveston, LA, SFO, Seattle. Owing synchronized nature of arrivals, ONI & CG boarding first light. This shipping doubly suspicious in view of attached msg fr SACEUR (see 312359 SACEUR file). ONI desires check Sov. shippg to establish whether they are carrying atomic or HE cargoes.
(2) Naval Attache's London report Brit. Admiralty concerned over identical arrival Sov. freighters Port of London, Southampton, Bristol, Liverpool, Glasgow. Moreover Air Ministry reports air recon saying unusual number Sov. Bears, Badgers, Bounders, Bisons operational Norwegian Sea, North Sea, Black Sea, eastern Med. JIC London has reports these movements part of reported late-winter maneuvers. However when allied to recent reports heavy Sovsub movement—16 Z class subs sighted in the arc Biscay–western approaches–Norwegian Sea–Barents Sea—Admiralty inclined to view this major power demonstration in connection with Berlin sit.
(3) Sigsint reports very heavy traffic between Sov. embassy DC and Foroff Moscow. Traffic analysis shows DC embassy has undertaken major cryptographic change.
(4) All attachés all eastern capitals report unusual troop movements, especially in areas Trieste–Bosporus–Greek frontiers. All report AFVs not (repeat) not combat-ready, although of course it would only take a week or so to bring them to combat status. All report widespread rumors Sov. late-winter maneuvers and power demos over Berlin.
(4) Ameramb. Paris reports Quai d'Orsay concerned Sov. agents' activity some Rhine bridges, also at Brest–Marseilles–Toulon naval bases.
ENDS

From   CINCFE G2
To   Pearl, Tokyo, Taiwan, Guam, Okinawa, Manila.
Info   G2 Washington, JIC Washington, CNO Washington, DNI Mel-
            bourne, DNO Singapore, G2 SEATO Bangkok.
310900Z   AI source reports Sov. FE fleet departs Vladivostok anchorage.
            Destination not rept not known. Airecon despatched. Consider-
            able Z and W class subactivity observed off Hokkaido, Pearl,
            Okinawa, Taiwan since mid-month.
ENDS   310918Z

CHIEF OF STAFF, WHITE HOUSE. MINUTES EMERGENCY MEETING
1 Jan 57.
Present: President, Vice-President, Cabinet, CJCS, DCIA, DDIA, DNSA.
Time: 0722 (all times GMT)
Reports received (see War File 1).
Agenda: Review various security reports received during the night of 31
           Dec–1 Jan. from all commands and all agencies. Steno report
           available noon 1 Jan. 57.

President's view. Crossing of Soviet land forces into American and British
zones grave act of war. All concur. Soviet land, sea, and air movements
indicate hostilities imminent or have actually begun. All concur. CJCS
requests permission to place all armed forces worldwide in condition
red. All concur. CJCS requests permission to place Emergency War Plan
Dropshot and Emergency War Plan (air) Trojan into effect. All concur, but
President stresses no attacks, especially with atomic weapons, to be
launched without his permission. All concur. CJCS requests further meeting 1200 GMT. All concur. President to broadcast 1300 GMT. NBC, CBS,
ABC notified. CJCS requests permission to place all key civilian and military installations under maximum guard. President concurs but stresses
armor must not be used. No desire to alarm civilian sector prematurely.
All concur.

METRIC TOP SECRET
From   SACEUR Versailles.   OP OP OP
To   All heads of state
011750Z Jan 57.

Major Soviet attack developing all along line between Arctic and Bosporus. French, British, American armies falling back onto Rhine line.
Berlin silent, presumed fallen. Casualties very heavy. Civilian situation
chaotic. Sov. parachute regiments on all primary Rhine bridges. British
destroyer Volage sunk by unknown sub 30 miles NNE Faeroes. Three
French warships attacked by three Sverdlov class cruisers off Corsica.
Fourteen merchantmen in North Atlantic fail to make position report as
scheduled. Opinion SACEUR: TOTALITY (war-telegram situation) exists.
End msg.

011756Z DFH Ack.

011757Z PTG Ack.

Christ!

METRIC TOP SECRET   OP OP OP
From   President
To   All CinCs
012216Z
                  TOTALITY. All ack. personally.
Ends message WH 012220Z

World War III has begun. With a splintering crash the Red army has launched two major offensives. Western Europe has been attacked by 100 line divisions supported by 4,800 combat tactical aircraft, units of the long-range air force, and elements of the air-transport fleet. A second arm of this thrust has hit Scandinavia: strength 13 divisions, 600–900 tactical aircraft. The second main thrust has developed against Turkey. There 33 Soviet divisions supported by 1,400 combat aircraft and the Black Sea fleet are lunging toward the Bosporus and the Dardanelles.

The Allies—primarily American and British—make a brief stand on the Rhine. But the front collapses on 3 January when Marshal Malinovsky's front establishes a bridgehead near Wesel—oddly enough in the same area where Montgomery crossed in World War II. Thousands of cannon and multibarreled rocket launchers backed by 90 squadrons of ground-attack aircraft smash a path through the shallow and exhausted Allied defense line.

Other Soviet spearheads dart across the Rhine near Koblenz, using bridges seized by Communist guerrillas and Soviet paratroops. Throughout Western Europe Communist action arms come out into the open and, using World War II weapons and explosives stored for this moment, are blowing bridges, road, rail, and telecommunications centers being used by Allied forces. At the same time small Soviet Asian forces strike at South Korea—presumably to divert Pentagon and White House attention from Western Europe.

On 6 January the Red flag is hoisted over Paris and the other Western European capitals. The remnants of the Anglo-American armies make attempts to stand at the mouths of the Cherbourg and Breton peninsulas. But the fighting will last only eighteen days. There is no natural defense line for a stand on either of the peninsulas, and the 92,000 survivors surrender.

By 12 January the Red army is on the English Channel preparing to invade its main strategic objective in this phase of the war: Great Britain.

London and the Home Counties are under heavy bombardment by aircraft, long-range artillery, and missile. The government is in the emergency underground command center at Box Hill, near Chippenham. The enormous ammunition dump in the Savernake Forest is blown up on 7 January by Communist guerrillas. The country is semiparalyzed by a weak but fairly general strike. The Home Guard is recalled to the colors by Royal Proclamation on 7 January. Soviet commandos land in northern Scotland, Ulster, the Faeroes, and Iceland on 8 January. Two out of three of the U.S.–U.K. air bases have been destroyed or neutralized by sabotage and air attack. The great oil docks at

Avonmouth and London are aflame, either through air attack or sabotage. Three Soviet agents are caught with plans to put the N and X biological-warfare agents into sixteen large reservoirs.

In Turkey, Soviet parachute battalions seize the passes through the Cistercian Mountains, and the spearheads of the Soviet army are crossing the Bosporus and taking Istanbul and are now on the Anatolian plain. On 6 January, they are moving toward the capital, Ankara, and agent activity indicates their targets are Tehran, Baghdad, Damascus, Beirut, Suez, and the great oil refineries of Abadan and Saudi Arabia.

In the United States the freighters boarded by ONI [Office of Naval Intelligence] and the Coast Guard are found to be laden with high explosive. But no atomic weapons are found—presumably because their use would invite retribution by the Strategic Air Command. The captain of the freighter at Los Angeles does succeed in pressing the button as the ONI and Coast Guard board. There is a gigantic explosion—some eight thousand tons of high explosive were thought to be aboard—and very serious damage has been caused to the dockland.

Red army commandos land in and around Seattle, Kotzebue, Bethel, and at several points along the Alaskan peninsula on 3 January. Paratroops and agents infiltrate near Fairbanks and at the neck of the Seward peninsula—the tip of which is close to Siberia. More Soviet marines take St. Lawrence Island on the American side of the Bering Strait, the Pribilof Islands, and Nunivak. The airfields in the Seward peninsula and the fighter defense base at Anchorage are destroyed by aerial attack. There are signs of Soviet marine and paratroop activity at Kodiak and the Alexander Archipelago between Juneau, Petersburg, and Ketchikan. The Soviets try to establish an artillery base on the British Columbian coast of the Strait of Juan de Fuca—presumably to interdict the movement of submarines and warships between the Pacific and the naval base in Puget Sound. The Soviet base is destroyed in eighteen hours and sixty-eight prisoners are taken. They tell how it was not until the early evening of D-1 that they were given their operational orders. Obviously, therefore, the Soviet general staff intended to surprise America and the West.

So far there have been no landings on the eastern seaboard of the United States. However, there is intense Soviet marine and commando activity on non-American territory between Godthaab in Greenland and Maracaibo in Venezuela. Agents are detained in the Panama Canal Zone, and attempts to sabotage the canal are expected at any moment. Soviet submarine activity is heavy in the Gulf of Mexico, there are many sinkings, and two submarines that manage to get into Galveston Bay succeed in sinking fourteen tankers in ninety minutes.

The most serious episode within the frontiers of the United States so far is the interception on 3 January of five B-29-type Soviet bombers over the Everett Mountains of Baffin Island, just south of the Arctic Circle. Examination of the wreckage of one of the aircraft (the other four were shot down into Hudson Strait) showed that it was carrying two atomic bombs similar in design and kilotonnage to the Mark III American bomb. Two crew members survive and interrogation elicits that their orders were to make one-way suicide attacks on Minneapolis–St. Paul, Chicago (two bombs), Detroit (two bombs), and Cleveland. One of the survivors reports that the commander and the men of the Third Red Air Fleet had protested the mission and that the chief of staff of the fleet had been shot as an example to the rest of the force. The survivor reports that morale is very high but that there are signs that it will decline unless there is a quick victory. Casualties in the air force, he says, are heavy, but in the Red army there has been only a "battle of flowers" at Paris. Anglo-American war prisoners are being Sovietized by the Antifa indoctrination process.

The American press is agitating for a full-scale SAC air program following the discovery of large quantities of the biological-warfare (BW) agents anthrax (N), botulinus toxin (N), and ammonium thiocyanate (AT) in a railroad warehouse at Abilene, Kansas, on 4 January 1957. It is thought that Soviet agents were about to spread this in the cattle and wheat areas of the Midwest. Following the deaths of ninety-four air-force research-and-development personnel at Edwards Air Force Base in California, a test of the water shows that a nearby holding tank had been poisoned with a substance resembling N. All commands order a water test, and a similar substance is found in reserve water tanks at Warren, Andrews, and McGuire air-force bases and at the Pentagon, Camp David, and Los Alamos reservoirs.

The presidential reaction to this rash of BW incidents—combined with an attempt to foment a general strike—is to place all bases and their surrounding areas under martial law from midnight on 4 January. A state of national emergency was proclaimed on D + 1, and general mobilization, both manpower and industrial, is under way. On 5 January the first trainloads of nonessential civilians leave the main cities of the eastern and western seaboards; 97,000 children and old people were removed from Manhattan in the first day. They are being taken to tented camps in the countryside outside Baltimore.

Re consequences of sabotage and subversion: the President outlaws all Communist activity. Those found guilty of sabotage or subversion are liable to execution by firing squad. The President gives the strongest warnings—he mentions the word *treason*—to the AFL–CIO and a number of affiliated trade unions in which the Communists are reported (by the FBI) to be making policy. One Communist in the National Maritime Union is sentenced to death for inciting seamen to disable their ships. Sixteen influential Communists in the International Longshoremen's and Warehousemen's Union and the United Electrical, Radio, and Machine Workers of America union are indicted for inciting strikes at Detroit, Jersey City, Duluth, Spokane, and Madison. Eight Communists belonging to the International Union of Mine, Mill, and Smelter Workers are found executed in gangland style at Pittsburgh—right-wing vigilantes in the union are thought by the FBI to have been responsible.

In the first such move the President orders the disbandment of the United Public Workers of America; the United Shoe Workers of America; the International Fur and Leather Workers; the Marine Cooks and Stewards; the Food, Tobacco, Agriculture, and Allied Workers; and the United Gas, Coke, and Chemical Workers. The reason: undue Communist or pro-Soviet influence.

The President, in his address of 5 January 1957, declares that the following unions are infiltrated by Communists and that some of their locals are Communist-dominated, although their national leadership is still in the hands of non-Communists: United Automobile Workers; United Packinghouse Workers; Marine Firemen, Oilers, Watertenders, and Wipers of the Pacific Coast, Inc., and the American Newspaper Guild. A very large number of organizations said to be Communist front organizations—they range from the Veterans of the Abraham Lincoln Brigade to the Washington Book Shop—are outlawed by Presidential decree.

As the President announces in his television and radio broadcast to the nation—quoting from a Joint Intelligence Group paper entitled "Intelligence Estimate on Espionage, Subversion, and Sabotage":

> Communist penetration of organized labor in the Western Hemisphere has been intensified with the object of interfering with the general economic life. Small groups of militant Communists have been able to wield power out of proportion to their numbers.

The President announces that "Communist guerrillas" tried to seize the Pentagon in a night-long military action on 7 January, and 282 soldiers, Pentagon employees, and guerrillas were killed or wounded. The Soviet embassy staff is placed in internment, and the United Nations is suspended.

The Communist party of Japan rises as Soviet marine regiments land on Hokkaido on 8 January, and the Communist insurgents of Siam and Malaya join up with Soviet Asian commandos landing on the Kra Isthmus and in the Malayan peninsula towns of Pattani, Narithiwat, Kota Baharu, and Kuala Terengganu. There is fierce fighting between government troops and the Huks on Luzon, and civil war breaks out in Borneo, Kalimantan, and Sumatra. Clearly everywhere the Russians are going for the oil.

American and British embassies throughout the world—but primarily in Latin America—have been attacked and bombed or burned.

The Communists in Venezuela and Aruba successfully attack the oil refineries, many of which have been left burning. Russian bombers strike the main refineries in Iraq, Iran, the Trucial Oman states, and Saudi Arabia on 4 January, and guerrillas throughout Arabia attack, bomb, and burn Anglo-American oil installations. Pakistan and India announce their neutrality; the Irish Republican Army hits British army installations in Ulster; black nationalists attack similar installations in Rhodesia, South Africa, Portuguese Africa, and the Spanish Sahara. Spain joins the new Grand Alliance, and the remnants of the Anglo–American–French armies are preparing to make a stand on the line of the Pyrenees. RAF and USAF heavy bombers make token high-explosive raids on

Moscow, Leningrad, Kiev, Volgograd, and other key cities in western Russia on 3, 4, and 6 January. Sixteen bombers are lost.

The Office of National Emergency sends a secret warning to the mayor of New York: Soviet submarines equipped with V-1 flying bombs—possibly nuclear-tipped—are cruising off the eastern seaboard. On 9 January the President sends a warning to the Kremlin: any air attack on any American city will be followed by an immediate all-out nuclear attack upon Russian cities.

The Kremlin ignores the warning, and on 10 January 1957 four V-1s land in Manhattan. The first hits an apartment block at 340 East 51st Street; 89 people are killed. The second hits Washington Square; 92 people are killed. The third falls on the tarmac of Eastern Airlines at La Guardia airport, destroying five airliners and killing 120 passengers and ground crew. The fourth strikes another apartment block at East 134th Street in Manhattan. The roof of the building clips the bomb's wings and the bomb hurtles down into the street below. Three tons of high explosives in the nose leave the entire block in ruins.

Simultaneously other bombs fall on Boston, Baltimore, the New Jersey oil refineries, and the Bay Bridge in Maryland—the eastern-shore spans collapse, tipping some thirty cars onto the decks of an oil tanker. The tanker explodes, a creeping fire of petroleum seeps across the main shipping channel, and three more tankers catch fire and explode. In turn the new fire surrounds an ammunition carrier. There is a gigantic explosion that destroys more spans of the bridge and sets fire to some ninety boats in a marina. Eighteen bombs fall upon Los Angeles, Beverly Hills, and Hollywood—the Beverly Wilshire Hotel is demolished with very heavy casualties and nearly two hundred people are killed when the Brown Derby is destroyed. At the Stanford University campus there is a particularly sad incident: a flying bomb hits the Hoover Tower and then airbursts over the lunchtime crowds. Hundreds of the students and faculty are killed and wounded as they stroll in the sunshine or eat their sandwiches. At San Francisco airport there is a bizarre incident: a V-2 rocket hits a DC-9 as it is landing. The aircraft explodes and the flames leap from aircraft to aircraft lined up for takeoff. The fire burns for eight hours, destroying twenty-two planes and killing some 190 people.

The overseas situation worsens. Soviet marines land near the USAF bases at Port Lyautey in Morocco, in the Azores, near Keflavik in Iceland. Paratroops land on Sicily, Crete, Cyprus, and Rhodes. Frogmen–paratroops limpet-mine the British carrier *Bulwark* in the Suez Canal, blocking the waterway. A regiment of Soviet paratroopers lands and takes Shannon airport in Eire, and commandos come ashore at Malta to take Luqa airfield. The petrol dumps at Castel Benito and El Adem airfields in Tripolitania and Libya are destroyed, and Egyptian fedayeen blow the great British dump at Abu Sueir in the Canal zone.

The Red army strikes out of Armenia and is heading for the Persian Gulf, and there is a naval battle between cruisers of the Royal and Red navies off Aden. The Admiralty claim that the three Sverdlovsk-class cruisers are sunk. In India and Pakistan the Communist parties try a general strike, and Red army engineers are reported to be in the Khyber Pass—presumably reconnoitering. Chinese Communist marines land in Taiwan. Red air-force long-range B-29-type bombers are shot down soon after takeoff from the Vladivostok area—their targets were the vast U.S. airfields on Guam and Okinawa. At Pearl Harbor four Soviet cruisers are intercepted and sunk as they make their way through a fog bank to bombard the oil and ammunition installations.

But why has the President not authorized the initiation of Plan Trojan, the emergency air-war plan against the Soviet Union? There are—it will emerge—two reasons. In the first place the Strategic Air Command has been temporarily paralyzed by sabotage, subversion, the loss of certain key bases and ordnance dumps (including three East Coast atomic-bomb dumps), and the inability of the Military Air Transport Service to get key personnel, ordnance, and spares to the British bases—they have been swamped by the need to get the battalions of the Eighty-Second Airborne to surviving SAC bases. Second, the President and the Chairman of the Joint Chiefs have wanted to establish whether the Kremlin is prepared to talk. But it is not prepared to talk. And so on 14 January at 7 A.M. the President consults with the National Security Council and the Joint Chiefs—Blair House is blown up as they talk in the Oval Office—and then decides. Plan Trojan is to go into operation immediately.

At 0810 on 14 January (as a memorial service was being held for SACEUR Europe, whose death at the hands of a Soviet commando had been announced the night before) the orders went out to execute Trojan. At noon that same day thirty-two Strategic Air Command bombers lifted off from the RAF station at Saint Mawgan in Cornwall, England—unaccountably it had not been attacked, probably because Saint Mawgan was known as a coastal command rather than as a strategic bomber base. Eight of the B-50s carried two atomic bombs apiece; the rest of the force were either decoy or reconnaissance bombers. Just after dusk the bombers placed eight of the bombs on Moscow. The aiming point was the great golden onion dome of St. Basil's Cathedral. The other four bombers were lost during the penetration. And at 2 P.M. twenty-eight B-50s took off from the RAF station at Leuchars in Scotland. Seven of the bombers carried atomic bombs and atomic mines. They laid the mines in the Leningrad naval base and then, from 35,000 feet, atomized Leningrad.

And at air bases around the world—or at least those that were still operational—scores of other USAF strategic bombers lifted off to begin the last bombardment.

APPENDICES

APPENDIX A: SUMMARY STRATEGIC ESTIMATE (AS OF THE END OF PHASE I)

I.SUMMARY OF OPPOSING SITUATIONS

1. Political Factors

a. *Alignment of Selected States and Areas.* As of the end of Phase I, the following significant changes in the alignment of states and areas since D-Day (pages 171–182, Volume II) are estimated to have occurred:

(1) The countries listed . . . have been forcibly brought within the Soviet orbit by virtue of having been overrun by Soviet forces as indicated: Denmark—completely overrun; Norway—completely overrun; Sweden—completely overrun; Germany—overrun east of the Rhine; Austria—completely overrun; Greece—completely overrun, except for Crete; Turkey—major portion overrun; Iran—major portion overrun; China—north China but not Formosa completely overrun and indigenous Communist forces in control of most of south China; Japan—Hokkaido captured.

(2) Most of Burma and considerable portions of Indochina are within the Soviet orbit by virtue of control by indigenous Communist forces.

b. *Attitude and Morale.* There are increasing indications of deterioration of morale in the USSR and satellite countries attributable to lack of promised success of initial Soviet offensives, to the Allied air offensive, and [to] the Allied psychological warfare effort.

2. Economic Factors

a. *Soviet and Satellite.* The success of Allied resistance to initial Soviet offensives has forced the USSR to expend the major portion of their initial stockpiles, and the strategic air offensive has caused a considerable dislocation of the Soviet and satellite war economy. The limited Soviet POL [petrol, oil, lubricants] refinery capacity has been drastically reduced, Soviet transportation systems have been interrupted, and losses of coastal shipping have been considerable. Soviet industry is currently unable to produce the supplies required for major offensive operations at this time, and Soviet stockpiles no longer provide the means for a major offensive effort.

b. *Allied Nations.* The overall economic situation of the Allied nations re-

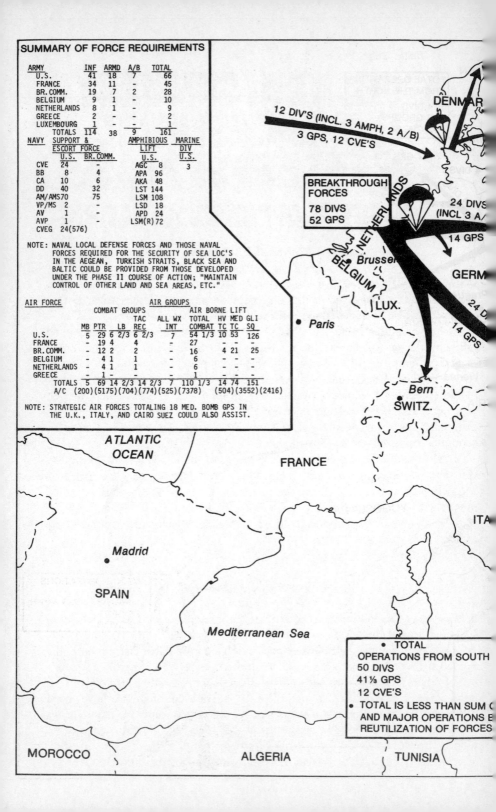

SUMMARY OF FORCE REQUIREMENTS

ARMY	INF	ARMD	A/B	TOTAL
U.S.	41	18	7	66
FRANCE	34	11	-	45
BR. COMM.	19	7	2	28
BELGIUM	9	1	-	10
NETHERLANDS	8	1	-	9
GREECE	2	-	-	2
LUXEMBOURG	1	-	-	1
TOTALS	114	38	9	161

NAVY	SUPPORT & ESCORT FORCE		AMPHIBIOUS LIFT		MARINE DIV
	U.S.	BR. COMM.	U.S.		U.S.
CVE	24	-	AGC	8	3
BB	8	4	APA	96	
CA	10	6	AKA	48	
DD	40	32	LST	144	
AM/AMS	70	75	LSM	108	
VP/MS	2	-	LSD	18	
AV	1	-	APD	24	
AVP	1	-	LSM(R)	72	
CVEG	24(576)				

NOTE: NAVAL LOCAL DEFENSE FORCES AND THOSE NAVAL
FORCES REQUIRED FOR THE SECURITY OF SEA LOC'S
IN THE AEGEAN, TURKISH STRAITS, BLACK SEA AND
BALTIC COULD BE PROVIDED FROM THOSE DEVELOPED
UNDER THE PHASE II COURSE OF ACTION; "MAINTAIN
CONTROL OF OTHER LAND AND SEA AREAS, ETC."

AIR FORCE	COMBAT GROUPS					AIR GROUPS				
				TAC REC	ALL WX INT	AIR BORNE LIFT				
	MB	PTR	LB			TOTAL COMBAT	HV TC	MED TC	GLI SQ	
U.S.	5	29	6 2/3	6 2/3	7	54 1/3	10	53	126	
FRANCE	-	19	4	4	-	27	-	-	-	
BR. COMM.	-	12	2	2	-	16	4	21	25	
BELGIUM	-	4	1	1	-	6	-	-	-	
NETHERLANDS	-	4	1	1	-	6	-	-	-	
GREECE	-	1	-	-	-	1	-	-	-	
TOTALS	5	69	14 2/3	14 2/3	7	110 1/3	14	74	151	
A/C	(200)	(5175)	(704)	(774)	(525)	(7378)	(504)	(3552)	(2416)	

NOTE: STRATEGIC AIR FORCES TOTALING 18 MED. BOMB GPS IN
THE U.K., ITALY, AND CAIRO SUEZ COULD ALSO ASSIST.

12 DIV'S (INCL. 3 AMPH, 2 A/B)
3 GPS, 12 CVE'S

DENMAR

BREAKTHROUGH
FORCES

78 DIVS
52 GPS

24 DIVS
(INCL 3 A/

14 GPS

GERM

24 D

14 GPS

NETHERLANDS

BELGIUM

Brusser

LUX.

• Paris

• Bern
SWITZ.

ATLANTIC
OCEAN

FRANCE

ITA

• Madrid

SPAIN

Mediterranean Sea

• TOTAL
OPERATIONS FROM SOUTH
50 DIVS
41⅓ GPS
12 CVE'S
• TOTAL IS LESS THAN SUM (
AND MAJOR OPERATIONS E
REUTILIZATION OF FORCES

MOROCCO

ALGERIA

TUNISIA

mains essentially sound. The United Kingdom has been severely damaged by air attacks and its war-making potential greatly reduced, and the Soviets have initiated air attacks against the economy of other Western Union nations. Sabotage, air attack, and raids initially caused serious delay to U.S. conversion to wartime production, but only a small percentage of U.S. war industry has been lost. The Allies have suffered the loss of most of the oil-refining capacity of the Near and Middle East by Soviet bombing, but the crude products of the oil areas are still available to the Allies. Communist successes in Southeast Asia have cut off supplies of strategic and critical materials from these areas, but stockpiles on hand in the United States are such that the loss of these areas is not yet serious. However, in the event that Communist forces should gain control of Malaya, the Allies would suffer a cumulative loss of 70 percent of the world's supply of natural rubber, which would constitute a serious blow in a long war.

3. Relative Combat Power

a. Strengths and Dispositions

(1) *Ground Forces.* Soviet land offensives have been stabilized generally along the line of discriminate containment outlined in the overall strategic concept.

North and South America, Alaska, Hawaii, Greenland, Iceland, and the Azores are safe in Allied hands.

In Europe the Soviets have overrun Denmark, Norway, and Sweden and are occupying Norway and Sweden with about 13 line divisions and 500 combat aircraft. Along the general line of the Rhine River–Alps–Piave River, 76 Allied divisions and 3,400 combat aircraft are holding against about 125 Soviet and satellite divisions and some 5,300 combat aircraft.

Greece, except for Crete, and much of Turkey have been overrun. The initial Soviet forces of about 33 divisions and 1,400 combat aircraft have been reduced in effectiveness by Turkish resistance and by Allied demolition and air interdiction of LOC [lines of communication], and a large number of them are being utilized in occupying overrun Turkey and in combating Turkish guerrillas. Fifteen Allied divisions (eleven of which are Turkish) and about 400 combat aircraft are holding southeastern Turkey. Similarly, in Iran the initial Soviet forces of about 16 divisions and 600 combat aircraft have been so reduced in effectiveness by Allied demolition and air interdiction of LOCs that 3 Allied divisions and 350 combat aircraft are able to prevent the passage of major Soviet forces through the mountain passes leading into Iraq and the Iranian oil areas and to control the Tigris River valley.

In the Far East elements of 20 Soviet line divisions and 2,800 combat aircraft have captured Hokkaido. Most of China is under the control of Chinese Communist forces. Indigenous Communist forces have acquired control of Burma

[and] considerable areas of Indochina and are threatening British control of Malaya. However, a total of 2⅓ U.S. divisions, 10 Japanese divisions, and about 5 U.S. fighter groups are holding the other Japanese islands and Okinawa.

(2) *Naval Forces.* Soviet submarine and air attacks, including mining, are causing the Allies considerable losses of both naval and merchant shipping, but so far those losses are tolerable.

Except for a few Soviet raiders Allied naval forces control the surface of the seas. However, in spite of continued offensive and defensive measures, Soviet submarines continue to present a threat to Allied LOCs, especially serious in the approaches to the United Kingdom and Japan. Allied shipping losses to enemy submarines, although considerable, are not exceeding tolerable proportions. The Soviet submarine threat in the Mediterranean, the Strait of Gibraltar, and the western approaches thereto has been reduced to such an extent as to be controlled by the ASW and escort forces available. Allied naval forces have been generally successful in preventing the Soviet Black Sea fleet from emerging into the Mediterranean. The Soviet air threat in the western Mediterranean is not of serious proportions and that in the central and eastern Mediterranean has been kept sufficiently under control by Allied air counteraction so as to maintain the sea LOC between Gibraltar and the Suez Canal.

(3) *Air Forces.* The Soviet air offensive against the United States and the U.K. has cost the USSR a considerable proportion of its original eighteen hundred long-range bombers as well as of their trained crews, and the Soviet long-range air force is limited to reconnaissance of and sporadic air attack on the United States, Alaska, Iceland, the U.K., the Cairo–Suez area, and base areas in the Far East.

Soviet and satellite tactical aircraft have suffered high attrition rates, but reserves of aircraft have been available to make up these losses, although the quality of Soviet flying personnel is deteriorating. The Soviet air-transport fleet has been reduced to an estimated 60 percent of its original 2,500 aircraft.

On the Allied side the air offensive has been conducted at a considerable cost but no greater than planning factors had anticipated. Consequently about three hundred U.S. heavy and medium bombers plus about one hundred British medium bombers are still operational, although bases in the U.K. can be used only with difficulty and at reduced efficiency.

Fighter defenses of the continental United States have been reduced for redeployment in Western Europe. Allied fighter defenses and tactical air groups in the U.K., Continental Europe, the Middle East, the Far East, and Alaska are being maintained but have suffered some loss in combat effectiveness due to lack of replacements. U.S. troop carrier, MATS [Military Air Transport Service], and civil airline organizations are still available for limited airlift operations.

b. Mobilization Capabilities

(1) *Ground Forces*. The Soviet capability for mobilizing over five hundred divisions with their necessary equipment by M + 12 months has been materially impaired by the effects of Allied strategic air attacks. Satellite mobilization capabilities have been similarly reduced because of their dependence on the USSR for equipment and because of Allied air attacks.

Allied mobilization capabilities have been strained to the utmost to keep abreast of combat losses, and no great increase in trained and equipped Western Union ground forces beyond those available on D + 6 can be expected until sometime between D + 12 and D + 24 months, when U.S. arms production has significantly increased. Additional trained and equipped U.S. ground forces would likewise be unavailable for combat in sufficient numbers for major offensive operations until D + 12 to D + 24 months.

(2) *Naval Forces*. Lacking a reserve fleet except for minor craft, Soviet requirements for initial mobilization have been readily met. Mobilization capabilities for expansion of naval forces have been greatly reduced by Allied air and naval activities. The reactivation and manning of Allied combat ships from reserve fleets is proceeding satisfactorily.

(3) *Air Forces*. Because of the effects of the Allied air offensive, no increase of Soviet air strength appears possible unless the USSR is allowed time to rebuild industry.

Since Allied air forces have come to depend almost entirely on U.S. and British aircraft production, which is currently unable to meet replacement requirements, no great increase in Allied combat air units can be expected until sometime between D + 12 and D + 24 months.

c. Combat Efficiency

(1) *Ground Forces*. The combat efficiency of Soviet ground forces has been reduced because of logistic difficulties, particularly shortages of POL and disruption of communications. Allied ground forces, despite supply difficulties caused by Soviet air and submarine action and serious losses from initial Soviet offensive operations, retain an effective mobility, and Allied divisions are superior to individual Soviet divisions in fighting power.

(2) *Naval Forces*. The Soviet submarine fleet has acquired considerable experience in undersea operations and has constantly improved its tactics; however, Allied countermeasures have kept pace, and loss rates of Allied shipping are being reduced.

(3) *Air Forces*. The combat efficiency of Soviet air forces has suffered a progressive reduction because of shortages of trained personnel, POL supplies, and equipment.

Allied air forces have maintained their qualitative superiority over Soviet air forces but have been unable to achieve air supremacy because of the numerical advantage of their opponents.

d. Logistics

The Allied air offensive has limited Soviet and satellite logistic capabilities to the extent that Soviet overall offensive capabilities have been materially reduced and drastically reduced in some areas.

Logistic support of Allied forces has been hampered by enemy air and submarine attack, but supplies reaching our forces have been sufficient to support operations thus far undertaken. However, the time required to convert to war production in the United States and to provide additional shipping will probably preclude major offensive operations until some time between D + 12 and D + 24 months.

II. ALLIED COURSES OF ACTION

1. A consideration of the foregoing factors indicates that the war has reached a temporary stalemate wherein the Soviets have lost the initiative and do not have the immediate capability of powering further large-scale offensives. Although Soviet offensives have been temporarily stabilized, the Allies lack sufficient balanced forces to launch an immediate offensive of sufficient weight to bring the war to a successful conclusion in conformity with our national objectives. This will result in a period (Phase II) of building up forces, while continuing unremitting pressure against the Soviets, in preparation for major offensive operations of all arms (Phase III). Phase II may be considered the offensive–defensive period during which the Allies would exploit local opportunities for improving their position along the general line of discriminate containment.

2. It must be recognized that the date D + 6 months, at which Phase II is assumed to commence, has been adopted for planning purposes only. The commencement of Phase III in point of time is actually a function of the progressive collapse of the Soviet ability and will to wage war as weighed against the Allied capability to create the forces required to launch the major offensive operations of all arms designed to overcome that Soviet will and ability. The progressive buildup of Allied offensive capabilities of all arms on an increasing scale can be calculated with reasonable accuracy from considerations of pertinent manpower and industrial factors. Should Soviet capabilities actually be less than is envisaged herein, fewer Allied forces would be required to overcome those capabilities, and major offensive operations could possibly be initiated as early as D + 12 months. On the other hand, should Soviet capabilities remain relatively strong as visualized herein, major offensive operations of all arms could probably not be launched until about D + 24 to D + 30 months. In order, therefore, that the most difficult contingency may be provided for in planning, the period of Phase II is assumed to extend from D + 6 to D + 30 months.

3. The following courses of action as discussed in subsequent paragraphs are open to the Allies during Phase II and III.

PHASE II

a. Continue the air offensive to include the intensification of the air battle with the objective of obtaining air supremacy.

b. Maintain our holding operations along the general line of discriminate containment, exploiting local opportunities for improving our position thereon and exerting unremitting pressure against the Soviet citadel.

c. Maintain control of other essential land and sea areas and increase our measure of control of essential lines of communication.

d. Reinforce our forces in the Far East as necessary to contain the Communist forces to the mainland of Asia and to defend the southern Malay Peninsula.

e. Continue the provision of essential aid to Allies in support of efforts contributing directly to the overall strategic concept.

f. Intensify psychological, economic, and underground warfare.

g. Establish control and enforce surrender terms in the USSR and satellite countries (in the event of capitulation during Phase II).

h. Generate at the earliest possible date sufficient balanced forces—together with their shipping and logistic requirements—to achieve a decision in Europe.

PHASE III

a. While continuing courses of action *a* through *f* of Phase II, initiate a major land offensive in Europe to cut off and destroy all or the major part of the Soviet forces in Europe.

b. From the improved position resulting from *a* above, continue offensive operations of all arms as necessary to force capitulation.

4. Phase II: Courses of Action

a. Continue the Air Offensive to Include the Intensification of the Air Battle with the Objective of Obtaining Air Supremacy

At the end of Phase I Soviet capabilities for opposing a continuing U.S. and British air offensive have been considerably weakened by the effects of Allied atomic and conventional bombing attacks. The Soviet fighter defense force is deteriorating and its operations are being seriously curtailed because of lack of POL.

In view of the effects which have been obtained by the conduct of the air offensive in Phase I, it is considered that the principal objectives of the continuing air offensive in this phase would be the attack on such targets of the Soviet powers as will achieve air supremacy for the Allies and obtain the collapse of the Soviet ability and will to wage war. Selected targets would therefore consist of those already attacked but requiring further policing together with such additional targets as current intelligence indicates are critical to the Soviet warmaking capacity.

Since the Soviet long-range force has suffered the loss of most of its offensive power by the end of Phase I, it is considered that policing attacks only would be required during Phase II against Soviet facilities for production and delivery of weapons of mass destruction.

It is also considered that the task of continuing offensive mining will not create any increased demand for Allied strategic air forces since existing Allied naval and air forces will have the capability of accomplishing the replenishment requirements of this task.

The remaining tasks, therefore, for Allied strategic air forces would be a continuation—with the maximum possible increase in intensity—of the air offensive against LOCs, supply bases, and troop concentrations and against important remaining elements of the Soviet and satellite industrial economy. This increase in intensity may be accomplished by an increasing tempo of operations as existing bomber groups are brought back up to strength by replacement aircraft and crews and as the enemy resistance becomes further weakened.

The rebuilding of the Allied strategic-bomber forces to their D-Day strength could probably not be accomplished until about D + 12 months. By D + 18 months, because of expanded production, it should be possible to augment the U.S. medium-bomber groups by one squadron each and to start committing additional groups to combat. The decision as to whether additional groups would be required should be made, however, in the light of the developing situation as it exists between D + 6 and D + 12 months. For the purposes of the situation as envisaged in this plan it is considered that no increase in strategic-bomber forces in Western Eurasia is required, except as would be accomplished by bringing medium-bomber units up to D-Day strength and by augmenting each U.S. group by an additional squadron. Two U.S. heavy-bomber groups should be maintained in the United States for use by staging through advanced bases wherever required to obtain coverage of those targets in central Russia beyond the radius of action of the medium bombers. A redeployment from the United Kingdom of two medium groups to the Near East and two to Italy should be accomplished as early in this phase as practicable to provide more feasible coverage of targets in central Europe. One strategic reconnaissance group should also be redeployed from the United Kingdom, ⅓ going to Italy and ⅔ to the Near East.

There is, however, an additional requirement for medium-bomber forces in the Far East and Southeast Asia to meet the developing threat in those areas. As soon as possible, consistent with the requirements of the preceding paragraph and after rebuilding and augmenting the existing groups in Alaska and Okinawa, one additional augmented U.S. medium-bomber group should be provided for Okinawa and one additional British Commonwealth medium-bomber group should be provided for Malaya. Two additional U.S. strategic reconnaissance squadrons would be required: one in Alaska and one in Okinawa. A British Commonwealth strategic reconnaissance squadron would also be required for Malaya. [See force-requirement chart.] . . .

b. Maintain Our Holding Operations Along the General Line of Discriminate Containment, Exploiting Local Opportunities for Improving Our Position Thereon and Exerting Unremitting Pressure Against the Soviet Citadel

The principal areas of contact with major Soviet forces along the line of discriminate containment are the Rhine–Alps–Piave line, southeastern Turkey, and the Iranian mountain passes. These areas also are the ones which it is most important be held against further Soviet encroachment. Although Soviet capabilities have been considerably reduced in these areas as a result of the initial air offensive and other Allied operations, it is possible that a gradual buildup of Soviet capabilities may be effected in some of them. In order to meet these increasing Soviet capabilities, Allied forces will have to be strengthened as necessary in order to maintain our principal positions. In addition, they should be prepared to exploit local opportunities for improving their positions whenever possible.

Along the Rhine line the Soviets could probably maintain a maximum of 125 divisions, although the offensive capability of these divisions would be limited. Their air strength, however, would probably not exceed about 4,800 combat aircraft because of the effects of the Allied air offensive. To provide the means for improving our positions along this line, it is considered that both ground and air forces of the Allies will have to be increased. An additional 18 Allied divisions would be required, increasing the total of Allied divisions defending the Rhine line from 60 to 78. Of the additional 18 divisions, 8 should be furnished by the United States and 10 by Western Union countries. As early as practicable the Allied tactical air forces should be augmented by a maximum possible buildup consistent with the capabilities of the Allied aircraft industry during this period and with the redeployment and neutralization capabilities of defensive fighter units released from the United States, Canada, and the United Kingdom. The buildup of fighters, light bombers, and tactical reconnaissance groups should continue until requirements for the support of ground forces needed for Phase III operations are reached. This requirement, estimated at 69 air groups, . . . can probably be realized well before the number of divisions required is met, and groups arriving in the theater of operations should be committed to action as soon as possible in order to enable the Allies to undertake Phase III operations at the earliest possible date.

The restrictions on maneuver imposed by the terrain, together with the effects of the air offensive, would probably preclude any further buildup of Soviet divisions or combat aircraft along the Alps–Piave line. Therefore it is estimated that Allied forces still holding this line should continue to be sufficient.

Although Soviet forces in southeastern Turkey probably could gradually improve their supply routes to the extent that some additional pressure could be applied against the Allied positions, the Allied forces—because of their superior defensive positions and their continuing ability to interfere seriously with Soviet LOCs—should be able to maintain their positions with moderate reenforcement. Therefore it is considered that 1 Allied division and 2 fighter groups should be scheduled to reenforce that area at approximately $D+9$ months. These forces should be furnished by the British Commonwealth; the division could be redeployed from the Rhine after $D+7$ months.

In spite of the initial and considerable disruption of Soviet LOCs leading through Iran and the continuing Allied capability to interfere with them, it is believed that the Soviets could, by diligent effort, increase to a small degree their offensive capabilities against Allied forces holding the Iranian mountain passes. Therefore it is considered that to ensure the Allied positions in these passes, 1 fighter group should be scheduled to reenforce that area at about $D+7$ months, and 1 additional division at about $D+9$ months. These forces should also be furnished by the British Commonwealth; the division would be redeployed from the Rhine after $D+7$ months. [See force-requirement chart.] . . .

c. Maintain Control of Other Essential Land and Sea Areas and Increase Our Measure of Control of Essential Lines of Communication

The stabilization of the Soviet land offensive, generally along the line of discriminate containment, has ensured the retention in Allied hands of the Western Hemisphere and overseas bases essential to the maintenance of sea and air lines of communication.

The Soviet occupation of Norway is not considered to warrant Allied occupation of additional North Atlantic islands in order to deny them to the USSR since neutralization of these islands by Allied bombing would be feasible in the event of Soviet seizure.

The USSR now controls the Skagerrak entrance to the North Sea by reason of occupation of Denmark, Norway, and Sweden. As a result Soviet submarines from bases in the Baltic together with those employed from bases being established on the North Sea continue to present a serious threat to Allied shipping by virtue of increased mining activity in the vicinity of U.K. and French ports and direct attacks on shipping in the approaches thereto.

Soviet air attacks from bases in the USSR, Norway, Sweden, Denmark, and

Germany have severely damaged port facilities in the United Kingdom. The unloading and distribution of cargoes presents a problem in logistic supply which requires considerable use of alternative methods of discharge and inland distribution of cargoes, e.g., through secondary ports or over beaches.

Except for the severe damage sustained by the United Kingdom, the security of Allied overseas bases has not been seriously threatened.

Communist successes in Southeast Asia are threatening the Allies with the loss of strategic and critical materials therefrom. Increase in forces in Malaya to counter this threat will require minor increase in local defensive naval forces at Singapore.

In order to maintain control of essential land and sea areas and to increase our measure of control of essential LOCs, Allied attacks on enemy submarines, their bases, and repair facilities must be continued and intensified. Attacks against Soviet submarine bases in the Baltic, the North Sea, and the Pacific should be increased to reduce Soviet submarine activity from bases in these areas. To this end two CVLs [small aircraft carriers] in the North Atlantic task force should be replaced by two CVs [aircraft carriers] from the Mediterranean and the CVLs employed in hunter–killer groups. Policing attacks in the offensive mining campaign—especially on primary targets in the Atlantic area and on secondary targets in the Pacific—should be continued by Allied aircraft. . . .

Hunter–killer operations and antisubmarine submarine operations—especially in the North and Central Atlantic and in the approaches to the United Kingdom and French ports—would have to be increased to provide greater security from submarine attacks in those waters. It is therefore considered that two additional hunter–killer groups in the Atlantic will be needed by about D + 7 months. Ten additional antisubmarine submarines (five of which should be British) should be provided for operations in the approaches to the United Kingdom by about D + 7 months.

As our buildup of U.S. forces in Europe progresses, increases in escort forces for convoys will be required, particularly for troop lift. An increase in naval local-defense forces will also be required in U.K. and French ports by about D + 7 months in order to intensify Allied measures of defensive control.

Certain other defensive forces in the United States, Canada, Alaska, and the United Kingdom may be reduced. In the United States, fighter defenses may be further reduced to about four groups at approximately D + 9; in Canada, from three groups to one at D + 9; in Alaska, from two groups to one group at about D + 9; and in the United Kingdom, a progressive reduction in fighter defenses from twelve groups at D + 6 to six groups at D + 12 may be effected. [See force-requirement chart.] . . .

d. Reinforce Our Forces in the Far East as Necessary to Contain the Communist Forces to the Mainland of Asia and to Defend the Southern Malay Peninsula

Except for the provision for medium bombers discussed . . . above, Allied forces already based in Japan, Okinawa, and contiguous waters should be sufficient without further reenforcement to contain Communist forces to the mainland of East Asia.

In Southeast Asia, Communist control of most of south China and Burma and considerable portions of Indochina, with its resultant inroads in the area of containment of the Soviet powers, must be accepted, since the necessity for husbanding Allied resources would preclude the allocation of the major forces required to control these areas.

On the other hand, the greater importance of Malaya to the Allies—first, because of its rubber and second, because of its location on our LOCs—warrants additional Allied action to secure it. The principal threat to its security will develop from indigenous Communist forces aided and abetted from without. Therefore to ensure its continued availability to the Allies, it is considered that at about $D + 7$ the British division already there should be augmented by additional forces totaling the equivalent of one infantry division. This increase is tabulated as follows:

Malaya	$D + 6$	$D + 7$	$D + 30$
Inf Divs	1	2	2

e. The Provision of Essential Aid to Allies; the Intensification of Psychological, Economic, and Underground Warfare; and the Preparation to Establish Control and Enforce Surrender Terms in the USSR and Satellite Countries Are Continuing Tasks for which Provision Has Been Made in the Development of Requirements for Phase I. . . .

5. Phase III

a. While Continuing Courses of Action a through e of Phase II, Initiate a Major Land Offensive in Europe to Cut Off and Destroy All or the Major Part of the Soviet Forces in Europe

(1) General

The conditions under which major land offensives might be launched in Europe have been set forth in Volume II, page 165. In summary, they consist of a reduction in Soviet and satellite logistic capabilities with a resulting loss of tactical and strategical mobility of their armed forces so that they can no longer rapidly move or reconcentrate in the campaign area. Soviet and satellite ground forces throughout the Eurasian land mass may total upwards of 650 line divisions, although they will be greatly reduced in capabilities because of their relative immobility [and] their lack of resupply of ammunition, equipment, and other supplies. Of these, 200 would be satellite divisions.

Soviet dispositions will probably reflect increases in the number of their divisions in Western Europe in anticipation of Allied offensive operations. Possibly 125 Soviet divisions could be maintained for defense of the Rhine. Along the North Sea coasts of Holland, Germany, and Denmark the Soviets could probably have 30–40 divisions, supplied partially by sea from the Baltic ports. Giving consideration to necessary dispositions of their forces in other areas, the Soviets could probably still have on the order of 125 divisions in reserve in Poland and the USSR.

Satellite ground forces would probably be, in general, in their own countries, with perhaps some utilized by the Soviets in occupational roles in Germany, Austria, and Greece.

Although lacking in mobility and in arms, equipment, and supporting air, the Soviet and satellite ground forces in Western Europe by virtue of their large numbers would initially be able to provide a considerable degree of defense against Allied operations.

Soviet and satellite air forces in Western Europe may still number upwards of 5,000 combat aircraft, but Soviet air operations will be greatly restricted because of lack of qualified pilots, POL, and other supplies.

A consideration of the estimated strategic situation indicates that major base areas in Western Europe and the North African–Near Eastern area would be available to the Allies for the projection of a major land offensive against the USSR. The base area in Western Europe would permit offensive operations to be launched through the north German plain into Poland, the Baltic States, and the USSR, if necessary. The base area in the North African–Near Eastern area would permit launching either a pincer operation consisting of a series of ancillary operations in conjunction with the foregoing to effect a junction of the arms of the pincer, possibly in Poland, or of launching major offensive operations through the Aegean Sea and Turkish straits, with landings on the northwestern Black Sea coast or in the Ukraine, while continuing holding operations in Western Europe.

Operations from Western Europe would have the advantages of utilizing the 78 Allied divisions and 53 air groups employed in the area in holding along the Rhine and the large base area already established to support these forces. At the start of the campaign it would also have the advantage of the best LOCs and could support all the Allied forces that could be made available for such operations. An additional advantage would be that the terrain is especially favorable for large-scale operations. On the other hand, a disadvantage would be found in long land routes of advance as the campaign progressed, with the bulk of Soviet forces in opposition.

A pincer operation would have the advantage of partially utilizing the advantage of seaborne mobility enjoyed by the Allies for a wide flanking movement to attack Soviet forces in Western Europe from the rear and sever them from the USSR. It would reduce Allied forces required for the operations in Western Europe by draining off Soviet and satellite forces to the south. On the other hand, preliminary operations to neutralize Soviet forces in western Turkey, to seize the Athens area, eastern Macedonia, Thrace, and the Turkish straits would also be required.

Major offensive operations through the Aegean Sea, Turkish straits, and Black Sea to the Ukraine, while continuing holding operations in Western Europe, would be most suitable for launching land operations directly against the home territory of the USSR. Such operations, although utilizing to the maximum the advantage of seaborne mobility enjoyed by the Allies, would have the disadvantage of the requirement for a considerable engineering effort due to the poor LOCs leading north through the Ukraine, which would not be especially good for large-scale operations. However, major offensive operations generally to the northwest through eastern Romania after landings on the northwestern Black Sea coast would have the advantage of excellent LOCs. As in the case of the pincer operation the movement through Romania would permit Allied forces to attack the Soviets in Western Europe from the flank and rear and sever them from the USSR. On the other hand, preliminary operations for the seizure or neutralization of areas in and adjacent to the Aegean Sea, the Dardanelles, and the Bosporus would still be required. In addition, there would be the requirements for establishing a large base area in the North African–Near Eastern area.

(2) Operations Through the North German Plain to Poland and East Prussia, Thence Southeast to the Black Sea

Allied operations against the Soviets along this axis would envisage initially a breakthrough in the Rhine positions north of Cologne together with simultaneous amphibious and airborne landings on the German North Sea coast.

Initial objectives of the breakthrough forces should be to seize the Berlin area and to link up with the amphibious forces in the Bremen area. Approximately 114 divisions and 73 fighter, light bomb, and tactical reconnaissance groups should be allotted for the breakthrough and subsequent exploitation. It is estimated that approximately 3 airborne divisions, included in the above total, would be required to assist in this breakthrough; 13 medium bomb groups of the strategic air forces in the U.K. and Italy could also assist in this effort.

Forces landing on the German North Sea coast should consist of an estimated total of 12 divisions, of which 3 should be amphibious and 2 airborne. These forces should seize a bridgehead to include the Bremen–Hamburg–Lübeck area, thus sealing off the Danish peninsula and securing the important ports of Bremerhaven and Hamburg. An estimated 12 CVEs would be required to furnish air support for the amphibious landings. As soon as the bridgehead is secure, a force of 6 of the 12 divisions should break out of the bridgehead and liberate Denmark. About 3 air groups would be required in support of this operation.

Approximately 24 divisions and 14 air groups of the breakthrough forces should be allotted to consolidate initially the Berlin area, link up with the bridgehead area, and protect the south flank of the breakthrough forces.

After seizure and consolidation of the Berlin area, the Baltic port areas of Stettin, Danzig–Gdynia and Königsberg should be seized. An estimated 6 divisions from the breakthrough forces would be required for the Stettin area, 6 for the Danzig–Gdynia area, and 6 for the Königsberg area. About 10 air groups from the breakthrough forces would be required to assist in these operations.

Simultaneously with the seizure of the Baltic port areas operations should continue from the Berlin area to seize the Warsaw and Krakow areas of Poland. These operations would cut the main Soviet LOCs to the west. An estimated 24 divisions and 14 air groups from the breakthrough forces would be required for the seizure and initial consolidation of each of those areas.

Approximately 24 divisions and 14 air groups holding positions south of Cologne should be prepared to advance to the southeast, as the situation becomes feasible, in order to seize the Vienna area. These forces should then link up with forces in the Krakow area.

After consolidation of Denmark and neutralization of the Soviet forces in southern Norway and Sweden, permitting movement of shipping into the Baltic, and after the Baltic ports become available, operations from the Krakow area should be launched to the southeast with the objective of reaching the Black Sea and seizing the Constanta–Danube mouth area. Basing their right flank on the Carpathian Mountains and their left flank on the Dniester River, an estimated 24 divisions and 14 air groups from the breakthrough forces would be required by the Allies for these operations. Such operations would complete the severance of Soviet and satellite forces in Western and Central Europe from the USSR.

As soon as practicable after consolidation of the Constanta–Danube mouth area, the sea LOC through the Aegean, Turkish straits, and Black Sea should be opened in order to supply Allied forces through the Black Sea ports. In view of the relatively slight opposition envisaged in the operations of opening this LOC, it is probable that at this time sufficient forces could be released from other tasks in the Mediterranean–Near East area—and from other areas if necessary—for this purpose. If airborne landings were required, airborne units from the north German area could be redeployed to this area.

In summary, the forces estimated to be required for all the above operations total 150 divisions and 90 combat air groups. It is estimated that this total should consist approximately of 108 infantry divisions and 37 armored divisions, 5 airborne divisions, 64 fighter groups, 13 light bomb groups, and 13 tactical reconnaissance groups. In addition, approximately 63 troop-carrier groups and 63 assault aircraft or glider squadrons would be required for the airborne operations outlined above.

About 13 medium bomb groups based in the U.K. and Italy could also assist in this effort. It is probable that a considerable portion of the 6 all-weather interceptor groups defending the U.K. and the 8 groups defending areas west of the Rhine could also be made available to assist in the above offensive operations, since Soviet air attacks during Phase III should no longer be a serious threat.

Naval forces for the amphibious operations on the German North Sea coast will have to furnish assault lift for three divisions and the necessary support forces. . . .

Naval local-defense forces and those naval forces required for the security of sea LOCs in the North Sea and the Baltic could be provided from those developed under the Phase II course of action: "Maintain control of other essential land and sea areas," etc., page 266.

It is estimated that the time required for the Allies to generate the required forces and supplies for these operations would preclude their initiation until about D + 24 months.

(3) Major Operations Through the North German Plain in Conjunction with Ancillary Operations Through the Aegean, the Turkish straits, and the Northwestern Black Sea Area to Effect a Juncture in Southern Poland

As an alternative it might be desirable and feasible to assist the campaigns described above by a series of operations from the North African–Near Eastern area which would eventuate in landings on the northwestern Black Sea coast followed by operations to the northwestward to effect a junction with Allied forces in Poland, possibly in the Krakow area. These operations would be designed to drain off Soviet and satellite forces from the north, reducing the Allied forces required in the northern campaign [and] preventing the escape of Soviet forces committed to the Balkans, and would close the pincers around Western Europe. It would also ensure that in the event of Soviet collapse Allied forces would be in a better position to exploit such a possibility.

Operations preliminary to Allied landings on the northwestern Black Sea littoral would include, as a minimum, the neutralization of Soviet forces in western Turkey, particularly in the Izmir area; the seizure or neutralization of the Aegean islands; and the seizure of the Athens area, eastern Macedonia, Thrace, and the Turkish straits.

The sequence of operations and scheme of maneuver to accomplish the above minimum requirements could be as follows: there would be a period of neutralization of Soviet air and naval power based in western Turkey and southern Greece by land-based air, principally from the Cairo–Suez area and

Crete, and by carrier-based air, followed by amphibious and airborne landings in the Athens–Piraeus area. Following consolidation and the buildup of air power in the Athens area, and after further and intensified neutralization of Soviet air and naval bases in western Turkey and elsewhere in the Aegean littoral, including the possible seizure of some Aegean islands, amphibious and airborne assaults would be made first in the Salonika area and later in the Alexandroúpolis area for the purpose of seizing eastern Macedonia and Thrace; the Turkish straits would then be seized by ground attacks launched from Thrace in conjunction with amphibious and airborne landings. Consolidation of these areas, with the buildup of air power in the Aegean littoral, would permit passage through the Turkish Straits into the Black Sea for major landings on the northwestern Black Sea coast.

Taking into consideration the reutilization of some forces during the successive phases of the above operations, it is estimated that the scale of forces required would be on the order of 27 divisions and 25⅓ combat air groups. The composition of this total would be approximately as follows: 3 A/B, 4 armored, 20 infantry divisions, and 5 medium-bomber, 10 fighter, 2⅔ light-bomber, 2⅔ tactical reconnaissance, and 5 all-weather interceptor groups. In addition, because of the time phasing of the airborne operations, troop-carrier aircraft for 2 divisions would be required, except for assault or glider squadrons, of which lift for 5 divisions would be required in view of their probable nonrecoverability. The total airlift would therefore be 4 heavy and 21 medium troop-carrier groups plus 63 assault or glider squadrons.

Consideration of time phasing of the amphibious operations would require the provision of naval forces for a 4-division assault lift. In addition to carrier task forces, hunter–killer forces, and submarine forces already operating in the Mediterranean, support and escort forces for these operations would be required approximately as follows: 12 CVEs with air groups, 6 BBs, 8 CAs, 36 DDs 108 DD/DE, 75 AM/AMS. [See Glossary for explanation of abbreviations.] Two squadrons of naval patrol planes together with necessary tenders would also be required.

It is estimated that to complete the series of preliminary operations outlined above, approximately three months' time would be required.

Following those operations, amphibious and airborne landings would be made against the northwestern Black Sea coast. The Bucharest–Ploesti area would be seized in conjunction with a thrust from Thrace across the Bulgarian plain to Bucharest. A major drive should then be launched to the north and west generally along the axis of the Prut River valley with the objective of linking up with operations from the north in the general area of Krakow. Containing operations to the line Iron Gate–Transylvanian Alps to protect the left flank and to the Dniester River to protect the right flank would be required.

It is estimated that approximately 30 divisions and 26 air groups would be required for the major operations outlined above. This total should consist of approximately 2 A/B, 8 armored, and 20 infantry divisions and 5 medium-bomber, 13 fighter, 3 light-bomber, 3 tactical reconnaissance, and 2 all-weather interceptor groups. Of the above forces, an estimated 7 divisions (1 A/B, 2 armored, 4 infantry) and 10 air groups (5 medium bombers, 3 fighters, 1 light bomber, 1 tactical reconnaissance) could be furnished from forces released from the preliminary operations. Airlift for the airborne operations could be provided by the troop-carrier aircraft employed in the preliminary operations, except that assault or glider lift for 2 more divisions (i.e., 25 squadrons) would be required.

The major operations in the Black Sea area would require no naval forces in addition to those allocated to the preliminary operations and as contained in other courses of action.

An estimated two months' time would be required after completion of the preliminary operations until completion of the major operations with the linking up of forces in the Krakow area.

Total forces for the entire series of operations from the south amount to 50 divisions (4 A/B, 10 armored, 36 infantry), 41⅓ combat air groups (5 M.B., 20 Ftr., 4⅔ L.B., 4⅔ Tac. R., 7 All-Wx. Int.), troop-carrier units composed of 4 heavy and 21 medium groups plus 88 assault or glider squadrons, amphibious lift for 4 divisions, support and escort forces composed approximately of 12 CVEs with air groups, 6 BBs, 8 CAs, 36 DDs, 108 DD/DEs, 75 AM/AMS, and 2 squadrons of naval patrol planes with necessary tenders therefor. Total elapsed time for all operations from the south would be approximately five months. Operations from the south would reduce ground and air forces required in the northern campaign by the 24 divisions and 14 air groups which had been allocated for the drive southeastward from the Krakow area to the Black Sea and by 1 amphibious lift which could be released from preliminary operations in the Aegean Sea area in time to participate in the landings on the German North Sea coast. In addition, some further reduction in ground and air forces required in the northern campaign probably could be effected because of the draining off of some Soviet and satellite forces to the south, which would have been expected to oppose the northern thrust. This reduction is difficult to determine, but for planning purposes it is estimated that it might be something on the order of 12 divisions and 7 air groups. On the other hand, 3 additional divisional amphibious lifts together with support and escort forces for an additional 3 amphibiously lifted divisions would be required.

Summarizing, the ground and air forces required for operations both from the north and from the south would total approximately 164 divisions and 110⅓ combat air groups. The estimated composition of this total would be approximately 117 Inf., 38 Arm'd., and 9 A/B divisions and 5 M.B., 69 Ftr., 14⅔ L.B., 14⅔ Tac. R., and 7 All-Wx. Int. groups. In addition, the total airlift required for all the airborne operations in both the north and south operations would be 14 heavy and 74 medium troop-carrier groups plus 151 assault or glider squadrons.

Naval forces for the amphibious operations of both arms of the pincer will have to furnish a total of six divisional amphibious lifts with the necessary support and escort forces. . . .

If the decision were made to launch operations from the south in conjunction with the northern campaigns, it would probably be desirable to phase the two arms of the pincers so that they would meet in the Krakow area at approximately the same time. It is estimated that Allied forces from the north could probably reach [the] Krakow area in from two to three months. Since the estimated time required for forces in the southern campaign to reach the Krakow area is approximately five months, it would be necessary to launch the thrust from the south approximately two to three months prior to the northern campaign.

Considering the probable additional forces required for both the northern and southern campaigns over those required for the northern campaign alone and the increased length of time needed for the generation of such forces, it is probable that a delay of something on the order of four to six months might be required before a major land offensive could be launched.

(4) Major Operations Through the Aegean, the Turkish straits, and the Northwestern Black Sea Area to the Baltic and Eastern Germany in Conjunction with Holding Operations Along the Rhine Line

If the major offensive against the Soviets were to be launched from the south, with only holding operations along the Rhine, the initial phases of operations in the south—to include the clearing of the Aegean and the Turkish straits followed by landings on the northwest Black Sea coast with a drive to the north and west as far as the Krakow area—would follow a similar pattern and would be on a scale comparable to those corresponding operations already described for the pincer movement.

In addition to operations to the Krakow area, however, it would be necessary to conduct operations northward to the Baltic and northwestward, probably to the general line of the Elbe River. These operations would sever the Soviet forces in Western and Central Europe from the USSR and would lead to the rapid destruction of these forces.

Concurrently with the thrust to the Krakow area, operations northward through Lvov to seize the Warsaw area should be launched. An estimated 24 divisions and 14 air groups would be required for the seizure and initial consolidation of this area.

After seizure of the Warsaw area the Baltic port areas of Königsberg, Danzig–Gdynia, and Stettin should be seized. An estimated 6 divisions would be required for the seizure and initial consolidation of each of these three areas. About 10 air groups would be required to assist in the operations.

After seizure of the Krakow area operations should continue to the northwest to seize the Dresden and Berlin areas and consolidate along the general line of the Elbe. An estimated 6 divisions and 4 air groups would be required for the seizure and initial consolidation of the Dresden area and 24 divisions and 14 air groups for the Berlin area.

Forces required for holding operations along the Rhine could probably be reduced to approximately 60 divisions and 41 air groups.

These forces should be prepared, as the situation becomes feasible, to advance eastward to link up with Allied forces from the east; northeastward to clear the Soviets from Denmark; and southeastward to seize the Vienna area with a subsequent linking up with forces in the Krakow area. Coincident with the consolidation of Denmark, neutralization of Soviet forces in southern Norway should proceed, together with naval operations, in order to permit movement of shipping into the Baltic ports.

Summarizing, the ground and air forces required for the above operations total approximately 182 divisions and 124⅓ combat air groups.* The estimated compositions of the above total would be as follows: 138 Inf., 40 Arm'd., and 4 A/B divisions and 5 M.B., 77 Ftr., 17⅔ L.B., 17⅔ Tac. R., and 7 All-Wx. Int. groups. In addition, airlift requirements would total 4 heavy and 21 medium troop-carrier groups and 88 assault or glider squadrons.

*Editor's Note: About 6 million men of all arms and services.

Naval forces required would be approximately the same as those required for the southern arm of the pincer, namely, sufficient amphibious lift for 4 divisions together with the necessary support and escort forces. . . .

Naval local-defense forces and those naval forces required for the security of sea LOCs in the Aegean, Turkish straits, and Black Sea could be provided from those developed under the Phase II course of action: "Maintain control of other essential land and sea areas," etc., page 266.

Considering the large additional ground forces required for the above operations, it is probable that these operations could not be launched until about twelve months later than the operations set forth in paragraph (2)—that is, about D + 36—and about six to eight months after the operations set forth in paragraph (3) or D + 28–30.

Summary and Conclusions

The force requirements for each of the three offensive operations discussed above are tabulated below.

A comparison of the force requirements and time phasings tabulated below— together with a further consideration of the principal advantages and disadvantages of each of the proposed major offensives—leads to the following conclusions.

(a) Major operations from the south require the generation of excessive ground forces. The time required for this generation would also cause a further and undesirable delay in launching the major offensive. In addition, these operations would be of questionable logistic feasibility because of both long sea

Operation North (D + 24)		Operation Pincer (D + 28–30)		Operation South (D + 36)	
Divisions		**Divisions**		**Divisions**	
Inf.	108	Inf.	117	Inf.	138
Arm'd.	37	Arm'd.	38	Arm'd.	40
A/B	5	A/B	9	A/B	4
Total	150	Total	164	Total	182
Combat Air Groups		**Combat Air Groups**		**Combat Air Groups**	
M.B. Gp.	—	5		5	
Ftr. Gp.	64	69		77	
L.B. Gp.	13	14⅔		17⅔	
Tac. Recon. Gp.	13	14⅔		17⅔	
All-Wx. Int. Gp.	—	7		7	
	90	110⅓		124⅓	
Troop Carrier Units		**Troop Carrier Units**		**Troop Carrier Units**	
Troop Carrier Gp.	63	88		25	
Assault or Gli. Sq.	63	151		88	
3-Div. Lift		**6-Div. Lift**		**4-Div. Lift**	
4 AGC		8 AGC		6 AGC	
48 APA		96 APA		64 APA	
24 AKA		48 AKA		32 AKA	
72 LST		144 LST		96 LST	
54 LSM		108 LSM		72 LSM	
9 LSD		18 LSD		12 LSD	
12 APD		24 APD		16 APD	
36 LSM (R)		72 LSM (R)		48 LSM (R)	
Support and Escort		**Support and Escort**		**Support and Escort**	
12 CVEs with air groups		24 CVEs with air groups		12 CVEs with air groups	
6 BBs		12 BBs		6 BBs	
8 CAs		16 CAs		8 CAs	
36 DDs		72 DDs		36 DDs	
70 AM/AMS		145 AM/AMS		75 AM/AMS	
		2 VP–MS		2 VP–MS	
		1 AV		1 AV	
		1 AVP		1 AVP	

Note: See Glossary for explanation of abbreviations.

and land LOCs. Therefore, notwithstanding the advantages previously discussed, the launching of major operations from the south is rejected.

(b) Major operations from the north—in spite of the smaller requirements in forces, the earliest date of launching, and the other advantages already set forth—have the major disadvantage of long land LOCs toward the end of the campaign with their attendant logistic difficulties. For this reason the launching of major operations from the north alone is not considered the most feasible.

(c) Major operations from the north in conjunction with ancillary operations from the south would have the important advantage of the shortest land lines of communication from mounting bases. The pincer operations proposed would lend themselves well to the best operational seasons of the year in that operations from the south could commence in the spring followed by operations from the north in the summer. Once the major operations from the north had commenced, it is probable that the pincer operations contemplated would conclude the campaign envisaged more rapidly than either of the other offensives. In addition, these operations would have the greatest probability of preventing the escape of Soviet forces from the Balkans, and they would also ensure that in the event of an anticipated Soviet collapse or capitulation Allied forces would be in a better position to exploit such a possibility. Therefore it is concluded from the principal advantages set forth above that the launching of major operations from the north, so phased as to obtain the optimum benefit from ancillary operations from the south, would be the most suitable and feasible. (For employment of forces, see map, page 260.)

Forces for the selected course of action should be furnished by the Allies according to the following approximations:

	Divisions			
	Inf.	Arm'd.	A/B	Total
United States	44	18	7	69
France	34	11	—	45
British Commonwealth	19	7	2	28
Belgium	9	1	—	10
Netherlands	8	1	—	9
Greece	2	—	—	2
Luxembourg	1	—	—	1
	117	38	9	164

Notes—(1) Divisions could be released from operations in other areas for reutilization in these operations as follows:

   2 U.S. Inf. and 1 U.S. Arm'd. from southeastern Turkey.

   1 U.S. Marine from Mediterranean area and 2/9 Marine from Iceland.

   1 Br. Comm. Inf. Div. from Basra–Abadan.

   2 Greek Divs. from Crete.

   (2) Of the total of 44 U.S. Inf. Divs., 3 should be Marine Divs.

				All-				
			Tac.	Wx.	Total	Hv.	Med.	Gli.
	M.B.	Ftr.	L.B.	Rec.	Int.	Combat	T.C.	T.C.	Sq.

Air Groups

	M.B.	Ftr.	L.B.	Tac. Rec.	All-Wx. Int.	Total Combat	Hv. T.C.	Med. T.C.	Gli. Sq.
U.S.	5	29	6⅔	6⅔	7	54⅓	10	53	126
France	—	19	4	4	—	27	—	—	—
Br. Comm.	—	12	2	2	—	16	4	21	25
Belgium	—	4	1	1	—	6	—	—	—
Netherlands	—	4	1	1	—	6	—	—	—
Greece	—	1	—	—	—	1	—	—	—
Totals	5	69	14⅔	14⅔	7	110⅓	14	74	151
A/C	(200)	(5175)	(704)	(774)	(525)	(7378)	(504)	(3552)	(2416)

b. From the Improved Position Resulting from a Above, Continue Offensive Operations of All Arms as Necessary to Force Capitulation

Further operations from the improved position held by the Allies depend to a large extent on the degree of disorganization and the willingness to continue fighting of Soviet and satellite forces cut off in Central Europe. Even if only large-scale guerrilla-type fighting continued, it would absorb large numbers of Allied forces to cope with it. Therefore first-priority operations would be those designed to force capitulation of the remaining Soviet and satellite forces cut off in Central Europe. When this has been completed, the Allied forces would have to furnish forces for routine control of the satellite areas. . . . These forces are estimated to total fifteen divisions and seven air groups.

Coincidentally with the mopping up of Soviet and satellite forces in Central Europe, Allied air forces should continue to intensify the air offensive against the USSR, advancing their bases eastward into Europe as necessary and feasible.

Subsequent offensive operations of all arms cannot be definitely determined at this time, but it is considered probable that the forces already generated would be sufficient to force the capitulation of the USSR.

APPENDIX B: WESTERN HEMISPHERE FIGHTER DEFENSES AND CONTROL AND EARLY WARNING COVERAGE

1.FIGHTER DEFENSES

The total number of Soviet bombers capable of reaching vital areas of Canada and the U.S. on one-way or limited two-way missions in 1957 is estimated at eighteen hundred to two thousand, of which perhaps four hundred may be jet bombers. This force would be subject to centralized control, and its objectives might differ widely geographically from day to day. Therefore any estimate of the proportion which might be devoted to any particular target area might be misleading and, at best, would be of doubtful value. The effects of the Allied counter-air-offensive, plus operational problems such as flying time per sortie (twenty to twenty-four hours), air-to-air refueling, cruise control, airfield complexes, and coordination would probably limit the scale of attack against the Western Hemisphere. Although there is no sound basis for estimating the probable scale of attack, for planning purposes it is reasonable to assume that for sustained operations something like one hundred aircraft per day up to approximately three hundred aircraft every third or fourth day might be employed.

U.S. and Canadian fighter requirements to meet the Soviet air attacks on the scale described above would be on the order of three hundred aircraft airborne if all aircraft were in a position to effect interception. Since fighters in some areas of the United States or Canada could in all probability not intercept Soviet bombers attacking other areas at considerable distances, the fighter requirement probably would have to be nearly tripled. Assuming a 75 percent operational availability factor and a deployment that would permit effective interception, the number of fighter groups required to be operational on D-Day would be about fifteen. These should consist of high-performance all-weather interceptors. About three groups of this total should be provided by the Canadians for defense of the most important areas in Canada and to provide initial interception of Soviet bombers attacking the United States. The remaining twelve groups should consist of U.S. interceptors, initially deployed approximately as follows (see also map, page 196) . . .:

Mitchel AFB, L.I.
Suffolk County Airport, L.I.
McGuire AFB, Trenton, N.J.
Otis AFB, Falmouth, Mass.
Andrews AFB, Wash, D.C.
Langley AFB, Hampton, Va.
Grenier AFB, Manchester, N.H.
Albany Airport, Albany, N.Y.
Wheeler-Sack AFB, Watertown, N.H.
Niagara Falls Airport, N.Y.
Greater Pittsburgh AFB, Pa.
Selfridge AFB, Mt. Clemens, Mich.
Saulte Ste Marie Airport, Mich.
Orchard Place AFB, Chicago, Ill.
Wright-Patterson AFB, Dayton, Ohio
Knoxville Municipal Airport, Tenn.
Scott AFB, Belleville, Ill.
Duluth Municipal Airport, Minn.

Lincoln AFB, Nebraska
Wichita Municipal Airport, Kans.
Tinker AFB, Oklahoma City, Okla.
Camp Hood AFB, Waco, Texas
New Orleans Airport, La.
Lake Charles AFB, La.
Houston Municipal Airport, Texas
Kirtland AFB, Albuquerque, N.M.
San Diego Naval Air Station, Calif.
Long Beach AFB, Calif.
Hamilton AFB, San Francisco, Calif.
McChord AFB, Tacoma, Wash.
Whidbey Island Naval Air Station, Wash.
Moses Lake AFB, Wash.
Portland Airport, Ore.
Salt Lake City Airport, Utah
Lowry AFB, Denver, Colo.
Santa Maria Airport, Calif.

Anticipating the probable losses of Soviet bombers to the Allied defenses, the expenditure of Soviet A-bombs, and the effects of the Allied air offensive, U.S. fighter groups could probably be reduced by one-third at about D+6 months.

Fighter defenses should also be provided for Alaska, Greenland, Labrador, Newfoundland, and the Caribbean area, for protection of these areas and for interception of Soviet bombers attacking the U.S. and Canada. These forces should also be all-weather interceptors. . . .

2.CONTROL AND EARLY WARNING COVERAGE

In order to provide the minimum land-based control and early-warning network for the air defense of the Western Hemisphere, a total of fifty early-warning [EW] radar stations, sixty-six combined early-warning radar and GCI [Ground Control Interception] radar stations (including thirteen air-defense control centers), and six separate GCI stations would be required. One additional EW radar and GCI radar would be required in Panama. As an added measure of control and early warning for the continental United States, a system of radar picket vessels (DDRs) and land-based reconnaissance aircraft employing airborne early-warning [AEW] radar will be needed off the northeastern and the western coasts of the United States.

APPENDIX C: ANTIAIRCRAFT DEFENSE OF THE CONTINENTAL UNITED STATES

1. The fighter defenses developed [on p. 283] . . . are designed to give area defense to those "most important" areas of the continental United States containing the greatest density of "vital," "critical," and "very important" facilities. . . .

2. Although it would be highly desirable to provide antiaircraft defenses also for the above areas, an examination of the requirements for defense of even the "vital" facilities alone in those areas reveals that those requirements are far beyond the capabilities of the United States without an unacceptable reduction in our offensive capabilities overseas. Therefore two major conclusions are reached: first, only those "vital" facilities must be selected for defense whose destruction and impairment would entail a risk so grave as to be unacceptable, and second, the scale of defense for each of those facilities must be only that minimum which is sufficient to give 360° coverage of the target area.

3. In the selection of facilities for defense and the type of antiaircraft protection given those facilities, as set forth in the table below, the following general principles were followed.

a. Facilities lying within the intercept capabilities line were given antiaircraft defense only where the facility was of highest priority; most of these facilities were given only AW defense since it was considered that the fighters could take care of the high-altitude defenses; some of the highest-priority facilities were, however, still given gun defenses because of their importance.

b. Facilities lying outside of the intercept capabilities line were also given antiaircraft defense only where the facility was of highest priority. In general these selected facilities were considered to require both gun and AW defenses. However, since the majority of these facilities, especially those in the southern states, would actually get considerable high-altitude protection because of their location behind areas of intercept capabilities, it was considered that only AW protection should be given except for those targets of paramount importance.

c. Facilities lying along probable axes of Soviet attack and closest to Soviet bases were considered to be, in general, the most vulnerable and consequently were given highest priority for defense.

d. Facilities which, while being extremely vital, were not considered to be particularly vulnerable or remunerative targets for bombing were placed low on the priority list for defense.

4. Applying the principles enumerated in the above paragraphs, the following table lists the minimum antiaircraft defenses required for the vital facilities in the United States. It is recognized that each of the facilities selected in the table below may not be those which will actually be defended in 1957. This, however, is not of significant importance at this time since changes resulting from more detailed planning would probably closely approximate the overall estimate of requirements set forth herein. These installations, together with the "critical" and "very important" installations, . . . are plotted on the map. . . .

Facility	Location	Fighter Protection	Gun Bns*	AW Bns
Admin. and Command	Washington, D.C.	Yes	5	3
Atomic	Sandia, N.M.	"	1	1
"	Los Alamos, N.M.	"	2	2
"	Hanford, Wash.	"	4	4
"	Miamisburg, Ohio	"		1
"	Oak Ridge, Tenn.	"	3	3
Thompson Products, Inc. (Parts for jet engines and aircraft)	Euclid, Ohio	"		1
Wyman Gordon Co. (aircraft components)	Worcester, Mass.	"		1
Ethyl Corp. (av. gas component)	Baton Rouge, La.	"		1
Dupont (sodium)	Niagara Falls, N.Y.	"	1	1
Dupont (av. gas component)	Deepwater, N.J.	"	1	1
Ethyl Dow Cml. Co. (av. gas component)	Freeport, Texas	"		1
Ethyl Dow Cml. Co. (av. gas component)	Wilmington, N.C.	No	1	1
Howdry Process Co. (av. gas catalysts)	Paulsboro, N.J.	Yes	1	1
Standard Oil, N.J. (petroleum processing for synthetic rubber)	Baton Rouge, La.	"		
Pratt & Whitney (aircraft engines)	Hartford, Conn.	"		1
Curtiss Wright (propellers)	Caldwell, N.J.	"		1
Bendix Corp. (aircraft components)	Sidney, N.Y.	"		1
Chrysler Corp., Dodge Div. (aircraft components)	Chicago, Ill.	"		1
Port of embarkation	Brooklyn, N.Y.	"	1	1
Allison Plant (jet engines)	Indianapolis, Ind.	"	1	1
GMC, Buick Div. (aircraft components)	Melrose Park, Ill.	"		1

Facility	Location	Fighter Protection	Gun Bns*	AW Bns
Am. Bench Corp. (aircraft components)	Springfield, Mass.	Yes		1
Packard Co. (aircraft engines)	Detroit, Mich.	"		1
Bendix Corp. (aircraft components)	Teterboro, N.J.	"		1
Wright Aero. Corp. (aircraft components)	Cincinnati, Ohio	"		1
Port of embarkation	San Francisco, Calif.	"	1	1
Port of embarkation	Seattle, Wash.	"	1	1
Port of embarkation	New Orleans, La.	"		1
Steam electric sta.	Buffalo, N.Y.	"		1
Hydroelec. sta.	Niagara Falls, N.Y.	"	1	1
Hydroelec. sta.	Massena, N.Y.	"	1	1
Alcoa Substation (electric power)	Alcoa, Tenn.	"		1
Hydroelec. sta.	Boulder City, Nev.	No		1
" " "	Mason City, Wash. (Grand Coulee)	Yes	1	1
" " "	Bonneville, Oreg.	"	1	1
Steam elec. sta.	Baton Rouge, La.	"		1
" " "	Hartford, Conn.	"		1
Locks and canal	Sault Ste. Marie, Mich.	"	3	1
Norton Co. (abrasives)	Worcester, Mass.	"		1
Carborundum Co. (abrasives)	Niagara Falls, N.Y.	"		1
GMC, New Departure Div. (bearings)	Bristol, Conn.	"		1
" " "	Meriden, Conn.	"		1
SKF Industries, Plant #1 (ball bearings)	Philadelphia, Pa.	"		1
SKF Industries (bearings)	Shippensburg, Pa.	"		1
SKF Industries, Plant #2	Philadelphia, Pa.	"		1
SKF Industries, Plant #3	Bridgboro, Pa.	"		1
Penna. Salt Mfg. Co. (aluminum-processing component)	Natrona, Pa.	"		1
Alcoa (aluminum processing)	Massena, N.Y.	"		1
" "	Alcon, Tenn.	"		1
Naval shipyard	Norfolk, Va.	"	1	1
" "	Boston, Mass.	"	1	1
" "	New York, N.Y.	"	1	1
" "	Philadelphia, Pa.	"	1	1
Aluminum Ore Co. (alumina)	Mobile, Ala.	No	1	1
Reynolds Metals Co. (aluminum processing material)	Hurricane Creek, Ark.	No	1	1
Permanente Metals Corp. (alumina)	Baton Rouge, La.	Yes		1

Facility	Location	Fighter Protection	Gun Bns*	AW Bns
Aluminum Ore Co. (aluminum processing)	East St. Louis, Ill.	Yes		1
RCA (electronic components)	Lancaster, Pa.	"		1
Corning Glass Wks. (electronic and optical-instrument components)	Corning, N.Y.	"		1
Superior Tube Co. (radio tubes)	Collegeville, Pa.	"		1
RCA (radio components)	Harrison, N.J.	"		1
Fansteel Metallurgical Corp. (electronic components)	Chicago, Ill.	"		1
Sperry Gyroscope (fire-control instruments)	Lake Success, N.Y.	"		1
Sylvania Elec. Products Co. (electronic components)	Emporium, Pa.	"		1
Electric Metallurgical Co. (electronic metals)	Niagara Falls, N.Y.	"		1
General Railway Signal Corps (fire-control instruments)	Rochester, N.Y.	"		1
General Aniline Wks. (electronic components)	Grasseli, N.J.	"		1
Consolidated Vultee (airframes)	Ft. Worth, Tex.	"		1
Boeing (airframes)	Seattle, Wash.	"	1	1
Grumman (airframes)	Bethpage, L.I., N.Y.	"	1	1
Republic (airframes)	Farmingdale, L.I., N.Y.	"	1	1
Lockheed (airframes)	Burbank, Calif.	"	1	1
Naval shipyard	Puget Sound, Wash.	"	1	1
" "	Mare Is., Calif.	"	1	1
" "	San Francisco, Calif.	"	1	1
Dow Chemical Co. (explosives and synthetic rubber components)	Midland, Mich.	"	1	1
Carbide & Carbon Chemical Corp. (chemicals for resins and plastics)	S. Charleston, W. Va.	No		1
Dupont (rayon and hexa-chlorothane)	Martinsville, Va.	"		1
Dupont (nylon salt)	Belle, W. Va.	"		1
Dupont (nylon)	Seaford, Del.	Yes		1
Total			44	89

*If guided-missile squadrons are available for use, they could be substituted for gun battalions on the basis of one guided-missile squadron per four gun battalions. Their use in lieu of gun battalions cannot, however, be determined at this time.

APPENDIX D: A TYPICAL STRATEGIC AIR OFFENSIVE PROGRAM

Tabulated below is a summary of three possible scales of attack on the three primary target systems, which when eliminated to the indicated degree would collapse the Soviet economy as shown. There is included an indication of the requirements and the results to be expected. Further details on the target systems are set forth in the maps hereto, pages 290, 294, and 296.

Soviet Industry:

Degree of Collapse of Industry	Several Years	1–1½ Years	1 Year
Target Systems to Be Attacked	Petroleum, Electric Power, and Steel	Electric Power and Steel	Petroleum and Electric Power
Atomic Bombs on Target (in 30 days)	180	141	109
Tons of Conventional Bombs on Target (by D + 4 mos.)	12,620 tons	10,420 tons	10,420 tons
Percentages of Industry Destroyed or Eliminated from Production.			
Electric Power	66–70	66	66
Petroleum	95	70	95
Steel	85	85	76
Alumina	100	100	100
Aluminum	100	100	100
Magnesium	100	100	100
Autos and Trucks	100	100	100
Hvy. Elec. Eq.	97	97	97
Syn. Ammonia	98	98	98
A/C Assembly	92	92	92
A/C Engines	89	89	89
Elec. Tubes	91	97	91
Lt. Elec. Eq.	82	82	82
Coke	100	100	100
Hv. and Med. Bomb Gps. Reqd. for Atomic Effort	7	5	4
Hv. and Med. Bomb Gps. Reqd. for Conv. Effort	6	5	5

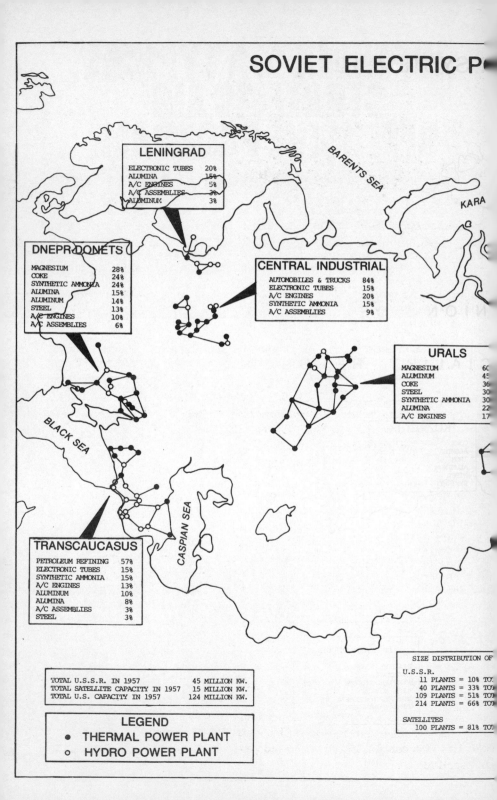

SOVIET ELECTRIC P

BARENTS SEA

KARA

LENINGRAD

ELECTRONIC TUBES	20%
ALUMINA	15%
A/C ENGINES	5%
A/C ASSEMBLIES	3%
ALUMINUM	3%

DNEPR-DONETS

MAGNESIUM	28%
COKE	24%
SYNTHETIC AMMONIA	24%
ALUMINA	15%
ALUMINUM	14%
STEEL	13%
A/C ENGINES	10%
A/C ASSEMBLIES	6%

CENTRAL INDUSTRIAL

AUTOMOBILES & TRUCKS	84%
ELECTRONIC TUBES	15%
A/C ENGINES	20%
SYNTHETIC AMMONIA	15%
A/C ASSEMBLIES	9%

URALS

MAGNESIUM	60
ALUMINUM	45
COKE	36
STEEL	30
SYNTHETIC AMMONIA	30
ALUMINA	22
A/C ENGINES	17

BLACK SEA

CASPIAN SEA

TRANSCAUCASUS

PETROLEUM REFINING	57%
ELECTRONIC TUBES	15%
SYNTHETIC AMMONIA	15%
A/C ENGINES	13%
ALUMINUM	10%
ALUMINA	8%
A/C ASSEMBLIES	3%
STEEL	3%

TOTAL U.S.S.R. IN 1957	45 MILLION KW.
TOTAL SATELLITE CAPACITY IN 1957	15 MILLION KW.
TOTAL U.S. CAPACITY IN 1957	124 MILLION KW.

SIZE DISTRIBUTION OF

U.S.S.R.
    11 PLANTS = 10% TO
    40 PLANTS = 33% TO
    109 PLANTS = 51% TO
    214 PLANTS = 66% TO

SATELLITES
    100 PLANTS = 81% TO

LEGEND

- ● THERMAL POWER PLANT
- ○ HYDRO POWER PLANT

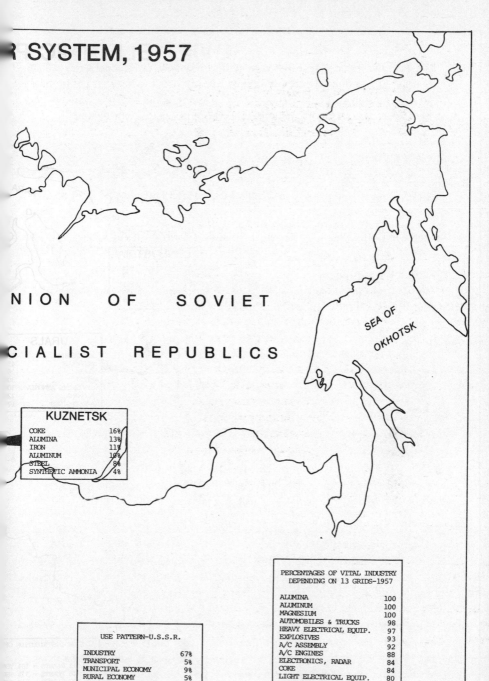

NION OF SOVIET

CIALIST REPUBLICS

SEA OF OKHOTSK

KUZNETSK

COKE	16%
ALUMINA	13%
IRON	11%
ALUMINUM	10%
STEEL	8%
SYNTHETIC AMMONIA	4%

PERCENTAGES OF VITAL INDUSTRY DEPENDING ON 13 GRIDS–1957

ALUMINA	100
ALUMINUM	100
MAGNESIUM	100
AUTOMOBILES & TRUCKS	98
HEAVY ELECTRICAL EQUIP.	97
EXPLOSIVES	93
A/C ASSEMBLY	92
A/C ENGINES	88
ELECTRONICS, RADAR	84
COKE	84
LIGHT ELECTRICAL EQUIP.	80
PETROLEUM REFINING	64
IRON AND STEEL	55

USE PATTERN–U.S.S.R.

INDUSTRY	67%
TRANSPORT	5%
MUNICIPAL ECONOMY	9%
RURAL ECONOMY	5%
TRANSMISSION LOSSES	7%
USE BY POWER STATIONS	7%
TOTAL	100%

If it becomes necessary to attack satellite industry, it is considered that initially only conventional bombs should be used in order to spare friendly masses of population and to minimize our tasks of occupation and postwar recovery. On this basis a summary of requirements would be as shown below.

Satellite Industry:

Degree of Collapse of Industry	Several Years	1–1½ Years	1 Year
Target Systems to Be Attacked	Petroleum, Electric Power, and Steel	Electric Power and Steel	Petroleum and Electric Power
Tons of Conventional Bombs on Target (in 6 mos.)	22,008	17,308	9,508
Percentages of Industry Destroyed			
Electric Power	80	71	71
Petroleum	98	85	98
Steel	77	77	60
Hv. and Med. Bomb Gps. Reqd.	8	6	3

If circumstances at the time dictate the substitution of atomic bombs for conventional bombs for certain appropriate targets in the satellite countries, the requirements would be changed as follows:

Atomic Bombs	73	65	64
Tons of Conventional Bombs	9,305	6,589	7,295
Hv. and Med. Bomb Gps. Reqd.	3	2	2

The above requirements are developed from air-force studies using operational factors estimated for 1957 planning. . . . The timing indicated in the above tables would require that most of the conventional campaign be delayed until the atomic campaign was completed. If attrition were higher than expected and if accuracy of bombing were less than expected, the above timetables would have to be changed. While the atomic effort should be completed as quickly as possible, it is considered that no great decrease in overall effect would result if the campaign were not to be completed until ninety days after it had begun.

A comparison of the three programs above reveals that the first program, when considered in the light of our overall requirements, would result in the most gains for the amount of effort expended. A total of seven heavy and medium groups is therefore selected as the optimum force for this task.

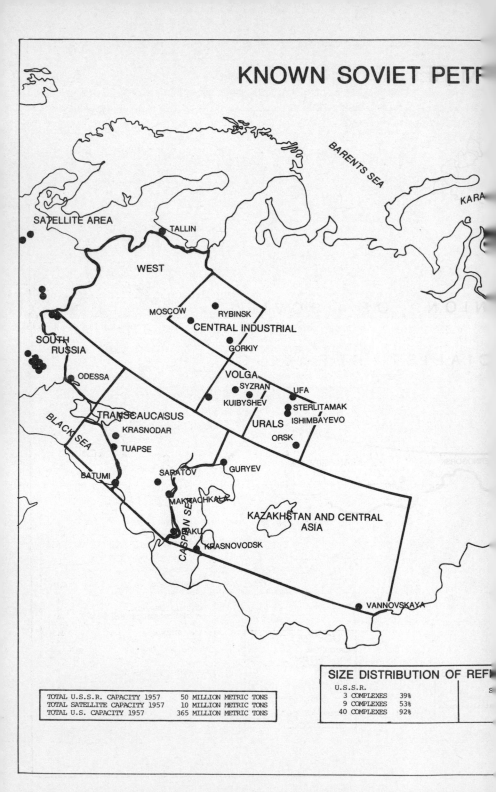

KNOWN SOVIET PETF

BARENTS SEA

KARA

SATELLITE AREA

TALLIN

WEST

MOSCOW   RYBINSK

CENTRAL INDUSTRIAL

SOUTH RUSSIA

GORKIY

VOLGA

SYZRAN   UFA

ODESSA

KUIBYSHEV

STERLITAMAK

ISHIMBAYEVO

TRANSCAUCASUS

URALS

KRASNODAR

ORSK

BLACK SEA

TUAPSE

BATUMI   SARATOV   GURYEV

MAKHACHKALA

KAZAKHSTAN AND CENTRAL ASIA

CASPIAN SEA

BAKU

KRASNOVODSK

VANNOVSKAYA

TOTAL U.S.S.R. CAPACITY 1957	50 MILLION METRIC TONS
TOTAL SATELLITE CAPACITY 1957	10 MILLION METRIC TONS
TOTAL U.S. CAPACITY 1957	365 MILLION METRIC TONS

SIZE DISTRIBUTION OF REFI

U.S.S.R.		
3 COMPLEXES	39%	
9 COMPLEXES	53%	
40 COMPLEXES	92%	

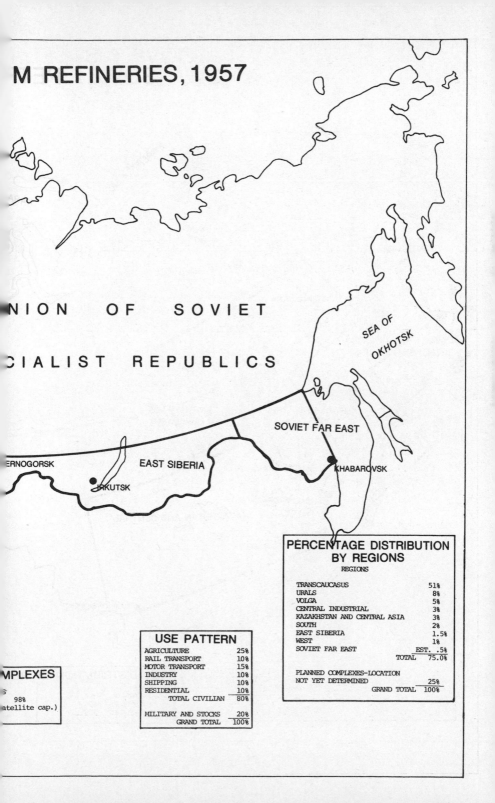

M REFINERIES, 1957

NION OF SOVIET

CIALIST REPUBLICS

SEA OF OKHOTSK

SOVIET FAR EAST

ERNOGORSK

EAST SIBERIA

IRKUTSK

KHABAROVSK

PERCENTAGE DISTRIBUTION BY REGIONS
REGIONS

TRANSCAUCASUS	51%
URALS	8%
VOLGA	5%
CENTRAL INDUSTRIAL	3%
KAZAKHSTAN AND CENTRAL ASIA	3%
SOUTH	2%
EAST SIBERIA	1.5%
WEST	1%
SOVIET FAR EAST	EST. .5%
TOTAL	75.0%
PLANNED COMPLEXES-LOCATION	
NOT YET DETERMINED	25%
GRAND TOTAL	100%

USE PATTERN

AGRICULTURE	25%
RAIL TRANSPORT	10%
MOTOR TRANSPORT	15%
INDUSTRY	10%
SHIPPING	10%
RESIDENTIAL	10%
TOTAL CIVILIAN	80%
MILITARY AND STOCKS	20%
GRAND TOTAL	100%

MPLEXES

98%
atellite cap.)

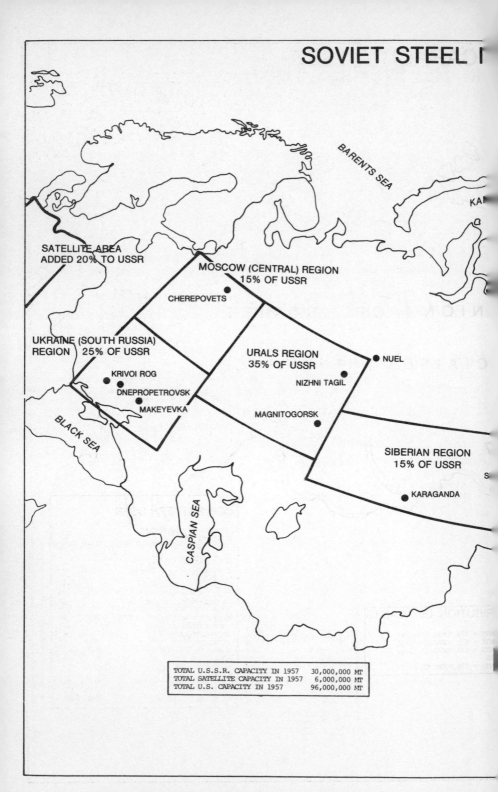

SOVIET STEEL I

BARENTS SEA

KAI

SATELLITE AREA
ADDED 20% TO USSR

MOSCOW (CENTRAL) REGION
15% OF USSR

CHEREPOVETS

UKRAINE (SOUTH RUSSIA)
REGION 25% OF USSR

URALS REGION
35% OF USSR

NUEL

KRIVOI ROG

NIZHNI TAGIL

DNEPROPETROVSK

MAKEYEVKA

MAGNITOGORSK

BLACK SEA

SIBERIAN REGION
15% OF USSR

S

KARAGANDA

CASPIAN SEA

TOTAL U.S.S.R. CAPACITY IN 1957	30,000,000 MT
TOTAL SATELLITE CAPACITY IN 1957	6,000,000 MT
TOTAL U.S. CAPACITY IN 1957	96,000,000 MT

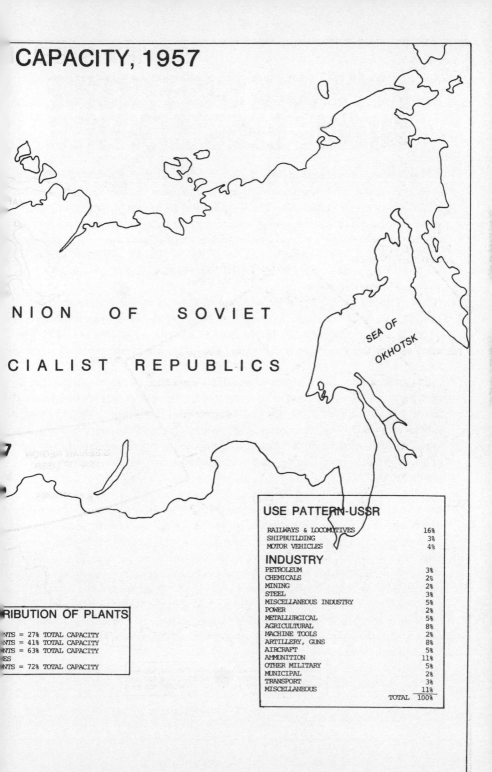

CAPACITY, 1957

NION OF SOVIET

CIALIST REPUBLICS

SEA OF OKHOTSK

USE PATTERN-USSR

RAILWAYS & LOCOMOTIVES	16%
SHIPBUILDING	3%
MOTOR VEHICLES	4%

INDUSTRY

PETROLEUM	3%
CHEMICALS	2%
MINING	2%
STEEL	3%
MISCELLANEOUS INDUSTRY	5%
POWER	2%
METALLURGICAL	5%
AGRICULTURAL	8%
MACHINE TOOLS	2%
ARTILLERY, GUNS	8%
AIRCRAFT	5%
AMMUNITION	11%
OTHER MILITARY	5%
MUNICIPAL	2%
TRANSPORT	3%
MISCELLANEOUS	11%
TOTAL	100%

RIBUTION OF PLANTS

NTS = 27% TOTAL CAPACITY
NTS = 41% TOTAL CAPACITY
NTS = 63% TOTAL CAPACITY
ES
NTS = 72% TOTAL CAPACITY

APPENDIX E: OFFENSIVE MINING REQUIREMENTS

1. The estimated strength of the Soviet submarine fleet in 1957 of 300–350 oceangoing and 200–300 coastal types would constitute a serious threat to Allied sea lines of communication. In addition to the employment of hunter–killer groups and defensive antisubmarine measures, offensive measures would be necessary to destroy submarines at source or to contain them. An important part of attack at source would be an intensive mining campaign. A secondary but highly important objective of such a campaign would be to disrupt enemy shipping in coastal waters.

2. Offensive mining could be accomplished by land-based and carrier-based aircraft and by submarines. In very limited areas the employment of surface forces would be possible, but the amount of air cover required would be prohibitive. Surface mine forces, therefore, should be used primarily for defensive mining.

3. Aerial mining is by far the most effective method of carrying out a mining campaign, but considerations of accessibility to the targets, terrain features, and probable limitations of availability of forces would make it necessary to employ submarines initially in some areas. Submarines would of necessity be limited to initial efforts because of the danger in subsequent operations of running into mines previously laid. Carrier- and land-based aircraft would augment the submarine effort.

4. The degree of effectiveness of the mining campaign based on requirements set forth herein cannot be predicted with accuracy because it would be dependent in part on the reactions of the Soviets, the effectiveness of their minesweeping techniques, and the degree of risk they would be willing to accept. Past experience, however, indicates that complete closure of any port or strait for an appreciable period of time is not possible. Replenishment of mine fields would therefore be a continuing charge on Allied resources.

5. Soviet submarines would initially be based in the Barents–White Sea area, the Baltic, the Black Sea, and the Far East. Analysis of Soviet naval bases indicates that the following primary targets should be mined immediately upon the outbreak of war.

European Area	Pacific Area
Kattegat	Vladivostok
Kiel Canal	Sovetskaya Gavan
Kola Inlet	Petropavlovsk
White Sea	Nikolaevsk
Bosporus	Paramushiro

European Area	Pacific Area
Pyechora Bay	Port Arthur–Dairen
Kara Strait	Hitokoppu Wan
Yugorski Strait	Otomari

6. Current intelligence indicates that bases listed below are either in limited use or under development by the Soviets and accordingly should be kept under surveillance and are classed as secondary targets. Plans should include provisions for mining of these targets as necessary. . . .

European Area	Pacific Area
Molotovsk	Aleksandrovsk
Petsamo	Anodyr Bay
Spalato	De-Kastri Bay
Other ports in Yugoslavia	Kommandorskie Islands
and Albania	Nagayevo
	Novgorod Bay
	Okhotsk
	Plastun Bay
	Uelen
	Grossevich Bay
	Karaginsky Island
	Kavacha
	Korff Bay
	Novik Bay
	Olga Bay
	Trinity Bay
	Tetyukhe
	Strait of Tartary

7. Of the primary targets listed the Kattegat and Kiel Canal should be the responsibility of the British assisted by the Norwegians and Danes. The initial mining of the Bosporus should be accomplished by the Turks, although pre-D-Day provision by the Allies of mines for this purpose may be necessary.

8. In addition to the primary and secondary targets listed above, it would be advantageous in some respects to mine the following straits: La Perouse, Tsugaru, Tsushima, and Korea. However, consideration of the large number of mines required, the depth of water, and strength of currents in some areas, together with the fact that use of these straits by our own naval forces may be desirable, indicates that the attempt should not be made.

9. In the tables below aircraft requirements are computed for naval land-based and carrier-based types which are considered to have a mine-carrying capacity of either five 2,000-lb. mines, ten 1,000-lb. mines, or twenty 500-lb. mines. Submarines could carry twenty-four ground or forty moored mines.

U.S. Air Force and British medium bombers could carry six to eight 2,000-lb. mines or twelve to fifteen 1,000-lb. mines. Of the mines indicated to be laid by aircraft, a portion would be laid by naval land-based and carrier-based types and the remainder by air-force sorties. Total minimum estimated mine requirements for six months' operations are 26,536. It is considered that an additional 50 percent should be made available to provide for secondary targets, for replenishment, or for further unforeseen developments. This would require a grand total of approximately 40,000 mines.

EUROPEAN AREA	Type of Mine	Initial Attack (1st Week)			Weekly (Policing Attack)		Tot Min
		No. of Mines	A/C Sorties	SS Sorties	No. of Mines	A/C Sorties	D ꞏ D +
Kola Inlet	2,000-gr.	150	30	—	25	5	
	1,000-gr.	150	15	—	25	3	
Total		300	45		50	8	1,5
White Sea	2,000-gr.	300	46	3	30	6	1,0
Bosporus	2,000-gr.	200*			50	10	1,4
Pyechora Bay	2,000-gr.	100	20	—	10	2	
	1,000-gr.	100	10	—	10	1	
Total		200	30		20	3	7ꞏ
Kara Strait	1,800-m.	240		6	—	—	2ꞏ
Yugorski Strait	2,000-gr.	96		4	10	2	3ꞏ
The Sound†	1,000-gr.	200			75	8	2,0
Little Belt†	2,000-gr.	150			25	5	7ꞏ
Great Belt†	2,000-gr.	400			100	20	2,9ꞏ
Kiel Canal†	1,000-gr.	200			50	5	1,4ꞏ
TOTAL MINES		2,286			410		12,5ꞏ
U.S.		1,136			160		5,1ꞏ
British		950			250		7,2ꞏ
Turkish		200					2ꞏ
TOTAL A/C SORTIES			121			67	
U.S.			121			29	
British						38	
TOTAL SS SORTIES				13			
U.S.				13			

PACIFIC AREA	Type of Mine	Initial Attack (1st Week)			Weekly (Policing Attack)		Total Mines
		No. of Mines	A/C Sorties	SS Sorties	No. of Mines	A/C Sorties	D to D+6
Vladivostok							
Including	2,000-gr.	928	186		100	20	
Russki Island		72		3			
Russki Bay	1,000-gr.	420	42		50	5	
Nokhoda Bay		80		2			
Ussuri Bay and approaches thereto							
Total		1,500	228	5	150	25	5,250
Sovetskaya Gavan							
	2,000-gr.	76	15				
		24		1	10	2	
	1,000-gr.	400	40		40	4	
Total		500	55	1	50	6	1,750
Petropavlovsk	1,000-gr.	380	38		50	5	
		120		3			
Total		500	38	3	50	5	1,750
Nikolaevsk	1,000-gr.	50	5		5	1	
	500-gr.	150	8		15	1	
Total		200	13		20	2	700
Paramushiro	2,000-gr.	300	60		30	6	1,050
Port Arthur–Dairen	2,000-gr.	100	20		10	2	
	1,000-gr.	400	40		40	4	
Total		500	60		50	6	1,750
Hitokoppu Wan	1,000-gr.	300	30		30	3	1,050
Otomari	1,000-gr.	200	20		20	2	700
TOTAL MINES		4,000			400		14,000
TOTAL A/C SORTIES			504			55	
TOTAL SS SORTIES				9			

Note: See Glossary for explanation of abbreviations.

*Initial mining would be a Turkish responsibility.

†British responsibility assisted by the Norwegians and Danes.

APPENDIX F:
THE SOVIET UNION[*]
MANPOWER AND POTENTIAL

Since 1955 the Soviets have announced reductions in their armed forces totaling over 2 million men. But it is unlikely that reductions of this magnitude have in fact been carried out. It is estimated that today the Soviet armed forces comprise a total of no less than 3.9 million men, which means that the reductions effected total approximately 1.1 million, if the estimate of a total of 5 million at the time of Stalin's death is correct.

This figure includes about 2,350,000 men in the army, 500,000 in the navy, 700,000 in the air force, and 350,000 security, border, and labor troops.

Soviet armed forces during the last few years have undertaken a comprehensive program of adaptation to atomic warfare. As far as new weapons are concerned, it must be assumed that the Soviets possess operational quantities of fission and fusion bombs with yields varying from one or several kilotons up to the megaton ranges. In the field of missiles they have now a variety of types in operational quantities: ground-to-ground in the short and medium ranges; ground-to-air; air-to-ground; and air-to-air. They are also capable of waging biological and chemical warfare on a large scale.

THE ARMY

If the Russians have considerably reduced the number of men in uniform, the reductions have been mainly in respect of rear units, headquarters, and auxiliary establishments. It is estimated that there are 2,350,000 men in the Soviet army, together with a further 350,000 men in internal security and labor battalions. The total number of divisions remains the same, that is to say approximately 175. Far from being reduced, it is thought that the effectives of each division have been increased: the infantry division from 11,500 to 13,000 men, the armored division from 12,000 to 13,670, while the mechanized division remains at approximately 16,500 men.

Seventy-five percent of these divisions, of which 75 are armored or mechanized and 9 airborne, are stationed in the Soviet Union along its western border and in Eastern Europe. In East Germany there are 8 tank divisions, each with 410 tanks, and 12 mechanized divisions, each with 260 tanks. Not all these

---

[*] Extracted from the *Institute for Strategic Studies Annual Report*, 1957 and 1958.

divisions are completely up to strength, but it is officially estimated that they comprise a total of 6,000 tanks. In Hungary and Poland there are 7 divisions.

The 175 divisions are augmented by approximately 60 satellite divisions—predominantly of the rifle type—in varying degrees of combat readiness. Finally, it is estimated that the Soviet Union could provide another 125 divisions within thirty days from the date of mobilization and that she has an overall mobilization potential of 7 million men.

Over the last few years the Soviet army has undergone a major reorganization in order to deal with the new aspect of war under atomic conditions. Its old equipment has been almost entirely replaced and its mobility, fire power, and flexibility increased.

The total tank strength of the Soviet army is estimated at 20,000 front-line tanks and 15,000 second-line tanks. The new tanks which are being introduced to the Soviet armored divisions are the T-54 medium tank fitted with a 155mm gun and the 53-ton heavy tank, which mounts a 130mm gun.

The artillery divisions are equipped with an atomic 203mm cannon with a range of twelve miles and a heavy 240mm mortar with a range of twenty miles.

Other elements of the army characterizing its modernity are airborne forces totaling approximately 100,000 men and supported by a lift capability that would permit about 10 percent of the force to be air-dropped or air-landed in any single operation.

THE NAVY

The Red navy has increased from a total tonnage in 1940 of 600,000 to 1.6 million tons today, which makes it the most powerful fleet in the world after the United States (4 million tons). The Royal Navy with 750,000 tons ranks third.

I. The surface ships of the Soviet navy consist of:

1. Cruisers	37
2. Destroyers and frigates	230
3. Minor craft	2,000

These are distributed more or less equally in the following theaters: the Baltic, the Black Sea, the Arctic, and the Far East.

The cruisers are of three different types:

(a) Twenty-four Sverdlov class, launched between 1951 and 1957, displacement 15,000 tons, speed 34 knots, armament twelve 152mm guns and twenty-eight antiaircraft guns.

(b) Five Tchalov class, launched between 1948 and 1951 of 11,000 tons displacement, with the same speed and armament as the Sverdlov.
(c) Six Kirov class, launched between 1936 and 1945, displacement 8,500 tons, speed 30 knots, armament nine 180mm guns and twenty antiaircraft guns.

The greater part of the destroyers are modern, having been constructed since 1950. Their displacement varies from 1,000 to 2,700 tons and their speed from 28 to 38 knots.

II. The main strength, however, of the Soviet navy lies in the submarine fleet, which according to Russian figures comprises 450 units, of which 95 are based in the Baltic, 75 in the Black Sea, 140 in the Arctic, and 140 in the Far East.

Before 1956 this fleet was essentially a coastal fleet and its ships rarely cruised the high seas. Nowadays, however, Soviet submarines are to be found in all the waters of the world, and long-range cruising has been greatly developed. Soviet submarines have been sighted off the coasts of the United States and Iceland as well as in the Mediterranean. It is considered that the figure of 450 may fall short of reality and that the real total may be somewhere between 500 and 600 submarines.

Of this total it is expected that in the foreseeable future 75 percent will consist of oceangoing craft, of which a proportion will be atomic-powered. The oceangoing submarines are at present of two types: the W class and the Z class, both of which include missiles among their armament.

(a) The W class is 245 feet long with a 1,050-ton displacement. It has a speed of 16 knots on the surface and 13 knots submerged and a radius of action of 13,000 miles. There are at least 150 of these in service.
(b) The Z class submarine is 310 feet long with a displacement of 1,850 tons. It is capable of 20 knots on the surface and 15 knots submerged with a radius of action of 22,000 miles. There are at least 75 of these in service and they are being constructed at the rate of 20 per year.
(c) The K- and Q-type submarines, which were built between 1945 and 1950, are also long-range vessels; their radius of action is about 7,000 miles and their displacement varies from 1,400 to 680 tons.
(d) In addition there are at least 250 short-range submarines.
(e) The atom-powered submarines on which work has begun will be larger than the W- or Z-class types, reaching 3,000 tons or more.

III. There are no aircraft carriers in the Red navy, but there is a land-based fleet air arm which comprises 4,000 fighter, reconnaissance, torpedo-carrying aircraft and bombers.

(a) The torpedo-carrying Ilyuchin 28 and Tupolev 14 have ranges of 1,500–1,800 miles.
(b) The Tupolev 16 bomber has a range of 4,300 miles.

THE AIR FORCE

During the last ten years there has been a revolutionary change in the Soviet conception and organization of air power. Hitherto, aircraft had been used primarily as a kind of long-range artillery in support of ground forces. Today the Russians possess an air force comprising 700,000 personnel and over 20,000 operational aircraft organized into five major components, namely: I. The long-range strategic-bomber force; II. The tactical-bomber force; III. The fighter force; IV. The land-based fleet air arm; and V. The air-transport force.

A vast complex of airfields has been constructed in Soviet territory and numbers now about one thousand. In Eastern Europe the number of airfields capable of handling modern planes has been tripled. Defensively, apart from the vast increase in the numbers of high-performance fighters, an extensive radar early-warning and control system is in operation, and ground-to-air missiles have been installed for air defense in great numbers.

It is estimated that in 1951 only 20 percent of the Soviet fighters were jet-powered, and all bombers and ground-attack aircraft were World War II types. Today all fighters and light bombers are jet-propelled; only the obsolescent TU-4s are piston-driven and form less than one-third of the strategic-bomber force.

I. *The strategic-bomber force* consists mainly of the following aircraft:

(a) 200 Tupolev 95 turboprop "Bears"; range 6,000 miles, bomb load 20 tons, maximum speed 500 miles per hour.
(b) 500 Myasishchev 4-engine jet "Bisons"; range 6,000 miles, bomb load 10 tons, maximum speed 560 miles per hour.
(c) 500 TU-16 twin jet-engine medium bomber "Badgers"; range 4,320 miles, speed 620 miles per hour, bomb load 4–5 tons.

This force is largely based on the Arctic coast, where it is supplied by the air-transport force. The rate of production of these heavy bombers is between 15 and 20 per month. Bisons and Badgers have also been adapted as tankers for in-flight fueling.

II. *The tactical-bomber force* consists of about 5,000 aircraft, the most modern of which are the supersonic twin jet-engine light bombers nicknamed the Ilyuchin "Blow lamp" and the "Backfin."

III. *The fighter and interceptor force* comprises 13,500 planes, all of them jets, the MIG-15, -17, and YAK-25 are subsonic, the MIG-19 and the MIG-21 and the Soukhoy are supersonic.

IV. *The land-based fleet air arm* (See under "The Navy").

V. *The transport fleet* is highly developed and consists of about 2,000 aircraft, a number of which, such as the TU-104, the TU-104A, the TU-114, and the IL-18 are either turbojet or jet-propelled. Other piston-engined types include the twin engine AN-2, AN-4, AN-8, the four-engine AN-10, the twin-engine IL-14, and the TU-70.

Rockets and Guided Missiles

In the field of missiles the Russians have made notable progress, and they have now in operational quantities missiles with nuclear warheads of different types: ground-to-ground in the short and medium ranges, ground-to-air, air-to-ground, and air-to-air. In addition, intercontinental and intermediate-range ballistic missiles have been in service since July 1958.

The principal Soviet missile bases, about one hundred in number, are situated along the Baltic coast mainly in northeast Prussia around Königsberg, in the area between Lake Ladoga and the White Sea, in the Thuringian Forest in East Germany, southern Ukraine, and the Carpathians. The principal Soviet production centers are situated in the region of Vorkuta near the 65° longitude and 68° latitude and around Tiksi near 125° longitude and 72° latitude. The personnel operating the Soviet missiles have been organized into what is virtually a fourth arm of the services numbering about 200,000 men under the command of an engineer general, who has under his control all factories in which nuclear bombs are manufactured, all testing sites, all factories in which rockets and guided missiles are produced, and rocket and guided missile units.

The following are details of Soviet equipment:

I *Atomic Artillery*
  (a) Atomic 203mm cannon mounted on a mobile platform with a range of about 15 miles.
  (b) Heavy 240mm mortar with a range of 20 miles.
II *Ground-to-Ground Ballistic Missiles*
  (a) T-1 is a tactical weapon and is the standard equipment of the tactical units of the missile arm. Propelled by one liquid-fuel engine, it has a range of 375 miles and reaches an altitude of 125 miles. Speed 5,000 mph, length about 52 feet. It can be fired from a mobile ramp.
  (b) T-2 is the Russian IRBM. It is propelled by two liquid-fuel engines, has a range of over 1,600 miles, and reaches an altitude of 260 miles. Speed 5,100 mph, length 91 feet.
  (c) T-3 is the Russian ICBM. It is propelled by three liquid-fuel engines, has a range of over 5,000 miles, and reaches an altitude of 375 miles. Speed 16,000 mph, 110 feet.
  (d) T-4 is a two-stage IRBM with a range of 1,000 miles. It has an 1,800-lb. atomic warhead.
  (e) T-4a is a boost glider missile. It carries a 3,100-lb. atomic warhead.
  (f) T-5 is a three-stage ballistic missile with a range of 100 miles.
  (g) T-5B and T-5C are smaller versions of the above carried on self-propelled launchers with ranges from 18 to 25 miles.
  (h) T-7a is a guided missile with a range of 100 miles.
III *Sea-to-Ground Ballistic Missiles*
  (a) Komet: This missile can be fired from surface craft or a submarine

whether submerged or not. It is already in service. It is propelled by one solid-fuel engine, has a range of 95 miles, and reaches a height of 45 miles. Speed 3,000 mph, length 40 feet. The Komet is relatively cheap to produce, and consequently large quantities have been ordered for the Soviet navy.

(b) Golem: This weapon is for submarines only but can only be fired from the surface. Mass production has already begun. It is propelled by a liquid-fuel engine. It has a range of 310 miles and rises to an altitude of 137 miles. Speed about 5,500 mph, length 50 feet.

IV *Ground-to-Ground Guided Missiles*

The principal weapon of this type is the J-1, which has two solid-fuel engines. It has a range of 350 miles, rises to an altitude of 4 miles. Speed 500 mph.

V *Ground-to-Air Guided Missiles*

(a) The T-6 is a radar-directed rocket which is already in service and is considered to be highly effective. It is propelled by two main and four auxiliary solid-fuel engines. Its range is 20–25 miles, and it rises to a height of 12 miles. It has a speed of 1,500 mph. (This is similar to the American Nike.)

(b) The T-7 is a high-altitude guided missile. Inertial guidance.

(c) The T-8 is an antiaircraft infrared missile; it has a range of 18 miles, and speed is over 1,500 mph.

VI *Air-to-Air Missiles* include the M-100, length 4 feet, which has a range of about 4 miles.

APPENDIX G:
THE NATO POWERS[*]

Ten years ago, when the North Atlantic Treaty was signed in Washington, the military position of the Western powers was very weak. Most of the ground forces available were badly equipped and were deployed not for defense but for occupation duties. Less than 1,000 operational aircraft were available in Europe and only about 20 airfields. Now, as the facts below indicate, the defensive position of the NATO powers in Europe, although in certain respects it leaves much to be desired, has changed out of all recognition. The ground forces in the central area have been built up to about two-thirds of the planned goal of 30 divisions and equipped with nuclear ground-to-ground and ground-to-air missiles. The air forces in Europe of the NATO powers can now muster about 5,000 tactical aircraft (strategic bombers remain under national control), which operate from some 220 operational bases. Joint production in NATO countries of modern weapons such as the Hawk and Sidewinder is about to begin, while a project for a NATO tank is under discussion.

ALLIED COMMAND, EUROPE

Allied Command, Europe, stretches from northern Norway to the Mediterranean. The minimum force requirement for the central area is 30 divisions. The Supreme Commander now has at his disposal 21⅓ divisions with the following national composition: United Kingdom, 3; United States, 5; France, 2 (the commitment is 4, but 2 divisions have been withdrawn for use in Algeria. France has promised to return those 2 when possible); Germany, 7 (the commitment is 12; 5 are yet to come); Belgium, 2; Netherlands, 2; Canada, ⅓. On the northern flank, the Danish commitment is slightly over 1 division and the Norwegian is 1 division also.

On the southern flank the forces allocated to NATO comprise 12 divisions from Turkey, 5 divisions from Greece, and 7 from Italy.

ALLIED COMMAND, ATLANTIC

Unlike the Supreme Allied Commander Europe [SACEUR], the Supreme Allied Commander Atlantic [SACLANT] does not have forces permanently as-

---

[*] Extracted from the *Institute for Strategic Studies Annual Report*, 1957 and 1958.

signed to him in peacetime. The eight maritime powers which form the Atlantic command maintain control of their naval forces in peacetime but have earmarked certain of them for SACLANT in the event of war.

Broadly speaking, in wartime SACLANT's dual roles are to strike at enemy naval bases and airfields and to meet the threat to Allied lines of communication in the Atlantic presented by the Soviet fleet of over 500 submarines.

For the first role, the Supreme Commander Atlantic has a considerable proportion of the American aircraft carriers at his disposal. For the purpose of antisubmarine warfare he has about 450 surface ships and 150 submarines.

The 450 surface ships include:

(1) About 16 modern aircraft carriers (5 American, 6 British, 3 French, 1 Canadian, and 1 Dutch), which carry either American S2F or Trackers, British Fairey-Gannets, or French Breguets. In all, NATO antisubmarine carriers could embark between 400 and 500 aircraft and helicopters (the latter are being increasingly used for this purpose) in the Atlantic and the Mediterranean.

(2) About 440 destroyers and escort types (200 American, 75 British, 75 French, 37 Canadian, 12 Dutch, 20 Portuguese, and 22 Danish and Norwegian. In certain circumstances the Dutch and Norwegian vessels come under Channel Command). A considerable proportion of these are of World War II construction, but many have been modernized, and steady progress is being made in building replacements.

With regard to submarines the trend in most NATO navies has been to change their role from commerce destruction to antisubmarine warfare. Of the 150 available for antisubmarine warfare in the Atlantic, the United States include in their allocation 22 built since 1945, of which 6 are atomic powered. The Royal Navy has 42 submarines in active service, France about 20, the Netherlands 10, and Denmark 1.

The surface and submarine fleets are supported by long-range patrol aircraft such as American Neptunes and British Shackletons. The most modern aircraft in this category is the Canadian turboprop Argus, which is the military version of the Britannia.

THE CHANNEL COMMAND

The role of Channel Command is to exercise maritime control of the English Channel and southern North Sea, to deny it to the enemy, to protect the sea lines of communication and to support operations conducted by SACLANT and SACEUR. To this end Channel Command has at its disposal a considerable proportion of the national naval forces of Belgium, France, the Netherlands, and the United Kingdom listed in Section 6.

THE NUCLEAR RETALIATORY
FORCES OF NATO

These remain under national command and comprise the United States Strategic Air Command, RAF Bomber Command, and the United States Sixth Fleet. In addition seven IRBM bases in Europe are in operation, under construction, or projected.

(a) Strategic Air Command is divided into the Fifteenth Air Force based in California, the First Missile Division also based in California, [and] the Second and Eighth Air Forces based in Louisiana and Massachusetts. The overseas units are the Sixteenth Air Force in Spain, the Seventh Air Division in the United Kingdom, and the Third Air Division based on Guam. Each of these overseas units operates several advance bases. SAC has a total of about seventy bases in the U.S. and overseas.

Strategic Air Command now has about 1,250 medium B-47 jet-engined bombers with a range of 6,000 miles and a speed of 600 mph, and over 450 heavy B-52 eight-jet-engined bombers with a speed of over 650 mph and a range of 6,000 miles. Both types of aircraft use in-flight refueling to extend their range. This is provided by a fleet of 120 KC-135 stratotankers capable of a speed of 550 mph. New aircraft being developed are the supersonic B-58 to replace the B-47 and the B-70 Valkyrie, which will travel at three times the speed of sound at altitudes above 70,000 feet and which will replace the B-52.

The First Missile Division is responsible for operating the ICBMs' Atlas (range 5,500 miles) and Titan (range 5,500 miles), which are based in the United States, and the IRBMs' Thor and Jupiter with ranges of 1,500 miles, which are based in Europe. In addition to these weapons there is the Snark, or intercontinental cruise missile, which has a range of 5,000 miles.

(b) RAF Bomber Command is equipped with Vulcan and Victor bombers capable of carrying a nuclear or conventional weapon. The performance of these aircraft compares favorably, as regards speed and altitude, with that of bomber aircraft in the Soviet and United States air forces. They are capable of refueling in flight from Valiant tanker planes. Progress is being made in the development of the propelled standoff bomb, which reduces the vulnerability of aircraft by enabling them to release these weapons a long distance from the target, outside the range of the missile defense system. Meanwhile the development of the Blue Streak ballistic missile (range 2,000 miles) is proceeding and Thor missiles are being deployed for training and operational purposes in England.

(c) The United States Sixth Fleet consists of approximately fifty ships including two or three heavy aircraft carriers, such as the Forrestal; escorting destroyers; and submarines. The carriers' armament includes the supersonic Skyray, Skylancer, Demon Crusader fighters, the Skyhawk transonic light-strike aircraft, and Skywarrior transonic medium bomber.

(d) Seven IRBM bases in Europe are sited in the following countries:

4 Thor bases in the United Kingdom
2 Jupiter bases (under construction) in Italy
1 Jupiter base (projected) in Turkey

Each base has fifteen missiles.

The State of National Forces

Belgium
General	Length of military service: one year
	Total armed forces: 120,000
	Defense budget: 20 milliard B. francs
Army	2⅓ divisions, of which 2 (1 infantry and 1 armored) are at the disposal of NATO
Navy	50 minesweepers
Air Force	Approximately 200 F-84 and F-86 fighters and reconnaissance aircraft

Canada
General	No military service
	Total strength armed forces: 120,000
	Defense budget: $1,818 million
Army	Total strength: 48,000
	Three brigade groups based in Canada
	One brigade group stationed in Europe
Navy	Total strength: 20,250
	1 aircraft carrier
	2 cruisers
	50 destroyers and frigates
	3 submarines
Air Force	Total strength: 52,000
	9 fighter squadrons equipped with the CF-100 integrated in North American Air Defense Command
	8 day-fighter squadrons and
	4 all-weather fighter squadrons in Europe
	4 transport squadrons

Denmark
General	Length of military service: 16 months
	Total armed forces: 45,000
	Defense budget: 985 million Krone
Army	1 infantry division
Navy	18 destroyers and frigates
	4 submarines (2 under construction)
	36 minesweepers

	20 patrol boats
Air Force	Approximately 100 F-84 and F-86 fighters and reconnaissance aircraft

France

General	Length of military service: 28 months
	Total armed forces: 1 million
	Defense budget: 1,622 milliard francs
Army	The greater part of the French army is engaged in Algeria; 2 divisions are at the disposal of NATO
Navy	4 aircraft carriers (plus 2 aircraft carriers and 1 helicopter carrier under construction)
	2 battleships
	6 cruisers
	92 destroyers and frigates
	18 submarines (plus 14 under construction)
	160 other craft
Air Force	There are some Mystere 4 and F-86 squadrons in Germany, as well as a larger number (which is classified) of fighter and attack squadrons in metropolitan France.

Germany

General	Length of military service: one year
	Total armed forces: 206,000 (to be increased to 350,000 in 1963)
	Defense budget: 7,882 million DM
Army	7 complete divisions at the disposal of NATO include:
	3 motorized infantry divisions
	2 armored divisions
	1 airborne division
	1 mountain division
	(A total of 12 divisions to be reached in 1961 will include a further 5 infantry divisions in the process of formation)
Navy	1 destroyer (12 + 6 frigates)
	2 submarines (12)
	12 patrol boats (40)
	40 minesweepers (54)
Air Force	1 transport squadron (5)
	5 fighter-bomber squadrons (8)
	1 fighter squadron (10)
	1 reconnaissance squadron (5)
	(The German air force at present has about 350 F-84 and F-86 fighters. The goal for 1963 is 1,000 planes)
	Note: figures in parentheses indicate construction in progress or planned

Greece

General	Length of military service: 24–30 months according to the arm of the service
	Total armed forces: 127,000
	Defense budget: 4,668 million drachmas
Army	1 armored division
	11 infantry divisions
Navy	1 cruiser
	18 destroyers and frigates
	4 submarines
	40 other craft
Air Force	20,000 men; there are 12 squadrons equipped with 400 F-84 and F-86 aircraft

Italy

General	Length of military service: 18 months for the army and air force; 24 months for the navy
	Total armed forces: 400,000
	Defense budget: 626 milliard lire
Army	10 infantry divisions
	3 armored divisions
	5 mountain brigades
Navy	3 cruisers (4)
	47 destroyers and frigates (7)
	6 submarines (2 under construction)
Air Force	20 squadrons, including 6 fighter squadrons equipped with F-84 and F-86 aircraft
	Note: figures in parentheses indicate construction in progress or planned

Luxembourg

General	Length of military service: 12 months
	Defense budget: 408 million L francs
Army	1 brigade

Netherlands

General	Length of military service: 18 months for the army; 22 months for the navy and air force
	Total armed forces: 130,000
	Defense budget: 1,745 million guilders
Army	2 infantry divisions at the disposal of NATO
Navy	1 aircraft carrier
	2 light cruisers
	34 destroyers and frigates
	10 submarines
	68 other craft
Air Force	Approximately 12 squadrons equipped with F-84, F-86, and Super Sabre F-100 aircraft

Norway
General
Length of military service: 16 months for the army; 18 months for the navy and air force
Total armed forces: 40,000
Defense budget: 1,036 million Krone

Army
1 division

Navy
19 destroyers and frigates
5 submarines
20 other craft

Air Force
Approximately 150 F-84F and F-86F fighters and reconnaissance aircraft

Portugal
General
Length of military service:18–24 months for the army; 36 months for the air force; 48 months for the navy
Total armed forces: 79,000
Defense budget: 2,566 million escudos

Army
54,000 (1 division at the disposal of NATO)

Navy
16 destroyers and frigates
3 submarines
33 other craft

Air Force
2,500 men; 350 aircraft including a number of F-84G fighter bombers (under national command)

Turkey
General
Length of military service: 24 months for the army and air force; 36 months for the navy
Total armed forces: 500,000
Defense budget: 1,435 million Turkish pounds

Army
22 divisions

Navy
1 cruiser
12 destroyers
7 submarines
30 other craft

Air Force
Approximately 400 jet fighters

United Kingdom
General
Length of military service: 24 months (to be abolished by end of 1962)
Total armed forces: 614,200
Defense budget: £1,608 million

Army
Total strength: 323,900 men (165,000)
New weapons such as the Corporal ground-to-ground guided missile, and the antiaircraft missile Thunderbird are coming into service
3 divisions in Germany

Navy
Total strength: 105,400 (88,000)
8 aircraft carriers

16 cruisers

175 destroyers and frigates

42 submarines (1 atomic-powered submarine under construction)

228 other craft

Guided-missile cruisers under construction will be equipped with the Sea Slug missile, and other ships will carry the Sea Cat missile for close air defense. Aircraft carriers are receiving the new Scimitar fighter bomber and Sea Vixen, which will be equipped with the Fire Streak air-to-air missile

Air Force   Total active strength: 184,900 (135,000)

The supersonic TSR2 will replace the Canberra for tactical purposes. It will be equipped with nuclear bombs and air-to-air guided missiles

For bomber command see Section 4; fighter command is being reequipped with supersonic P-1 Lightning fighters carrying the Fire Streak missile and with the Bloodhound ground-to-air missile

Note: figures in parentheses indicate total strength in 1962 when national service ends

United States

General   Military service: although there is a form of military service for 2 years, the majority of men serving in the U.S. forces are volunteers

Total armed forces: 2,435,000

Defense budget: $44,994 million

Army   Total strength: 850,000

The 14 divisions of the army include a Strategic Army Corps, consisting of 2 airborne and 2 infantry divisions and 5 divisions in Europe

MISSILES

(i) Jupiter—an IRBM liquid-fueled rocket with a range of 1,500 miles and speed between 10,000 and 15,000 mph

(ii) Tactical surface-to-surface short-range missiles include:

Redstone—range 200–500 miles, speed 8,000 mph

Corporal—range 70–100 miles

Sergeant—to replace above, range 70–200 miles, has a self-contained guidance system

Honest John—unguided field-artillery missile; range 16 miles, speed 750 mph

La Crosse—a solid propellent rocket for use against field fortifications; range 20 miles, speed 1,500 mph

Little John—unguided field-artillery lightweight missile, range 10 miles, speed supersonic

Dart—antitank rocket, range 1–3 miles

Pershing—a solid-fuel development of Redstone, range 700 miles +, speed 8,000 mph

(iii) Surface-to-air:

Nike–Ajax—liquid-powered antiaircraft rocket, range 25 miles, speed 1,500–1,800 mph

Nike–Hercules—improved Nike–Ajax with nuclear warhead, range 60–85 miles, speed 2,700 mph

Nike–Zeus—antimissile missile, range 200 miles, speed 5,000 mph

Hawk—antiaircraft rocket for use against low-flying planes, range 25 miles, speed supersonic

Navy Total strength: 600,000

103 aircraft carriers

68 cruisers

421 destroyers

390 escorts, etc.

125 submarines (including 6 operative nuclear-powered submarines and 27 projected or under construction)

MISSILES:

(i) Surface-to-surface missiles:

Polaris—IRBM solid-propellent rocket for shipboard launching, range 1,500 miles, speed 6,000 mph

Regulus I—jet-powered winged missile for ship-based launching, range 500 miles, speed 700 mph

Regulus II—improved version of Regulus I, range 1,000 + miles, speed 1,000–1,200 mph

(ii) Surface-to-air missiles:

Terrier I & II—ship-based solid-propellent AA rocket, range 10–20 miles, speed 1,800 mph

Tartar—lighter and smaller improved version of Terrier, range 20–30 miles, speed 1,800 mph

Talos—long-range ship-based AA ram-jet missile, range 65 miles, speed 1,800 mph

(iii) Air-to-air missiles:

Sidewinder—solid rocket with infrared guidance, range 6 miles, speed 1,800 mph

Sparrow III—range 5–8 miles, speed 2,250 mph

Air Force Total strength: 825,000 divided into 105 wings (each wing has 45 aircraft in the case of bombers and 75 in the case of fighter-bombers and fighters); see also Section 4

The equipment of fighter and tactical bomber squadrons includes the F-100 Super Sabre, RF-101 Voodoo, F-102A, F-104 Starfighter, and the most recent F-105; all of these aircraft are supersonic

MISSILES:

(i) Surface-to-surface missiles:

Atlas—ICBM liquid-fueled rocket, range 5,500 miles, speed 15,000–20,000 mph

Titan—ICBM liquid-fueled rocket, range and speed same as Atlas

Thor—IRBM liquid-fueled rocket, range 1,500 miles, speed 10,000 mph

Snark—winged missile powered by turbojet, range 5,500 miles, speed 700 mph

Matador—jet-powered winged missile, range 300–500 miles, speed 650 mph

Matador–Mace—improved version of above, range 700–1,000 miles, speed transonic

(ii) Surface-to-air missiles:

Bomarc—long-range ram-jet missile interceptor, range 400 miles, speed 1,600–2,000 mph

(iii) Air-to-air missiles:

Genie MB-I—missile with a nuclear warhead carried by fighter-interceptors, range 2–4 miles, speed supersonic

Marine Corps   Total strength: 160,000

Note: With regard to the figures for naval vessels, these represent the totals that would be available in the event of war. Not all these ships are in commission at present, a considerable number being laid up in reserve.

APPENDIX H: MEMORANDUM FOR THE SECRETARY OF DEFENSE FROM THE PLANNING COMMITTEE FOR PLAN DROPSHOT (EDITED)

2. . . . . The development of the plan has been premised on the following:

a. That we should achieve optimum use of ALL the resources of ALL the probable allies to advance the common security interest both in preparation for and during war; and

b. That United States' expenditures in its security interest for the Department of Defense, European Recovery Program, and military-aid program must not be so great as to endanger the national security by jeopardizing a stable economy in the United States.

3. While this plan is essentially a war plan directed at the only foreseen potential enemy on a certain date, the Joint Chiefs of Staff consider that because of its long-range nature and subject to the tests indicated in paragraph 1 above and subsequent periodic review, it will serve as a basic blueprint of long-range guidance for the national security from the military point of view. The successful implementation of the strategic concept contained therein, in the degree required, presupposes an ad interim consistent and positive national policy on the part of the United States vis-à-vis the USSR along the lines indicated in NSC 20/4. Specifically there are certain corollary elements of national policy, the successful implementation of which would enhance the national security from the military point of view; would create conditions favorable to the execution of the plan; and, of great importance, would reduce the cost to the United States of the degree of security which must be maintained ad interim.

4. These elements of national policy are in general beyond the sole purview of the Department of Defense. The Joint Chiefs of Staff are of the opinion, however, that they are in furtherance of the national policy as set forth in NSC 20/4 and that they should be accomplished in correlation with the implementa-

:ion of that policy. While it is realized that certain of these elements are in the
process of implementation and that imminent action on others is contemplated,
for the sake of emphasis and completeness they are set forth as follows. It is
recommended that they be submitted for the consideration of the National Security Council with a view toward their accomplishment in correlation with the
implementation of NSC 20/4. They are:

a. The provision of appropriate economic and military aid to the nations of
   Western Union, other signatories of the North Atlantic Treaty, and to Turkey, Greece, and non-Communist China.
b. Resumption of diplomatic relations and the institution of economic cooperation with Spain. Advocacy of participation of Spain in a Western Europe security system.
c. Arrangements with Saudi Arabia and Bahrein which would permit the introduction of U.S. forces into the Bahrein–Dhahran area prior to D-Day to
   protect the Arabian oil-bearing areas.
d. Arrangements which would assure the D-Day security of the oil production
   of Aruba, Curačao, and Venezuela.
e. Arrangements which would permit the D-Day security and use by U.S. military forces of Iceland, Greenland, and the Azores.
f. An increase in the military effectiveness of Italy beyond the present peace-
   treaty limits.
g. Fostering of political and economic cooperation between Yugoslavia and the
   non-Communist nations of Western Europe, particularly Italy, with a view
   toward encouraging a complete break militarily from the Soviet orbit and,
   as a minimum, obtaining her neutrality in case of war.
h. Arrangements with Sweden, Greece, and Turkey to assure maximum collaboration with overall Allied strategy.
i. Adoption of such courses of action with respect to China as will reduce or
   eliminate the influence of Moscow over whatever government or governments evolve from the present civil war.
j. Modification of the present policy toward West Germany and Japan to permit the creation of indigenous defense forces.
k. Arrangements for the provision of operational air bases in the United Kingdom and the Near and Middle East from which immediate post-D-Day
   operations could be undertaken.
l. Increase in the scale and effectiveness of intelligence efforts to determine
   Soviet capabilities and intentions.
m. Intensification of psychological warfare against the USSR, penetrating the
   Iron Curtain to the maximum:
   (1) To develop internal dissension within the Soviet orbit and disagreements
       between the USSR and Soviet satellites.
   (2) To develop among the Russian people the conviction that the United
       States is, and has been, friendly to the people of the Soviet Union but

not to the Soviet dictatorship that has seized control of the governmen
and is depriving them of the material benefits and religious freedom tha
would be theirs if they were not cut off from most of the civilized worl
by the policies of their rulers.

APPENDIX I: FINAL REPORT ON PLAN DROPSHOT (EDITED)

. . . In treating with this plan, it must be constantly borne in mind that it is a REQUIREMENTS STUDY. It is a REQUIREMENTS STUDY limited only by the approximate fiscal ceiling of 10 percent of U.S. national income required for the implementation of its concept. . . . The committee has weighed and reweighed, considered and reconsidered the many imponderables inherent in such a study. Every attempt has been made to provide a REASONABLE SOLUTION in cases where various views differ widely or where available studies are inadequate to provide a firm basis on which to proceed. Your committee fully recognizes that the Allied operations envisaged herein are not the only ones which could be undertaken in a war on the assumed date; that some of those selected might be of greater scope while others might be of lesser scope or not required at all due to a Soviet decision not to implement certain of those courses of action which we credit as capabilities and for which we provide a counteraction; that the developments of the changing situation, politically, economically, and militarily, would undoubtedly result in many modifications before the assumed date is reached; and that war-gaming of Phase I of the outline plan may also indicate desirable modifications. The committee submits for your careful consideration, however, our strong feeling that the study determines the requirements for a "scale of effort" in a war commencing on the assumed date which would accomplish our national objectives at optimum cost. The details of courses of action and tasks could be cast up in various alternatives, but the committee feels that the total "scale of effort" as envisaged in this plan would not vary materially—assuming no change in basic intelligence or other such basic factors—from that which would accrue from the forces developed by such alternatives. . . .

5. CONTROLLING FACTORS IN PREPARING THE PLAN

a. That we should achieve optimum use of all the resources of all the probable Allies to advance the common security interest both in preparation for and during war; and

b. That U.S. expenditures in its security interest for the Department of Defense, European Recovery Program, and military aid to allies must not be so great as to endanger the national security by jeopardizing a stable economy in the United States. To this end your committee was then, and still is, of the opinion that a maximum of 10 percent* of the national income could be devoted to expenditures on account of the national-security interest without jeopardizing a stable economy. The committee therefore has attempted in this plan to hold preliminary costing of the requirements to an average annual total expenditure of $20–22 billion for the Department of Defense, European Recovery Program, and military aid to allies.

*Editor's Note: The reality is that in 1953 the United States spent 14.8 percent of its GNP on defense. In 1958 the figure was 11.1 percent, 10.4 percent in 1962, and 9.8 percent in 1963. The next highest big spender was Great Britain (11.3 percent, 7.8 percent, and 7.2 percent). France was third (11.3 percent, 8.1 percent, 7.1 percent and 6.4 percent). While Franco–U.S.–U.K. defense expenditures dropped, those of West Germany during the period reviewed tended to rise from 4.9 percent and 3.4 percent to 5.6 percent and 6.1 percent.

6. GUIDED-MISSILES WEAPONS SYSTEMS

With respect to your committee's conclusions as to the use of guided-missiles weapons systems . . . we now consider that exceptional progress has been made in research and development. We believe that the development of certain new weapons may have a significant effect on the strategy of a war in 1957, although we do not attempt to judge the degree at this time. We believe the development of supersonic air-to-air and surface-to-air guided missiles has assumed increased importance in view of the greatly increased Soviet A-bomb capability as presently assessed. Also, in view of the anticipated development of special-type warheads for the larger surface-to-surface and air-to-surface guided missiles, we further consider that research and development of these missiles should be expedited.† . . .

†Editor's Note: The research, development, and manufacture of these weapons was expedited and, if the ISS study for 1961–1962 is correct, altered the strategic picture very significantly—and not only in the area of missiles.

COMPARATIVE ESTIMATES
OF STRATEGIC STRENGTH
(1961–1962)

	WEST	EAST
ICBMs	63	50+
MRBMs	186	200

COMPARATIVE ESTIMATES
OF STRATEGIC STRENGTH
(1961–1962)

	WEST	EAST
LRBs	600	190
MRBs	2,200	1,100
Carriers	58	—
Nuclear subs	22	2
Conventional subs	266	480
Mobilized manpower	8,195,253	7,994,300

8. CONSIDERATIONS AFFECTING THE DEVELOPMENT OF TASKS

a. The relative importance of courses of action . . . highlights the importance of holding the United Kingdom and maximum areas in Western Europe.

b. In developing the forces to hold maximum areas of Western Europe, your committee contemplated maximum use of the manpower of the Western Union nations in containing the initial Soviet onslaught. United States participation on D-Day would consist of military aid to provide a maximum feasible ground and air strength to Western Union; U.S. forces then on occupation duty or deployed in Europe (estimated to be about two divisions and two fighter groups [see ISS study for an estimate of the actuality in 1959]); and the operations of the air offensive. U.S. divisions and air units were redeployed from the defensive tasks in the Western Hemisphere as early as it was considered the requirements therefor could be reduced. No German combat units were contemplated, although it was considered likely that German constabulary units would be in existence and they would be of some assistance in harassing and delaying the initial Soviet advance. In view of the prospective emergence of Western Germany as a sovereign nation, it may be well in future revisions of this plan to consider Western Germany in a more active military role.

c. In treating with the course of action for limiting Soviet advances in China and Southeast Asia, your committee has assumed that initial Soviet domination at the outset of a war in 1957 would not extend beyond the Asiatic mainland nor into the Malayan Peninsula. Should events . . . result in Soviet domination of Formosa, Hainan, Malaya, or parts of the East Indies, forces additional to those developed by this plan would probably be required initially in the western Pacific and Southeast Asia. This is a matter for future treatment in reviewing this study and is mentioned at this point to highlight the contingent military liability which our national policy may well bring upon us.

9.PSYCHOLOGICAL, ECONOMIC, AND UNDERGROUND WARFARE

The committee considers that the progress of planning within the Department of Defense for implementation of the course of action "Initiate or intensify psychological, economic, and underground warfare" leaves much to be desired.
. . . Economic and underground warfare should be given similar treatment within the Department of Defense and studies prepared which would result in immediate definitive action in these important categories by the United States and her allies in event of war. Intensive study and planning for the utilization of these categories of warfare not only during but in preparation for armed conflict will, in the opinion of the committee, materially reduce the cost of war. Further, and of even greater importance, the existence of plans and programs in these categories, when properly correlated with planning for overt military action, may well result in decreased requirements in preparing for war.

10.MILITARY AID TO ALLIES

a. In developing this plan, your committee has assumed from the start that the United States would implement a military-aid program for its probable allies and has therefore assumed a potential capability on the part of several of the principal Allies to furnish forces to meet the requirements of the plan, PROVIDED A SUITABLE MILITARY-AID PROGRAM IS IMPLEMENTED. Your committee considers such an assumption to be mandatory . . . and believes that such an approach to the problem would be the cheaper way to provide, first, the forces deterrent to war, and second, the forces necessary for war.

b. Your committee adheres firmly to the beliefs that:

(1) A U.S. military-aid program is an essential part of any long-range program to attain national security.
(2) A U.S. military-aid program involving an average annual expenditure of $2–2½ billion over the next seven years would adequately support the long-range security program envisaged in this plan, PROVIDED THE AIDED COUNTRIES MADE A MAXIMUM CONCURRENT CONTRIBUTION OF THEIR OWN RESOURCES IN THE COMMON INTEREST.
(3) A detailed long-range military-aid program based upon this plan is required to assure that each U.S. dollar spent on military aid makes a maximum contribution to the accomplishment of the overall strategic concept. . . .

e. The cost of the military-aid program for the period FY 1950 to FY 1957 . . . based on U.S. costs and use of U.S. transportation, was approximately $21 billion . . . [This] figure of $21 billion would now have to be revised upward by nearly $2 billion due to the receipt of additional information which has reduced estimated French capabilities in combat aircraft for 1957 from 1,450 to 500. . . .

11. DETERMINATION OF IMPACT UPON THE ECONOMY AND INDUSTRIAL CAPACITY OF THE UNITED STATES

a. Your committee considers that the long-range military-aid program, . . . although representing an assessment of the MAXIMUM probable cost to the United States in implementing the concept of this plan, furnishes a valuable first approximation of dollar costs to the United States to build up forces of our major allies to support the strategic concept of Dropshot and to satisfy the requirements of other friendly countries in order to augment our collective war potential by reciprocal economic, military, and political assistance. . . .

14. ADEQUACY OF INTELLIGENCE

. . . The committee is now informed that the Joint Intelligence Committee has available a revised estimate of the 1957 Soviet atomic-bomb stockpile. As a result, the Joint Intelligence Committee considers that it must make a complete reexamination and further study of the Soviet strategic intentions and campaigns and that this study will require a prior examination of the vulnerability of atomic bombing of the United Kingdom, the United States, and Canada together with a reexamination of the validity of 1956–1957 as a planning date.

b. The results of this reexamination may well have implications of such gravity as to require major modifications in our long-range planning. It is considered, therefore, that upon completion of its study, the Joint Intelligence Committee should immediately review the intelligence aspects of this plan, and the Joint Strategic Plans Committee should thereupon determine the resultant modifications, if any, that must be made therein.

c. Thereafter it would be most desirable, in the opinion of the committee, to charge the Joint Intelligence Committee with maintaining a continuous review of intelligence applicable to the plan and with collaborating with the Joint Strategic Plans Committee in periodic future revisions. . . .

15.THE POL POSITION

During more than a year of study of this problem the committee has maintained a continuing review of the prospective POL [petrol, oil, lubricants] position for the Allies in 1957. While recognizing that many factors could operate to eliminate a firm requirement for Near and Middle East oil products, the committee remains of the opinion that prudent planning requires the adoption of a future strategy that would provide reasonable assurance of the retention of at least a part of Near and Middle East oil products for Allied use. Further, assuming that the United States will have a continuing political commitment in this area, as presently indicated by our national policy, the military requirement to hold the oil-bearing areas is but a slight increase over that otherwise required and considerably less than that which would be required were our strategy to envisage abandonment with subsequent retaking of these areas during the war's progress.

16.COST IMPLICATIONS

a. Your committee has carefully considered the cost implications of this plan. . . .

b. The tremendous cost of war is illustrated by the following:

(1) World War I cost the United States $25 billion.
(2) World War II cost the United States $340 billion.
(3) The current approximate annual charges against our budget in payment for past wars is:
  (a) For pensions, bonuses, disability benefits, etc., $2.355 billion.
  (b) For interest on the national debt, $5.450 billion.
  (c) For a total continuing commitment of $7.805 billion.

c. If the cost of the next war should increase in a comparable ratio as between World War I and World War II, it could be in the neighborhood of $3 trillion, or roughly twelve times the value of the current annual industrial production of the United States. The annual expenditures of 10 percent of U.S. national income or approximately $20 billion per annum, amounting to 0.6 percent of the possible cost for World War III, would not appear to be too much to pay as insurance for success in a future war. Even if the probable cost of this future war were to be estimated at only three times that of World War II, roughly four times the value of the current annual industrial production of the United States, or approximately $1 trillion dollars, the insurance premium would then amount to but 2 percent of the possible cost of war. . . .

18. PROSPECTIVE UTILIZATION OF DROPSHOT

a. It is the responsibility of the Department of Defense to provide military guidance to the government of the United States:

(1) As to how the cost of a future war, should it become inevitable, may be held to a minimum, and
(2) As to how the military cost of maintaining the peace and being prepared for war may be so minimized as not to jeopardize a stable economy in the United States.

b. The continuing charge on the Department of Defense thus becomes one which:

(1) First, provides the studies leading to those arrangements and forces within the United States and among its allies which will deter the Soviets from seeking armed conflict, and
(2) Second, determines the requirements and makes maximum preparations for possible war at the most probable future dates.

c. Your committee considers that plan Dropshot is aimed at accomplishing the second of these continuing charges. The first continuing charge is accomplished through the process of the annual budgetary considerations and emergency war planning. The many imponderables of political, economic, and military changes within our own country and throughout the world which are termed "the changing situation" make difficult an assessment on a long-range basis of the force requirements to provide this deterrent factor. An annual reconsideration of these forces is therefore indicated. But these annual considerations cannot be intelligently formulated and successfully defended before the government and the people unless they are guided by a long-range objective which indicates the requirements for war.

d. The cost of war has not been cheap in the past and will not be cheap in the future. There must be developed within the government of the United States [and] within the consciousness of the people of the United States and those of our allies as well, a realization, a full awareness of the cost of war. Our government and our people must accept the continuing cost essential to our security which will, as a minimum, provide a deterrent force against war, and should the threat of armed conflict become high, they must be prepared to accept the increased cost necessary to prepare for war. Only by so doing can the United States hope to assure the provision of those forces required to accomplish the deterrent against war.

e. In discharging its responsibility to assess and state to the government and the people not only the force requirements to maintain the peace but also those force requirements and the cost thereof which would be required for war, the Department of Defense should, in the opinion of your committee, utilize Dropshot in the interim. It provides a tentative statement of those requirements, which, if a decision to wage war in 1957 were to be made today, would be capable of being realized without jeopardizing the economy of the United States.

f. The annual budget considerations to provide the forces deterrent to war will, of course, have an effect on the long-range ability to provide the forces for war. Thus there develops the necessity for dynamic treatment of the long-range plan and its periodic revision in the light of the changing situation from year to year.

g. The committee therefore considers that Dropshot should be accepted, subject to periodic review and modification as required, as an initial approach to long-range basic guidance for possible war in the next decade. . . .

h. Ad interim the committee considers that Dropshot should be utilized as objective military guidance for long-range planning for the security of the United States. It should provide the basis for discussions with Allies; it should provide the basis for a long-range military-aid program; it should provide the tentative basic guidance for long-range mobilization planning; and it should provide objective guidance for the annual military-budget considerations. . . .

GLOSSARY

SYMBOLS OF NAVAL VESSELS AND AIRCRAFT

Battleships ....BB
Cruisers:
   Heavy ....CA
   Light CL
   Hunter–killer ship ....CLK
   Antiaircraft cruiser ....CL(AA)

Aircraft carriers:
   Aircraft carrier CV
   Large ....CVB
   Small CVL
   Escort ....CVE
Destroyers ....DD
   Destroyer escorts ....DDE
   Hunter–killer destroyer ....DDK
   Radar picket ....DDR
   Escort vessels ....DE
Submarines ....SS
   Antisubmarine ....SSK
   Radar picket ....SSR

Amphibious vessels:
   Amphibious-force flagship ....AGC
   Cargo attack ....AKA
   Transports, attack ....APA
   High-speed transports ....APD
   Dock................................LSD
   Medium ....LSM
   Medium (rocket) ....LSMR
   Tank ....LST

Mine vessels:
    Minesweepers ....AM
    Auxiliary-motor minesweeper ....AMS

Patrol vessels:
    Submarine chasers (173′) ....PC

Auxiliaries
    Ammunition ships ....AE
    Store ships ....AF
    Cargo ships ....AK
    Oilers ....AO
    Transports ....AP
    Seaplane tenders (large) ....AV
    Seaplane tenders (small) ....AVP
    Aviation supply ships ....AVS

FLEET-AIR-WING-TYPE AIRCRAFT SQUADRON DESIGNATIONS

VP(HL)	4-engine land-plane patrol
VP(ML)	2-engine land-plane patrol
VP(MS)	2-engine seaplane patrol
VH(MS)	2-engine seaplane (hospital version)
VP(AM)	2-engine amphibian patrol
VPP(HL)	4-engine land plane (photo version)
VPM(HL)	4-engine land plane (weather recce)
VPM(ML)	2-engine land plane (weather recce)
VH(AM)	2-engine amphibian (hospital version)
VP(HS)	4-engine seaplane patrol
ZP	Lighter than aircraft

AIR GROUPS

Air groups for individual aircraft carriers ....CVBG, CVG, CVLG, CVEG
Marine fighters (day) ....VMF
Marine fighters (night) ....VMF (N)
Marine-aircraft control group ....MACG
Marine transport ....VMR